THE RULE OF THUMB

WRITTEN BY
STEVE DEW-JONES

INTREPID BOOKS

First published 2010 by
Intrepid Books, London, W12
www.ruleofthumb.co

Printed in the UK by Sarum Colourview
www.colourview.co.uk

Copyright © Intrepid Books 2010

ISBN 978-0-9567162-0-0

FOREWORD AND PHOTOGRAPHY
BY WILL JACKSON

ILLUSTRATIONS
FROM
PHILIPPE NASH

CONTENTS

⋆ FOREWORD ⋆

BY WILL JACKSON

It came upon a Sunday lunch. "We should drive to India" were the exact words I heard coming from my mouth. It wasn't as random a comment as first seemed; in fact I'd been to India a couple of years prior and had come back raving to Steve about curry for breakfast and reckless driving to match our own, urging him to join me in a return trip at some, unspecified point in the future.

Now Steve was in his final year at university and I was finishing a job at the same time he graduated; the timing was perfect. We were sat in the dining room of Mr. & Mrs. Gill, with whom I was lodging, alongside an eclectic mix of invitees to whom the lady of the house would extend her weekly offer of a roast dinner.

"Perfect!" replied Steve, in his typically over-exuberant fashion, before the rest of the dinner guests jumped in with their own appreciations of what a "great idea" it was and how we should "seal the deal" by shaking on it before the end of lunch. And so it was agreed, come July 2008 we were driving to India.

The first issue we faced was quite a large one and a fundamental flaw in our otherwise very well thought through plan. We didn't have a car. Issue. However, being two eternal optimists, we decided that this small, insignificant factor should not deter us from accomplishing our goal and it was at this moment that Steve suggested hitchhiking. Having hitched from the UK to Morocco for a university challenge, he claimed it would be a "doddle," and a lot less hassle than driving, especially as neither of us knew the slightest thing about fixing any of the inevitable mechanical problems we would face if we were to obtain a vehicle from somewhere.

At this point in time my hitching experience consisted of being too lazy to walk home from school – the insurmountable distance of 2 miles – and so standing on the side of the road and picking up lifts from friendly West Country farmers. The thought of hitching all the way to India seemed like going from riding a bike with the stabilizers on to being plonked on the seat of a Kawasaki super bike. Never one to shy away from a challenge, I hastily agreed that hitching was an agreeable solution and our already ambitious trip had become even more so within an hour of that fateful handshake.

Considering it was already late April at the time of Steve's visit, we didn't have much time to plan our continent-spanning adventure, but Steve and I both operate on an 'It'll be alright on the day' mindset, which is fairly counter-productive when the obtaining of visas is involved. A month later and still no plans, routes or visas had been sorted, although I did watch Ewan McGregor and Charlie Boorman's *The Long Way Round* series, which seemed to sum-up quite accurately what we faced.

It was at that point that I received the phone call.

"Hi mate, how's it going?" said Steve, in his trademark chirpy voice.

"Yep, fine thanks. How's planning going your end?" I responded, knowing that Steve was almost certainly set to have done nothing.

"Well… I was thinking… You know how much I love my girlfriend Jo…" His voice was becoming more sheepish with every word. I thought for sure that he was about to whimper out of the trip, tail between his legs, as he didn't want to be away from his beloved for so long. I was just about to respond with the pertinent advice of "Bro's before Ho's" when Steve dropped the bomb: "…Well, she's going to be travelling around Southeast Asia at the end of our trip and I thought we could end in Malaysia instead of India so we can be reunited on the other side of the world." Something in his voice seemed to echo the romantic sentiment of The Pretenders song, '*I Would Walk Five Hundred Miles*'.

"Brilliant, of course. It can't be that much further to Malaysia than it is to India anyway. They're practically next door, I think," I replied, with all the geographical confidence of an American trying to point to Iraq on a map.

And so it was decided; we were going to be hitchhiking from England to Malaysia for charity. The charity addition was another rather last-minute plan. We figured that not many people had or could achieve such a feat and thus it was worthy of some fundraising for nominated local charity, *The Trussell Trust*. The phone call I made to the charity was a rather amusing one as I was already supposed to be doing a 10 kilometre run for them, but this was scheduled to be taking place after our planned departure date of July 12th.

"Hi, Molly. I'm really sorry but I'm not going to be able to do the 10k run. I know I said I was free but something's come up. Well, how about, because

I can't run the 10k, Steve and I hitchhike from England to Malaysia for you instead? You can't say fairer than that!"

Mid-June came and went and we were still to attain our first visa, or that huge TV sponsorship deal we'd been dreaming about. However, even though Steve and I hadn't committed any money or even much time to our planned expedition, we were as determined as ever that we were actually going to go through with it. Those around us also realized that we were becoming quite serious about our little escapade and began to question whether it was the wisest move, especially crossing through the Middle East in its "current political climate."

It seemed that all of our friends and families – even the most daring and out-going – were set on dissuading us from making the trip. My dearest Mum just couldn't understand why we couldn't just hitchhike to Eastern Europe and then fly from there to Malaysia, whilst our best friends were making bets on which country we'd be in before we gave up and caught a bus or flew home – the majority of whom thought we'd return before Turkey. We even had phone calls just days before we were set to leave warning us of the dangers before us and that we should really reconsider, or at least postpone the trip. We were well aware of the dangers and trials that we faced, but by our estimation the odds were in our favour. We figured that the chance of one of us dying was probably around 25%, and therefore the chance of both of us surviving was 75%; and I like those odds.

Seven months without Mrs. Gill's roast dinners. Would we survive?

THE RULES

1 NEVER PAY FOR TRANSPORT

2 NEVER SAY NO TO AN OFFER

THE THUMB

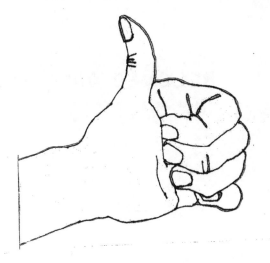

TO MY BELOVED WIFE JOANNA,
THANKS FOR WAITING

1. HOW MUCH DOES A POLAR BEAR WEIGH?

DAY TWO:
CAROLINE SCARTH'S COTTAGE, MOUSSAC, VIENNE, POITOU-CHARENTES, FRANCE, SATURDAY 12TH JULY 2008, 11.42AM

I think we're staying with a bunch of raving nudists. The bathroom is covered with photographs and pencil sketches of family members in their birthday suits, and while I'm all for life drawing being taken seriously as an important art form, it is quite disturbing to get to know your hosts quite so well – anatomically speaking – so early on into a relationship. Will reassuringly whispers into my ear that they might just be swingers as I try to collect my thoughts for the first time since leaving home twenty-four hours ago.

My surroundings are as follows. I sit with my back pressed up against the pillows of a comfortable double bed in the spare room of the Scarth family's holiday home on a beautiful summer's day in the remote French village of Moussac – a second home to our travel-loving hosts: Caroline, daughter Jessica, and Jess's Texan boyfriend Brady – who appears to be filling in as Mr. Scarth's replacement for the integral role of man of the house. Of course Will and I would be happy to offer ourselves for that role, but perhaps it is just as well that we haven't, given that we've only known the Scarths for one day – most of which was spent bonding over a game of cards on our afternoon ferry from Portsmouth to Caen.

By the end of that seven-hour crossing we had evidently managed to appear charming and unthreatening enough to convince our new friends that it would be a pleasant experience for all concerned if they were to allow us to squeeze into the back of their tiny yellow *Skoda*, joined there by Brady and pet dog Bahla – who, as they had warned us, never did stop panting down our necks until we finally arrived. Mother-daughter navigational and driving disputes overcome, we pulled up at their quaint cottage home in Moussac in the small hours of this very morn and were swiftly welcomed as if we were firm family friends, even given our own boudoir when a sofa would have been generous enough.

So how did we end up here? Well I suppose that you could say that it came upon a Sunday lunch...

The hustle and bustle of London living and the hopeless struggle to avoid unemployment might be attractive options to some, but from the very moment a prospective hitchhike to Asia had been suggested (midway through Will's nonchalant attempt to devour a whole chicken leg in one go) there was only ever going to be one outcome.

Two months later – not a whole lot of time for planning really, which probably explains why we haven't *done* a whole lot – and we find ourselves hitching a ride on a ferry across to France, scouring the decks of the ship to find anyone – yes, *anyone* – who will give us a lift anywhere in the vague direction of Malaysia.

The Scarths weren't the first people that we'd tried to befriend on the ferry, as we trawled through potential drivers – taking into account each candidate's age, apparent level of good nature, and potential space in vehicle. It proved quite a lengthy challenge, but we were certainly game – the excitement of the first day of our adventure had sparked an even greater level of optimism and self-confidence than the two of us feel on your average day. Will and I firmly believe in our abilities to charm our way into or out of any situation, so our approach was typically unrestrained: we must have asked almost every passenger on board, going from person to person, trying to get across (through a mixture of English, pidgin French, or even – in the case of Spaniards or other anomalies – the occasional hand gesture/map point) that we were hitching to Malaysia *for charity* (yes, that's right; there's a certain nobility about our efforts too), and first wanted to get as close to Spain as possible.

Now, for the geographically aware, you might realise that Spain isn't exactly on the way to Malaysia in the strictest sense, but we had already bought tickets to Benicassim's music festival and weren't going to miss out. The first hitch had been planned accordingly and we'd given ourselves a seemingly comfortable five-day target to hitch down to the festival only about 200km south of Barcelona.

The initial response to our inquiries was mixed. Most people had good excuses – having a full car, not travelling great distances in their car, or not actually possessing a car – whereas it was clear that some people simply didn't want to be bothered by a couple of cheeky freeloaders – "charity or no charity."

We had actually spoken to Jessica and Brady very early on in proceedings, but they had apologetically informed us that there wasn't enough room in the car for the two of us and our whopping great rucksacks – what with all their baggage, Jessica's mother, and a large dog.

Thanking them all the same for giving us the time of day, we had gone off to explore other avenues. But after over two hours of roaming, the best offers we'd received were a lift just to the other side of Paris with a middle-aged French woman (who had an unwarranted amount of facial hair) and a lift with an elderly British chap to some unknown destination in Normandy.

Nevertheless, we felt sure that a better offer lay out there somewhere. Moving our attentions towards lorry drivers, we went to the one place upon a ferry that you are sure to find them: the smoking room.

When we arrived at the doors of this cloudy room, it almost seemed as if its entire population was made up of truckers, such was the contrast between these burly, single men and the masses breathing the clean air outside. But when we'd finally summoned up enough courage to approach this assortment of intimidating gents, our inquiries were brought to an instantaneous halt because of the unhappy coincidence that we had decided to cross the Channel during the anniversary of Bastille Day – a French festival that has apparently got something to do with a mass people's uprising in the eighteenth century and, so I'm told, holds enough significance to bring all cargo lorries to a standstill for one weekend of every year. Of course we had no idea about Bastille Day (when it occurred – July 14th apparently – or even what it was), but having been bizarrely informed by three or four foreign truckers that they would be happy to give us a lift to Spain, but not until Tuesday morning, we eventually found an Englishman amongst the bunch who helpfully translated the reasoning behind it, and turned our attentions back to cars.

* * * * *

It had been a few hours since we had first spoken to Jessica and Brady and I suppose that we must have seemed a little down because, when we met for the second time, they seemed saddened by our lack of progress, took one quick look at each other, and offered to introduce us to Jessica's mother, who would have the final word.

Caroline was taking some time out to herself, reading a book in one of the ferry lounges as we were brought before her. It seemed that she had already been informed of our situation, and immediately took a shine to us as we enthused about the beginning of our great adventure. Moments later and this well-groomed lady had kindly offered us a lift half the way through France to their cottage near Poitiers (the one place that I could pin on a mental map in the long list that she gave us of bigger towns near to Moussac).

"I don't have any problem squeezing you in," Caroline had said, "but, I must warn you that the offer comes with a price…"

"Please go on," Will encouraged.

"Well," Caroline continued. "You will have to share the back seats with Brady here – not a small chap, as you can see – as well as our rather large, slobbery old dog, Bahla, who, and believe me when I say this, simply will not stop wetly panting on you throughout the journey."

"A small price to pay!" we agreed, hastily replying so as to remove the slightest inclination that she might have had that, for some reason or other, we might refuse the lift.

"Great," said Caroline, "So long as you're sure!" Caroline smirked at her daughter as she said these words, but there was no chance that Will and I were going to refuse an offer like this, no matter what small inconveniences we might have to suffer along the way.

The sun was setting when the ferry finally arrived in Caen, presenting the perfect backdrop to the scene of two excited young travellers alighting from the passenger section and making their way to the car park outside to meet their very first drivers en route to Malaysia.

Anxious thoughts flashed through our minds as we contemplated the possibility that we might not find the Scarths again. Although we felt sure that they truly intended to give us a lift, perhaps we would miss each other as the streams of cars departed the ferry, and the Scarths would assume that we'd gone off with somebody else, briefly shed a tear (or perhaps not), then sadly drive off without us.

But there they were, waving at us from the other side of the dimly lit car park. Breathing sighs of relief, we jogged over and helped fasten our bags underneath the cover of the handy trailer that was attached to the back of Caroline's yellow *Skoda Octavia*, the dog was relocated to the boot, and off we set. Six hours later and we would arrive in Moussac, wipe thick layers of canine slobber from the backs of our necks, and crash out in the comfort of our very own room.

You join me now, the following morning, as the corners of my mouth curl into a smile – a reaction to the glorious sunshine that peeks in through the cracks in the jolly, wooden shutters of this typical French cottage, and I dwell upon the sense of kinship that I feel towards our hosts, who are preparing breakfast downstairs to the welcome accompaniment of a *Van Morrison* record.

DAY THREE:
CAROLINE SCARTH'S COTTAGE, MOUSSAC, VIENNE, POITOU-CHARENTES, FRANCE, SUNDAY, 13TH JULY 2008, 19.24

Oh my! What a wonderful time we have had here in Moussac. We have been well fed, treated like family, and given licence to make ourselves at home here for as long as we like.

Making the most of the glorious sunshine, Will and I got thoroughly lost this afternoon as we went for a long walk around the surrounding countryside, giving our hosts a bit of time to themselves, away from these unexpected special guests. On our return, we enjoyed a fine French espresso, nibbled upon a couple of baguettes, and played a game of pétanque in their spacious back garden.

Will and I truly hope that in each new country, we doest as the natives do, thus ensuring that our experiences are as authentic as possible. We're off to a flyer: on our first full day in France we've started the day with croissants, had baguettes for lunch, at least three espresso breaks during the course of the day, and Caroline has put a casserole in the oven for dinner. How very French!

Day Four:
...Still in Moussac, Caroline Scarth's Cottage, Moussac, Vienne, Poitou-Charentes, France, Bastille Day! Monday 14th July 2008, 15.32

A ghastly crime took place this morning in the infamous bathroom of the Scarths' Moussac cottage. On the advice of our American friend, Brady, Will and I foolishly decided to completely shave off our underarm hair in the name, apparently, of "better travelling hygiene." I feel naked, and fear the long-term implications of such a regression.

Masculinity lost, we had a little breakfast (croissants, café, bol du chocolat; you know the score) and headed out to the Charente River for your typical family afternoon out. Who would have thought that we have only known each other for three days?

Last night we took our sense of belonging to a new extreme, as we were taken for dinner at the home of the Scarths' old family friends and neighbours, Simon and Karen. Treated to a banquet of fine food and French wines in the run-down barn that takes over the garden of this Kiwi couple, we engaged in deep discussions about all the important matters of life until the small hours of this morning. And it was fifty-something year-old former model, Simon, who led the way, vehemently defending his particular views, which, as far as I could understand, fell somewhere in between liberal Christianity, Buddhism and even the farcical beliefs better-relating to that idiot David Icke (who, if you haven't heard, really does believe that the world is ruled by lizards).

Blonde-locked Simon is quite the talker; he won't allow anyone else to get more than about five words into a sentence before interrupting and going off into his own stream of consciousness.

"I just don't understand how anybody can believe in one religion," Simon protested.

"Well, I think..." I began, but before I could get any further in my response, Simon felt it high time that he should speak again.

"You know, don't you think it's just a little mean to think that only one way can be the right way? I'm not just talking about Christians here, you know; I'm talking about the whole Goddamned lot of them. I just think that we would all be better off without religion, don't you?"

Of course Simon didn't allow anybody else the time to respond, but the thoughts that our conversation (actually, "lecture" would be better suited to the description) provoked lived long into the night and remain with me the following day. Why is it that we decide to limit the grace of God to one particular religion? Why does every religious trend insist upon its own superiority and, in fact, claim to be the *only* way? Seven years as a Christian – three of which were spent on a theology degree – have given me plenty of time to think through this particular issue, but I still find myself without any satisfactory answer to the problem of salvation. Perhaps, come Malaysia, I will have one.

As I sit out on the veranda sipping another espresso I am overwhelmed by the difference that a healthy dollop of sunshine can make to one's mood; better here than in the torrential downpours that have best typified English summers of late, that's for sure. It would appear as if this will be my last entry in Moussac; a mixture of itchy feet and the potential to outstay our welcome looming large has led us the point at which, when we have summoned up the courage, we will approach Caroline and make everyone's lives a lot easier by offering to leave before they kick us out, leaving them to enjoy the *family* holiday that they came here for.

As welcoming as the Scarths have been, there comes a point in every relationship where the honeymoon phase runs out and tenuous bonds are exposed for... Well, being tenuous. We have thoroughly enjoyed our time as part of this family, but can certainly sense the unspoken tension surrounding our lingering presence and the lack of a set ETD (estimated time of departure). Perhaps the biggest stepping-stone for Will and me is knowing that once we leave the surety of a place where we can rest our heads and enjoy home cooking, we will be stepping out into the unknown for only the second time since stepping onto that ferry in Portsmouth. Although the prospect also excites us, there is a niggling doubt that suggests that it would be easier to stay for just *one* more day. Yet, regardless of the distinct uncertainty of the road ahead, onwards we must go. We leave tonight. Next stop Barcelona, or as close to Benicassim as we can get in the few daylight hours remaining for us to secure a decent hitch.

DAY FIVE:
TUDELA, NAVARRE, NR. ZARAGOZA, SPAIN, TUESDAY 15TH JULY, 2008, 13.33

We finally left our surrogate family late last night and headed out onto a *station de service* in the middle of the N10 (the motorway that runs all the way south from Poitiers to Spain) just in time to catch three Ukrainian truckers partaking of their evening snacks. It took us a little while to communicate exactly what we were after – none of the men being particularly adept at English or French, whilst my very basic Russian did little more than surprise these Slavonic gents – but eventually, thanks to a mixture of hand gestures and attempts to say the word "Spain" in as many different dialects and accents as we could muster, we had done enough to convey our intentions to their ring-leader: a man by the name of Valera.

The only member of the trio that seemed to possess the vaguest notion of what it felt like to smile, we warmed to Valera instantly, and were delighted when he managed to convince one of his pals to help out by taking me in one truck, whilst Valera took Will in another. Of course we never intended to split up, but any ride is better than none and we had no choice but to comply with Valera's stipulations.

In the cabin of a regular European lorry, there is generally one driver's seat (a necessity really, complete with an impressive suspension system that sees the driver comically bounce up and down in line with the truck's movements), one passenger seat (without such mod cons) and one bed (usually of the bunk variety). Unfortunately for us, Valera informed us that the bed does not meet up to the strict safety regulations required for its use as an extra seat, and we were left with no choice but to separate. And so it was that Will and I set off in two separate trucks, not really knowing where it was that we might end up, but under the blissful assumption that Valera seemed like a nice enough sort, and had hopefully arranged some sort of meeting point with his friend on the other side of the border.

So, I hear you ask, how did it go? Well, let's just say that Will and I have since vowed never to split up again, even if next time we might have to wait around for a few extra hours to secure another lift.

Even though I tried all my best lines in English, French, Russian and even the more universal communication method of body language, my driver was obviously not the talkative type and would reply to my various questions (Are you married? Do you have children? What is your name? How are you? Etc.) with one word answers – that is if he bothered responding at all.

Three hours later, by the time we had finally proceeded to the other side of the Spanish border, and my useless attempts to ask how we were going to meet up with the other lorry were answered – even if this wasn't by the regular verbal means – as we pulled up on the hard shoulder of the motorway and he angrily gesticulated that I was to leave.

Shocked, and slightly mystified as to what I might have done to displease my taciturn friend so much, I watched with alarm as the lorry pulled away, leaving me on the hard shoulder of the N10 with streams of traffic whistling past and not a Will in sight.

Nervously I made my way towards a slip road a couple of hundred metres I front of me and reached inside the inner pocket of my rucksack for my phone. It was fortunate really that both of us had decided to take phones on the journey for use in an emergency such as this, and more fortunate still that my contract was not set to expire until the following day.

"Where are you?" I asked Will, fretfully pondering how difficult it might be to explain my exact location as I stood by the side of what appeared to be a slip road much like every other.

"Hard to say really," Will replied. "We got off the motorway a few minutes ago and we're in some sort of trucker stop now. How about you?"

"Difficult to say," I responded. "I don't think he liked me very much. A couple of minutes ago he just pulled up on the hard shoulder and gestured that I should leave. Now I'm by the side of this cylindrical slip road and I can just about see a roundabout near the bottom. Sound familiar?"

"Oh yeah, know the one," Will responded. "Don't worry, I'm pretty sure we came off at that slip road a couple of minutes ago; I'll come and get you."

"Thanks babe," I said. "But let's never split up again."

"Agreed," Will replied.

Searching for a spot to put up a tent on the outskirts of a small Spanish town (later found out to be Irun) at midnight is no walk in the park. There seemed to be a whole lot of concrete options to choose from, but not a lot of grass, so when we finally found the smallest patch of green on the other side of an abandoned car park, we pounced at the opportunity. There were a few street lights around and assumedly some new neighbours safely asleep in their warm, comfortable houses, and we hoped that no-one would mind too much if the following morning they awoke to find two travellers sleeping in the car park outside.

* * * * *

We made it through the night undisturbed and recommenced our hitching efforts early this morning. Finding ourselves a good spot that met all the hitching criteria (right road, easily visible, good space to pull in, and cars moving slowly), it wasn't long before a smiley Spanish chap named Roberto had pulled over to give us a ride.

An hour later and we were dropped off by the side of a roundabout and pointed towards an exit that was signposted for Zaragoza. After a slightly longer wait than we would have liked, a proficient English-speaking Peruvian named Juan rescued us from the scorching gaze of the summer sun and took us into the shade of his car.

After Juan we received a lift from two middle-aged Spanish chaps whose names were slightly too Spanish to comprehend, and it was they who dropped us off at the Tudelan café in which we now sit, mercifully shaded from the Spanish sun for a further few moments as we await the clock to strike three – the time that we have informed the sun that we would really rather appreciate it if it cools down a little.

It's a tough business hitching in this sort of weather. We've drunk copious amounts of water to compensate for dehydration and have also implemented the highly recommended slip, slop and slapping of sun cream; and yet we're still very glad for this brief respite from the midday glare. I doubt that we'll reach the festival tonight (although it remains a possibility) and my biggest concern is getting out of Tudela now that we have inadvertently made it into the centre of this town, far away from the decent position that Juan left us in on the main road to Zaragoza. Will's hungry belly was the reason we ventured into this town – my own stomach seemingly incapable of feeling hunger pangs – and I have this niggling fear that the detour might cost us.

DAY SIX:
RESTAURANT ALMADRABA, BENICASSIM, CASTELLÓN, SPAIN, WEDNESDAY 16TH JULY, 2008, 17.06

Tired, jaded, and suffering a considerable headache: these are all fitting ways to describe my current state, even if we have had a mildly spirit-lifting turn of events in the last few hours to take us out from a desert wilderness in the middle of nowhere to the very destination that we have been striving towards ever since leaving Moussac on Monday evening.

It all started going wrong in Tudela, where I left you. We had eaten our lunch and were back on the road, patiently waiting for a lift. Only, instead of the instantaneous pick up that we were hoping for, two hours went by and we still hadn't moved, and were beginning to wonder if we ever would. Meanwhile we were sweating buckets in 40-plus degrees heat and taking it in turns to take breaks in the shade, while the other would hopelessly attempt to stop a car from our unfavourable position off a roundabout in pretty central Tudela.

Other than the agonising waiting, the only incident worth reporting in those stagnant hours was a chance meeting with a British nomad by the name of John. An odd chap, it seemed that forty-eight year-old John had become rather disenchanted by his life in England and had left behind his mundane existence to follow his dream of cycling around the world, starting off in Spain by getting to grips with a new culture and language until either his money ran out or he decided to move somewhere new.

To the untrained eye, John's appearance was similar to that of a vagrant: tattered clothes and an unkempt beard perfectly complemented the stale stench of last night's (and possibly a bit of this morning's) alcohol. But, as with many people, there was more to John than his immediate appearance suggested. He was obviously an intelligent man, who spoke articulately in English and seemed to have a fair grasp of Spanish – as much as we could gather from his best attempts to speak to passing drivers on our behalf.

He told us that he had left behind a high-pressured job in computers for a new challenge, fed up with constantly falling in and out of relationships with girls with whom he shared no common ground. Consequently he had upped and left seven months ago, searching for that missing *something* that seems both to captivate and to elude most people in life. Just what it was John was searching for I'm not sure that he knew, but he had at least made a change to his life so as to stand a better chance of finding it.

If we had met John in a less stressful situation, I think that we might have chatted for longer and generally been more polite. We always try to be courteous to every person that we meet along the way, but when you have been stuck in the same place for two hours and have a dishevelled hobo comes along to cramp your already laboured style, it becomes a little more challenging.

We thanked John for his kindness in both attempting to help us to get a ride and also buying us both a drink (non-alcoholic as we had specified), then decided that it was high time for a change of approach. I think that John must have followed us for most of the four or five kilometre hike to what we considered to be a better spot on the edge of town, but he had evidently got lost or distracted at some point along the way because, when I looked behind, he had vanished. It briefly came to mind that perhaps he was no more than a figment of my fanciful imagination, but I concluded that this was a rather fanciful thought in itself.

* * * * *

The change of scenery obviously did the trick. We were soon picked up by the cheerful Mita – a shop assistant who had just finished work at the nearby Dia supermarket. At 29 years of age, Mita was a recent divorcee and now looked after her young daughter at her mother's house, which, handily for us, lay somewhere between Tudela and Zaragoza. The lovely Mita was another example of what makes this hitching business such a worthwhile exploit. It might be quicker and easier if we were to simply catch buses or trains all the way to Malaysia, but then we would have missed out on the chance to meet so many interesting people, including this rather sad girl.

Even though our conversation was a bitty combination of French, English and the morsel of Spanish that we have picked up, we were still able to communicate well enough to encourage Mita that she was a pretty young woman with a lot to offer the world.

She beamed as she drove away from us. Despite long waits and the associated huffing and puffing that goes with it, meeting with folk with whom we can chat on profound levels certainly gives hope for a richer vein of purpose as an undercurrent to our adventure. It is amazing to be completely reliant upon the good nature and kindness of complete strangers; and that will be our privileged position for this entire trip.

Unfortunately, the actions of the kind people that we meet along the way can very soon seem like a distant memory whilst helplessly waiting by the side of the road for hours on end. Not for the first time yesterday, this was our predicament.

Mita, as lovely as she was, dropped us off in the most unhelpful of places: the middle of a fast-moving road with no available space to stop. Having made no progress in a further hour of waiting, we made the five-kilometre hike up a never-ending hill and took our place by the side of a slip road near the summit.

Eventually our desperate attempts at hitchhiking were rewarded by a kind man named Andres. He had seemed alarmed by our desperate flagging of arms and legs and, good natured man as he was, felt obliged to stop and lend a hand. Andres' generosity stretched so far that he proceeded to take us all the way to the other side of the Zaragoza ring road until he had found an exit that would put us onto the road to Benicassim.

One thing that one notices whilst hitchhiking is that one's mood is almost entirely situation-dependent. Progress (be it good or bad) completely dictates one's current state of mental health and can dramatically swing one way and then the next in a matter of seconds. The unbearably upsetting experience of standing and waiting by the side of a road with no idea of when your next lift will arrive is flipped around into boundless elation as soon as a lift finally does come. A complete stranger like Andres becomes your favourite person in the world for the time that he is helping you out, and is then forgotten as a new saviour is awaited.

There are long days, and then there are those days that are so long that they wind you up to a point of near breakdown. This was how we felt at 9.45pm last night, four hours since the moment Andres had dropped us off, and still rooted in the same spot. Apart from about a twenty-minute break for dinner at the petrol station café, the rest of this four-hour stretch was spent vainly attempting to get a ride… to anywhere. Petrol stations are generally great hitching spots because you can chat to drivers, they can see that you seem unlikely to harbour maniacal tendencies, and should darn well consider giving you a helping hand.

But none did. No saviour came. We tried everything: speaking to drivers as they filled up, waiting by the exit of the petrol station that led to the very road we wanted to go on, and if it was an air of desperation that they wanted, I think that that was plastered all over our faces after only about half an hour of standing there like lemons.

Perhaps the worst thing about the experience was this sarcy old Spaniard who would come up to us every ten minutes and convey a message of eternal doom:

"Oooh, you won't get picked up here," he would say. "Nobody hitchhikes in Spain. People used to pick up hitchhikers but there have been too many incidents of violence," and so on in that vain.

This sort of negativity is the last thing that one needs to hear when spirits are already at an all time low. We longed for a bunch of cheerleaders encouraging us, rather than old stooge who seemed only to delight in our misery.

Try as we might to laugh off this old man's insistence on the futility of our efforts, by 9.45pm – the moment when both daylight and our spirits had sunk sufficiently for us to call it a day – we had to concede that, as much as we hated to admit it, this evening the old man had been right. Drearily, we dragged our bags away from the petrol station, crossed over the busy spaghetti junction that had been our changeless view that evening, and hunted for a patch of grass suitable for a tent.

Even this was harder than expected: there were plenty of fields around, but they were all full of the spikiest of crops – not a patch of regular grass in sight. In the end we had to settle for doing our best to smooth down what we understood to be a field of corn before the light completely faded and we would be forced to erect the tent in the dark.

This was the lowest point of the trip to date and we barely said a word to each other throughout. We had at one stage contemplated making the most out of a bad situation by leaving the tent and going to get a *cerveza* (Spanish for *beer*) or two, but knew that to do so we would have to return to the spot that had been the bane of our existence for the last four hours. Instead, we settled for an early night, tiredness taking us off to sleep as soon as we hit the ground, preventing us from worrying too much about the potential grief we might encounter if disturbed in the middle of the night by an angry farmer, incensed by our flattening of his once lofty corn.

* * * * *

We were awoken at first light this morning by the barking of what we fearfully assumed to be either the farmer's dogs, or, worse still, a pack of snarling police Alsatians. Aghast at this unnerving introduction to the new day, we were petrified as what seemed like four or five large dogs encircled our tent, their shadows drawing ever closer. I have always put my fear of dogs down to being bitten by one at the age of two, and I whispered this again to Will so that my friend knew that it was he that would have to deal with the situation.

"Hola," he whispered, using the only word that he knew in Spanish to try and calm down these snarling mutts.

"What are you doing? The dogs don't speak Spanish," I said, shaking my head in disbelief.

"Hola," he repeated, unmoved by my cynicism, and then... *then* the dogs left!

I shook my head again in disapproval as Will proudly raised his palms up to the skies as if to praise mighty God for the powers that had been bestowed upon him. Make of it what you will, but I remain rather sceptical that this budding dog-whisperer was the reason for their dispersal.

Cautiously we crept out of the tent, looked around for any lingering farmers or policemen and, seeing none, sleepily made our way back to the road. We avoided the petrol station and, as if we needed any further proof for how much luck plays a part in hitchhiking, we received a lift in our new spot after waiting for only about two minutes.

Our first driver this morning was a talkative chap, who told us that we could call him either "Pepe" or "Jose Miel." Pepe or Jose Miel? Someone please tell me why Spaniards have the right to possess two names?

Pepe/Jose Miel drove us a good distance away from our hated town of the moment, Zaragoza. It seems that our opinion of a place correlates almost entirely upon the ease with which we get picked up there. Bearing in mind that there is probably a good dollop of chance involved (i.e. one day we might wait for hours; the next we might be picked up within ten minutes by a man with two names), this is perhaps unfair, but it is difficult to feel any warmth towards a place in which your only two experiences were standing in a fume-filled petrol station (is it possible for petrol stations to be anything but?) and sleeping in a prickly field with stray dogs.

Tangents aside, Signor two-names was kind enough to take us for a good hour's drive, dropping us off in the small town of Alcañiz, from where he assured us that we would be much more likely to find a lift to Benicassim.

The day had started so well and we felt sure that we were deserving of a continued upturn in fortunes – anything to make up for the horror of last night – as we stretched out our thumbs again.

Things didn't quite go to plan. We began to watch in disbelief as streams of cars passed us by, giving a full range of expressions – from the sympathetic to the outraged – but not once did anybody look even vaguely likely to pull over into the helpful space that we had allocated for them just a few metres beyond where we stood.

Equally the most humorous and frustrating expression came from the many drivers who would point in an abstract direction (anywhere other than straight on) as if to suggest that they were, unfortunately, going a different direction to you, although they hadn't even stopped to enquire where it was that you were actually trying to get to – especially boggling of the mind when the road ahead doesn't exactly lend itself to a plethora of decision making. We had but one road ahead of us and every single passer-by *was*, by the very fact that they were passing by us, heading our way. Other firm favourites of ours are drivers who decide it might be fun to mimic the dying art of thumbing a lift, or even those special few who go so far as to raise their middle finger in the air. We have made a habit of looking all drivers in the eye as they drive past, hoping that this will play upon their better nature and make them feel that they are lesser people if they choose not to stop. And yet, even our most manipulative/suggestive tactics were tried and tested, but ultimately failed.

Almost two hours went by before a vehicle finally stopped, and when it did, we took the lift only because we figured that *anywhere* would be better than there.

Upon reflection, this was a bad decision. We were taken only 14km up the road and, instead of being well positioned at the start of a main road, we were now in a generic spot somewhere in the middle of it. Streams of traffic were still passing us by, except that now they were travelling at about three times the speed with little hope of finding a safe spot to pull in, even if they did miraculously manage to spot us as they whizzed on by. It had been hard enough hitchhiking in a relatively good spot; *here* it was practically impossible.

It had been a mixture of impatience (we were fed up) and ignorance (you can never be sure of what lies ahead) that had led us to take this ill-advised hitch, and now we were stuck in what felt like the middle of a single-carriage motorway. We quickly lost heart again and it seemed as if we would never reach Benicassim, let alone reach it by the end of the day, even though we felt sure we couldn't be very far away.

Pacing up and down the road in search of a better position, the only half-decent spot that we could find was a run down petrol station opposite a restaurant – neither of which seemed to be buzzing with potential lifts.

"Come on Steve. This is getting ridiculous. Let's go get some food in the restaurant," Will said. As usual it was his belly doing the talking for him.

"No Will," I replied, desperate to carry on hitchhiking until we got a decent ride. "We can't just give up now. How can you be hungry again already? We only just had breakfast!"

Finally, a compromise was reached: we would wait for another ten minutes and if nobody had stopped by then, we would cross the road, have a bite to eat, not to mention downing at least a few gallons' worth of rehydration therapy each, and then we would return for phase two of our efforts.

It cannot have been more than a minute before a beaten up old banger – the car of a friendly old Moroccan chap named Chirky – chugged uncomfortably towards us, noticed our clear distress (forget your concept of hitchhiking that suggests we might have been motionlessly standing there with thumbs outstretched; we were going bezerk!) and pulled over to give us a ride.

"Gracias! Gracias!" we yelped in unison, rather alarming our docile new friend. "Where are you going?"

Chirky disinterestedly informed us that he was driving towards Benicassim and proceeded to show further alarm at the reaction of the two strangely distressed foreign men before him. Whooping, high fives and a thousand graciases; we'd done it!

What an emotional roller coaster we have been on already, and this is only a tiny fraction of the journey that lies ahead. As we assured our Moroccan friend that we were glad to listen to his warbling Arabic chants – in the apparent absence of any common language with which to converse – we dwelt upon what had been an exhausting two days since leaving the Scarths.

Since leaving home on Friday afternoon, it had taken us five days to get to Benicassim and we had already seen and experienced so much. There was an air of calm that had arisen through the storm as Will and I breathed deep sighs of relief and, for the first time that day, sat and blissfully watched the world go by.

A scorching summer seemed to have dried up what could otherwise have been lush green hillsides surrounding us, and yet there was still beauty in the arid desert-land that now, to our minds at least, glistened in acknowledgment of our success.

DAY SEVEN:
CAMP FIB, FESTIVAL INTERNACIONAL DE BENICASSIM, BENICASSIM, CASTELLÓN, SPAIN, THURSDAY 17TH JULY, 2008, 9AM

I woke up in a rather frenzied state some twenty minutes ago and tried surreptitiously to nudge my companion so that he could reassure me in the midst of my current mental crisis, but Will was fast asleep and I couldn't bring myself to nudge too insistently and disturb him from what was a well-deserved rest.

How I wish *I* were still asleep right now! This is the second night in a row that I have woken up, unable to shift worried thoughts from my mind. The marathon nature of the hitch thus far has highlighted the scale of what lies ahead. Malaysia isn't round the corner after all; we're looking at going through about twenty more countries before we get there, and that is going to be no small feat when one considers that we are firmly bound to the fundamental rule of *only* hitchhiking. I cannot believe the topsy-turvy nature of the past five days – full of the most extreme highs and excruciating lows – and that was only to get us as far as Benicassim!

Of course the future excites me, but it all seems a little surreal. All the other people here at the festival probably arrived through a combination of no more than one flight and a couple of connecting train rides, whilst we have already been given lifts by ten different drivers, stayed in a cottage in France, slept in a car park, then a field, and nearly been eaten alive by a pack of wild dogs – not to mention the long hours spent stressing out by different Spanish roadsides. And it took us five days!

I suppose that it just seems a little overwhelming that we are caught up in what is only a one-week beach holiday for others, but represents just the beginning of a much bigger, five-month adventure for us. I'm starting to find it hard to believe that we've even taken a little detour through Spain en route to Malaysia – as if it wasn't far enough already!

Perhaps stress has been mounting because we have finally been given the opportunity to stay still for a few days. Sometimes it can be so much easier to just keep on moving, not allowing your brain to catch up with you, as you ignore the constant worries that accumulate over days of uncertainty that lie ahead.

Waking up dripping with sweat inside the confines of a tiny plastic cage is hardly the ideal start to a day for a mildly claustrophobic man, who is occasionally liable to thinking things through too much. For the first time since setting sail I have had time to dwell upon the significance of a five-month absence from Jo, my beloved girlfriend/future wife. I miss her, and more, I know that there is no point dwelling on this because this absence is not going to end for a very long time.

Escape plans flash through my head. Could I just pack it all in and go back to a comfortable 9-5 and the occasional weekend break with Jo? Would I be satisfied? Or, more likely, would I hate myself for giving up?

The conviction that I certainly would, spurs me on to overcome the battle going on within me. I cannot give up because this is something Will and I have promised that we will do; I cannot give up because we are raising money for a charity; I cannot give up because we've got bags full of clothes, malaria tablets and other medical supplies to last us five months on the road; I cannot give up because I would be letting Will down; but, finally, I cannot give up – clichéd though it might appear – because I would be letting myself down.

This trip must go ahead, and for some months yet. I just have to will myself to enjoy each moment and not think about the alternatives too much. What use is there in undertaking a trip if you are constantly wishing yourself away? I am doing this trip; I am here in Benicassim and I even get the chance to see Sigur Rós tonight.

DAY NINE:
BENICASSIM BEACH, FESTIVAL INTERNACIONAL DE BENICASSIM, BENICASSIM, CASTELLÓN, SPAIN, SATURDAY 19TH JULY, 2008, 15.39

As I marvel at the panoramic view before me, I am comforted by a peace that has steadied me over the last few days of festival life. Frenzied dreams and tormenting worries regarding the length of this grand adventure are faded and gone.

Sigur Rós and Hot Chip have been the musical highlights at a festival whose only routine revolves around the bands that play from 6.30pm until 8 o'clock the following morn. Festival-goers blearily traipse down to the beach as soon as the roasting sun forces them to face the day (at no later than 10am), proceeding to doze on the beach as their bodies blister in the heat of the day.

My own body is red raw (entirely Will's fault) because of a failure to observe that spray-on sun creams might actually need also to be rubbed in a little. There is currently a towel protecting my sore back from any further long- term damage as my weary brain struggles to readjust to this nocturnal pattern of life. But this is the way of life for every festival-goer and I have to sacrifice the grandad inside of me that cries for bed at about 11pm (the time we generally make it to our first gig) and summon the required energy to stand up for a further nine hours and nod my head in time with the banging electro beats.

To be honest, I rarely make it past 3am, when I leave the more hardcore elements of our group to continue raving to their hearts' content, whilst making my own return to our plastic cell, and the few hours of sleep available until the sun wakes me up dripping again, gasping for the fresh air outside, but finding only a sticky heat that parches lips and makes me thirst for water.

All my concerns regarding time spent away from Jo have been assertively dispelled by the unavoidable truth that this trip will be a part of my life until Christmas at the very earliest, and I had better make the most of every experience until then. I would hate to make a mockery of what is a once in a lifetime opportunity by whingeing about it for its entirety, letting the amazing people and places that we run into simply pass me by, while others slave away at their 9-5s back home.

As you can see, this is my version of a rallying cry to myself; I feel better already.

DAY ELEVEN:
CAFÉ JOTA, FESTIVAL INTERNACIONAL DE BENICASSIM, BENICASSIM, CASTELLÓN, SPAIN, MONDAY 21ST JULY, 2008, 13.06

Sipping a *café con leche* (coffee with milk) and nibbling upon croissants in our favourite coffee shop, *Café Jota*, has become a regular morning exercise during our time in Benicassim, which is now coming to an end. Tonight there will be a grand finale on the beach and we have heard exciting rumours of a rave involving lasers in the sea. The music has been a great success over the last four nights, highlights ranging from dance acts *Justice* and *Hot Chip* to rockers *Sigur Rós* and *Leonard Cohen*. Mr. Cohen rather stole the show last night, his famous *Hallelujah* performed with surprising adherence to tunefulness by a choir of some twenty thousand spectators in what almost felt like a mini-religious experience, even though the song is only ironical in that sense.

I think I'll miss the festival atmosphere, even if I won't miss being asked if I want an ecstasy tablet or some cocaine every five seconds. I usually reply that I only deal in heroin, but this does little to impress the most street-cred of users (normally aged anywhere between about 15 and 25) and once got me into a spot of bother when I pretended to be selling some myself.

"How much you got mate?" I was asked in a thick cockney accent by a child of no more than sixteen years of age.

"How much you after?" I replied, looking around to my friends for support in the charade, but finding none.

I was quickly out of my depth and mumbled something about "50 grams, eight ounces, or... however much you want mate," then burst into laughter.

The boy and his cronies sniggered at my obvious lack of knowledge regarding all the different measurements and terminologies that are involved in an average drug deal.

"You should be more careful mate. Watch yourself," one small child told me.

Perhaps I should have cheekily retorted that this is something very difficult to do without the appropriate reflective glass on hand, or that it was *they* who needed to be a touch more careful with what they were shoving into their bodies. It's probably just as well that I didn't.

My eyes have just been alerted by the protruding underarm hairs of a lady at a nearby table – well, we are in Spain after all: it's the European dream. But wait, I think the girl's English, or maybe Australian. Either way, I must applaud her for her lack of care about what other people think of her. It may not be the most attractive sight, but I guess that it used to be the way in ancient times, before shavers were invented, and I'm all for traditionalism providing it isn't hurting anyone.

In a seamless link, not wishing to move on too swiftly from physiology, and metaphorically speaking at least, Will and I are beginning to get rather itchy feet again. It feels like high time to move on. Tomorrow we're making tracks for Barcelona. Who knows at what time and in what state we may arrive?

Day Fourteen:
Illegal Hostel, Nr. La Rambla, Barcelona, Cataluña, Spain, Thursday 24th July, 2008, 10.16am

The beach party on Monday night was a huge letdown. No rave in the sea and not a laser in sight. The only "entertainment" on offer was watching, horrified, as a bunch of British louts set about destroying that pretty little town by setting fire to anything and everything that they could get their grubby mitts on. No wonder we Brits have such a poor reputation overseas. The miscreants, struggling to find much firewood upon a sandy, treeless beach, decided to rip up wooden pathways and deck chairs, throwing all that they could assemble onto the blazing fires.

It was an absolute disgrace, and soon enough these kids were jumping through the fires, risking death in order to win the greatest number of macho points from their drunken compadres. We watched in disbelief from a safe distance so as not to appear to be supporting their misdemeanours, nor involved enough to take the rap that finally came in the form of an approaching squadron of police cars.

We seem to be developing quite a rapport with the Spanish police during our short time in the country. The incident around the fire that night was followed the very next day by another crime by association – this time with Spanish drug-dealing duo, Victor and Eric.

Deciding that our best bet of a lift to Barcelona was to wait in the festival car park until we found some hip young fellows eager to take us in, we spotted Spanish ravers Victor and Eric approaching, and let me tell you, they don't come much hipper. We hadn't been in Victor's *Fiat Punto* for long before Will did his usual falling asleep trick, soon to be joined by the obviously fatigued Eric. As I admired the back of Eric's extraordinary hairdo (a kind of short back and sides with an additional thirty centimetre-long rat-tail dangling off the back of it), I decided to get to know Victor a little better, whilst making sure that I gripped him in conversation so that he didn't feel overly tempted to join in with this nice little slumber party.

Victor is currently in the middle of an Economics degree at a University in Barcelona and seemed more than happy to help us out by taking us as far as his hometown, which isn't far outside the bounds of the Catalan capital. Quite how this quiet-spoken, considerate gent ended up with Eric, I do not know. His companion was a loose cannon by all accounts. When roused from his slumber during a short break at a service station, our rat-tailed friend needed little invitation to boast about his exploits at the festival.

"I just made 4,000 Euros at that gig by shifting pills!" Eric squealed as he rolled a joint with some of the stash that he had left over.

"Not a bad week's work eh Victor?" he continued, rat tail proudly swinging in the wind as he spoke.

His friend reluctantly nodded his head and apologetically informed us that he had also made about 500 Euros at the festival.

"You know, just enough to cover the cost of the festival," Victor ensured us, aware that Will and I weren't particularly impresses by Eric's endeavours.

Whilst I was slightly surprised to learn of Victor's involvement, there was still such a huge contrast between the two men. Eric spoke with such pride as he relayed his success, whilst Victor's was a rather penitent admission of the same offence. Eric walked and talked with a swagger, whilst Victor seemed to have a little bit more depth to him than that which comes from mere bravado. During our long conversation in the car I had become rather fond of Victor, thus making the next turn of events seem all the more tragic.

We had almost reached Victor's hometown – in fact we were passing through the very last toll station – when we were pulled over by La Policía. They seemed to be doing spot checks of all traffic heading back from the festival and took only one look at our scruffy chauffeurs – and a slightly longer gaze at the cigarette-type object that Eric was not so subtly attempting to stub out against the glove compartment – before signalling that Victor was to pull over.

Will and I glanced fearfully at each other, knowing that the boys were in big trouble. There was no way that they would have shifted all the gear at the festival – at least Eric clearly had some left – and it might seem more than a little suspect that both of them had wallets jam-packed with Dineros.

Sure enough, the police found heaps of drugs upon both of our shell-shocked friends. Eric looked a real mess, clasping his head in his hands and muttering Spanish expletives to himself as the police found a whopping 7 grams of weed upon him – not to mention the endless number of little drug packets that they pulled from all over his belongings. The strange thing was that, with every new packet they discovered, Eric would let out a remorseful squeal as if it came as a surprise!

Eric was in trouble: his eyes glazed over (not only with the effects of the marijuana that had hot-boxed the car throughout the journey), and for the first time, he was speechless.

Victor had seemed quite calm throughout the proceedings, but underneath this façade of nonchalance, his blood was boiling. As soon as the search was done and both men had been ceremoniously given official-looking pieces of paper (which presumably held their fate), Victor started removing all of Eric's belongings from his car and set about throwing them at his friend. When every last piece had been removed, Victor beckoned Will and me back into the car and would certainly have left Eric by that roadside if the police hadn't ordered Victor to at least take the man to the next junction.

Not a word was said in the remaining five minutes that Eric was with us before he was ceremonially chucked out at the very next junction. I don't even think that Victor looked at Eric, keeping his hands tightly fastened to the steering wheel as if to prevent them from naturally flying up to strangle the prime offender.

"We're sorry Victor," I said, breaking a long silence since Eric's departure. "Are you going to be OK?"

"Yes, it's OK," he replied slowly. "Don't worry about me. I got lucky. I was given a suspended fine, but one time a friend of mine got caught with twice the amount that I did and has never paid."

"What about Eric?" Will inquired hesitantly.

"I don't know about him!" Victor snapped. "Maybe it will be worse for that idiot, but I don't care!" Victor paused for a moment, breathing heavily as he took time to let recent events sink in. "Do you know...?" Victor stopped short and let out a wry chuckle, before continuing. "Do you know I only met him a couple of days ago? Man, I'm such an idiot! Why did I get involved with that loser?"

* * * * *

When we eventually arrived in Victor's hometown, our friend was profusely apologetic for tying us up in such an embarrassing situation, but we tried our best to show only thanks and sympathy as we waved goodbye. And yet, for all of Victor's good intentions, he did drop us off in a rubbish spot.

We had to hike for about half an hour just to find our way back to the motorway and, even when we had arrived there, we still had to wait for two hours before a big friendly giant named Pedro came to the rescue.

Will had lost his patience a long time ago, and his impatience in turn irritated me (a vicious circle indeed), but just at the moment when we were considering a change of locations, or even giving up entirely, Pedro pulled over in his flashy 4x4, and we were on our way to Barcelona.

Language barriers stopped us from being able to learn much about our kind chauffeur and his partner, Goncha, but we humorously attempted the exchange of personal details, using Franglais, Spanglish, and a good amount of gesturing too, enough to satisfy and amuse our merry friends. We ascertained that Pedro and Goncha had been together for some eight years and had three sons by different partners. They lived in the same town as Victor and were on their way to the *Supermacado*.

I'm sure we learned a few more things than these during that thirty-minute ride, but no more immediately spring to mind this Thursday morn as I sit in our grotty, but mercifully cheap, illegally-run hostel... I'll explain later.

DAY FIFTEEN:
RANDOM FIELD JUST ACROSS FRENCH BORDER, NR. PERPIGNAN, PYRÉNÉES-ORIENTALES, FRANCE, FRIDAY 25TH JULY, 2008, 9AM

Bonjour! We found ourselves back in France late last night, thanks predominantly to the happy coincidence of bumping into a couple of Italian hippies driving their campervan all the way from Lisbon to Milan. I have just woken up and crawled out from our tent to the welcome realisation that Etso and Christina's van is still parked up next to us in this random field just over the border. But before I fill you in on the details of yesterday's story, I must first give an account of our two nights in Barcelona.

Pedro dropped us off right in the heart of the city, at the famous *Plaza Cataluña*, where we soon arranged to meet a few of our festival friends who had joined in the fun by also hitching up to Barcelona. Whilst we waited for Jamie and Chris to arrive, for no particular reason we decided to play some songs on our little travel guitar, and before you knew it we were busking.

I had thrown down Will's cap as our collecting plate more in jest than in expectation as we began to pull out all the classics: Ronan, Clapton, Mayer, Rice, and Taylor all made appearances. With no real agenda we had started to make friends and attracted quite a crowd.

A group of Russian school kids gathered to our right and began clapping, whilst a friendly French family listened intently on our left, just the other side of the flowerpot that made for us a footstool. We asked the mother of two young girls and a teenage boy if she would like to request a song and, glancing at her youngest daughter, she suggested some James Blunt. Luckily for them, *You're Beautiful* was pretty much at the top of Will's repertoire and I was soon tapping a drumbeat on my knees and attempting vocal harmonies to Will's exemplary cover. We even did a slightly cheesy French translation of the chorus, which seemed enough to win the affections of the shy eight year-old and, with it, her family.

Their eighteen year-old son, Jean-Baptiste (great name), spoke much better English than we did French, so he quickly took on the role of group translator, despite our best efforts to persevere in la langue d'amour. It turned out that the Richelme family live in Nice, which, funnily enough, stood somewhere between Barcelona and Malaysia.

Alerted by this helpful coincidence, we told them about our trip and suggested that they might like to offer us a ride. Being a family of five, they apologetically informed us that they didn't have enough room for us in the car, but would be more than happy to invite us round for dinner on Friday night (that is tonight!).

We gratefully accepted and I cheekily remarked that they might even fancy letting us put our tent up in their garden for the night. Slightly taken aback by my unabashed approach, M. Richelme told me that we would "see what happens"... I reckon that's a definite "yes."

Thus, after about half an hour of busking in the centre of Barcelona we had been invited round for dinner (and likely accommodation) in Nice and somehow made about 8 Euros too. Not a bad earner by all accounts. Now we just have the small challenge of making it across the breadth of France for dinner tonight. I just came off the phone with Mme. Richelme, who seemed mildly perturbed when I told her that we might not arrive until the Sunday. In fact, she seemed so offended that I quickly changed my mind and told her we'd be there by about 9pm... We've got some work to do.

* * * * *

... Just to clear up a little something thus far unaccounted for, how much does a polar bear weigh? Well, as Will proudly told Caroline Scarth and family in what may have been the moment that we firmly secured our very first hitch, I don't really know but it's enough to break the ice!

2. "FREE FRANK!"

DAY SIXTEEN:
LE CAFÉ DELL'ARTE, VIEUX NICE, PROVENCE-ALPES-COTE
D'AZUR, FRANCE, SATURDAY 26TH JULY, 2008, 14.26

As you may be able to ascertain from the header, we made it to Nice, but for cliff-hanger purposes, I won't tell you just yet whether we arrived in time for dinner last night. For the time being it's back to Plaza Cataluña and the story of our two nights in Barcelona.

So where were we? Busking profits bagged, we were finally joined by Chris and Jamie, who had had a much less interesting ride with a couple of English lads who made them fork out for petrol money, thus breaking our fundamental rule on their first attempt. We weren't impressed.

Leaving Plaza Cataluña in search of food and a bed for the night, Will remembered that a festival friend had given him the number of a lady who was said to own a cheap (if not strictly street-legal) hostel and, upon realising that most of the other hostels were fully booked, we decided to give this "Francesca" a call. We wolfed down some pretty dire food at a cheapish restaurant (the chef somehow managed to make a simple omelette taste bad) and then went to meet the wonderfully eccentric, and slightly drunk Francesca, who shiftily gave a few looks around to make sure that we weren't being watched, before ushering us into a grotty apartment block down a back alley just off La Rambla (the main street running away from

Plaza Cataluña).

When I think of Francesca, the image that springs to mind is of an eighties hooker in a seedy suburb of New York (from what I've seen in films, that is) and her apartment served only to enhance this profile. The interior seemed to suggest that it couldn't remember the last time that anyone had cleaned it, clinging on to the dirt and cobwebs that had become its only friends. The walls were unpainted and the banister had long since rotted in its place; fortunately for us, the appearance of our quarters was our last concern. We would have put up our tent in the middle of La Rambla if we thought we could have gotten away with it, but this dodgy hostel at least gave us a place to leave our heavy bags, whilst we made a short circuit of the perimeters to get a better feel for our surroundings.

La Rambla seems to be home to all the city's performers. Mimers, singers, dancers and artists fill the streets throughout the day, and the night's most popular vendors are immigrants selling beers on the cheap. We decided to make the most of this booming trade and bought a few cans from the first man to approach us, taking them with us on our tour of the harbour.

Barcelona is a beautiful city and the evening serves only to highlight its grandeur as the city lights shine out majestically over the surrounding waters. We walked along the port, envious of the flashy yachts docked there, and found a nice spot to smoke a victory cigar, which at least helped feign some sense of fitting in with the city slickers as the night drew to a close.

* * * * *

The following day we enjoyed our first lie-in (and our first bed) since leaving Moussac, then headed out for a café con leche and croissant breakfast in a local café. The rest of the day was spent wandering the streets of Barcelona, marvelling at the many architectural works of genius left by the highly acclaimed Antoni Gaudi. He has more than left his mark on the city for practically every attraction worth seeing was his creation. There is a bizarre looking temple – the famous *La Sagrada Familia* – which is more bright, colourful, and generally positive-looking than any other Cathedral I've seen. There is a multicoloured house that would fit in quite well in the fairytale of *Hansel And Gretel*. It seems that everywhere you go in Barcelona there are signs of the Master's legacy. Postcards are all Gaudi-inspired, books are entirely devoted to his work, thus it was quite fitting when Will and I finished the day by eating in a restaurant named after the great man: *Tapas Gaudi*.

Barcelona was a city in which we really let our hair down (metaphorically speaking at least; our hair remains rather coarse). We walked around all the big streets, gawped at the thousands of richly dressed men and women, and even rather cheekily climbed our way up the spiral staircase of *La Sagrada Familia*, bypassing a "No Entry" sign and winding our way heavenwards, occasionally stopping and pretending innocently to stare out of a window or take a better look at the decaying steps, so as not to arouse the suspicions of the paying customers making their descent.

Our justification for this minor law-breaking is twofold. Firstly, they had already charged us a whopping 20 Euros each to get in, and wanted a further 2 Euros for the privilege of seeing anything more than the construction sight that currently dominates the interior of the famous temple. Secondly, we believed that Gaudi would have wanted us to. After all, did not the great man once say: "The great book, always open and which we should make an effort to read, is that of Nature?" [We read that little gemstone in the Gaudi exhibition downstairs]. One thing we also read was that Gaudi met a premature death when he was run over by a tram, so he can't have been *that* clever after all.

DAY SEVENTEEN:
LE DEUXIEME MAISON DE LA FAMILLE RICHELME, PEYRESQ, ALPES-DE-HAUTE-PROVENCE, FRANCE, DIMANCHE 27TH JUILLET, 2008, 14.57

Will and I have been with the delightful Richelme family for two days now and are about to spend what sadly looks to be our third and final night at their home in Nice. It is strange to think that just five days ago we had no idea that they even existed and now we have been welcomed into their home and absorbed into their family as if we have been friends for years.

This is definitely going to be the best bit about the trip: meeting new friends and getting a real taste for their different ways of life and expressions of culture as we move from place to place. Our time with the Richelmes – most of which has been spent enjoying the gastronomic delights of French cuisine upon their terrace – brings back fond memories of our time with the Scarths. The French really do exhibit the best of European culture, with their long lasting family dinners outside in the glorious sunshine (of course, in Nice they do have a slight climactic advantage) and their fine appreciation of what rich sauces and red wine can bring to a meal.

It is such a lovely thing to be able to attempt to converse in each other's languages, not just being typically British and assuming that all the world should go out of its way, as it does, by conversing only in ours. Christian and Martine Richelme have very kindly opened their home to us these past two days and *did* even allow us to erect our tent in their back garden, which just so happens to include a private outdoor pool. The only drawback to our "bedroom's" location is the number of bugs that it seems to attract: I was bitten alive by mosquitoes last night, whilst Will thinks that he may have unknowingly slept with a spider... I've always told that boy he needs to be more careful about such things.

The Richelme family's hospitality has extended so far that this morning Christian even took us to visit their second home in a tiny village called Peyresq at the heart of the French Alps. Currently we sit precariously upon an enormous rock, looking down at a drop of what must be several hundred metres, feeling generally overawed by the sheer number of breathtaking peaks that surround us (at the moment I can count nine), the furthest of which majestically fade in and out of sight in the distant horizon with each change of the wind.

But, for this moment, I wish to take your minds far away from here, back to the centre of Barcelona and a little café that was the location for our final breakfast in the Catalan capital, *Casa Joan*...

Whoever Joan might be, I'm a big fan. Oh, and I don't think we're talking about an English lady here; I prefer to think of Joan as a rotund, old Spanish man with a fine moustache and a pizza in hand... no, wait, that's a bit Italian. Scratch that, I think that Joan – pronounced something more like "Jo-an" with a silent "j" and possibly a replacement "h" (but certainly two syllables) – is a seventy-two year old Spanish gent with an innumerable supply of wrinkles (think of Churchill in canine form), who once designed a funky coloured Cathedral in the centre of Barcelona... Hold on a minute, that's it: Joan was actually Gaudi's alter-ego/pseudonym.

I should probably use this moment swiftly and officially to disclaim everything that I've just written as pure speculation. Whoever Joan is, we stayed at his/her café for the best part of two hours until we felt sufficiently rested and ready to undertake the next phase of the journey. Then off we went, backpacks reinstated, the sun already making us pant as it warmed into the day and followed our every step as we huffed and puffed out of the city centre and into the unknown. The target was simple: we had a little under two days to make it back into France and travel all the way along the southern coast to Nice.

* * * * *

It wasn't long before our standard combination of cheek and charm had landed us our first lift, which came in the form of a nice young Australian man named Daniel, whom I accosted at a set of traffic lights by frantically waving at him through the window until he wound it down to be told that we wanted to hitch a ride anywhere out of town.

Never having picked up a hitcher before, Daniel was uncertain at first, but soon warmed to us and, once he had reassured himself that we were highly unlikely to rob him, even took us a little further than he was originally intending, so that we might end up in a better spot. Daniel dropped us by the side of a petrol station and we can't have been there for more than five minutes before we bumped into two Italian hippies, who casually invited us into the back of their van, apologetically informing us that we were going to have to fight with their two black Labradors, Zango and Mina, for pride of place on the bench in the back.

To undertake the work of describing our bohemian friends, perhaps the best thing would be to start by describing their respective dogs – both of which seemed to pay an uncanny resemblance to their owner.

We start with Zango (Etso's boy), who, in a world of his own, would playfully bound around the back of the van, jumping on and off Will and me (who had beaten the dogs to our precarious perch in the back) to his heart's content, whilst appearing to share the attention span of a goldfish.

Mina, on the other hand (Christina's docile companion) seemed happy enough just to curl up underneath our feet and stay motionless for the entire journey, oblivious to everything going on around her, but clearly comforted by the ever-presence of her bouncy boyfriend, Zango. Now, replace the names Zango and Mina for Etso and Christina and you pretty much know all you need to know about our Italian friends, who were driving home from a year in Lisbon.

This really was *the* stereotypical hitchhike. We were in the back of a campervan with two dope-smoking hippies, who actually *did* play Bob Marley tracks on loop for the 24-hour period that we travelled with them. The top speed of the van must have been about 50mph – slashed in half when driving up hills – but the relaxed pace didn't seem to bother our friends in the slightest. Switching between the roles of driver and chief spliff-roller, it was just as well that our vehicle didn't move very fast because our friends would burst into hysterics every time a butterfly flapped past the window or one of them nearly forgot to apply the brakes in time.

Now, I feel as if I am selling our friends a little bit short in my descriptions. Just before you write our friends off as complete no-hopers, let me inform you that both Etso and Christina spoke very good English, Spanish, French, Portuguese and, presumably, Italian, and they were currently returning to their home in Parma (near Milan) so that Etso could finish his medicine degree – the last year of which had been spent on an Erasmus scheme in Lisbon. Christina, meanwhile – at 25, one year Etso's junior – had followed her partner of three years to work in Lisbon as head chef in an Italian restaurant, thereby earning their keep. This was another example to us of the uselessness of making snap judgments about people dependent solely upon their physical appearance or way of life.

As it was, it wasn't Etso and Christina who needed to fight for our affections; quite the opposite, Will and I were desperate to make as good an impression as possible so that our new friends might take us as far as possible on our route to Nice – if you hadn't worked it out already, Nice happens to lie somewhere in between Lisbon and Parma, so there was a good chance we'd found ourselves a lift the entire way!

At first it had seemed as if it might be a little tricky to win their respect; Etso in particular was hesitant to trust two British strangers (he told us that he didn't like English people), especially given that these strangers were encroaching upon what had once been a private sojourn for these two loved-up hippies.

It is difficult to pinpoint the exact moment when Etso's mind had finally been made up, but I think that it must have happened somewhere near the time when we arrived at the *Libertat Franki* (Free Frank) rally. "Free Frank" has since become our latest catchphrase – always accompanied by raising one arm to the side, pointing the fist skyward in a defiant gesture akin to the manner in which I imagine a 1960s flower-power extremist might have done. But before I give too much away about our night in Girona – which ended with a protest for releasing Franki from his shackles – I must take you back to the beginning, which started with a search for some squatters.

It turns out that not only do Etso and Christina subscribe to membership of the intangible universal society of hippies, but they are also part of what I understand to be a similarly universal secret society of squatters. At first we were a little bemused by this new concept, only vaguely possessing the notion that there did exist some people in the world who liked to house themselves in derelict buildings, but not linking this with any sort of membership within a club or society.

That was our mistake.

"You can find squatters anywhere," Christina told us, giving her dreadlocks their regular flick away from her eyes. "We do this every time we go to a new city. It's easy."

"But how do you find them?" Will enquired, bemused at this slightly ethereal concept.

Well, as we soon learned, that's the easy part. All you need to do is look for a few distinctive traits of appearance. Dreadlocks and a pet dog are a good start, whilst a not so healthy smell of marijuana lingering nearby and, if possible, an actual joint in hand, will confirm suspicions.

If only we'd have known these character traits from the start, we could have immediately discerned that our friends were part of this international squatters fellowship and, as such, were sure to be pros at the dying art of searching for squatters.

Sure enough, it wasn't long before they had directed our path towards the steps of a Cathedral, where a lady squatter (ticking off every item on the checklist) was sitting and waiting as if she had taken one glance into a crystal ball and had ever since been awaiting our arrival. The surreal nature of the experience rose to new levels as this squatter – who had the vacant expression of a lady who'd abused far too many drugs over the years – mumbled something barely audible in Spanish and, before we knew it, was leading us to the Free Frank Rally.

What we had once thought was a simple search for somewhere to sleep that night – and perhaps a community to share our homelessness with – ended with a full-on protestation against the apparent injustice that had seen Catalan political activist, Francesc Argemi Anglada, sent to prison for burning a Spanish flag.

This was the first protest either of us had ever been to, and it certainly fitted the stereotype. There were posters, petitions, refreshments, recording equipment and, of course, a considerable number of people who I now feel qualified enough to refer to as squatters. If it weren't for the lofty 12 Euro asking price for food, I'm sure we would have stayed long into the night, but as it was, the four of us departed as one, each echoing spirited cries of "Free Frank" and raising our right arms up to the sky in unified protestation.

DAY EIGHTEEN:
CHEZ RICHELME, POOLSIDE, NICE, PROVENCE-ALPES-COTE D'AZUR, FRANCE, MONDAY 28TH JULY, 2008, 9.10AM

A long weekend in Nice with the Richelme family is something I would certainly recommend. We have been well fed, washed (not by them), have been advised as to the best places to visit in Nice, and have even been chauffeur-driven all the way out to their beautiful cottage in the Alps for a day out with *Dad*. Yet, before I divulge too much more regarding the details of this long weekend (now about to end), I must fill you in on the remainder of what you might refer to as our not-so-speedy version of *The Italian Job*, which somehow took us from a field just inside France on Friday morning all the way to Nice in time for dinner.

Mme. Richelme had sounded so put out by the notion that we might not make it in time that I couldn't help reassuring her, no matter how hopeless our cause appeared. But, now that I had made my hasty pledge, we had the small problem of attempting to convey the situation to our hippie pals, who weren't in any rush to get home because this was as much a holiday for them as it was a matter of getting home.

The Italians were partaking of a leisurely breakfast as we went over to speak with them early on that Friday morning.

"Good morning guys," Will began. "I don't suppose you are planning on making it to Nice in time for dinner tonight, are you? We've kind of got ourselves a date, you see..."

Etso and Christina smiled back at us and said nothing, their familiar vacant expressions as confusing as they were endearing. What were we thinking? There was no way that our Italian friends were going to understand our urgency.

"Nice?" Christina replied nonchalantly, after thinking the matter through. "Si, perhaps."

To be honest, I doubt that the thought even registered in their minds. At least you wouldn't have thought so, judging by their incredibly relaxed approach to what Will and I now considered should be a *race* across southern France. We were crawling along, regularly stopping for all "necessary" detours (such as seeing a beach here, or a nice view there) and by lunchtime we had only made it to Montpellier – barely a third of the way.

Will and I were in a quandary. It wasn't our friends who wanted to get to Nice in such a rush; they hadn't asked to be our personal chauffeurs, and yet with every added minute of dawdling, we were becoming increasingly less fond of them, and more eager to leave.

There was still time, however, for our Italian friends to compound our misery by deciding that this lunch break was perfect opportunity for them to showcase their hidden talents at the Brazilian martial art of *Kapawera*. Languidly they exchanged weight from one foot to the other, flipping onto their hands in an acrobatic attempt to floor the other, whilst Will and I were encouraged to perform makeshift drumming beats upon our knees to accompany the entertainment, but what might usually have been a fun day out in the park with new friends felt excruciating like torture to Will and me, desperate as we were to get back on the road to Nice, toute suite!

It was almost 4pm by the time the entertainment finally drew to a close and we lethargically wandered back to the van. With about 330km still separating us from our target and only five hours to get there, it was decision time. Surely there was no way that our friends would make it to Nice that night. It had taken us more than twenty-four hours to make the same distance from Barcelona to Montpellier and it hardly seemed as if Etso and Christina were about to employ a change of pace. If we were to stand any chance of making it in time, we were going to have to do something we had never dreamed possible: spurn the chance of a certain lift to a destination (however slow it might be) in preference of the distinct uncertainty of waiting by the side of the road again for the slim chance that we might instantly find someone heading our way.

How I long to tell you that that was the end of it; that we got out our stuff, jumped out of the van and stuck our thumbs out right there and then, by the side of that Montpellien park. But no. Against our better judgment, when asked whether we would like to get out of the vehicle in Montpellier or stay with them until they reached the next town of Arles, we took one quick look at our new map of Europe, decided that it couldn't hurt to stay with them for just one more stint, and told them we would stay.

At only about 30km away, we had naively assumed that we would be in Arles in no time at all, but alas, Etso and Christina – unfazed by what now must surely have been an unmistakable look of concern in our eyes – trundled along as slowly as ever along a deserted coastal road, before casually informing us that they were searching for a place to go for a "bath!"

I don't know what it was about our manner that was so easy to misunderstand. Maybe we were simply being too polite and British about the whole thing, but whatever it was, we weren't having the least bit of impact upon our bohemian buddies. Facial expressions that, to us, screamed of urgency had been misunderstood to be the faces of those that longed to find a beach to hang out for a while, whilst they took a bath! We were never going to make it to Nice with these two jokers.

Thankfully, however, that is not the end of it; the story does not end there. Something, somehow was about to conspire to turn our misery into a chain of events that I simply cannot but refer to as miraculous...

DAY NINETEEN:
DUE RUOTE SNACK BAR, VENEZIA, VENETO, ITALIE, TUESDAY 29TH JULY, 2008, 11.27AM

It is not every day that two young, rather strapping, English lads walk into Venice over the 3850 metre bridge, yet this was romantic way that Will and

I huffed and puffed our way into the former merchant hub of Europe this morning, in a moment that Shakespeare himself would have been happy to relate.

To be honest, we tried our best to avoid it, but this was the only option remaining because of the inconsiderate way in which the Venetians seem to have closed off all potential hitching spots for the several miles of motorway that precede the bridge to the island. The only other method that we might have tried – which perhaps would even have surpassed the romanticism involved in our marathon walk – would have been to try and hitch a ride with a merchant vessel, or any other boat for that matter.

We chose to walk, and although four kilometres might not sound like much, when carrying twice one's bodyweight upon one's back, it is no mean feat. Furthermore, it is amazing how deceptively close a city can appear as you look at it from the other side of a straight bridge. For much of the walk it seemed no closer at all, until we looked behind us to see the distant speck that marked our beginnings.

We have been in Venice for about one hour now, taking time to get a feel for this otherworldly city from one of its many canal-side cafes. As you may be able to ascertain from the date and time of my previous entry, we've come quite a long way in a relatively short space of time. Since leaving Nice at about 11am yesterday morning we have crossed the Italian border and proceeded to flash past much of the breadth of northern Italy. We feel like we are cheating Italy somewhat by spending such a short time experiencing the wealth of culture that this country boasts, but we have begun to realise that we have been dawdling of late and will never reach Malaysia if we don't quicken up a little. Italy is the necessary sacrifice; our defence, the knowledge that we will surely visit again.

Now, when I left you, we were in Nice and I was talking about miracles. This deserves further justification, so back in time we go, to the moment we parted ways with Etso and Christina as a result of a freak weather-fluctuation…

* * * * *

I think that one could fairly safely presume that a weatherman in the south of France can probably afford to take a day off from time to time during the long summer months – such is the consistency with which the sun doth pleasantly shine. That Friday was one day upon which he should certainly have called into work.

The morning had been the same old sunshine story. We had been cooped-up in the back of their van with a wet Zango upon our laps and the scorching summer rays threatening to bake us alive. Lunchtime had carried on in that vein and, in fact, I cannot remember seeing even one cloud in the sky.

Then suddenly (and for once I feel entitled to use this overused narrative-cliché) we were enveloped in an eerie mist like none I have ever seen – not in the south of France anyway! This thick mist followed us all the way along our coastal path to Arles and was the one saving grace that prevented our friends from stopping to take the bath that would have certainly ended our hopes of reaching Nice that day.

Now, I cannot honestly say that I have studied the weather conditions in that particular portion of French land in enough detail to certifiably conclude that what we experienced was a violation of the laws of nature (which, by Hume's definition, would denote a miracle), but there did seem to be a superabundance of holiday-makers along the coastline by Arles, and I doubted whether the foggy marshland that formed the road to Arles on that particular Friday would attract such a crowd.

Baths duly omitted, our bohemian friends were forced to stew in their own juices for another day (goodness knows how long it had been since the last one!) and finally bade us farewell at a petrol station on the Nice-side of the little town of Arles.

What followed was a string of extraordinarily quick lifts, beginning with the crutch-laden, thirty-something year-old Jerome. En route to Aix-en-Provence, poor Jerome – whose leg did not seem in any fit state to drive – kindly agreed that we could ride with him and, about an hour later, dropped us off at a second station de service.

Our sympathy for Jerome somewhat dwindled, however, when we later found out that he appeared to have stolen Will's phone – or at least this is how I would like the story to read. Truth be told, I think that somewhere in the midst of exchanging details, I seem vaguely to remember putting the phone down in what is probably the very spot that it remained long after we had exited the car.

Not only was Will understandably perturbed by my minor hiccup – in what was the latest of a long line of articles that I have been (for "bag weight" related reasons, of course) shedding recently – but this latest blip had caused us to lose the only method of communication that we had with the Richelmes. It was *his* phone on which we had logged Jean-Baptiste's number and it was *his* phone from which we soon expected to receive their call, having recently updated them of our progress from Jerome's car – a vehicle we would surely never see again.

In the time that it took me to work out what had happened, we had already hopped into our next lift, in what was definitely the nicest car to have picked us up so far. It was a *Hummer* (one of those huge American 4x4s that look more like moon-buggies than cars), which, we whispered to one another whilst running over to it, *must* belong to a rock-star.

Lo and behold, upon bundling into our next vehicle, who should be behind the wheel but a M. Victor Bosch – a self-professed rock-star, who certainly looked the part with his flowing grey-brown locks and leather jacket. Living in Lyon and working as a producer for a man he described as the French *Bob Dylan*, Victor told us that he was also currently producing a musical of the famous French cartoon, *Kirikou*, and spent any spare time in the studio, composing and recording new pieces. I must confess to being slightly star-struck, especially as Victor told us that he was currently on his way to Tommy Hilfiger's annual party in Saint Tropez.

Obviously we asked for an invite, but the best that Victor said he could do would be to mention our names to Tommy and co., and give our details to his "good friend" Ewan Mcgregor, who, he told us, would also be attending.

Slightly miffed that we weren't instantly presented with invitations ourselves, we remained grateful that Victor hadn't lost himself in his own ego – as one might expect celebrities to do – and was happy to pick up two bedraggled hitchhikers, to supply them with crisps and drinks, and to talk about them to his high-flying friends that night. This was good enough for us, and we started to dream of the TV crews that would soon be in touch, asking to fly out and join us, surreptitiously tailing us with video recorders for an exclusive documentary about the *hitch*.

But wait... where was the phone? We had been so caught up in all the drama of our latest hitch that we had completely forgotten about our approaching date with the Richelmes and, when I finally thought to give them a call, we realised what had happened.

Victor had taken us the bulk of the way by that stage, and wished us well as he headed off to the party, leaving us in our fourth petrol station of the day to rack our brains in search of the faintest relics of Jean-Baptiste's 14-digit number. In the midst of the brain-racking, a young man named Gellus kindly stopped to pick us up on his way home to Cannes, which, he told us, was "*tres près*" to Nice.

We'd made remarkable progress in the last few hours and would be but twenty kilometres away by the time this particular lift was through, and yet, painful as it was to think, we were now forced into considering the likelihood that we *would* make it to Nice on time, but have no way to contact our friends, thus rendering all our efforts vain; and we would have to find somewhere else to eat and to pitch our tent that night.

When Gellus dropped us off at yet another petrol station, he kindly approached another driver on our behalf. As a lawyer, Gellus' skills as our advocate were never in doubt and he had soon acquired a lift for us with the good-humoured Jennifer (a fellow lawyer), who was on her way home... to Nice!

Cautious at first, this blonde-haired mother of two gradually warmed to Will and me as we told her about our trip and shared with her the story of the lost phone, which now seemed sure to have scuppered our plans. We tried our luck by asking Jennifer if she had heard of the Richelmes and might possibly be able to help us find them, but what were the chances of that? Nice is a big city and she told us that *Richelme* is a fairly common French family name.

"Je suis désolé," Jennifer responded. "I am sorry I cannot help you, but I do have a telephone if you can remember the number."

Oh the irony! How unlikely had it seemed that we would make it to Nice on time, and now that we were here, there was no chance we would remember a number as long as Jean-Baptiste's, was there?

One last time Will and I scoured the very depths of our brains.

"00… 33… 06"… We were beginning to piece together the number! Surely we couldn't remember the whole thing, could we?

For security reasons, I had better not reveal Jean-Baptiste's number completely, but I can honestly reveal that, as miraculous (there's that word again) as it may appear, with a combined effort we remembered the entire 14-digit number and we were soon listening to his vaguely familiar voice bellowing out over the speakerphone of Jennifer's car. Twenty minutes later and we were pulling up outside the doorstep of the Richelmes' family home, just thirty minutes late for dinner.

DAY TWENTY:
SAN MARGHERITA SQUARE, VENEZIA, VENETO, ITALIE, WEDNESDAY 30TH JULY, 2008, 9.15AM

There truly is no place like Venice. A maze of avenues adjoins a web of canal passages and together make up one of the world's easiest places to get lost in. Although we have only been here for a little over twenty-four hours, it feels like we have walked the place three times over and still have no idea how to get back to our hotel.

I suppose it's just as well that we are leaving. As soon as the effects of our morning cappuccinos have kicked in, we'll sleepily make our way back to that killer bridge, and onwards to Slovenia. One can only hope that we will receive the same sort of luck that saw us make it from Nice to Venice in pretty much one ride, all thanks to a Brazilian trucker by the name of Helio.

After three glorious days of wining and dining with the Richelmes, Christian had kindly driven us out of the centre of Nice, dropping us off at a service station on the beginning of the autoroute towards Italy, and we had been employing rather upfront tactics ever since. Approaching drivers as they went between petrol pumps and the kiosk, we finally knew how it feels to be one of those on-the-street salesmen that everyone crosses the street to avoid.

"Excusez-moi," we would start, plastic smiles plastered across our faces; "we're trying to get towards Ita…"

But before we could finish the sentence the driver would usually have passed us by, muttering something or other about leaving the gas on at home, or how the cat had just called to alert him that he needed rescuing from the neighbour's tree; then off he would go, waving apologetically and giving us one of those, "Oh, I'm so terribly sorry" faces, which really translate as: "I could not care less about the two of you freeloaders and would much rather you didn't bother me again."

Luckily for us, on this particular day, it wasn't only grumpy workaholics with too much money and not enough time on their hands to pay anyone else the slightest bit of regard; on this day, there just so happened to be a warm-hearted Brazilian trucker by the name of Helio, stopping off for refreshments in between his long drive from Lisbon to Venezia. Barely ten minutes of waiting time had elapsed before we were hopping into the cabin of a truck (together this time), and we would not leave again until we had crossed much of the breadth of Northern Italy.

3. THE FRENCH CONNECTION

DAY TWENTY-ONE:
KAVARNA MAČEK BAR, LJUBLJANA, SLOVENIA, THURSDAY 31ST JULY 2008, 14.36

Having experienced quite enough romance since stepping into Shakespearian territory the previous morn, we quickly ruled out a long return hike over the Venetian bridge and set about finding a lift from the petrol station just before it.

As tends to be the way when hitchhiking, our patience wore thin after a comparatively short space of time and we found ourselves irrationally considering the possibility that no lift would ever come along, after what had only been about half an hour! This alarm rose to such an extent that we soon changed techniques, moving from our tried and tested petrol station position to a more erratic approach.

Our new, more in your face method, involved walking up and down the line of traffic before the bridge, attempting – through a mixture of waving, thumb wagging and slow motion, overemphasised lip movements that read something like: "Just... to... the... oth... er... side... of... the... bridge..." – to coerce these poor, unsuspecting drivers into taking us anywhere.

Subtle, our approach was not, but effective it certainly turned out to be. Barely a few minutes had elapsed before a chap named Andrea hurriedly beckoned us into his car – ensuing the wrath of a hundred honking drivers behind him as he did so – and on we proceeded to Venezia Mestre (the part of town that isn't just an island).

OK, so it wasn't the longest lift, but Andrea knew the place well enough to drop us off in a superb spot for catching a much more substantial ride, leaving us by the side of a petrol station on the edge of town, where, he told us, we should ask for a ride to Trieste.

Petrol stations on main roads are always a good option for finding long lifts because, more often than not, drivers will be filling up on their way to somewhere quite far away. Sure enough, a young Frenchman by the name of Mickael fitted the bill entirely. During the previous two days, this twenty-eight year-old carpenter had driven all the way from his home in Mont Saint-Michel to Venezia, and was now filling up on gas as he prepared to travel on towards Slovenia, Croatia, and beyond. And if the distance that he was travelling wasn't already enough to secure our interest, the fact that Mickael was driving in a rather plush BMW Estate sealed it.

The only drawback was that Mickael didn't appear to have even the slightest grasp of the English language, but this gave Will and me the perfect platform with which to perform French skills that had been honed during our time with the Richelmes.

"On va faire du stop de l'Angleterre á Malaysie," I said slowly and clearly in my Franglais accent. "Maintenant, on va aller á Slovenie. Ou est vous allé?"

Mickael seemed understandably shocked. It's not every day, I suppose, that a Frenchman hears a couple of foreigners trying to tell him, in his own language, that they are attempting to hitchhike towards Malaysia.

"Á Malaysie?" he repeated, giving us the time change our aims to a more believable target.

But, of course, there was to be no change.

"Ouais," we coolly puffed together, shrugging our shoulders as we dropped our bags into la derrière of Mickael's Beemer, and headed off together towards Slovenie.

* * * * *

We arrived in Koper/Copadistria in the early evening and went straight for a dip in the Mediterranean. It is rare that one finds a town that clearly hasn't made up its mind between two potential names, but frustrations at such indecisiveness aside, we immediately fell in love with the place – our very first taste of Slovenia.

Probably the first Slovenians I had ever met were the three street vendors whom we encountered as we made our way back from our swim – dripping wet, but happy enough to drip-dry in the evening warmth, whilst we stopped to chat to Boris, Simona and an old lady called something like "Gor-sheeba" (the names are getting harder).

A row of five or six huts selling local produce and touristy treats lay between the main street that ran to the coast and the sea, but it was Boris and co. that had gone out of their way to invite us to their particular stand for some free samples of the local liquor. To be honest, it pretty much just tasted like vodka, but perhaps this should not have come as such a surprise now that we have entered the old Russian block.

Having some previous knowledge of basic Russian from months spent in Kazakhstan a few years ago, I was intrigued to see the clear similarities between the two languages, as Boris – who looked like an archetypal Russian – enthusiastically took us through our first steps in the language.

"Dobre Dan," which means "Good Day," aroused my suspicions about the origin of the language (the phrase is exactly the same in Russian), whilst the generally gruffer twang to the accent confirmed them. For the time being at least, it appears that we have left behind the romantic sounds of the French, Spanish and Italians for a harsher, less rhythmic tone.

This potentially traumatic transition was softened slightly by the presence of our new French friend, Mickael, who deserves a fuller introduction.

Tall, thin, and a little odd, Mickael was the reclusive type, which perhaps suggests why he was travelling tout seul. His English was even less impressive than my French and he didn't appear to have grasped that neither Will nor I had the faintest chance of understanding him unless he spoke a little slower.

"Parler un peu plus lentement, s'il vous plait!" we would say to the man, but he never listened.

The reason for my lack of detail in the description of the journey from Venice to Koper (I have recently been informed that Copadistria is the Italian name for it) was that there really wasn't much to talk about. Language barriers and Mickael's timid nature conspired to give us our quietest hitch thus far. We did our best to ask Mickael all our favourite questions, but had no chance to catch more than the gist of his answers, such was our friend's inability to perceive the weakness of our comprehension.

Perhaps it's a little unfair to label Mickael as "odd" because the language barrier probably wasn't helping, but then again, there really was just something a little... different about the lad. He just had a slightly... special way about him, which came across in his poor social skills, and eyes that didn't appear able to fix upon any one object for more than half a second at a time.

Again I realise that I am treading on rather thin ground in judging a man on such things as the fact that his eyes didn't move in regular ways, but I'm just telling it straight. There was nothing *wrong* with our friend, per se, but he just made us feel a little... uneasy.

Perhaps he was a cannibal, I thought, reflecting upon the difficulty with which one can be sure of these things. I suppose that there would be no way of knowing until it was too late. You would be in the oven, onto a plate and into his mouth before you had time to file your suspicions.

"A very difficult thing to catch a cannibal," I remarked to Will, as we made light of the language barriers that had brought a little awkwardness into our relationship with dear Mickael.

I'm fairly sure that neither Will and I, nor Mickael himself, wanted this relationship to go on much longer, but none of us took steps to end it because *we* wanted a driver and *Mickael* either couldn't bring himself to tell us that he'd rather go on alone, or just wanted to eat us.

Cannibalism aside, let me take you back to the moment we left Boris and friends, and looked for some dinner. On our way to finding the restaurant that Boris had recommended, we bumped into a friendly foursome of inebriated fellows, who shook our hands merrily and patted us on the back with such vigour that the word "patted" doesn't quite do it justice. Like I said, we were in Russian territory now.

Sore backs in tow, our awkward trio wandered through the pretty little town in search of our first authentic Slovenian cuisine. When we arrived at the restaurant, we were glad to see a "local specialities" page translated into English, but found it a touch disappointing that they'd simply stolen their "local" specialities from their Italian neighbours; Will and I went for calamari, whilst Mickael had gnocchi.

Perhaps the only thing authentically local about the meal was the red wine that we bought, hoping that they might have also learnt that trade from their Italian friends. We won't be making that mistake again. Matching up to the Spanish, French and Italian wines of the last few weeks was always going to be a tough ask, but Will's description of Slovenia's attempt as "sour" doesn't tell the half of it. I think we'll stick to spirits in the future – something they've hopefully had better tuition in from their time in the Union.

The beer's not too bad. Beer such as we enjoyed during the night's main event: a music festival à la Slovenie by the name of J.E.F.F. (Jazzy. Etno. Funk. Festival.). The headliners of the event were a Brazilian samba band, whose blend was certainly funky enough, but, unsurprisingly, failed to be in any way Slovenian. Is nothing authentic in this country? The Slovenian attitude seems to be one of... well, there's plenty of good stuff going on in the world already, so why don't we try producing an eclectic mix of them all in our own not-so-unique way?

Festival over, it was time to find somewhere to pitch our tent for the night. Our big friend Boris alerted us that we would be likely to be arrested if we tried to pitch a tent anywhere in Koper, so Mickael drove us out to the little village of Sveti Anton (a wonderful name for a village, but I feel sorry for whoever Anton is), where we pitched-up in the back garden of a local school for the night.

I didn't sleep particularly well – perhaps still conscious of fears regarding a certain cannibal sleeping beside us, whilst Will pestered me regarding his own fear that the strange noises outside were coming from a group of wild bears. More logically, perhaps we were also wondering if Mickael might run off with our stuff. Foolishly we had left everything – passports and money included – in the back of his car.

But when we arose, our docile friend was still there, as friendly and inoffensive as ever. As much as we were obviously grateful for Mickael's help in taking us into Slovenia, I don't think that either party regretted the parting when Mickael decided not to take us to the Slovenian capital today. The language battle had tired us all out and we were ready to let our time together remain relatively unspoilt by cutting it off before it could become, like Slovenian wine, a little sour.

Mickael took us to a decent spot just before the motorway and we were soon in the cabin of our first Slovenian truck with a lovely guy called Ivan, who – in accordance with the theme – wasn't actually Slovenian, but a Serb.

DAY TWENTY-TWO:
CASTLE CAFE, LJUBLJANA CASTLE, LJUBLJANA, SLOVENIA,
FRIDAY 1ST AUGUST, 2008, 14.26

I am a firm believer in the importance of fidelity. A strange opening gambit you might think, but one that is on my mind this lunchtime because of a conversation that we have just had with two GB athletes from the highest heights of Ljubljana's hilltop castle. Des and Kermit (apparently his actual name) are competing in the European Masters this week in what they referred to as the "elite division" – which, as far as I can gather, basically means a bunch of old boys staving off retirement for another year. Our friends are somewhere in their early forties, so perhaps not *that* old, but for athletes, I guess you'd say they've passed their peak.

Physically speaking, they looked like your average athletes (big and black) and seemed like really decent guys, but what has stuck in my mind the most was their casual approach to fidelity. Kermit, at least, is a married man, and both he and Des seemed to pay little regard to that symbol, chatting to us about girls they had met, whilst referring to a metaphorical stick that they carry around the world with them, adding new notches onto it with every "new bird." In the same vein, they asked us about our own exploits since leaving home and seemed a touch surprised when we told them that we'd left our own "sticks" at home with our girlfriends.

It has just occurred to me that if we had been different sorts, we might well have reacted differently to the waitress currently serving us – a pretty, young Slovenian girl called Mateja. She has brought us two fabulous (if a touch expensive) iced coffees and we have been gradually getting to know her, whilst even asking her if she knows of anywhere that we might stay for free tonight.

"Maybe we could stay with you," Will cheekily suggested a moment ago, desperate that we won't have to spend another night like the last one, which saw us in the corridor of an overcrowded hostel with an automatic light switch that would ping on every time a new person came through the door. They even had the cheek to charge us 20 Euros for the privilege!

We're trying not to pin too much hope upon Mateja, who is currently on the phone with her parents to check out if it'd be all right to have a couple of random English guys back to stay. If, as we expect, she is unsuccessful, we'll hitch tonight to the apparently "unmissible" Lake Bled, which lies in a slightly northern and anti-Malaysian direction, but we've never liked to make things too easy for ourselves. From Bled we have decided to opt against the straightforward route through Zagreb to Sofia, preferring a waltz along the Croatian coastline, a dip into Montenegro, perhaps even a few dodged bullets in Albania, before finally heading up through Macedonia towards *The Trussell Trust's* second home in Bulgaria.

DAY TWENTY-THREE:
GOSTILNA MURKA RESTAURANT, BLED, SLOVENIA, SATURDAY 2ND AUGUST, 2008, 22.21

Have we finally found the much-anticipated Slovenian speciality?

Slovenian sausage with cabbage and apples, served in a vinaigrette – a little bit too much of the latter in my opinion, but flippin' good otherwise, and potentially actually authentically and originally Slovenian. Is it too good to be true? The fact that it marks our second successive evening of authentically Slovenian grub excites me… a little more than you might expect.

The first of these experiences came yesterday as a direct result of the cheek with which we had approached unsuspecting waitress, Mateja. Just five minutes after expressing the doubt that anything might come from our conversation, Mateja approached us with the news that, although her parents had refused, she had also tried her good friend Anna, who was always on the lookout for strangers to welcome into her home, and she had instantly offered us a place to stay.

"She's like that. Free spirited. You'll see what I mean," joked Mateja. "I've arranged for her to meet you at the three bridges at 8pm."

For those of you that have been to Ljubljana, you'll know exactly what she meant. Sometimes it can be hard to pinpoint the exact centre of a city, but not with Ljubljana. *The* landmark of the city is this trio of parallel bridges (each parted by only a few metres), which span a river that links the castle to the city main.

When we arrived at said bridges at 8pm, we began to worry whether we might choose the wrong bridge, or whether Anna, not knowing us, might invite someone else home by mistake, but our big bags were the clue that this "free-spirited" girl needed and we hadn't waited long before we were approached by a small brunette with a surprising shyness and apparent ignorance of English for someone with such a confident approach to strangers.

This problem was soon overcome and Anna came into her own and blossomed into the lovely, free-spirited character that Mateja had so highly acclaimed. We found Anna to be just as Mateja had described her. Anna had her head in the clouds and displayed the unblemished innocence of a child who, as of yet, had no reason to presume anything but the very best in new friends. Her childlike nature was infectious. It was a joy to meet this wide-eyed, bubbly girl, whose beautiful view on life can be so difficult to find in a world increasingly scared about new things.

"Don't talk to strangers" is one of the first lessons you learn as a child, but just think about the experiences that we might already have missed if we were to implement such a philosophy upon this trip. Our personal attitude of never refusing an offer is quite the opposite. Instead of expecting the worst in people and constantly being on the lookout for danger, we believe the very best of everyone – stemming from the complete trust that we are simply required to put in people because of our utter dependence upon them for getting anywhere.

DAY TWENTY-FOUR:
BLED CHURCH, BLED, SLOVENIA, SUNDAY 3RD AUGUST, 2008, 10.41AM

It's Peter's birthday today. You have not yet met Peter, so I shall give you a short description of the turn of events that led us to meet this lonely soul. I must take you back to the time before we met Anna and just after the point at which Mateja had arranged a place for us to lay our heads that night.

After walking down the steps that led away from the castle, we were crossing over one of the bridges as he approached us. At twenty-six years of age, Peter has the look of someone whose life has been harder than most. A relatively clean appearance for a guy without a home, his beard was tidy enough and his clothes were not in tatters, but it was the sadness in his manner that startled us most. He appeared to be selling the Slovenian version of the *Big Issue*, but not wishing to buy the paper itself – having no way of deciphering the native tongue – we decided to offer Peter some food instead.

At his request, I went to buy him something from the universally prevalent McDonalds franchise. We had hoped never to enter into a Western establishment during the trip – wishing to make the most of this unique opportunity to enjoy the native foods of the different lands that we pass along the way – but I hope you can forgive me on this occasion. It was worth it just to see the look on his face when we told him that the McChicken Sandwich Meal was all for him.

"Thank you, thank you friends," Peter said, before hastily devouring the contents.

When he had finished, and had given me the remnants of the paper packaging, he began to relate the family troubles that had brought him to this sorry state at such a tender age.

"My mother not like me and send me from home when I fourteen. I go find father, who I do not know, but he very bad to me too. I am depressed and live on street for eight years," Peter said, with a face that seemed rather devoid of emotions. "My life full negative energy. Whole life people say bad thing to me," he continued.

How can people voluntarily create a life if all they are going to do then is to abuse it? I think of where Peter might be on this, his birthday, whilst Will and I enjoy the calm that has been instilled by our first church visit of the trip. The service is impossible to fully comprehend due to our rather elementary understanding of Slovenian, but we still revel in the peace that one always finds in Holy places...

Got to go; it's time for Mass.

DAY TWENTY-FIVE:
PEKARNA PLANIKA CAFE, BLED, SLOVENIA, MONDAY 4TH AUGUST, 2008, 9.12AM

Last night we decided not to sleep in a tree. Perhaps I should explain this decision, which to you might seem rather obvious.

It all started on the very first night that we arrived in Bled, thanks to our random decision to go for dinner at what was soon to become our favourite Bled-ian restaurant: *Gostilna Murka*.

We had arrived in Bled a little before sunset (only an hour since leaving Anna's place) as a result of a remarkably quick pick-up. Anna had directed us to a spot on the road to Bled, which she told us was actually an official hitching spot (apparently they have them here), and barely had we stuck out our thumbs before the lovely "..." (insert Slovenian-sounding name) pulled over, ushered us into her car, and proceeded to take us all the way to Bled, even though her home was a good 15km short of our intended destination.

Upon arrival, we were stunned by the natural beauty of this little town, which is dominated by the gigantic lake that sleeps deep in the valley between a set of breathtaking mountains. For our first hour in Bled, all that we did was to sit silently upon a bench, looking out over the lake until the final rays of light had kissed goodnight to the waters and somehow brought Will's belly to the realisation that it needed some food.

It was purely by chance that we decided upon *Gostilna Murka*, but we ended up staying in that place for the rest of the evening – largely as a result of not knowing where else we might go once night had fallen.

Every other customer had long since departed and it was with a sympathetic tone that Adiosh – the rotund and balding waiter with whom we had developed the first strands of a friendship – approached us to tell us that the restaurant was closing.

Unfamiliar with our surroundings, we sought help from our new friend.

"Do you know anywhere that we could put our tent?" I asked, secretly hoping that Adiosh was going to ignore the mention of a tent and invite us home to stay with him in his lakeside mansion.

My fanciful hopes were raised when our friend's sole response was to give us a wink and a smile, before telling us to follow him. Soon we were scrambling over hillsides, wrestling through fields, making our way to what Will and I were sure to be Adiosh's secret palace. However, unless Adiosh happened to live in a field, this was a strange way of getting there.

No, what were we thinking? He lives here; he is bound to know a shortcut. Slovenian palace, here we come!

Twenty minutes or so later, when Adiosh finally stopped, there were no royal grounds; in fact, there was no house at all. We had simply halted in one of the many fields that we had now walked through, and there did not seem anything at all out of the ordinary about this particular field to distinguish it from any of its predecessors.

"Go on then Adi" (seemingly we felt close enough at this stage for nicknames), Will urged after a short, slightly uncomfortable pause. "Where is it?"

Adiosh smiled back at us and, with one more wink, pointed his long fingers up towards one particular tree within the copse on our right, in which we could just about make out the outline of what looked remarkably like... a tree house!

"*There* is your bed," Adiosh stated proudly, as if he really *had* taken us to a royal kingdom. And with that he was gone.

Will and I exchanged quizzical glances. Was he mad? We found it rather amusing that our dear friend had got so excited about taking us to sleep in what seemed essentially to be a rather bog-standard tree house. Oh well, we were tired by then and just wanted to get some sleep.

Having clambered up the ten-metre wooden ladder, we were somewhat taken aback by the rather cramped quarters above. The space cannot have been more than about 5 ft square, and a pile of wooden logs hardly makes for the most comfortable bedding. Nevertheless, we were there now, and the charm of sleeping in a tree house was enough to help us persevere through initial concerns.

I have to say that the romantic nature of our lofty dwelling far outweighed its practicality. Even with our bags perched out of the way upon the thin bench that hung across the middle of the hut, and our feet stuck out of the doorway, trying to sleep upon a floor made up of tree stumps was hardly ideal. By the end of a long night, we must have tried about ten different arrangements of clothes, bags and bedding to fashion any kind of near-comfortable matting, but cannot have had more than an hour's unbroken sleep.

Bearing this in mind, spirits were surprisingly high when morning did finally arrive.

"That was awful!" Will groaned, which, although to you might sound like a rather disappointed state of mind, was actually spoken with the light-hearted glee of a small child who has just spent his first ever night in a tree house.

If the novelty of the venture wasn't enough to win us round to its appreciation, our morning view certainly sealed the deal. Looking out of what I suppose you might have referred to as our "bedroom window," we were stunned into silence by the majestic array of mountains shining brightly in the distance, hovering proudly above the glistening lake, whose surface we could just about make out in the foreground.

"Good old Adiosh," I said, "The old fella knew what he was doing, after all."

Will agreed, but once was certainly more than enough. The following night (last night), having spent the bulk of the day attempting to swim across the enormous lake, we took our aching backs and weary heads on a trip down memory lane by spending the night as squatters in a derelict building just round the corner from *Gostilna Murka*, which made for an equally dirty, but slightly flatter, and thus sleep-inducing night.

DAY TWENTY-SIX:
MERCATOR SUPERMARKET CAFE, PORTOROZ, SLOVENIA, TUESDAY 5TH AUGUST, 2008, 9.02AM

One thing that has particularly stood out to us during our stay in Slovenia is the large variety in attitudes amongst the people here. I'm sure that such contrast can be found in every culture, but we have noticed a huge gulf here between people who will go out of their way to help you and others who seem to want quite the opposite.

Bojan I, as he shall be known (there are a lot of them around here) was one of those who certainly fitted into the former category. Our second driver of the day, Bojan could offer us a lift of only about thirty kilometres in the Croatian direction, but evidently wanted to help us out so much that he welcomed us into his home, in a town called Kranj, for what he had suggested would be a "bite to eat," but turned out to be more like a feast. Even though we had travelled less than 50 kilometres at that stage and had already consumed a *burek* (a really nice Slavonic pastry that comes in meat or cheese form) for lunch, we felt compelled to accept – *never refuse an offer* and all that!

Plying us with alcohol in the form of beers and his own homemade "medicine" (which just tasted like vodka again), our host really looked after us, but we were seriously made to regret that burek when obliged to accept a second helping of his Slovenian sausage stew (they really like sausage here).

For the briefest of moments, I have to admit that Will and I wondered whether our new friend might have some impure thoughts regarding other uses for us. There was something a little bit Mickael about him and he was plying us with a lot of alcohol, but we were soon made to feel a little silly for harbouring these irrational concerns because Bojan proved to be the perfect gent. I mean, the man didn't even force us to kiss on the first date!

In all seriousness, Bojan really was just a very nice man. What is it about our modern culture that introduces us to this bizarre idea that any person who offers an abnormal amount of kindness should be regarded as suspicious? Bojan was only after two things: one, he wanted to help us out; two, he wanted company, admitting being a little lonely, having been a divorcee for the past eighteen years and still living alone. His kids are all grown up now and he had picked us up on his way home from visiting his new girlfriend, whom he has vowed never to marry.

Bojan seemed to have completely lost his faith in love, describing to us the "foolishness" that had seen him marry at "such a young age" (20), only to find that the honeymoon phase was quickly replaced by the stark and bitter reality of living this life with someone else. Bojan was your typical middle-aged divorcee, intent on having some fun without the commitments – a way of life that was exemplified by his next comment; and I quote:

"If a man cook, the girl's knickers come down!"

After imparting to us this little gemstone, Bojan helpfully nipped into the kitchen for a moment, giving Will and me the time needed to process such a bizarre statement, whilst deliberating whether he might want a similar sort of reaction from us…

Whatever Bojan's intentions, our panties remained firmly in place until every last morsel had been dutifully slipped away and we had been taken back to the side of the main road leading back to the capital.

* * * * *

Unfortunately for us, a day that had started with such promise transformed into easily our worst day's hitching since Spain. We eventually made it from Bled back to Ljubljana (a journey that had taken 45 minutes on the first leg) in about five hours, thanks to one short lift from Bojan II and a second, more substantial ride from the aged Peter – an absolute hero by all accounts.

Like a knight in shining armour, his silver hair blowing in the wind, Peter took one look at us, slammed on his brakes, and mounted the curb in front of us, welcoming us into his vehicle with a smile that stretched from ear to ear. And as if the man's warm-hearted nature and flowing silver locks weren't enough to win our affection, Peter sported a McEnroe-esque sweatband (presumably in place to stop his straggly locks from impeding his view) and designer stubble to complete the appearance. This old man's carefree attitude certainly gave us a lift (if you'll excuse the pun), even if it also regularly endangered us – Peter seeming never to decide which lane he preferred to drive in – but perhaps our favourite thing about the old chap was his claim to have "a wife of 22 years and a daughter of 21."

I'll let you make up your own mind about just what our eccentric friend was attempting to tell us, but it amused us to consider that this old dog might have somehow managed to find a wife who was just one year older than his daughter. All other, more logical conclusions were forgotten – you've got to use this language barrier stuff to your advantage sometimes!

And yet, for all Peter's good intentions, he dropped us off in the middle of absolutely nowhere – a couple of motorway exits short of Ljubljana – and even the most amusing anecdote from our time with the man did little to save desperation from kicking in as we approached the start of our fourth hour of waiting in exactly the same position!

We grew so desperate that ordinary hitchhiking tactics soon gave way to a performance of strange hat tricks (a sort of Michael Jackson-esque flipping of hats onto heads) and even the occasional song on the guitar – anything to get some attention – but nobody seemed the least bit impressed with any of it. Our best attempts at appearing friendly served only to alienate us further from our potential redeemers, many of whom were so suspicious that they would pull up a few metres short of the traffic lights by which we stood, or even, in one instance, physically reverse away from us so as to protect themselves from whatever evil tricks we had up our sleeves.

The only man who seemed to take even the vaguest interest in our plight was a lonely motorbike-mounted policeman, whose sole response was threatening to arrest us if he saw us standing on the road again – yes, that's right; our desperation had even led us to try and stop a few vehicles with a cunning human blockade.

It was all just becoming a little too much. Where had all the good people gone? The best civilian response that we were getting was feigned sympathy, but they may as well have sworn at us for all the good it did us. Finally, when one man stopped and began to reel off this well-rehearsed line about really wanting to help us, but unfortunately not going very far, we simply could not take it anymore.

"Please, please!" we cried. "We don't care where you're going; just take us somewhere other than here!"

On reflection, I feel a little sorry for poor Eztok (I'm guessing the spelling here, but it's a pretty cool name however you write it), who lived only a few miles away, but finished by driving us all the way around the Ljubljana ring road until he had dropped us off in another one of those "official hitching spots" on the south side of the city.

How we longed for this new spot to produce a similar level of success to that first official one that we had tried the last time we were in town, but it just wasn't our day.

A further two and a half hours went by and we hadn't moved! Can you believe it? Could this day get any worse? We were trying everything again: hats, no hats, guitar, no guitar, harassing people at the lights, or simply standing still with our thumbs out. What was it with the Slovenian people? That's right; our opinion of the country was seriously dwindling by now. Those highs and lows that I've talked about are really quite extreme during the long, long waits, when you simply have no idea if anyone is ever going to save you from misery.

"This is worse than Zaragoza!" Will whinged, tired, stressed, and generally fed up with life. We had waited two and a half hours, on top of the three that we had waited only ten kilometres up the road, plus the many hours that had preceded the lifts from Bojans I and II and Peter, and we still hadn't made it more than about sixty kilometres since leaving Bled at about 10am that morning!

To make matters worse, not one, but two fellow hitchers had come along to share our hitching spot (this was an official spot after all), and we felt sure that these new guys would get first dibs because they were Slovenian.

Sure enough, our fears were soon realised as the latest arrival stole a lift right from underneath our noses. What could we do? There was no law about these things. It is *every man for himself* out on the road. Next time we were just going to have to be a little more assertive. Two hitching parties remained, but next time there would only be one winner.

We might as well have had sprinting blocks with us for the speed with which we pounced upon the next vehicle to stop. Poor Jelena seemed a little shocked to see us arrive with such eagerness, but, fortunately for us, she wasn't scared enough to refuse us the chance to ride with her. This marginally crazy and wildly talkative girl had done some hitchhiking herself, so she sympathised, at length.

It is unbelievable how quickly one's mood can change when hitchhiking. From the pits of despair just moments before, we were suddenly on top of the world as we calculated that we were about to be taken twice as far in one lift as we had made throughout the entire day.

When we arrived in Portoroz – Jelena's sister's town, a few kilometres south of Koper – we summoned up just enough energy to thank Jelena, stumble into a restaurant for our first food since Bojan I's, and slump into the tent that we had pitched in possibly the least subtle place thus far – a patch of grass just off the main high street.

No-one seemed to mind.

* * * * *

A long-haired gentleman has just informed me that the café in which we have just breakfasted is only 1km from the Croatian border. We will wander that way in a few moments and get as far as we can along the Croatian coastline by nightfall. Well, surely it can't be as bad as yesterday, can it? Making only 150km in some ten hours of hitching must be some sort of record; and not one I wish to emulate anytime soon.

DAY THIRTY:
ROADSIDE, LITTLE VILLAGE (LATER FOUND OUT TO BE CALLED GRUDA), SOUTH OF DUBROVNIK, HRVATSKA, SATURDAY 9TH AUGUST, 17.55

"Hrvatska? Who's she?" I hear you ask, as we contemplate leaving this beautiful country (better recognised as Croatia) before she has even been introduced. We have much catching up to do if I am to relate the details of the five days that we have spent passing through Croatia since last speaking on Tuesday morning – in that town that, we were reliably informed, was just 1km the other side of the border.

It had all sounded so simple, but we didn't account for the possibility that our long-haired friend just might be lying to us. We must have walked in excess of five kilometres before we saw the first sign to the border, which informed us that we were going to have to walk the same distance again before we would eventually arrive in Croatia.

Tired out already from an unexpectedly long walk, we decided to hitch the rest, and after what seemed like a disproportionate length of waiting time for the comparatively short hitch required, we were finally picked up by a friendly Slovenian man named Mirko, who took us just over the border, where he plied us with coffee and cigarettes.

We've really got to get this *never refuse an offer* thing sorted out, before we incur some sort of permanent damage to our health. At the moment, it encompasses all offers – from places to stay, to the two packs of cigarettes that Mirko gave us to keep – and we don't even smoke! All of a sudden and we're averaging about two-a-day. I'm already feeling a little wheezy.

Mirko was going to a beach only just over the border and, not being particularly knowledgeable in our understanding of Croatian geography, we took one quick look at the map and decided that we should head away from the coast (for then at least) and do our best to make a shortcut across the land to a port called Rijeka.

It all started off all right. Will and I persuaded a group travelling from Austria to squeeze us into the back of their camper van, but, unfortunately for us, this bizarre ensemble – a quirky wine-seller named Roland, his Swedish apprentice (22 year-old Helena) and a 70 year-old named Adi (who had obviously lost it a little bit upstairs, spoke not a word of English and had never seen the sea) completely misunderstood our intentions and took us off the road to Rijeka (by goodness knows how far), whereupon they simply shrugged their shoulders, apologised, and dropped us off in the middle of nowhere as they continued on to their own remote beach resort.

So little idea did we have of where we were that Will and I went to opposite sides of a junction and began hitching in completely opposite directions. We weren't being fussy; all that we were after now was a lift from *anyone to... anywhere.*

An Italian couple – or, as it turned out, former couple – were our saviours this time. Ricardo and Annalesa, like the rest, were on their way to the Croatian coastline for a holiday on some beach resort or other, and we felt more tempted than ever to accept their offer to join them, but decided that we really should try and make it *some* distance into this new country before giving up entirely and sunning ourselves on a beach.

Kindly, Ricardo and Annalesa at least gave us some idea of where we were, taking us back to what they told us was at least *one* road in the direction of Rijeka, even if it wasn't the main one.

Here we were again, no more than about 50km from where we had begun, baking in the midday sunshine as we vainly attempted to hitch a ride towards Rijeka. The lack of cars wasn't the problem, and I don't think that our scrawny frames can have appeared particularly intimidating – although our fixed smiles may have drooped a little by this stage – but an hour soon came and went, hat tricks and singsongs having been performed on loop, and *still* there appeared not even the faintest sign that anybody wanted to pick us up.

Entirely fed up, we dragged our bags across to a handily-placed restaurant on the other side of the road, taking the weight off our feet for a while as we indulged our poor young waiter, Ivan, in the tale of our miseries.

"You know, Ivan, life can be cruel sometimes," I began.

"All we want to do is hitchhike towards Rijeka. Why won't somebody just pick us up?" continued Will.

Poor Ivan, who was rather helpless in the whole ordeal, simply gave us his most sympathetic wince and offered to get us a couple of coffees "on the house," before alerting us to the fact that he was finishing his shift very soon and could give us a ride to Poreç, "if we wanted."

Needless to say, we didn't have to think about our answer for very long. We hadn't even looked to see if Poreç was even vaguely in the right direction, but I think we would have taken Ivan up on his offer even if he had been driving completely in the opposite direction – just for a change of scenery.

It turned out that Poreç, latitudinally speaking, was about as far away from Rijeka as Portoroz had been at the start of the day. For those of you who are equally unfamiliar with Croatian geography, there is a strange bump on the western tip of an altogether bizarrely-shaped country, and this dip has a road right along its coastline, which runs in a substantial "V" shape. Now, bearing in mind that Rijeka is on the top eastern side of the "V" and we started out on the top western side, one would think that a more lateral route across the dip would have been more sensible. But since when have we liked to make things easy for ourselves?

At least we'd had that change of scenery. One of the most demoralising things about hitchhiking is to find oneself staring at the very same landscape – however impressive – for hours on end. At least we were avoiding that.

And yet, it wasn't long before morale sank further. Perhaps we should change our perspective about what it is that counts as a "regular" wait for a hitch because every time (and it is *every* time at the moment) we wait for more than an hour, we feel that the world is about to end.

Here we were again, waiting by another stretch of road that we had never been to before and were unlikely to ever see again, trying those same hat tricks and guitar playing that had gone so… badly the last time. You'd think that trying to entertain people would help them feel more comfortable in giving you a ride, but it seems only to engender anger – in Slovenians and Croatians at least (two particularly ungenerous races, it would seem). We encountered more tasteless middle-finger gestures and thumb-wagging mimics during that hour than I think we had done in the previous three weeks!

To make matters worse, our not-so-new spot was one of those official hitching spots that they seem to have in these countries and we were soon joined by three fellow hitching parties – all of whom clearly had a much better chance of getting a ride, simply because they could speak the language.

I think we should probably have our blood pressure checked out at the end of all of this. Not only is this trip proving bad for us because of the damaging, nicotine-filled products that people keep "forcing" upon us, but we are also being put under extreme stress all the time, and it isn't just the sun that is making us sweat our weight in water whilst waiting for each new lift to come along.

Fortunately for us, just before we could succumb to stress-related heart attacks, a couple of young Croatian punks rocked-up. Simon and Babo took us further and faster than anyone else had done that day and we appreciated their laid-back attitude, even if we would have preferred driver Simon to have been a little bit less reckless on the road – he was one of those who likes to drive in an imaginary third lane down the middle and hope for the best.

We had no idea where we were when they dropped us off, but figured that we couldn't be any further from our destination than we had been before. In fact, life in the fast lane had given us that extra boost that we needed and we even felt that old impostor, optimism, creeping in again on the realisation that a nearby signpost marked out our prospective destination at but 50km away. Wonderful! We were in the perfect spot on a slip road that fed onto the motorway towards Rijeka. In no time at all, we would surely be there...

Day Thirty: (continued...)
Katica's House, Gruda, Hrvatska, Saturday 9th August, 22.51

Oh, the joys of unfounded optimism! All that talk about "perfect spots" and "only 50km away" seemed grossly over-optimistic forty minutes later, when we found ourselves still standing in exactly the same place and watching as the very few cars to pass us by did so with vehement avoidance. Normally it would take us a little longer before panic gripped us, but it had been a hell of a day, on the back of a pretty rotten one before that, and we had just had about enough of hitchhiking.

We were certainly in need of some rescuing, and as if somebody, somewhere, was listening to our heartfelt pleas, who should come along a few moments later but a couple of French boys doing what all the French seem to like to do in these parts – driving around in a camper van.

"Salut!" said the driver, greeting us with the warmest of smiles. "Where you want to go?"

Truthfully, it mattered little to Will and me where exactly it was that these two travellers were going. All we wanted to do was to secure a ride as far away from our current location as possible.

"Quelque place," I replied eagerly.

"Anywhere at all, s'il vous plait," Will added.

That same smile shone back at us and we were hurriedly beckoned into the vehicle, where Will was given the chance to take a snooze on the bed in the back, whilst I got to know our new chauffeurs in the front.

Alex, a 27 year-old waiter from Le Mans (près de Paris) was my favourite from the very beginning. There was a certain *je ne sais quoi* about the man, revealing itself in his warm smile and the laid-back attitude that oozed from his every word. Enthusiastically, Alex revealed that he was a regular hitchhiker himself. Apparently he and his friends organised an annual race from Paris to a random destination in Europe (this year's target had been Bucharest) and Alex had always dreamed of going one better and hitching that little bit further.

"I'm very jealous," he confessed. "Can I come with you?"

At the time I chuckled and told him that I couldn't see any reason why not, whilst secretly assuming that he didn't really mean it. Come to think of it, however, I'm not sure Alex was joking after all.

Guillaume, a 26 year-old carpenter from Laval (près de Le Mans) and owner of the van, was the much quieter of the two, although it didn't help that the man could hardly speak a word of English. This made it rather difficult to grasp the finer details of Guillaume, but I just about understood that he was no stranger to hitchhiking himself, having partnered Alex on one of their previous hitching races across Europe.

Basic introductions dealt with, I wasted no time in getting down to business. Pleasantries could only get us so far; now for the matter in hand. Where were these French boys going and would it seem entirely unreasonable for them to consider having another two bodies on board for a few days?

Having only just met us, Alex and Guillaume understandably took a minute to decide, but Alex soon shone back at me with that same old grin and voiced the affirmative response that I was after:

"Ouais," he said, nonchalantly, puffing out cigarette smoke as he spoke in what I considered to be the quintessentially French equivalent of "cool."

"Pourquoi pas, eh?" he added with a wink.

And that was that. For the next four days we would travel around Hrvatska with these Frenchmen, who were especially keen on seeing the very best of Croatia as they trundled southwards towards Montenegro. No more standing aimlessly beside different roadsides or finding hidden areas to pitch our tents; for the next few days we had found ourselves a home.

DAY THIRTY-ONE:
HOTEL TUETA, RISAN, KOTOR MUNICIPALITY, MONTENEGRO, SUNDAY 10TH AUGUST, 11.07AM

It has been two days now since we left Alex and Guillaume behind, not far from the Montenegrin border. The fact was that they were going just a little too slowly for our liking and we felt compelled to continue our journey towards Malaysia apace. I found precious little time to write during our time together, but finally I have a moment to draw breath and I am determined to rack my brains in order to recall the details of what was a whirlwind tour of Croatia...

The first night was the worst. There we were, contemplating the joys of finding ourselves a home – however temporary – only to be cruelly driven up to the top of a mountain to attempt to sleep in what felt a lot like the midst of a hurricane to Will and me. We spent the bulk of the night vainly attempting to assert just enough downward pressure upon our tent to prevent our being blown away. If it weren't for the fact that we had attached a guy rope to the wheel of the van, I'm not sure we'd have survived the night. As it was, we got hardly a wink of sleep because the gale was so strong that the tent itself simply would not stop banging against our heads throughout the night.

Sleepless nights rarely seem worthwhile, but waking up to be confronted by a scene of astounding natural beauty certainly provides some compensation. Peeking through the opening to our tent, it was at this moment that we realised just how far above sea level we had driven. Blue horizons stretched into the distance. Sky and sea blues were both invaded by flashes of white, which, I imagined, were probably scars from their own respective sufferings under the onslaught of the fierce hurricane of the night before.

And as though that magnificent scene wasn't enough to make amends for a rough night, the moment our slumbersome friends awoke from the safety of their own, windproof sanctuary, we set off on the road towards what I now know to be Croatia's own little haven of natural beauty: the stunning National Park of *Plitvička Jezera*, where torrents of water tumble from the dozens of waterfalls that envelop this gigantic park, and fish of the ensuing valley lakes captivatingly follow your every step as you trot along wooden pathways.

Plitvička truly takes the breath away and we felt determined to make the most of the experience. All around the park there were signposts telling us what we could not do – *don't smoke, don't take a dog off its lead, don't be Chinese* (well, maybe not, but you get the gist) – but the one that really amazed us was the one that forbade any sort of swimming in lakes that simply screamed at us that they wished to be swum in!

Since when had a miniscule detail such as a sign ever stopped us? Winding our way down an overgrown path to a point that we adjudged to be fairly secluded, we fought our way through the undergrowth and jumped straight into the ever-so-inviting water. We hastily, and rather stealthily, swam over to the nearest cascade, staying under for a very short while as the water hammered down upon our heads, before darting back and hurrying out of the water, realising that, by now, every park-goer and security guard had become aware of our forbidden escapade. Cameras were flashing and commotion mounting as we exited the lake to a generous (if a little conspicuous, and thus unhelpful) round of applause. We felt like kings among men as we scrambled back up through the undergrowth, unscathed and undetected by authority, to rejoin the more timid Guillaume on the shore. Victory cigarettes came next, taken with our toes dipped into the warm waters, looking out over the beautiful lake and waterfall, the scene of our conquest.

For the rest of the day we bent the rules at every available opportunity. Stop signs became open invitations and we chose the most exciting and adventurous paths around this breathtaking natural maze. We stood under waterfalls, clambered over ancient rocks, and sauntered our way through untouched undergrowth. Together we ruled the day, set our own rules, and slept much more peacefully that night, pitching our tent in what later turned out to be someone's back garden!

* * * * *

The next day we made tracks for Split, stopping off only very briefly at Zadar and the charming coastal town of Šibenik along the way. Not long before we had arrived at the latter, Alex and Guillaume's hitchhiker-friendly approach ensured that our van (legally limited to three passengers) had picked up a further three hitchers, taking our tally to seven. This trio of lady hitchers (two Brits and a Pole) provided an amusing wake-up call to Will, who had once again been asleep in the back, but I don't think that he can have been in the best of moods because the girls soon seemed very eager to leave us.

When the girls had departed we took a moment to wander through the cobbled streets of Šibenik and dangled our feet over the harbour's edge, watching as the sun faded over the distant horizon, before heading off towards the next Croatian city on this whistle-stop tour. I have to say that every moment with Alex and Guillaume felt a little surreal, simply because we weren't having to hitchhike the whole time in order to get between places. Usually we would simply pass the bulk of these cities by, without sparing a thought for what we might be missing, but our French friends ensured that we were actually given the opportunity to experience a little piece of Croatia.

At sunset we were back on the road again, driving towards Split, hitting easily the highest speeds that we had achieved since entering our beloved van because this was our first stretch on a motorway. The Frenchies were keen to make the most of the chance to drive along more scenic routes than mere monotonous motorways, but there wasn't much to see now that the sun had set, and Will and I were secretly glad for the increase of pace.

Surmounting a hilltop to be greeted by the spectacle of thousands of shining bright lights – this was our introduction to the sizeable city of Split. If only the evening's accommodation could have matched such splendour!

Unfortunately, we ended up on a dirty pavement, surrounded by blocks of flats in what felt awfully like inner-city London. Just to give you an idea of the type of place we had encountered, our bedroom wall (the wall on the other side of the patio, that is) had been taken over by a bunch of yobs, who had spray-painted a huge mosaic in dedicated worship of that fiercely-supported Croatian football team, Hadjuk Split F.C.

Croatia's answer to Brixton, I distinctly remember emerging from the tent the following morning to be greeted by the unmistakable aroma of urine – possibly, no, probably, coming from the exterior of our tent. I'm a little surprised that we weren't awake at the time of the urination because I don't remember being not awake for very much of the night. It was ever so hot and, even though we were sleeping naked as usual (these are insatiably warm countries, after all), there was just no escaping it. So unbearable was the heat that we had even unabashedly slept naked with the tent door thrown wide open, in what was probably the least secure environment in which we had slept. Thinking about it, I'm surprised the urinator(s) didn't decide to shed their load all over us... Actually, perhaps they did, but if so, then I'm pleased to say that I've fully repressed the memory.

It would have been a most welcome morning's dip in the Ocean, but this was the one morning that we didn't find the time for it. Instead, we found ourselves stickily traipsing around the town, past the quarters of the ancient palace and a surprisingly popular statue of a man whose main feature of interest was a ginormous golden foot (apparently it's a good luck charm to kiss the thing), until we found a suitable place to stop for morning coffees, pastries, and copious amounts of water – this rehydration fluid itself coming out of a fountain acclaimed (by us) to possess healing powers.

Breakfast devoured and gigantic foot dutifully kissed "goodbye," we made haste towards our last destination with Alex and Guillaume, Dubrovnik. The very next morning and we would bid a final adieu to our fair friends and make our journey onwards alone. It would be strange to reunite our backs with their erstwhile friends (our heavy rucksacks), but it was high time that we moved on. There were new places to see and new friends to encounter, but who would have thought that our next friendship would come about as a direct result of one of Will's regular bouts of flatulence?

4. IN SICKNESS AND IN HEALTH

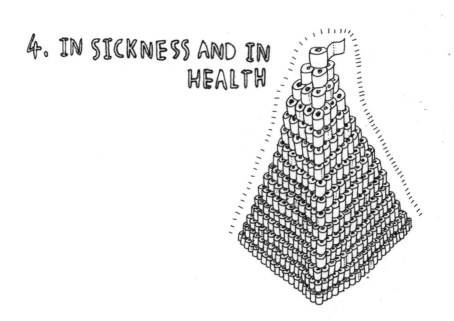

Day Thirty-One: (continued...)
Hotel Tueta, Risan, Kotor Municipality, Montenegro, Sunday 10th August, 18.49

Will may or may not be dying. This is the serious diagnosis of the most qualified doctor in the room at the moment: me. OK, perhaps it is a little misleading to refer to me as at all qualified in the field of medicine, but I do possess a pair of pretty good eyes (I reckon 20-20) and they are quite capable of concluding that what is going on inside Will's posterior at the moment is not right.

At a purely observational level, Will appears to have developed what I can only assume to be some sort of purple tumour that is currently making his generally pretty regular and explosive toilet habits a little bit less frequent, and certainly less expulsive. My purely speculative diagnosis is as follows: Will has either developed a cancerous tumour, or, whilst going for one of his regular episodes, has somehow managed to push a little too hard – thus causing some of his intestines to pop out.

... I have just used the novel combination of a mirror and my own posterior for means of comparison. Being not particularly well schooled in the specific inner buttock area, I was momentarily unsure whether Will's horribly deformed purple-headed exit hole was in fact simply the norm. After further inspection, we can at least certifiably conclude that whatever is going on down there needs some attention, and fast.

DAY THIRTY-TWO:
HOTEL TUETA, RISAN, KOTOR MUNICIPALITY, MONTENEGRO, MONDAY 11TH AUGUST, 2008, 9.22AM

It turns out that my diagnosis was not 100% correct. Will simply has what I am told is a fairly common case of haemorrhoids. The process by which we managed to determine just what was the cause of Will's considerable discomfort downstairs was one of the most amusing experiences of the trip so far, for all concerned, except perhaps Will. Three new Canadian friends of ours were able to pool their resources – one a doctor, another a nurse, and the third an ex-haemorrhoids sufferer – and together come up with this definitive conclusion, which at least means that Will won't die just yet, even if he may have forever surrendered his dignity.

Haemorrhoids. Who'd have thought it? I suppose it is rather fitting – given how ardently William's posterior has been striving to get our attention of late – that it might finally get its comeuppance.

The last time Will's bottom took charge we were standing by the roadside of a little village called Gruda, from where his bottom piped up that it needed the toilet, and a bush and some leaves simply weren't sufficient this time. Off my dear friend had trotted, not to be seen again for what amounted to just long enough for me to start seriously worrying about him, before he had finally re-emerged, smiling from ear to ear as if he had had a slightly disturbing amount of fun performing one of man's basic functions.

I now know that it was far more than toileting that had gladdened my companion. Will (as only he can) had gone knocking from door to door until he had found a friendly enough homeowner who might take pity upon his desperate need for the loo and provide the suitable facilities. I had assumed that nobody would be silly enough to let in a travelling bum (excuse the pun) like him, but I was wrong. Katica, whose husband was out at work at the time, had not only invited Will in to use the toilet; she had then asked him if he would like something to eat or drink. Of course, my insatiably hungersome friend had replied in the affirmative and was now coming to collect me for what would turn into a whole night enjoying the hospitality of Katica and her lovely family in their beautiful cottage in the obscure, sub-Dubrovnik-ian Croatian village of Gruda.

When we had first arrived at Katica's home, we had assumed that we would be invited only for a few sandwiches and would soon outstay our welcome, so we had both been nervously keeping a constant eye on the clock, contemplating the ever-reducing number of daylight hours remaining to secure a decent lift.

Bellies full from said sandwiches, we were just preparing to thank our host for her kindness and readying ourselves to get back on the road, when Katica insisted that we first get a tour of her delightful home, which had been entirely designed and built by her architecturally astute husband, Mikhael, who would be home soon, and whom we must stay and meet.

The tour had been stopped almost as soon as it had begun because of William's discovery of the piano room. For the next few hours we sang and played, regaining that sense of calm that is so often absent on the road, whilst little Eva (Katica's six year-old daughter) gazed up at us with her big brown eyes. Just at the moment it had seemed that we might finally stop, Eva had hopped up next to Will in search of tuition; dutifully it was given, and we were promptly invited to stay for the night.

A few hours later, after taking the blessed opportunity to give ourselves a good rinse under a hot shower, it was time for the evening meal. Joined by husband Mikhael, cousin Tea and Tea's Italian husband Franco, we sat underneath the trellis of Katica's patio and enjoyed a seafood platter of mussels, calamari and sardines, complimented exquisitely by the home-made red wine donated by a friendly neighbour. The hours rolled by as we chatted to our new friends and grew especially fond of Tea and Franco, who even pleaded with us to stay another day. Our well-fed friends were each a second spouse to the other and seemed to have been given a new lease of life by the success of this second attempt. Tea shared with us how she had longed for a large family, but had been unable to have children with her first husband, which had taken its toll upon their relationship and, in time, had led to their separation. She also shared the tragic story of both her sister and mother dying when she was only twenty-two years old. Franco was a former priest and a heavy smoker and he had been Tea's light through all those dark times, and they had been happily living together for over twenty years, and now had a grown-up son.

* * * * *

Our fondness for our new friends made the events of the following morning even harder to take. The invitation to stay for a second night had been confirmed just before bed, and we were sleeping peacefully in this knowledge until an alarmed Tea woke us up at 9am to tell us that Franco was being rushed to hospital because his heart was failing.

It transpired that Franco had had his third breathless night in a row and his worrisome wife had finally persuaded him to do something about it. Understandably we were asked to leave as soon as we could so that they could lock up the house and make for A&E. We packed our bags as quickly as we could, gave Tea a big hug and marched onto the road, eager to secure our first lift before Franco and co. drove by, so that they might not feel too guilty for having to usher us out sooner than expected.

Our prayers were immediately answered by a man called Nicola, who took us just that little bit closer to the border to a place where we wouldn't be seen by our friends, a place we were standing for just long enough to contemplate walking the remaining distance to the border; the place where Bojan III picked us up.

Big Bojan was travelling with fellow Serb, Marco, and a Norwegian lad called Gjermund, all on their way to a Christian conference at Hotel Tueta in

Risan, where you join me. To my right, Will is slipping down another stool softener – the medicine prescribed by our Canadian friends for Will's unfortunate and rather embarrassing condition.

DAY THIRTY-FOUR:
BOILER ROOM, GLASNOST, SKOPJE, GREATER SKOPJE MUNICIPALITY, MACEDONIA, WEDNESDAY 13TH AUGUST 2008, 9.13AM

I cannot believe that we managed to make it all the way from northwest Montenegro to Macedonia on Monday. Even if we had left at the crack of dawn we could never have expected to get so far, so after doing our usual trick of lazing around the entire morning, then struggling desperately to get even one lift before midday, I am amazed that by the end of the same day (or the small hours of the next, I suppose) we were in the Macedonian capital, hooking up with some old friends of mine.

As I said, the first lift was a tough challenge in itself. Standing outside the hotel under the watchful gaze of our friends and doctors from the previous day, the pressure was on, and we were struggling. Our typically slow start had meant that it was already the hottest time of the day and we were highly relieved when we were finally given a lift – a blessed relief from the sun.

Three short lifts in quick succession – from two Dutch couples and a French family – left us in a petrol station on the main coastal road of Montenegro, next stop Budva. And that was the moment when we spotted the hardly inconspicuous couple of a Serbian "Cabaret dancer" (code for "stripper") called Olja and her pimp-daddy boss and boyfriend, Boris. Soon we were speeding around in Boris' black BMW and hearing all the stories from his business in Novi Sad, which, funnily enough, is where the two had met. It really was like something out of a film: imagine a seedy David Hasselhoff lookalike with flowing mousey-blonde locks, an unzipped leather jacket and no t-shirt, paired with his blonde bimbo girlfriend, who sported spandex trousers and a tiny top, which revealed acres of cleavage. This surreal drive lasted for only about twenty minutes, but this was clearly sufficient time for us to make enough of an impression to be awarded a free lighter (courtesy of Boris' Cabaret club), which really did have a topless picture of Jennifer Rabbit on it.

Our stripper mates dropped us off on the other side of Budva in a perfect spot to hitch a ride towards the capital, Podgorica, and it wasn't long before a young, self-professed "football hooligan" by the name of Sal had screeched to a halt, taken us in, and then tried his best to kill us by overtaking around countless blind corners on treacherously mountainous roads.

Sal informed us that he was driving all the way to Podgorica, but needed to stop off halfway at a town called Cetinje so that he could pick up some gear for his work as a joiner.

"I back twenty minutes," Sal assured us, as he left us in a restaurant on the outskirts of Cetinje.

Happy enough in the knowledge that we would eventually be on our way to the capital, Will and I removed our bags from the car (well, we weren't going to leave them with a hooligan, were we?) and set about waiting for his return.

... But our skin-headed friend never showed up.

My first instinct was that we had somehow offended the boy by showing him the lack of trust that we did in choosing to take our bags out of the car while he went on his errand (rather than risk the potential/inevitable theft), but perhaps Sal really had only wanted to steal our stuff and had only taken us as far as he did that he might have a better chance of doing so.

I so desperately want to believe the best of him – that maybe his work took longer than expected, he simply forgot about us, or he really was upset that we hadn't trusted him – but perhaps a more logical explanation of events would be that we narrowly escaped our first mugging.

Whatever the reason, we never saw Sal again. To us, he will always remain a mystery; we will remember him for his two girlfriends, football hooliganism and kleptomaniac tendencies.

No matter. Post-Sal we had to wait a cumulative total of only one hour on the road that day, before we had secured back-to-back lifts to take us first to Podgorica, and then Skopje!

Initially we had been concerned, and with good reason. It had taken us a good twenty minutes to walk out of Cetinje and find a spot that we deemed suitable to hitch from. The strange thing was that we weren't the only ones who saw the advantages of the spot – just your everyday t-junction on the road from Budva to Podgorica. A host of fellow hitchhikers joined us, the size of which I doubt that the world can ever before have seen.

Surely this couldn't be another one of those countries with official hitching spots, could it? Originally, we had assumed that the place was an unmarked bus stop, but then had to watch, horrified, as first an old lady was picked up – well, we could hardly shove her out of the way, could we? – and then a scruffy looking gentleman (possibly a hooligan) was preferred to us.

We did our best to communicate with the remaining handful of competitors and to persuade them that ours was the noblest cause, but it's a dog-eat-dog world out there and they were having none of it. We tried everything; being the furthest forward in the line (so that we would be the first to be seen), then the furthest back (so that we would probably be closest to the car when it eventually did stop), but nothing was working and a further trio of hitchers stole our rides before us. The sole source of solace was the frequency with which hikers were getting lifts – there must have been ten of us when we started, and now there were only three.

Giving ourselves acres of room away from the other hitchers, finally we had our chance to get a ride. But, oh no, there they were, as plain as daylight: those four large letters that we have become so accustomed to seeing: "TAXI."

"No, no, we don't want your sort around here, thank you very much," Will scoffed, waving the man away. "We're hitch-hiking!"

The young man behind the wheel looked a little put out by our gestures, rolled his eyes, and then, much to our amazement, proceeded to tell us that if we wanted a free ride to Podgorica, we had better get in. It turned out that our new best friend had just dropped off some paying customers in Budva and needed to return home to Podgorica anyway. Kindly, this man not only took us with him free of charge (we still harboured fears that once we got there he might change his tune), but then proceeded to take us all the way through the capital to the other side so that we might have a better chance of catching a lift anywhere towards the Kosovo border that evening.

From our new spot on the other side of town, we had barely waited five minutes before a minivan pulled over and the driver, Boban, coolly proceeded to inform us that he was on his way to Skopje.

"Skopje?" we shrieked in unison, high fives and girly screams exchanged.

Boban seemed understandably taken aback, but nodded and watched as we leapt frantically into the back. What had at one stage seemed like a couple of potentially shifty border crossings over eight hours' worth of driving terrain were about to be done and dusted in one fell swoop.

Dear Boban turned and toiled through the mountains of Montenegro, bumped over the pot-holed paths of Kosovo, and charmed his way through four passport-stamping border checkpoints (two at each border) until we had eventually arrived by the side of a Skopje-ian road by 1.30am yesterday morning.

Unfortunately, our opinion of him will always be slightly tainted by his cheap attempt to get some money off us at the very end.

"Taxi... Podgorica... Skopje... 200 Euros," he stuttered in his best Macedonian English as soon as we had arrived, having made no mention of such cost in the previous eight hours. Fair enough, I guess; he was clearly an opportunist, determined to make the most that he could from two potentially rich foreigners.

Reluctantly, we had prepared ourselves for this eventuality in advance, noticing the increasing frequency with which the stocky Boban and his weasel-like sidekick, Faton, mentioned the dreaded t-word ("Taxi") over the last leg of the journey.

The winning combination of our hardest stares and a cool, yet determined, shaking of our heads seemed to do the trick, or perhaps it was our impeccable behaviour on the journey that led to their leniency. Either way, we escaped the hefty, unexpected fare, and watched the back end of Boban's minivan fade into the distance as we discussed the need to be a little more upfront in the "no money" aspect of the trip in future – now that language barriers really start to take their toll.

Ten minutes later and the fruits of our labour – during those moments when Boban and ourselves were getting on so well that he allowed us to use his phone – came to fruition as my old pal, Dejan, emerged over the hilltop to take us home.

DAY THIRTY-FIVE:
FASHION COFI, KRIVA PALANKA, KRIVA PALANKA MUNICIPALITY, MACEDONIA, THURSDAY 14TH AUGUST 2008, 14.37

Tonight I will return to René and Svetan's house near Botevgrad for the first time since I was part of the first student team to go out with nominated charity, *The Trussell Trust*, to help out with the orphanage way back in 2003. I'm really looking forward to seeing them again and I anticipate many a pang of nostalgia.

Our time in Macedonia has been short, but thoroughly enjoyable. The first two nights were spent on the floor of Dejan, Alex, Alpin and Dejan II's flat – a quality apartment on the 15th floor of a central Skopje-ian apartment block – and last night was spent at Jana's – just two minutes down the road. It was such a blessing to spend time with my crazy Macedonian mates, who are all passionate ex-drug addicts that have devoted their life to tattoos and Christianity.

Alpin is actually considered to be the best tattoo artist in Macedonia (so I'm led to believe) and is covered from head to toe in them, although most of them are cover-up jobs, such is the dramatic way in which his life has flipped around since becoming a Christian. It's a bit like Ed Norton in *American History X*, who has a swastika tattoo, which he later covers up after dramatically abandoning his neo-Nazi opinions during a stretch in jail. Whilst I'm fairly sure that Alpin never had a swastika tattoo, he certainly did have a few demonic/devilish things going on underneath tattoos that are now mostly pictures of Jesus, verses from the Bible, or just "STRENGTH" written in massive letters across his chest, and coming as a result of the dramatic nature of inner change to which he confesses.

When we weren't hanging out with our ex-addict pals, the rest of our time in Skopje was spent with Jana, a former child prodigy on the ski slopes (before her knees packed-in), whom I had once met on a train from Athens to Belgrade. This morning Jana was kind enough to drive us out of the centre of Skopje, leaving us at a toll station on the road to Bulgaria, but not before she had treated us to one of the best breakfasts of the trip so far. Her Mum owns a bakery, don't you know, and we had burek and other Slavonic pastries coming out of our ears as we left.

Since giving Jana's old banger a push start goodbye, we have made great progress. We're now within touching distance of the Bulgarian border, thanks to two almost instantaneous pick-ups by two guys called Drago (I suppose it's the Macedonian equivalent of the Slovenian *Bojan* or the English *Dave*), the second of which we are currently waiting for in a bar in Kriva Palanka.

Macedonian by descent, Drago II is driving from his new home in Venice all the way across to Bucharest in Romania for a holiday, and has just taken a short break to "meet a friend" in this town, not very far from the Bulgarian border. We anxiously await his return in this little bar, where we have just ordered a second round of iced coffee and set up another game of chess. Given that he told us that he would be no longer than an hour, the fact that it's already over forty minutes beyond that estimate is concerning; surely he's not going to be another Sal!

I don't think we have done anything to annoy him or give him reason to want to leave us here, but perhaps his so-called "visit to a friend's house" was just a cunning ploy to leave us by the wayside and drive the remainder of the journey to Bucharest on his own. Perhaps when he first stopped he had thought that we would only want a lift a short distance and now he was looking at having to take two strangers all the way to Sofia. Come to think of it, he hadn't sounded nearly as excited as we had when he had learned that his route was taking us exactly where we wanted to go, so maybe this was his way out. Or maybe it was the incident with the police that put him off.

We had been in the car for only about two minutes when he was pulled over for speeding and Will and I had been our usual, cheeky, loud-mouthed selves, which could potentially have put him off having us in the car over a border crossing. He might have thought that we were liabilities and could jeopardise his cover if he were, I don't know, carrying drugs with him, or thought that we might be.

Oh the possibilities! The worst thing about the entire affair is that we are completely powerless to do anything about it. We have no way of making contact with him and no way of finding out whether he intends to return. One hour and forty minutes ago, we felt certain that in only a few hours time we would be arriving in Sofia. We had the driver; all we needed to do was to wait for him to come back and pick us up. But where is he? In my heart I want so desperately to believe that he will return, to believe that all of this worrying is just me working myself into a fuss over nothing. I mean, he's only forty minutes late. He might still come back, mightn't he?

DAY THIRTY-FIVE: (CONTINUED...)
PETROL STATION, SOUTH-SIDE OF SOFIA RING ROAD, SOFIA PROVINCE, BULGARIA, THURSDAY 14TH AUGUST 2008, 21.47

Drago never came back, and we shan't ever reach Botevgrad tonight.

I just don't get it. Why would he have promised to take us to Sofia if he never intended to do so? I find myself trying to make excuses for him, but doubts prevail because of the unsavoury incident with Sal the other day. It just seems a little far-fetched to believe that in both of these situations the perpetrators intended to return. We have promised each other that the next time we are dropped off by a driver who promises to return, we will at least take down their number so that, if they should mysteriously decide not to reappear, we can call them to find out what's going on.

We did not have that same luxury earlier on and clearly misjudged Drago's character. When he was only one hour late, Will and I discussed the matter and concluded that we just couldn't think of a reason why he wouldn't come back. He seemed like an ordinary guy. He had been happy enough to pick us up in the first place and had sounded genuine in his promise to return, but it was these misplaced conclusions that saw us stay for a further two hours, continually assessing and reassessing the situation until there was no hope left. He wasn't coming back.

Cursing our luck, we traipsed out of town, back onto the road that we had first arrived on four hours earlier. It had seemed a dead certainty that we would reach Botevgrad by the end of the day, but that guarantee had now all but vanished; the time had crept past 5pm and we still hadn't even crossed the border into Bulgaria.

It was about time that our fortunes took a little upturn, so we were grateful for the smiling faces of one Bulgarian woman (called something like Hristina), who dropped us off at the border, and an old chap called Nicoli, who welcomed us into his Sofia-bound truck. For all of Nicoli's charm, however, he didn't have the slightest grasp of the English language (whilst our Bulgarian's a little ropey too these days), thus rendering his next move – as he dropped us off here, on completely the wrong side of the Sofia ring-road – that little bit less surprising.

Frustrated by what has been a thoroughly unsatisfactory day on the road, we haven't given hitching too much of an effort tonight. Light had faded long before we arrived at this petrol station and brief conversations with various drivers filling up here haven't led us to believe that this next hitch will be particularly easy to come by. Thus, we have settled for a night in at the petrol station.

It's homely enough. There's a little café where we can get some food and we've even found ourselves a stray dog to befriend (we're calling him Kermit), and we are currently training him to stand guard over our tent tonight. A couple of minutes ago we tried ringing our mates over in Botevgrad to see if they'd fancy driving over this way to give us a lift, but they just informed us that they didn't even know we were coming! I don't know, you try and do your bit for charity, and that's the thanks you get!

DAY THIRTY-SIX:
THE HOUSE OF JOSHUA, SKRAVENA, BOTEVGRAD, SOFIA PROVINCE, BULGARIA, FRIDAY 15TH AUGUST 2008, 16.27

"You can't hitchhike here. This is [insert country]... Bulgaria."

These were the familiar words that haunted us for the first ninety minutes of hitching this morning, following our nine o' clock awakening by an agitated petrol pump attendant, who seemed put out that we were using his office as a hotel.

It's the same story wherever we go. Locals will swear blind that it is impossible to hitchhike in their country – for a number of reasons ranging from the bad nature of their fellow countrymen to the notion that it was once possible, but times are a changing. The only thing that's worse than trying to persuade someone that it is actually possible to hitchhike in their country is trying to persuade them that it might also actually be possible in a bordering country. This has become the theme of our journey thus far and we are becoming quite fond of the doubters, especially when we get to see the look on their faces at the moment a lift eventually does come.

It took longer than expected to find a ride this morning and the duration of the waiting was trebled, psychologically speaking, because of the fact that we had been at the same spot since the previous night. Just at the moment we were about to give up and start walking along the hard shoulder of the motorway to find a better spot, a student named Alex came to the rescue, and this lift was certainly worth the wait.

Alex had been the first man to show us even the slightest bit of interest during our vain attempts at persuading any Bulgarians to give us a ride, so we hadn't even bothered asking the man where he was going when we launched ourselves into his car. I would say that the chances of this young man going towards Botevgrad were about as likely as finding someone on the south side of the M25 going towards Cambridge, so when our new friend – who spent the bulk of the journey trying to stop his mischievous kitten from resting underneath the brake pedal – eventually dropped us off only 4km from our friends' house, we were thinking about miracles again.

Ten minutes later and we were wandering along roads that we hadn't seen in years, attempting to remember our way to René and Svetan's house, when who should screech past in one of his unmistakable 4x4s – complete with tinted windows and a trailer perfect for picking up hitchhikers – but Svetan himself.

"Svetan!" we cried in unison, as his familiar face appeared from the other side of the lowering electric window.

He hadn't changed a bit and seemed vaguely to remember Will and me, although he might just have assumed he should know us because it's not every day that two backpackers stroll into the tiny village of Skravena (just a few kilometres from Botevgrad), let alone two backpackers that call him by name.

Day Thirty-Seven:
The House of Joshua, Skravena, Botevgrad, Sofia Province, Bulgaria, Saturday 16th August 2008, 13.03

There is simply no-one quite like Svetan Miniovski. Exuding an aura of alpha-male superiority, his ego is just about large enough to match a man of his physical stature. I doubt that there is one man in Bulgaria that doesn't know who Svetan is; there certainly isn't one in Botevgrad. Svetan is the king of that town and he certainly knows it. And whilst Svetan rules the roost, his glamorous wife René is the queen who complements him.

A blonde bombshell who appears only to get better with age, the only thing about René that keeps her from perfection is the croaky voice that has developed from forty cigarettes a day since she was her daughter Stella's age. Stella herself, at only nineteen, is well on her way to matching René's defining attribute, but just don't tell her mother. Stella is just how I imagine that René would have looked at her age, and just as sweet too; and if there were marks for completing the perfect family picture of an identical mother-daughter and father-son combo, then eighteen year-old Gallin would bring the prize home for the Minovskis.

Gallin must have been about thirteen when I first met the Minovskis and even at that age he was still happily filling in for his father as our personal chauffeur if daddy was too busy. There is nothing that the Minovskis cannot do (let's be honest, they probably own the local police) and Gallin has always known it. The only challenger to his father's throne, Gallin almost matches his father's physical and psychological stature these days and seems always to have a flock of pretty girls around him, playing out of his oversized hands. It's quite something to see the man at work, racing around town in his dad's flash cars and swaggering into the local clubs simply reeking of persona.

The Minovskis certainly have their fingers in a lot of pies and it is just as well for *The Trussell Trust* that this includes the charity pie because they probably wouldn't even have a Bulgarian leg to stand on if it weren't for our showbiz mates in Botevgrad. What Svetan says goes this side of the world and he is well behind the good work of chief operator, Mr. Petkov, in Skravena. "Gospod Petkov" as we lovingly refer to him (*Gospod* literally means *Lord* in the Slavonic tongue) is Svetan's right hand man, and he takes care of the charity side of things, whilst the King is off playing with his toys.

The Trust's work in Bulgaria has really come on since I was last here, just five years ago. Back then it was all about the orphanage at Lipnitza – home to some fifty or sixty children (mostly Roma gypsies), who would otherwise have little chance of education, a home, or any real sense of self-worth. The gypsies in Bulgaria are the victims of real prejudice, shunned by average white Bulgarians, who often stigmatise them as little more than a bunch of thieves.

I clearly remember one occasion five years ago when I was walking along with a group of young Roma girls and a couple of slightly older white girls walking by, stopped, and slapped one of the girls I was with. Upon asking my translator what on earth had just happened, I was simply told that "nobody likes *them* around here," and off we walked as if nothing had happened. Living in a country that is largely free from racism and prejudice is a privilege that we often take lightly, but for the Roma gypsies, life is an uphill struggle.

Svetan and Lord Petkov have deemed it best for Will and me to spend the next few days at the brand new *House of Joshua*, which is a new halfway house *The Trussell Trust* has set up to help the youngsters find work after they graduate from the orphanage. It used to be the case that when they reached eighteen, the children would largely be left to fend for themselves, but now *The Trust* looks to support them until they can truly support themselves – helping them turn away from what can often be lives that revolve around drugs, thieving and prostitution.

As with most forms of prejudice, there is some truth to the generalisation that says that: "All Roma gypsies are thieves." There probably are more Roma gypsies thieving than white Bulgarians, but when one looks at the reason behind this, one finds that it is, of course, nothing to do with their caste. Rather, the reason is a perpetual cycle of never having enough to survive unless they steal, which is because they can't find work, which is because they are the victims of prejudice, and so they steal, which is why a stereotype forms and they can't find work... And so, you see, the cycle continues.

DAY FORTY-TWO:
CASA RENÉ AND SVETAN, SKRAVENA, BOTEVGRAD, SOFIA PROVINCE, BULGARIA, FRIDAY 22ND AUGUST 2008, 9.11AM

This morning the bus left for Varna without Will and me. It is the start of the annual summer camp today and a new team from *The Trussell Trust* has come along to take the youngsters away to the Black Sea for a week that they will never forget – for some this can be the very first time that they have seen the sea!

Given that Varna is quite a way east of our current location, we had previously hoped to hitch a ride with them, taking the opportunity to spend time with the children from the orphanage whom we hadn't seen in years, but a mixture of not wishing to encroach upon the efforts of the new team, and the small matter of waiting upon our Indian visas to arrive, has ensured that we will make the journey alone.

Organisation has never been a particular strength of ours, and so it should come as no surprise to learn that the only visas that we had previously arranged (and these came in a frantic final five days of dashing around London and paying huge amounts of money for the privilege) were the ones for Iran and Pakistan. The rest, we decided (more out of necessity than preference), would be obtained along the way, and the first of these – the Indian visa – is the one we currently await from the Indian Embassy in Sofia.

Our time in Skravena has been the timely break that our fading energy reserves required. We have been very well looked after as we have flitted between René and Svetan's home and *The House of Joshua*, but our feet are beginning to itch again. It is time to move on. Bulgaria marks the end of the first leg of the journey, but there is still a very long way to go and the next leg is somewhat of an unknown quantity. You know where you stand with Europe, but Turkey marks the start of a brand new era: Asia here we come.

DAY FORTY-SEVEN:
STELLA'S PAD, SOFIA, BULGARIA, TUESDAY 26TH AUGUST 2008, 11.15 PM

Marking my twenty-second birthday with a Turkish bath in Istanbul was the dream, but when the 24th came around we were still stuck in Skravena, waiting for the Indian Embassy to get their act together. In the meantime, not wishing to be caught kicking our heels, we put our legs to better use by getting to grips with the very best that the Bulgarian music scene has to offer, which is... Well, not a great deal by the look of things.

On the eve of my birthday, we assembled all our Bulgarian pals to head down to the Rock Club. Now, I'm not sure if you've ever been to a rock club on home turf, but I can assure you that, even if you have, it would not prepare you for what you would find in this particularly karaoke-crazy section of Eastern Europe. If you've ever wondered just what goes on behind closed doors in the land that brought us the touch of Dimitar Berbatov and the unbelievably cheesy tones of one-hit wonders, *Ozone* (the ones who gave us "*Numa Numa Yay*"), then think karaoke, think cheap perfume, and think Jon Bon Jovi on loop.

It doesn't get any worse, but this was the surreal way that I entered into my twenty-third year – the very same way that I entered my first year, I imagine: kicking and screaming. The worst thing about it was that this wasn't even our first time there, so there can be no excuses; this was the second time that we had been there in two days and was objectively considered to be the "best chance" that we had of enjoying a night out in Botevgrad. And if you're wondering if we joined in by getting on stage, then yes, I'm afraid we did. Eagle Eye Cherry's "*Save Tonight,*" Natalie Imbruglia's "*Torn*" and Clapton's "*Wonderful Tonight*" were the three that Will and I managed successfully to murder, presenting the Bulgarians with an unfairly dire picture of England's musical tastes and abilities – not that our merry friends would have remembered much about it the next day.

* * * * *

And as if that birthday "treat" wasn't enough, we decided to give the Bulgarian music scene another chance last night by going to a club in the Bulgarian capital of Sofia with Stella and a group of her mates from Uni. This was our last night before we were scheduled finally to pick up those visas and make for Turkey, so Stella and her Uni mates were determined that we should finish with a bang. By 9pm we were all tarted-up, entering into a taxi and trundling down the road, ready to be thrust bizarrely into an entirely alien world that I never want to revisit: the world of *Chowder*... And I'm not talking about the soup.

For Bulgarians, Chowder is about music – if you can call it that. Somehow, Bulgarian "artists" (I shudder; referring to them as *artists* makes me feel uneasy) manage to create a musical blend out of warbling voices, cheesy dance beats, tarted-up girls with too much make-up and not enough clothing, and tunes that are impossible to dance to, unless you are a Bulgarian girl – in which case you'll simply take the lead from Beyoncé and start shaking that booty around, while lecherous Bulgarian men drool over you in uncomfortably close proximity.

The music itself sounds as though it would work better in Egypt than Europe. I don't know what instruments are used to create the warbling sounds that the singers so painfully imitate, and I don't really want to know. Every song has the same beat, same singing voice, same awkward timing and, as far as we could tell, pretty much the same words. "Obicham te" (which means "I love you" in Bulgarian) must feature in over half of the songs, but, come to think of it, I suppose that isn't so different back home these days. The Bulgarians' musical tastes do also widen to include rock ballads and American R&B, but if they had a choice, I'd wager that 99% of Bulgarians would opt for Chowder… Again I shudder.

Day Forty-Eight:
A1, Outskirts of Svilengrad, Haskovo Province, Bulgaria, Wednesday 27th August 2008, 10.40am

This is it. The first visa-requiring border is just around the corner and we simply have no concept of what lies beyond it. Just what will it be like to hitch in Turkey? I have only ever associated Turkey with hostile borders and unfriendly football fans, so the territory ahead is very much an unknown quantity and, whilst we are excited, this is tempered with a healthy dollop of trepidation.

Not long after we spoke yesterday, Will and I headed to the Indian Embassy for the third time in a week, where we were finally furnished with our Indian visas. Swift progress on the road soon followed and we had made it to Plovdiv by sundown, whereupon we somehow managed to convince a lovely hotel manageress to let us stay, free of charge, on the floor of an empty room. The only conditions were that we left the room exactly as we had found it and departed by 6am this morning (before her superiors could find out).

True to our word, at 5.45am this morning, bags were shouldered and off we set in an easterly direction again. A little motorway walking and hapless car-flagging later and we have arrived on the outskirts of Svilengrad, where our fourth driver of the day (a trucker) has left us, while he makes his own way on to Greece.

Istanbul is the final target today and we are determined to reach there by sundown. Only 285km now separate us from our target, thanks to lifts from two Stanimars, one Angil and one Tirano (spelling, of course, is sheer guesswork), and I should imagine that most of the traffic crossing the nearby border will be heading towards what I am told is the European capital of

Turkey. I've never heard of a country that has two capitals before, nor have I heard of a country that is a part of two Continents, but Turkey claims both of these attributes. Apparently Istanbul is the European capital and Ankara the Asian one, but that seems to make it rather challenging to work out just where Europe ends and Asia begins.

One Turkish man told us that everything further east of formerly world-dominating Constantinople is considered to be Asia, but another Turk informed us that the divide is actually made somewhere in the middle of Istanbul itself. To make matters easier, as far as we're concerned, Asia will begin the very minute we cross over into Turkish territory. Come to think of it, it's approaching midday, so we'd better get back on the road to make sure that we arrive in this, one of the world's busiest metropolises tonight.

5. INTO THE UNKNOWN

DAY FORTY-EIGHT: (CONTINUED...)
A1, BULGARIA-TURKEY BORDER CROSSING, EDIRNE
PROVINCE, TURKEY, ASIA (?), WEDNESDAY 27TH AUGUST
2008, 15.16

They say that the waiting is the hardest part and I'm starting to agree
with whoever it was that coined that phrase. We have been sitting on the
other side of the immensely busy Turkish border for a little over ninety
minutes now, and there is still no sign of Nafis – the truck driver who
promised to pick us up as soon as he made it through customs.

Nafis is on his way to Istanbul and, if it weren't for the recent
disappointments of Sal and Drago, we would be completely confident in his
promise to return. Since those sad events, however, our faith in humanity
has weakened and we are now staring in the face of what seems likely to be
our third poor judgment-call in a matter of weeks.

Such is the measure of trust that we have haphazardly placed in this
particular Turkish stranger that we have even left a few of our belongings in
the cabin of his bright yellow truck and haven't even bothered taking down
the man's telephone number. With every passing truck that has even the
faintest tint of yellow, our hearts race and expectancy rises, but it's amazing
how one's memory of a vehicle can diminish after such a short space of
time. I'm not even sure that it was yellow anymore and have absolutely no

idea what logo was written on the side. Almost every passing truck *could* be his, but none has been so far and I suppose that soon we will just have to give up on dear old Nafis, who seemed like such a cheerful, trustworthy sort... But don't they all?

DAY FORTY-NINE:
HOTEL DENIZLI, AKSARAY, ISTANBUL, ISTANBUL PROVINCE, TÜRKIYE, THURSDAY 28TH AUGUST 2008, 20.08

Third time lucky! Nafis did return and we did make it to Istanbul last night, even if we didn't get all the way into the centre in his bright yellow (we remembered correctly) truck, due to the colossal traffic jam that brought vehicles to a standstill within about a twenty-kilometre radius of the city centre.

Nafis was having none of it. As soon as the sea of cars started to slow down, he pulled his truck onto the hard shoulder and informed us that he was going to set up camp there until the small hours of the following morning, when the traffic might have subsided a little. A fine plan, we thought, but no good for us. Here we were, on the edge of a swarming metropolis, without the foggiest idea of how we were going to make it into the centre.

At least the vehicles were moving slowly, which made the hitchhiking side of things ludicrously easy. All we had to do was walk around to the other side of Nafis' truck, nervously hold out our thumbs, and we were invited into the van of a chap named Mohammed – I suppose we'll meet a lot more of them now that we have left the predominantly Christian Europe and arrived in the mainly Muslim Middle East

Mohammed kindly wove his way through traffic for us for about forty-five minutes, before leaving us by the side of a relatively-central tram station, from where, he told us, we were to head to Aksaray.

Now, let me clear a little something up here (if I haven't mentioned it already): our rule of never paying for transport applies only to the getting to and from each city. Once we have arrived in a city, we liberate ourselves to make the most of inner-city bus, tram and taxi services (it does wonders for the local economy, don't you know). Frankly, it would be inconceivable to do otherwise. Try hitching a ride from Piccadilly Circus to Westminster sometime and you'll see what I mean!

One short tram-ride later, then, and we had arrived in Aksaray – the place we assumed would mark the focal point of the city...

What a disappointment! Upon arrival, all that we could see were lots of grey buildings, a host of street-sellers, crowds of people and... not a lot else. Surely this couldn't be the centre! We stopped a few Turkish-looking folk to ask them the way to the centre, but all we got were a host of bemused faces suspiciously staring at us as if we had asked them the way to Istanbul.

This was it!

Thoroughly dissatisfied with a city about which we had heard so many good things, we trudged over to the nearest Turkish restaurant to console ourselves with the finest kebabs known to humanity, and it was here that we met Arash and Farhud.

Perhaps it was the uncouth manner in which we scoffed these Turkish treats that caught their attention, or maybe it was the writing on our foreheads that must have read something along the lines of: "We are totally out of our depth in this city; please help us!" Come to think of it, we exhibit rather a lot of distinctive features that could have caught the eye – white faces, red shoulders, clumpy backpacks, Will's blonde hair, my blue eyes – and so it shouldn't have come as much of a surprise when these two friendly Iranian men came to lend us a hand.

"Salam Alecum," the fatter of the two greeted us.

"Alecum Salam," we replied, vaguely familiar with this famous Arabic greeting.

"Where are you from?" the fat one continued, unusually forward in his manner.

"Um, we're from England," Will replied cautiously.

"England! Really? I have lived in England for two years. My name is Arash and this is my friend Farhud. We are from Iran. Can we help you?"

Wow! What a strangely kind offer. What had we done to deserve the help of these men? Was it a trap? What were they after? Cautiously, we confirmed that we could do with a cheap place to rest our heads and would be grateful for their help because we feared that we could be ripped-off, rich tourists as we might appear.

Without hesitation our two new companions agreed to help and we spent the next hour going between hotels in the local area until we had found one with a rate that Arash deemed appropriate. Then, as if this wasn't enough, our talkative friend proceeded to offer us a tour of the city and we spent the rest of the night being shown why exactly this cosmopolitan city is rated so highly across the world.

Istanbul simply has everything: mosques, churches, history, modernity, land, sea, black, white (and the range of colours in between). Our first perceptions of the place have been flipped around by a city that has it all.

DAY FIFTY:
HOTEL DENIZLI, AKSARAY, ISTANBUL, ISTANBUL PROVINCE, TÜRKIYE, FRIDAY 29TH AUGUST 2008, 19.37

It's time to introduce our new friends a little better. Farhud, at 25 years of age, is essentially a ladies' man. Physically speaking, I suppose one could say that he looks Iranian, although I never really had an image of what Iranians look like before. He has darker skin than we Caucasians, considerably more body hair, and a fine jaw line; Farhud is as slick as an Italian and as attractive as the French (with a nose to match) and his favourite word is "Jooooo...ne!" which, we are told, translates directly from Farsi as "Wooooo...w!" Let me give you an example.

So, imagine we're walking down the street and an attractive girl walks by. Farhud, unabashed, swivels to get a better look, raises the tip of his nose as if to take a whiff of her scent, purses his lips, and produces an elongated "Joooo-ne!" which is itself pronounced in the deepest, most seductive tone known to mankind. It's just as well that he isn't in Iran because at least the bulk of the girls here can't quite understand what he is saying. Then again, they probably get the gist.

Arash is shorter, older and fatter than his friend. He tells us that he is 26, but he could easily pass for 35 and bears the middle-age spread befitting a man ten years his senior. Arash blames the belly on his recent marriage to a Polish girl, but he's been blaming a lot on her recently. Apparently her family agreed to the marriage only on the condition that Arash renounce his Muslim faith and take up Catholicism. Whilst he doesn't seem to mind the loss of what wasn't exactly a passionate faith, Arash does feel a little miffed that he daren't return to Iran, in case he gets lynched.

Much the better linguist, Arash is the bolder and more intense of the two, embracing his self-imposed tour-guide status and marching us off around the city, whilst Farhud spends the bulk of his time in silence, waiting for the next pretty girl to pass by.

Other than a fascinating visit to our first mosque of the trip – none other than the aptly named "Big Mosque" – our favourite thing to do in Istanbul is what I understand to be the quintessentially Istanbul-ian thing to do: to smoke flavoured tobacco through water-pipes that we most commonly refer to as "shisha" pipes, but are known here as "narghilè." Amidst a maze of Turkish rugs (draped over every chair and even covering the very walls of the smoking chamber) we sit for hours, supping "çay" (black tea) out of tiny glasses and smoking narghilè, whilst chatting over the day's events. It's the Turkish equivalent of French coffee and cigarettes, and we love it just as much.

Our time in Istanbul is fast drawing to a close, so it's just a shame that an argument between friends has led to Farhud's absence on this, our last day in the city. We're not exactly sure what Arash said to the boy, but it can't have been kind and may even have jeopardised our chances of staying with Farhud in Tehran. Arash has thus been relegated to our bad books and we shan't be inviting him along for our hitch to Izmir tomorrow, however insistently he may plead. We aren't particularly looking forward to what is likely to be a rather tricky first few hours on the road as we somehow try and navigate our way out of this teeming metropolis, and we could well do without an extra body (especially one with such mass) cramping our style.

Day Fifty-Three:
ŞÜKRÜ BEY'IN YERI CAFÉ, IZMIR, IZMIR PROVINCE, TÜRKIYE, MONDAY 1ST SEPTEMBER 2008, 13.35

You join us as we sit upon the authentically-carpeted cushions of a shisha bar in the middle of Izmir, narghilè in one hand, Türk kahvesi (Turkish coffee) in the other. We are thoroughly warming to the culture of this new Continent and particularly enjoying the friendliness of the local businessmen, who rarely leave us to sit for more than a minute without interruption. The charming owner of this particular bar has just handed us one of his business cards, complete with a little caricature of the man himself, big smile on face, Türk kahvesi in hand. The likeness is accurate to the point of our friend's follicle recession and healthy moustache, but the colour of his remaining hair has greyed a little.

Opposite us stands Murat, working hard as ever. He has already given us two complimentary tastes of the authentic local cuisine from his restaurant. *Çi köfte* (a tofu-stuffed lettuce leaf) was the first, shortly followed by the sweeter *kerebic* – a bright green cake with a nutty filling, complemented superbly by a cream sauce that has apparently been made from natural plant juices!

A third man to have come to our table at regular intervals is the talkative Hisar, who runs a souvenir store next to Murat's restaurant. This elderly gent has imparted much wisdom to us over the past hour, teaching us how very wrong we were to presume anything about his country. Hisar has set us straight. We now know everything (well, maybe not quite) from grammatical correctness to which King ruled over the empire in the Sixteenth Century!

Speak of the devil, here he comes again. You'll have to excuse me. What a privilege it is to sit here and not even have the time to write or to collect our thoughts before we are interrupted once again by our friendly hosts...

* Interval (approximately forty minutes) *

... Phew! Finally we have another moment to ourselves, and I shall use it (before another of our friends comes along) to tell of the events that led us here from our time with the Iranians in Istanbul.

It was about as tough as expected to hitchhike out of the centre of Istanbul. In fact, if it weren't for the help of a friendly student named Mehmet, I'm not sure we would ever made it out of the European capital that Saturday. Mehmet had been watching us with curiosity for some time before he approached us to ask if there was any way in which he could help. He certainly could, and did. Forty minutes, one ferry-hop, and a cheeky bus-ride later and we had finally arrived at what we considered a suitable hitching spot on the outskirts of the city.

The rest of the day was split evenly between two drivers with contrasting names. The first, a fisherman called Ismael, kindly escorted us the remaining distance along the north-western strip of Turkey (Turkey is another one of those awkward countries with sticky-outy bits), before a lorry driver called Sin could turn us back on ourselves, towards the south-westerly Izmir.

The navigational nightmare that is the north-western tip of Turkey is our excuse for not making it the whole way to Izmir that day, although the fact that we were not on the road until 1pm probably didn't help. In the end, we had to settle for the town of Bursa (some 200km short!), as bad light brought an end to the day's proceedings. We try never to hitchhike in the dark for fear that we would only be hastening our inevitable demise, so after twenty minutes of fruitless car-flagging, we gave up and started looking for a place to spend the night.

Little did we know that ten minutes later we would be lounging around on beanbag chairs, smoking narghilè and playing *Tavla* (the Turkish name for *Backgammon*) with one of several groups of youths that frequented the lawn outside a funky little local café.

The joker of the pack was a chubby twenty year-old by the name of Onur, whose bulging belly would have been his most noticeable attribute if it weren't for his ridiculous mullet and wild sense of humour.

"Are you Muslims?" Onur asked us with almost his very first three words.

Our negative response led on to what became his favourite joke of the evening. Every now and then he would gaze over to us, eyes wide open, bite his bottom lip, flicker his eyebrows, and imitate the cutting motion of a pair of scissors with his middle and index fingers. The meaning was simple: Onur wanted to give us "the snip" to properly integrate us into the group.

"We're all Muslims here," he jested, paying particular attention to Will because I had somehow given the impression that I was already circumcised.

* * * * *

I'm pleased to report that both William and I managed to survive the night unscathed, foreskins intact, and awoke to find Onur and co. happily slumbering next to us upon those same bean-bagged cushions, with not a pair of scissors in sight.

Onur and pals suggested that we should stay around for a few hours, to be shown the "best" Bursa had to offer. Foolishly we agreed. Having been promised a beach, mosques and kebabs, we were more than a little disappointed when the only place we managed to visit was a giant shopping mall. Why on earth would we want to go and visit a shopping mall in Turkey when we have carbon copies in England (and all the rest of the way across Europe, for that matter)?

Apparently this *was* the boys' favourite place, so I suppose that we did see the "best bits" of the city as far as they were concerned, but, whilst we did have kebabs for lunch, the mood had soured in the last few hours and we were eager to get back on the road to Izmir.

It took us longer than expected to arrive here yesterday, but I guess the main thing is that we did. Back-to-back lifts out of the centre – including a strange ride spent sitting on a rug in the back of a white van, smoking cigarettes given to us by a boy who looked no older than twelve – had left us stranded at the top of a hill on the side of a motorway, considerably vexed because we were sure that no-one would ever stop for us *"here!"*

We were flagging down cars even more desperately than usual and it wasn't too long before a boy racer heeded our call, screeching to a halt on the hard shoulder and nodding to us to get in. His engine had that familiar boy-racer tone and the reverberations shook us in our seats, adding to the alarm already induced by the frequency with which the engine choked and spluttered. If the boy had spoken English, I might have recommended that he take the poor car to a doctor... I suppose it's a good job that he didn't.

At top speed, we zoomed along for over an hour until, at some non-descript junction, our friend repeated his opening gambit by slamming on his brakes, skidding onto the side of the road and nodding for us to get out.

The light was already fading, so we didn't even give ourselves the time to regain our senses before we had successfully approached a truck-driver and hopped into his cabin to be confronted by that familiar smell of cheap cigarettes and aftershave.

The next moment we were bumping along the road to Izmir, smoking copious numbers of said cigarettes (so as to avoid offending the man) as we went. At one stage we stopped at a petrol station for some food, and thought it a nice gesture to buy our friend (let's call him Mohammed) a couple of packs of his favourites... It didn't quite go as smoothly as planned.

Upon receipt of said cigarettes, Mohammed, who seemed more offended than grateful, jumped out of the truck and raced over to the kiosk, returning with another two packs of the same, which he ripped open and immediately started offering to us again. We should have seen this coming. Far from successfully avoiding to steal all of this man's cigarettes, whilst generally wishing to smoke less, we had ended up by buying two new packs that we were going to have to keep, *and* we were still being offered a new cigarette as soon as the previous one was out. This "never refuse an offer" malarkey is really getting us into trouble.

It was approaching midnight when we finally arrived in Izmir, surreptitiously leaving the three remaining cigarette packets behind with Mohammed as we went off in search of a place to pitch our tent. The trouble was that we had come just far enough into the town for grass to become a rarity. In fact, the greatest supply of greenery on offer happened to be in the middle of the roundabout by which we stood, but we'd probably get arrested if we tried to sleep there!

The only other patch in sight was a little sliver wedged between two corrugated-iron roofs (later found out to be the top of the Izmir underground metro) that popped up a few feet above the ground on the other side of the roundabout, which, we mused, might conspire to provide just enough cover to keep us (and our tent) out of sight.

OK, it could have been subtler, but this was the best that we had on offer and we thoroughly enjoyed the scene when we awoke this morning to the sight of endless streams of traffic whizzing by our faces, drivers craning their necks and straining their eyes to work out why these strange foreigners were sleeping in the middle of the road.

DAY FIFTY-FOUR:
PIDE VELAHMALUN RESTAURANT, SELÇUK, NR. EFES, IZMIR PROVINCE, TÜRKIYE, TUESDAY 2ND SEPTEMBER 2008, 11.55AM

Sometimes it appears that, no matter what time of day we start hitching, we always arrive at our destination – a rather handy stroke of luck, given our regular tardiness, which was exemplified yesterday when we began our journey to Efes (formerly known as Ephesus) with not one hour of daylight remaining...

The reason we had been so late in the departing was that overdue longing to unclothe ourselves within the idyllic setting of the infamous Turkish bath: the *Hamam*. This authentic Turkish experience, which mixes male nudity with steamy temperatures, differs from my previous experience of a naked sauna in Kazakhstan, in that, instead of being whipped with palm leaves by naked children, we were rubbed, slapped and massaged by a hairy Turkish man.

As bizarre an experience as it was, we thoroughly enjoyed the entire episode, which started off with a steamy sauna, led on to a vigorous exfoliation, was brought to a climax by a creamy soap massage, cooled down with a swim in a pool, and finished by a final hose-down.

It's not every day that a hairy Turkish stranger sensually rubs you all over your naked-apart-from-loincloth-body with creamy soapsuds, and as the bubbles rose up to our nostrils and tickled our most sensitive areas, we couldn't help but giggle at the surreal nature of what was happening. Our heavily-moustached Turkish friend seemed equally amused by events and would give us each a healthy, reassuring slap on the thigh, before returning to the work that his heavy hands had clearly been made for.

Prudish natures were broken down to the extent that I decided that it was time to take it to the next level. We had trodden far more than just the baby steps towards intimacy by this stage and my loincloth (no more than a glorified tea towel) was sodden through so much that I felt it more a hindrance than a help. When it came to the time for a dip in the pool, I casually removed my tea towel and strolled through the mosaic-covered halls of this Turkish Hamam completely *starkers* to be met by the startled faces of my two friends, whose tea towels were still very much in place.

I don't know exactly what the Turkish man said, but the gist of it must have read something along the lines of: "What the hell are you doing? Get that tea towel back on now!"

Mildly red-faced, I cupped my privates, and complied. Will and I wouldn't stop giggling about the event until long after we had re-clothed, paid our dues, and started out on the road to Efes.

DAY FIFTY-FOUR: (CONTINUED...)
EPHESIAN AMPHITHEATRE, EFES, IZMIR PROVINCE, TÜRKIYE, TUESDAY 2ND SEPTEMBER 2008, 19.25

The sun is setting on our time in Efes. An otherwise empty, and thus serenely quiet, amphitheatre in the ancient city of Ephesus is the majestic stage for our final moments here, following a glorious day spent casually strolling around the ancient ruins.

We arrived here late last night, after one of the most fortunate rolls of the hitching dice that we have had thus far. It was 7pm when we finally left Izmir, so we never really expected to reach Efes, courtesy of only one lift, and this mild pessimism was further enhanced by the seeming lack of any cars heading in our direction.

The sun had almost completely faded out of sight and we were contemplating calling it a day before we had even really begun, when a kind man with an incomprehensible name (such has become to us the norm in this part of the world) pulled over to lend a hand. Language barriers ensured that we hadn't the slightest clue where he was taking us, but we pulled into a petrol station about ten kilometres down the road, whereupon the man chanted the word "Efes" at us a few times (just to make sure) and proceeded to ask every person in the petrol station if they were driving our way.

When I said "every" person, I might have given the impression that there were a lot of them. In actuality, there can't have been more than about five, and apparently none of these was heading our way. Our friend (whatever his name was) seemed to be in a rush to leave, so he apologetically shrugged his shoulders, bought us a couple of glasses of çay, and passed on the ambassadorial role of finding us a lift to the owner of the station café, who seemed to be a personal friend.

Quite relaxed about the whole thing, we had already earmarked the petrol station to be a fairly good spot to put up our tent for the night. We had friends here and they would be sure to look after us until the next morning, when we would be certain of covering the remaining fifty-or-so kilometres to Efes. But just before we thought about ordering ourselves a narghilè and some dinner, we were approached by what appeared to be a man in his forties taking his twenty-year-old daughter out for a night in the petrol station café.

Cadir, the father, told us that they could give us a lift most of the way, but such was the homely nature of this high-octane joint that we almost refused! In fact, if it weren't for the "never refuse an offer" rule, we might well have done, but soon we were in the back of their car, singing songs and getting to know our new friends, Cadir, and Tuna.

"So, is this your daughter, Cadir?" I enquired, assuming that it was a pretty safe question.

Cadir and Tuna turned to each other, laughed (actually, I think Cadir winced) and Tuna calmly turned round to me and said: "No, I'm his girlfriend," smiling and reassuringly stroking the neck of her aged lover.

I must remember in the future that it's probably a safer option not to assume such things. Next time I'll have to start with a more open, "how do you two know each other?" or "are you related?"

Oh, the embarrassment. Luckily for Will and me, my little blunder didn't seem to mar our relationship with our chauffeur and his companion at all. If anything, they seemed to warm to us all the more. In fact, perhaps this hiccup was the very reason that Cadir and Tuna kindly drove us for at least thirty kilometres beyond their own home, eventually taking us right up to the gates of the ancient city. It's just a shame that finding a place to sleep wasn't quite so simple.

When we arrived at the gates, Cadir asked the security guard if it might be possible for us to pitch our tents somewhere nearby, but this guard was one of those solemn types who don't like to speak too much and he simply shook his head and waved us away.

Three kilometres away from the ruins at Efes, we were driven back to the less ruinous town of Selçuk, where we were sure to have a better chance of finding a place to sleep, but not in our wildest imagination could we have expected to end up where we did last night.

Cadir and Tuna had driven us around Selçuk until they spotted a campsite, but the stern campsite attendant refused us a free pitching spot and we weren't going to pay to put our tent in what was just a glorified field. Not wishing to keep our friends for too long, we told them that we would take it from here, gratefully waved them goodbye and started wandering around in search of a patch of grass.

It can't have been more than a minute before we spotted Selami. A pint-sized Turk with a rounded belly and a goatee, Selami runs a little tourist shop on the edge of town. Behind his store, there is a garden area that wouldn't look out of place behind a regular house, and it was in this area, underneath the shadow of a drooping tree, that we were allowed to put up our tent and, essentially, to "move in" to Selami's garden for as long as we should so choose. Saying that, quite what our midget friend knew of the stipulations of the contract, it is hard to say, but he seems happy enough we're still here.

Selami can speak only about five words in English and our twenty words of Turkish have done little to facilitate communication. We have been trying our best to get to grips with the Turkish word for "thank you," but it must be a strong contender for the longest and most difficult word that I have come across. "Teşekkür ederim," we attempt to say, but it probably comes out something more like: "Tess... acorn... a... dear... rim."

A little bemused by our nonsensical phrases last night, Selami seemed impressed enough that we were trying, and moved his fat fist in a way that seemed to indicate we were to follow him. Follow we did, and we were soon sipping çay and smoking narghilè on the chairs set up at the back of his store. A fine introduction to Turkish hospitality, we thought...

* * * * *

And now here we are, basking in the silence that we have found on the top step of the enormous amphitheatre that towers above former Ephesus. Even during the middle of the day, there weren't many tourists around to clutter up the place and spoil the definite sense that, once upon a time, an important letter was written to instruct the Christians of this once great city. Paul himself is believed to have walked down the very road that we have now trodden, and there is an unquestionable sense of the spiritual still lingering here. Will and I particularly enjoyed pretending to bathe in the old baptismal font and mimicking preaching at the altar of a once renowned church. We sang a few songs, read the letter to the Ephesians, and ended the night by bellowing out *Amazing Grace* from the stage at the bottom of this ancient feat of amplification.

DAY FIFTY-EIGHT:
ROADSIDE CAFÉ, SERIK, ANTALYA PROVINCE, TÜRKIYE, SATURDAY 6TH SEPTEMBER 2008, 12.10PM

Two days have come and gone since our happy time in Selçuk. We left Selami and friends on Thursday morning, after many a narghilè and far too much Turkish *Raki* – an anise-flavoured brandy that tastes like medicine and seems to be the favourite Turkish alcoholic beverage.

On our last day together, Selami and his mate (another Mohammed) took us to visit the farcical "probable home" of the Virgin Mary (we didn't stay long) and a beautiful hilltop-village called Şirince, which shares the same kind of charm one might expect from a Tuscan dwelling in northern Italy or a petite village in the south of France. Apparently the wine's pretty good too, but we simply cannot see past an offer to drink Turkish tea and coffee at the moment.

Turkish coffee is like no other coffee you'll ever experience. A chocolaty-black shot melts in the mouth, while thick grains cling to the taste buds. I once remember trying a Greek coffee and finding the thickness of the powder at the bottom slightly overwhelming, but Turkish coffee seems to get the blend just right. There are no bits in the mouth and no residue at the bottom of the cup. Thick and bitter, yes; unpleasant, no. Two big thumbs-up from Will and me.

Later that night Selami had promised that he would take us to visit his house (apparently he doesn't always live in the shop, although he did sleep outside it on a bench every night that we were with him) to show us his two hundred birds (the feathered kind) and a "special" narghilè that he was crazy about, but when 11pm came and went, and we still hadn't left our familiar seats at the back of his shop (where we sat and drank yet more Raki), we wondered if we would ever have the opportunity to see his home – the one reason that we had stayed another day.

Selami was quieter than usual. I mean, he was never a great talker, especially not with the pair of us and our twenty-five-word cumulative vocabulary, but this night he was particularly quiet. I think he felt embarrassed, for whatever reason, that he hadn't taken us to see his home as he had promised, and his nervous twitch (a flickering of his bushy moustache and a quivering of the lips) was going haywire.

In a flash, Selami was up, and we were getting into his bright red Escort XR3 on our way to an impromptu bar-crawl in the centre of town. Well, I say "bar-crawl"; it was more like one bar, filled with about twenty-five middle-aged blokes, all throwing back the Raki and, tragically, awaiting the advances of a prostitute. I can tell you that they wouldn't have had any trouble that night; the place was packed full with them.

A new girl would wander up the stairs every five minutes and trot on over to us, mimicking the moves that might better befit a catwalk, or perhaps even a strip-joint. Each girl looked pretty much the same on the outside (caked in make-up and clad in a mini skirt, fishnet stockings, a tiny top and a push-up bra) and as they came over to our table, one by one, the girls would normally hone in on the fresh-faced Will, stroking the back of his neck and ruffling his hair, looking out for the slightest indication that any one of us might want to ask them to sit down for a drink – an invitation that would surely have promised so much more.

This was the most strange and uncomfortable moment of our time with Selami and we didn't know what to do. Quite what was going on in our friend's mind was uncertain. To be honest, he just looked like the rest of the regulars in that place and would knock back the Rakis to calm his nerves at our obvious displeasure. We tried not to offend our friend by seeming too judgmental of this place (a place he had probably presumed to be right up our alley), but it wasn't too long before he had read our minds, paid the bill, and hurried us out of those seedy, dimly lit quarters.

"Teşekkür ederim," we said, with growing panache, as we quickly vacated the premises and made our way over the road to get ourselves what seems to be the Turkish equivalent of a kebab after a night out: some soup! [I suppose that the Turks have far too many kebabs during the day, so they need to try and mix things up at night.]

Selami went for the chicken soup, and I thought it best to follow his lead. Will, on the other hand, was not so clever, preferring the choice of the generic "meat soup" option, and proceeding to retch with every mouthful. Quite what "meat" was involved in the dish, I do not know, but the over-riding flavour was so unpleasant that it forced Will to heap a mass supply of whole chillies into the dish in a vain attempt to clear his palate.

After what was a night that we will struggle to forget, we left Selami's late on Thursday morning to start out on the long road towards Kapadokya – a World Heritage Site that we have been told not to miss.

At some 850km distance away, this was one trip that we were going to have to break up a little. The first target would be Antalya, slightly more achievable at 550km, and also a route that would see us stroll happily close to the Turkish coastline – something we're rather glad of, given that our last shower was way back in Istanbul. Even though the Hamam in Izmir probably atoned for much of the ensuing pong from the first few days, the following six or seven have left their mark.

Lifting my arms for a quick whiff just a second ago, I can acknowledge that it is likely to be the growing repulsion I feel towards my own scent that led to our immunity from the stale stench that lingered around our friend, Selami – presumably itself a result of his never-changing outfit of a "*blue jeans*" t-shirt, three-quarter length jeans and, as far as we were aware, the same underwear.

Personal hygiene is a concern in this part of the world (or certainly should be), but the rapid increase of smelly men all around us at least helps us to fit in, now that showering has become drastically less available.

Day Fifty-Nine:
"Esentepe Lokantasi," Ali's Trucker stop, Konya Province, Türkiye, Sunday 7th September 2008, 9.56am

It is becoming increasingly difficult to find the time and space to write. This morning I am surrounded by a group of truckers, all of whom have found their way to Ali's popular *lokantasi* (this seems to be the Turkish word for a cheap restaurant), which, like all other restaurants in this country, specialises in kebabs. Şiş (shish) kebabs are our favourite, but I don't know how long we can go on living off kebabs for breakfast, lunch and dinner. It's not exactly healthy...

Day Fifty-Nine: (continued...)
Another Lokantasi, Aksaray, Aksaray Province, Türkiye, Sunday 7th September 2008, 14.35

Coincidentally, my thoughts still revolve around kebabs, having just devoured the latest in this growing line of greasiness. Old Ali – our host and landlord for last night's kip on a rug-covered platform outside his lokantasi – kindly drove us to the other side of the large city of Konya (we've come a long way since Selçuk) and we have received a further two lifts to land us in this petrol station lokantasi on the outskirts of Aksaray, now only about 100km away from Kapadokya. But before I tell of the fascinating folk we have met since Ali's place (the last of whom were a couple of homosexual Australians!), I really do have some catching up to do...

Hitching is proving much easier here than it was in Europe. On our first day on the road from Selçuk, we were picking up lifts almost as soon as we had stuck out our thumbs. The first came from a (presumably) heterosexual Aussie called Izzy, who took us up the road to a place that he enthused would be "perfect" for getting a more substantial ride. He was right. Barely had a moment gone by before two burly Turks pulled over and invited us to join them for the next 200km, as they travelled in the direction of Antalya towards the village of Ortaca. Perhaps we might have thought twice about accepting an offer from these intimidating folk, if it weren't for the fact that they were going such a long way, but 200km is not something to be sniffed at, and we were in before we had given it another moment's thought.

Conversation with the slightly-less-enormous Mustafa (the driver) was just about achievable thanks to our shared proficiency in French, whilst Şerif in the passenger seat both amused and terrified us with his booming baritone voice, which, we speculated, must have been audible several kilometres away. Perhaps if we had felt a little less scared, we might have advised Şerif to get his blood pressure checked (so voluble was he in his aggression towards his latest telephone victim), but Will and I were stunned into silence, glancing at each other in sheer terror as we observed a vein on the side of his neck pulsating to the point of near-explosion.

I suppose that it should have come as little surprise when we pulled over a few moments later and were told to stay put while our chauffeurs jumped out and stormed into a building to undergo what we assumed must be some kind of shifty business transaction. Half an hour quickly came and went, and by this time we had conjured up the most elaborate of reasons for this delay. Şerif and Mustafa were in the mafia; there was no doubt about it. The raised voices, the money laundering, the obvious discontent and high blood pressure on the part of Şerif, and wait... what was that hiding sneakily beside the driver's door other than a baseball bat, which, we concluded, must have been used on the last people who attempted to cross these heavyweights.

Forty minutes had gone by before Şerif came out, sweating heavily and veins throbbing as usual. He snarled at us to get back into the vehicle and off we went... without Mustafa. Will and I exchanged worried glances. What had become of Şerif's sidekick? Where was the only man with whom we could actually communicate, and where on earth was Şerif taking us to?

Fraught with worry, Will and I did the only thing that we could do: sat and waited in silence, contemplating the likelihood that Mustafa had been the latest victim in a long line of mafia killings and Şerif was going to "get rid of us" so that there wouldn't be any witnesses. Our only hope was that Şerif's interpretation of "getting rid of us" might be to drop us back on the road to Antalya, where we would promise not to utter a word to anybody, and proceed to attempt to get another lift with a more mentally-stable driver.

It was a little disappointing in the end when Şerif didn't get rid of us anywhere at all, but instead took us to sit and wait outside a police station. At least this confirmed the dodgy dealing that was going on, but it seemed as if they were going to end it on the level by getting the law involved.

"The mafia *are* normally in cahoots with the police, aren't they?" Will whispered to me in Şerif's absence, trying to keep our conspiracy theory alive.

Solemnly, I nodded. We weren't out of the woods just yet.

Five minutes later and Şerif stormed out of the police station, still fuming.

This brief interaction with the police had clearly done little to improve his mood. We raced back to the scene of the crime – an ordinary-looking shop in the middle of an ordinary-looking town, but isn't it always the least suspicious places that one should be most wary about?

As soon as we arrived, Şerif leapt back into action, almost taking the shop door off its hinges as he re-entered the scene, but this time we weren't just going to sit there helplessly while our new friends got shot on the inside. Someone was going to have to do something. *We* were going to have to do something.

Before I could even think twice, I had reached around the side of the driver's door and picked up the baseball bat, whereupon Will and I crept over to the shop. Through the window we could see Şerif angrily gesturing at two strangers, arching his frame over their desk to get right in their faces, whilst the more sedate Mustafa waited in the wings. Phew! At least he was still alive, but for how long?

I'd had enough; someone had to act. Bursting through the door, I wielded the baseball bat and dealt the two strangers one hefty blow apiece that sent them sprawling across the room to lie unconscious upon the floor.

"Let's go," I said nonchalantly to our flabbergasted friends, who stood still for a moment in disbelief, mouths opened wide.

Casually, Will and I strolled back over to the car and waited for our friends to join us. Two hours of driving later and we would be left, unscathed, by the side of the road in the village of Ortaca…

It's up to you how much of the above account you choose to believe. I will tell you that all of the events up to the wielding of the baseball bat were exactly as we perceived them. Also true was our conviction that our friends were part of the mafia. An alternative ending to the dramatic one given above would be that Will and I stood outside the shop, petrified, whilst, with every minute that went by, we decided that our chances of survival were less, until, eventually, our friends left the shop – presumably leaving the two strangers for dead – and we were deposited, unscathed, by the side of the road in the village of Ortaca.

6. FASTING AND FISTICUFFS

DAY SIXTY:
ROOFTOP OF UMUT AND FAMILY'S HOUSE, GÖREME, NEVŞEHIR PROVINCE, KAPADOKYA, TÜRKIYE, MONDAY 8TH SEPTEMBER 2008, 8.52AM

This is the eighth day of the Muslim festival, *Ramazan*, a holy month of fasting for Muslims across the world. The rules are simple: no food or water between the hours of sunrise and sunset, which for Turkish Muslims at the moment means about fourteen hours of fasting from 5am to 7pm! Now, I can just about imagine not eating for a day, but to go without a single droplet of water as well... That's commitment!

So impressed are Will and I by their efforts that today, for one day only, we are joining in. It would have been easy enough for us to fall back upon our tourist status and profess a real, yet detached, interest in proceedings, but we've decided that we would rather see what all the fuss is about from close hand. Thus, at about 3.30am this morning our friendly host, Umut, woke us up for the morning feast before the fast.

Joining his loving wife, Mehtap (who had been busily preparing food for goodness knows how long), we all sat cross-legged upon a mat on the floor (some more accomplished in this art than others) and tried to take on the copious amounts of food and water required to last us through the rest of the day.

The beginning of the fast is signalled by the unmistakable howl of the Call to Prayer, after which our Muslim friends dutifully went off to pray, whilst Will and I were equally submissive towards our own summons back to bed.

It's been four gruelling hours so far (the bulk of which have been spent asleep) and we're still going strong. To be honest, I doubt whether we'll manage to last the day without *any* food or water – especially in this heat – but we're going to give it a shot, and will allow ourselves to cop out only if any fainting or extreme dizziness should occur.

DAY SIXTY: (CONTINUED...)
ROOFTOP OF UMUT AND FAMILY'S HOUSE, GÖREME, NEVŞEHIR PROVINCE, KAPADOKYA, TÜRKIYE, MONDAY 8TH SEPTEMBER 2008, 16.03

Phew! Thirteen hours through; we've almost made it. I dread to think what our breath smells like right now. With parched lips and horribly dry throats, we have panted around the magnificent humps that make up the bizarre natural phenomenon that is Kapadokya without a single drop of water between us. Come to think of it, maybe we are just tripping out, and the giant pink anthills surrounding us are only figments of our imagination.

Hallucinogenic tendencies aside, we have much catching up to do. It is now time to cast your minds back to the moments following our scrap with the Turkish mafia, and our subsequent efforts to flee far away from the scene of the crime, tout de suite...

Three speedy lifts took us to within 200km of Antalya, but the last of these (with a Brazilian ex-pat) would see us stranded in a pretty shoddy spot on the corner of a near-empty minor road – in what seemed to be the middle of nowhere – and it wasn't long before those same old fears returned to haunt us.

Where were we? How on earth were we going to get a lift from *here*? Why didn't we stay in the last spot? At least in *that* spot there were places to eat and, if necessary, to sleep. To make matters worse, the sun was setting fast and we reckoned we had only about one hour left before we would find ourselves completely blacked-out.

In the open fields in front of us, we noticed a trio of shepherds, whom we had already earmarked as our potential helpers should darkness ensue. And, as if they had been listening to our thoughts, one of these old-timers gradually shuffled his way over to us, presenting two pears with his grubby old paws, which he proceeded to shake in our direction in a blasé fashion.

"Teşekkür ederim," we said (our best impressions of the phrase thus far), accepting his pears.

The shepherd nodded disinterestedly.

Language barriers being what they are, we didn't feel in any sort of position to converse with our new friend, who hadn't moved a muscle since bringing us the pears. Was he dead, we wondered?

No, signs of life exhaled noisily from his heavily thatched nasal area and we started going through the motions of our best remaining Turkish phrases. How are you? What is your name? We were just wondering whether it would be disrespectful to ask the man how old he was, when he suddenly sprang into life.

With his last remaining ounce of strength, the man (whose name he never did reveal) stumbled over to our bags and started shaking them. Looking up at us, he fingered the tattered old garment upon his torso and pointed towards our own, still rather white, hitch t-shirts.

"Oh, I get it," I said to the man, as if he could understand. "You want one of our t-shirts as a way of saying thank you for the pears, which, by the way, won't be ripe this side of the next century."

The man nodded, as if he comprehended fully and agreed wholeheartedly.

There was nothing for it; we were going to have to give the man something. After all, he had made the effort to come all this way with what had at first seemed like a truly generous offering. I ruffled through a few of my things and, not wishing to part with one of only four hitch shirts, produced a white vest and gave it to him.

I don't know what it was about the vest that displeased him so, but he shook his head and appeared forlorn.

"Try again!" his eyes seemed to suggest.

Now it was Will's turn to produce two vests of his own, but still he wasn't satisfied. Once more he pointed towards our pristinely-white t-shirts.

The phrase "beggars can't be choosers" came to mind, but I thought it best to keep this one to myself, given that he had seemed to have so well understood my last phrase.

Perhaps he has an aversion to vests, I thought, rifling through my belongings again, before offering him a green t-shirt with the proudly displayed yellow slogan, *Morocco Hitch*.

"Much better," he seemed to say, and off he trotted, leaving us two pears better off, but down one t-shirt, as off he went, presumably to contemplate what "Morocco" was and why anyone would want to "Hitch" there.

By this time the sunset was painting the sky in a pretty array of reds, pinks and purples, but we were more concerned about the blackness that was sure to follow, as we set about trying to hitch again. The strange incident with the shepherd had only cost us about three missed opportunities – such was the sporadic nature with which vehicles would pass by – and it was another three or four minutes before another did.

As tends to be the case during more desperate times of hitching, we weren't thumbing anymore; this had long been replaced by a wild flapping of the arms, as if we were trying to co-ordinate a take off for a Boeing 757 or the like.

Our aeronautics seemed to do the trick. We were picked up by the very next truck to pass by and, before we knew it, we were on our way... to Antalya!

What a day! Starting out 550km away, we never really believed that we would make it to Antalya in one day, but here we were, just one ride away from our destination… It's just a shame that our own idea of "going to Antalya" didn't quite coincide with that of our driver, Vulcan.

At twenty-four years of age, Vulcan was easy to get along with. His English was by no means perfect, but was sufficient – combined with our meagre offering of Turkish – to get most of the essentials across, and we warmed to Vulcan immediately.

Up to this point, Muslims (practising Muslims at least) have been few and far between, but Vulcan certainly claimed a sincere belief in Allah and told us that he would be adhering to the Ramazan fast if it weren't for the fact that he were on the road. Apparently travellers are exempt from the rules, and it's just as well because Vulcan had driven all the way from Izmir that day (further than us) and would hardly have been fit for driving had he had nothing to eat or drink since the small hours. Our friend was tired enough as it was and soon told us that we would stop for the night in Kaş and continue towards Antalya the next day.

Not exactly in a position to argue, Will and I nodded our approval, and we were soon smoking narghilè and drinking çay at one of the many cafés there. Unfortunately, Kaş is just another of those naturally beautiful coastal towns abroad that has become overrun with tourists – most of whom are British or Australian. It seems to me that the tourist industry, however beneficial it may be for the economy, does tend to ruin the lives of the locals. Imagine living in a place that doesn't feel like your home anymore because a bunch of raucous foreign strangers keep disrupting your everyday existence. That night, Will and I simply added to the number.

When the evening was through and the narghilè had puffed its last breath, we made our way back to Vulcan's lorry and started making preparations for a night on the roof. It turned out that the back of our friend's truck was crammed full of Turkish rugs and Vulcan's idea was that we could place a few rugs on top, where we could spend the night underneath the stars, safely out of sight. I mean, who's going to be looking for people sleeping on top of a truck?

Rugs duly arranged and tooth-brushing in full flow, we were just preparing ourselves for the ascent when we were rudely interrupted by a shifty-looking Turk, who had sidled over to the truck and begun to converse with Vulcan.

Will and I looked on with suspicion, thoroughly unimpressed with the way in which this stranger's wandering hands were busily feeling the contents of our bags from behind his back.

Such was our distrust in this man, whose blue cap was pulled over his head so tightly that it cast a dark shadow over his unfriendly face, that we didn't take our eyes off him for a minute. Vulcan himself had looked a little uneasy at whatever this strange man was saying to him and, as soon as the man had gone out of sight, Vulcan signalled to us that we were leaving… "Now!"

Everything happened so quickly that we didn't have a chance to work out what was going on before we had hastily retrieved the rugs from the roof, bolted them tightly shut in the back, and were off again. What had seemed like your average night on top of a truck had suddenly been abandoned, but what on earth could the man have said that would have led to such a hasty getaway?

Vulcan hesitated before answering our musings, quietly, in his broken English.

"He was... He was bad man," Vulcan began, pausing to let out a sigh. "He wanted we take your things," he continued. "We take passports. You sleep and... And, he kill you." Again Vulcan sighed. "I'm sorry."

"What!" Will and I cried simultaneously as we began to think through the connotations of this man's intentions. "He kill us?"

There was a long silence. Vulcan was noticeably upset, whilst Will and I reacted in a way that might not have been expected. We weren't so much upset, nor scared, as we were angry – really angry! Expletives were flowing regularly from what are usually rather squeaky-clean lips.

"Why did this man want to kill us?" Will asked, wondering what on earth we had done wrong to induce a complete stranger into wishing us such harm.

"It because you English," Vulcan replied.

"What does that matter," I protested, amazed that such an insignificant thing as our nationality could have caused such malcontent.

"He is Kurd. Kurds bad people," Vulcan continued, apologising again.

"No, Vulcan, don't apologise. It's not your fault," Will reassured our friend. "If it weren't for you, we would probably be dead!"

Hold on a minute. That was it. We might *actually* be dead if it weren't for our friend. If Vulcan hadn't liked us, or if he had thought that we might be carrying enough riches with us to make it worth his while splitting them with this murderous man, then perhaps we could be lying asleep on the top of his truck right now, moments from death!

Vulcan was tired. As soon as we had driven far enough away to deem us safely out of reach of murderous Kurds, we pulled over into an abandoned petrol station. The rugs-on-the-roof idea was vetoed this time and we settled for a night upon the stone cold floor of an abandoned office, minds still racing with the thought of what might have been.

* * * * *

The next day was slow, really slow. We must have stopped off at about seven or eight different locations on the way to Antalya (for rug-dealing purposes) and, in the end, it took us a total of nine hours to reach a destination that cannot have been more than 150km away! If it weren't for the kindness of our travelling companion, we might have decided to try our luck with a faster vehicle, but we liked Vulcan and didn't want to be rude after all that he had done for us the night before.

After countless stops, an unwelcome touch of heatstroke, and a lot of frustration, we finally arrived in Antalya, where Vulcan proceeded to take us to the one place on earth that could compound our misery: a shopping mall!

We couldn't believe it. What is it about Turkish shopping malls that are so impressive that people insist upon taking us there? This was a carbon copy of the one in Bursa and felt just like another piece of England. I don't know, you make all this effort to get somewhere new and people insist upon taking you to see something you could very well have seen at home!

Day Sixty-One:
Rooftop of Umut and family's house, Göreme, Nevşehir Province, Kapadokya, Türkiye, Tuesday 9th September 2008, 13.08

Last night there was a horrible family argument, such that I have never experienced before first-hand. Shortly after we had eaten the post-fast feast together, Mehtap's oldest brother, who had been quiet throughout the meal, suddenly burst into the conversation. Although we couldn't understand the words, we knew that something wasn't right because this man's demeanour was so different from the peaceful and sweet manner of the rest of his kin. We had just left the table and gone back to our rooftop dwelling when suddenly it kicked off.

Shouting, screaming and fighting swiftly resulted in weeping, sadness and pain as the abusive older brother tore the family apart. Will and I watched despairingly from the rooftop, not knowing what to do. It wasn't our place to go downstairs and get involved, no matter how much we wanted to, so we did the only thing that we could think of at the time, and started to pray.

The argument ran on for over half an hour and, when it eventually died down, we did our best to leave unnoticed so that we wouldn't add to the awkwardness of the situation, but as we passed by the side of the house, there was Mehtap, five-year-old daughter Eva cradled in her arms, make-up smeared around her eyes and tears still streaming down her red face.

As we walked past, we offered our sympathy and commiseration as best we could, but, in truth, words seemed inadequate. Poor Mehtap didn't respond, except with a reluctant smile, and off Will and I went to try to get out of the way for as long as we could.

Returning at 3am this morning, we were shocked to find grandmother Layla still awake, cradling her head in her hands as she cried out to Allah for help.

For the briefest moment, as with Mehtap earlier on, we thought it best to walk on by, allowing her the time and space to consider the evening's events alone, but we couldn't just leave this clearly distressed old lady like that. We had at least better say good night.

Cautiously approaching Layla, we muttered a quiet "Bon nuit" (she speaks fluent French) and were about to turn for the exit when she erupted into sobs again.

We couldn't just leave her now. In between sobs, Layla began to open up about the situation with her eldest son, who has a drinking problem. This wasn't the first time that there had been a family row and *he* was always the initiator. Apparently Layla's husband had passed away a few years ago and the older brother had been hit the hardest.

"Pour quoi, mon Dieu? Pour quoi?" Layla lamented, with the rasping voice of a woman who has smoked far too much over the years.

Well out of our depth by now, Will and I offered to pray with her. Gratefully, Layla accepted, and together we offered our prayers to Almighty Allah.

What a wonderful thing it was: two Christians and one Muslim calling upon the God who, if He exists, must surely be God of both Muslims and Christians alike. When the prayers were over, Layla said that she had felt as if an electric current was passing through her, and we had felt it too.

As we left a comforted Layla to return to our beds that night, we wondered at the Providence that had brought us to this house. This was no co-incidence. We were simply *meant* to be in this situation at that exact time. Layla knew it too.

"Merci," she shyly exclaimed.

"De rien, Layla," we replied, shaking our heads in amazement at what had just taken place. The real wonder and praise belonged to God.

"Merci mon Dieu," was our final cry last night.

DAY SIXTY-ONE: (CONTINUED...)
RAMAZAN'S VILLE, TALAS, KAYSERI PROVINCE, TÜRKIYE, TUESDAY 9TH SEPTEMBER 2008, 21.40

Our relationship with Vulcan ended in the most sudden and unexpected fashion. No sooner had we exited that dreaded shopping mall than Vulcan received a phone call from his parents to alert him that his younger brother had been in a fight and was now in hospital. Before we knew it, we were back in the truck and back on the road towards Izmir. Vulcan said he would drop us off on the outskirts of Antalya and we had the time that the journey took (about fifteen minutes) to work out what we would do from there.

The hour was growing late and, as we arrived at a non-descript petrol station on the edge of town, Will and I soon decided against continuing our hitching efforts that day. Wishing Vulcan safe passage on his midnight trek home, we set about looking for a place to sleep, and crashed out upon a couple of benches outside a nearby school.

Tiredness overrode discomfort and we slept as soundly as the logs upon which we lay until the moment that we awoke to behold seven curious faces, hovering above us with a look that may well have been disgust, but we preferred to perceive as curiosity.

Sunday morning though this was, it appeared that the school was in full-flow and the man in charge of the group (possibly the headmaster) sent us packing with a couple of rolls and takeaway cups of çay – quite a nice little take on a *B&B*, by all accounts!

Wandering wearily back to the petrol station, we duly recommenced hitching efforts towards Kapadokya, only to be informed by the first passing driver that we were going the wrong way. Naively assuming that this man was far more likely to know the way than ourselves, we crossed over the road and set about hitching a ride back towards Antalya.

The next couple of hours were arduous and sweaty. It wasn't for a lack of people stopping for us. Rather, none of our drivers were going very far. We were given one lift back to Antalya, another two to get onto the "right" eastward road, and two further lifts before we had reached the intersection that marked the start of the "right" northward road.

All this to-ing and fro-ing (plus an enforced two-hour lunch break from the debilitating midday sunshine) had somehow seen the clock tick forward seven hours since our 8am awakening, and we were really only just beginning.

So desperate were we for a decent lift that, when three shepherds pulled over in their stable on wheels (with not one spare seat between them) and offered us a ride to Konya (some 200km away), we took no time in accepting.

If the distance had been any less substantial, I should think that we might have thought twice about getting into this cramped cabin with three old, sweaty, and extremely pungent shepherds, but our situation felt desperate, and desperate times...

Bearing in mind that their cabin was built for one driver and two passengers, they were already at full capacity without our help, so we fully expected to be chucked into the back with the sheep's wool.

No such luck, I'm afraid. Our bags were given the nice, woolly coating, whilst Will and I had to sandwich ourselves between the two non-driving shepherds, taking it in turns to sit upon each others' knees! Every time we stopped – and we stopped a lot – we would switch it over, but whilst you might expect that it would be better to be on top, I can assure you that being below had its benefits. Benefit number one was that you would avoid having your head thrust against the low ceiling with every bump (there were a lot of them too); benefit number two (my personal favourite) was that you would avoid a knee massage by the shepherd with the particularly stenchy breath.

As surprising as it may seem, I have to admit that I actually quite enjoyed the experience, in spite of the fact that it was a tad uncomfortable and, on occasion, more intrusive than I would have liked. Our shepherd friends, Yeshur, Mustafa and Memed, were an absolute joy to be around and, although regular communication wasn't possible, we were able to say so much through other means.

Mustafa, the less touchy-feely shepherd of the sandwich, was our favourite from the start. Whilst we couldn't understand exactly what he was saying, the *way* in which he would say it was hilarious enough and almost everything that he said was accompanied by wildly exaggerated facial expressions and hand gestures – Yeshur (the touchy-feely one) was almost always the butt of the joke.

It turned out that this tactile shepherd was the only one of the three to be observing the holy fast of Ramazan, and it quickly became clear that the other two found this rather amusing. During every çay break Mustafa would make the same joke, steering his glass in Yeshur's direction to question the commitment with which Yeshur was devoted to this fast.

"Ramazan?" he would ask his friend jovially, whilst the rest of us broke into hysterics.

The joke was played with such regularity that we soon joined in and, before long, we had all but forgotten our friend's name because we had started referring to him simply as "Ramazan." Yeshur was a good sport about the whole thing and seemed to find the joke almost as funny as the rest of us. Anyway, it served him right for touching us up.

The second joke that Mustafa insisted upon extending Ramazan's way was something about the Ukraine, but we never really caught the gist. At regular intervals, Mustafa would lean out of his seat, turn his head to Ramazan, and say: "Ukraine... sex; Ukraine... sex," as if the two were inextricably linked and we should know exactly what he was talking about. We didn't, but laughed along as if we did, not wishing to upset our friend, nor put an end to what was our greatest source of entertainment on this long journey.

Now, to give you a little more of an insight into the frequency with which we stopped, I can honestly say that in the 200km journey I think we stopped for çay no fewer than seven times! Don't get me wrong; we do like the stuff, but there are limits.

Bearing in mind that the vehicle averaged about 55km/hr (when we were actually moving), a journey that could have been done in about two hours still wasn't complete after five, come sundown, when the boys decided to call it a day at Ali's trucker stop, about 30km short of Konya.

We tried not to seem too disappointed at covering so short a distance that day because, after all, this trip isn't supposed to be about the speed with which we get between places; it is supposed to be about the people that we meet along the way. Yet, after a third long day on the road in succession, the fact that we were still a substantial distance from Kapadokya was a tough truth to contemplate.

* * * * *

Ali didn't even ask us for so much as one Turkish lira for his hospitality that night, which extended to dinner, breakfast, at least a further five glasses of çay, and then the morning's drive to the perfect hitching spot on the other side of Konya. Like so many of the others that we have had the privilege to meet for a very short time, it is highly unlikely that we will ever see Ali again, but his help will not be forgotten. If it weren't for his aid we might never have reached Kapadokya, and we would surely not have had the pleasure of meeting our next drivers, Geoffrey and partner, Matthew.

As you may be able to ascertain from their not particularly Turkish-sounding names, these middle-aged men weren't from around these parts. Geoffrey and Matthew were travelling Aussies, driving themselves around the ancient historical sites of Turkey and currently on their way to visit a few caravanserais on the old Silk Road (that we were apparently about to reach).

"Caravan... sir... what?" I enquired, after a moment's pause, during which I failed to convince myself that I had the least understanding of what they were talking about.

"Caravanserai!" Geoffrey enthused, proceeding to inform us that these places were "faaaa...bulous" rest stops (the ancient equivalents of service stations) for weary travellers or tradesmen, who could park their camels and find somewhere to shelter, pray and trade.

"Why don't you come along with us to this fasssss...cinating place?" Matthew asked and, we being yes-men, there are no prizes for guessing our response.

The caravanserai itself was indeed as faaaaa...bulous and as fasssss... cinating as our friends had suggested, but it was the events which followed our visit that really stick in the mind.

When we had first arrived at the site, we had been surrounded by a hoard of little people, each trying to sell us their own set of tacky postcards and jewellery. Turning out our pockets, Will and I had repeated the Turkish phrase, "Para nahi," which means "no money" (a very important phrase to learn indeed in these parts), whilst our flamboyant friends had simply ignored them.

Yet, we all know how forgetful children can be, and these ones were smart too. As soon as we had finished the tour, there they were again, jumping up and down and tugging upon our various limbs in the resolute belief that one of us must have something!

Pointing towards the gate of the site, the ringleader of the pack (no older than twelve and no taller than about four feet) rubbed his thumb and forefinger together, and then proceeded to hold out his hand, conveying his belief that it must have cost us a few lira to get into the site at all, so one of us must have been lying.

He was right and before long the sympathetic Geoffrey had succumbed to the growing pressure, first dipping inside his pocket to hand round a pack of sweeties, before – upon realising that this clearly wasn't enough – pulling out a great wad of notes and holding them high above these frenetic children.

Pulling one note away from the wad, Geoffrey was just determining which child was the most deserving when five or six of them clambered up his arm and tried to wrestle it from his grasp.

Incensed by their savagery, Geoffrey taught these greedy children a lesson, ripping the note away from their grasp, shoving it into his mouth and noisily devouring it in front of them as they watched on with horror.

Our Geoffrey had had quite enough. Taking firm hold of the rest of the wad, he marched us back to the car, where we had to lock ourselves in to make sure that the little blighters couldn't get at us.

"Would you believe those little rogues, Geoffrey?" Matthew shrieked as his partner began to drive us away.

"Savages. Pure savages, Matthew," Geoffrey replied. "What say we teach them a lesson?"

One wink and a nod of confirmation from Matthew, and Geoffrey proceeded to drop every single note out of the window, one by one, sending swarms of children racing after the car and brutally fighting over the plunder.

I must admit that Will and I hadn't the foggiest idea what was going on and had started to wonder if our friends were mad, or had simply lost their heads in the moment. Why on earth would they have given these kids (especially such an annoying bunch of them) so much money? Geoffrey and Matthew hadn't even flinched in releasing the notes and they seemed to be enjoying themselves, hysterically laughing as they watched the children fighting over the spoils in the rear view mirror.

And then they explained.

"We like to keep hold of fake money just in case we get robbed along the way," Matthew said, amidst fits of laughter.

"Serves the little beggars right," Geoffrey agreed.

Our Aussie mates dropped us off a few hundred metres down the road – just far enough so that the swarms wouldn't chase after us – and, as we waited for the three lifts that would eventually see us to Göreme by the end of the day, we thought about how long it might be before these poor children were met with the bitter realisation that all that they had fought over that afternoon were worthless pieces of paper.

DAY SIXTY-FOUR:
ÖZDEMIR ISI VIESSMANN, FATIH'S OFFICE, ŞANLIURFA, ŞANLIURFA PROVINCE, TÜRKIYE, FRIDAY 12TH SEPTEMBER 2008, 10.50AM

Pakistan was bombed today. The news came like a nasty shock to the system, as Will and I contemplate the ever-growing likelihood that we might run into trouble over the next month or so in Iran and Pakistan. I suppose that there is even the possibility that we might have to consider avoiding Pakistan completely – such is the threat posed by the recent U.S. air-strikes – but we fear that the implications of such avoidance would threaten the completion of the trip in its entirety.

For the moment, we will just have to hope that the U.S. will abate further strikes until after we have safely navigated our way across Pakistan and into less potentially-volatile territory within India.

Everyone seems to hate America in this part of the world, and we are all too aware that being British isn't much better, nor is it particularly obvious to the eye which particular Western force the two of us represent.

One of the most telling examples of anti-Western protest that we have experienced came during our post-Ramazan feast the night that we left Göreme and joined a group of Muslims on the top of a hill in a place that we now affectionately refer to as "Ramazan's ville."

Six bitty lifts took us away from Göreme that Tuesday afternoon and eventually landed us upon the hilltop on the other side of Kayseri, from where we had an awesome view of the city below.

With the pitifully inadequate sum of 4.50 Turkish liras (less than 2 pounds) to our names, and the lack of any obvious place upon this hill where we might buy some food (even if we had the money), we found ourselves contemplating the stark reality that very little separated us from the plight of homeless men. We had no home, no food, and no money to get either of these things; the only difference was that we were not homeless by necessity, but rather out of our own, somewhat questionable, decision-making. Whilst the homeless man might desperately wish to change his situation but have no means to do so, we could change our situation tomorrow but choose not to. It is our choice to be homeless and, along with it, I suppose it is our choice that has led us to need to beg once in a while.

Luckily for us, this hillside above Kayseri was no ordinary hillside, and options for begging were increased dramatically because of the presence of some fifty or sixty picnic-benches and outdoor barbeques – presumably erected specifically for the daily Ramazan feasts.

With no previous concept that any such place existed, we could not believe our eyes as groups of Muslims came together to celebrate the end of the day's fasting by sharing a meal in this glorious community setting. Now all that we needed to do was to summon up the courage to approach one of these groups and to beg for them to let us share in their feast.

Spotting a group of lads in their twenties, we decided that they represented our best bet and nervously dragged our bags up the hillside a little further to approach these men.

"Merhaba" (which means hello), we said hopefully. "Ramazan?"

Of course, to you and me, a simple "Hello, Christmas?" at the time of our own annual festival would be unlikely to induce much response beyond perhaps an, "Um, yes, indeed… It is Christmas." But to these wonderful gentlemen our intentions could not have been clearer and two places were instantly prepared for us at their table and we were given enough food to last us through to the end of the month!

Our friendly Turkish hosts asked us those same old questions with which we have become extremely familiar (names, ages, occupations, girlfriends), but there was one question that one man, in particular, was desperate to ask.

"American?" he asked accusingly.

"No! England. English," Will answered, slowly and clearly, looking quickly to dispel any conception that they might be dining with the "enemy."

"Good!" said the man abruptly. "I hate America, and George Bush!" The man spoke this name with such ill feeling that it looked as if he was about to explode, and with these words he brandished a knife and plunged it deeply into the table.

So that's what they think of America, then! Perhaps we'll pretend to be Swiss from here on in. The Swiss are peace-loving folk, after all, and we can even speak a little French. Anything to avoid being confused with an American, or one of their closest allies!

The most frustrating thought that crosses my mind is the niggling question of whether or not we are being foolhardy in continuing to hitchhike through political hotspots over the next few months. Our drivers have warned us, again and again, not to trust anyone now that we are in the land of the Kurds. To be honest, drivers have been warning us of much of the same since the day we left England and we've never given them much time, but is the Middle East going to be a step too far?

The funny thing is that every time we get warned about the next town or the next country, all we experience there is another dose of wonderful kindness and hospitality. We have heard similarly positive tales of Kurdish hospitality, but these have also been tempered by a host of recent warnings by the locals: "Be careful"; "Be *very* careful"; "Kurd no trust"; "Kurd bad people," etc, etc.

...After all, it was a Kurdish man that tried to kill us!

* * * * *

Our journey to this most Eastern part of Türkiye has taken a little longer than expected. Upon leaving Ramazan's ville, we made awfully slow progress until mid-afternoon the following day. The problem was twofold. Firstly, we really didn't know the area at all well. Secondly, our map of the country had not accounted for the recent addition of a new and better road between Kayseri and Pinarbaşi – our prospective destination that morn. There were so few cars going down our worn-out old road that we seriously contemplated retracing our steps to Kayseri and starting again. Perhaps we should have done so, but then we would never have made the acquaintance of a wonderfully kind-hearted family in the tiny village of Bişakbinat.

Only about twenty kilometres from Kayseri, Bişakbinat was hardly where we were hoping to find ourselves that lunchtime, four hours and four negligible hitches later, but here we were, tired, frustrated and desperately hungry. We hadn't consumed anything since the post-Ramazan feast the evening before, so when we asked some friendly locals if there was anywhere we could get some food, we were glad that their curiosity (upon meeting two travelling Swiss men) was sufficiently aroused that they themselves prepared a great feast for us. This was no small miracle considering that it was Ramazan and that the further we go east, the more strictly religious are the people we encounter.

As we sat down to enjoy a feast that none of our friends could share, we recalled our old friend Vulcan's sentiments when he had told us that travellers are exempt from the Ramazan rules. Needless to say, we were very grateful. Here we were, eating all this food and drinking all this water, whilst our friends sat and watched, graciously allowing us to feast, despite their own state of voluntary privation.

Food duly devoured, we thanked Ahmed (our host), his father, two brothers, mother, grandmother, and around half the rest of the village who had gathered to see these strange beings, and resumed our course towards Pinarbaşi.

From here on in, the journeying was much improved. We received a kind lift from a Pinarbaşi-bound minibus (completely free of charge), and the rest of the day was plain sailing (albeit incredibly slow sailing) in the cabin of a Turkish truck with a man whose name was just a little bit too Turkish to comprehend, and whose manner was a little too stern for us to want to ask him to repeat himself.

Despite his standoffish approach, we had a good laugh with this macho man from somewhere in the northern echelons of Türkiye. One of the things that we have enjoyed the most about the men of Turkey is their sheer volume and directness. Our trucker friend was a prime example. Seldom did a moment go by when he wasn't making the loudest of noises by smacking his hands together or simply bellowing out a sentence at a volume that could easily be confused with shouting.

Well, if you can't beat 'em, join 'em, we thought. And so it was that for the next three hours we continually slapped our hands together, showed off our puny biceps, and attempted to talk in louder, deeper tones – just by means of fitting in/ playing along with our new friend's amusing manner.

Sadly, it appeared that somewhere along the line we managed to offend him because he kicked us out some fifty kilometres short of his destination, Kahraman Maraş, and we were left to fend for ourselves again.

Taking one look at the clock, we realised that only twenty minutes remained before the end of the day's fasting and decided to wait along with everybody else until the familiar sound of a warbling voice would call us to feast. To be quite honest, it seems as if we choose to do this Ramazan thing only when it suits us. We will respectfully refrain from food when in the presence of other fasters, but as soon as we are in the clear we will secretly scoff as much food and water as we physically can, only to cause great surprise in the presence of our next driver by the frequency with which we need to relieve ourselves.

Fast finished, our first kebab in a few days was a surprisingly welcome sight, but not nearly as welcome as the offer that we received from the chaps on an adjacent table, who whizzed us the remaining fifty kilometres to Maraş in a swish sports car.

One of them, a self-acclaimed "big shot," spoke pretty good English, and we had hoped that this might lead on to better things – such as, perhaps, a complementary penthouse suite for the evening, but it wasn't to be.

Instead, we were dropped off right in the centre of Maraş and told to look for a tent-pitching spot inside the local park or mosque – both of which were swarming with people, and were, thus, terrible suggestions.

Gloomily, we trudged across the road into the courtyard of the mosque, where a group of giggling children and three startled gentlemen surrounded us; I suppose that it isn't every day that two pale-faced, backpack-wielding

Brits stroll into a mosque.

Two of the trio were off-duty policemen and we suggested that they might like to arrest us that we might spend a free night in a cell, but even after we had offered to commit a felony (such as punching them or stealing from the mosque) their refusal was unwavering.

"Well, you must know *somewhere* that we can sleep, then?" Will insisted, after briefly outlining the details of our hitchhiking trip, and our hopes to continue on towards Şanli Urfa the following morn.

The men conferred for a moment, before one of them beamed back at us and told us that he knew the "perfect spot"...

Ten minutes later and we wound up at the bus shelter. Oh, the frustration! It seems that everywhere we go, no matter how many times we attempt forcefully to reiterate that we are trying to travel by "hitchhiking" – "you know, Auto-stopping, with *no* money!" – our best efforts fall upon deaf ears and we are met by blank faces and the same old question... "Bus?"

Well, I suppose that our chosen method of transport isn't the most ordinary, and we shouldn't be too hard on people who probably don't have the foggiest idea what it is that we are trying to do, or why on earth we might want to do it.

That night we ended up in a taxi rank outside the bus station, where we made friends with some taxi-drivers who kindly allowed us to sleep in their little shack. It wasn't the most comfortable of sleeps, but the benches that we found there were at least relatively safe in what seemed like a rather rough part of town. It's just a shame that the taxi-drivers who had agreed for us to stay weren't the same ones who angrily confronted us at 6am the following morning, and hurried us on our way.

Blearily, we made our way out onto the road again. Next stop Şanli Urfa, "*inşallah*"... They say that a lot here.

DAY SIXTY-FOUR: (CONTINUED...)
ÖZDEMIR ISI VIESSMANN, FATIH'S OFFICE (AGAIN), ŞANLIURFA, ŞANLIURFA PROVINCE, TÜRKIYE, FRIDAY 12TH SEPTEMBER 2008, 18.05

Before I can tell of the rather frustrating day that we have had here (which has been almost entirely spent sitting in this office), I must first introduce the man responsible: our new friend, Fatih, whom we met yesterday on the road to Şanli Urfa.

Starting off at 6am certainly seems to have its benefits and we must learn from this lesson in the future. Barely had we waited for two minutes when the first Fatih of the day pulled over and took us along to the service station down the road (where he worked), kindly bought us some breakfast – including a tub of the apparently "world famous" Kahraman Maraş ice cream (never heard of it, and was a bit of a strange way to start the day) – and wished us a safe journey to Urfa, "inşallah" (it means God-willing).

I reckon old Allah might just have been listening because it wasn't too long before a chap called Serdan had taken us to the other side of Gazi Antep, departing from us with a stern warning regarding truckers and how they weren't to be trusted, before (sure enough) we caught the very next truck going our way, driven by a friendly Kurdish man named Ibrahim.

Just thirty kilometres from Urfa by this stage, we barely had to wait a minute before the next ride came along – this time in the form of a minibus, the attendant of which wrongly adjudged our hitching thumbs to be a request for a lift in his money-driven wagon.

Apologising for the inconvenience, Will and I did our best to wave the bus along, only to be told that money really wasn't an issue. For the second time in two days, here we were on a minibus in Eastern Turkey (a notoriously shifty part of the world), practically forced to accept a free ride!

Ushered to the back of the bus, we were contemplating the growing generosity of these eastern Turks when the smiling face of Fatih popped up from the seat in front of us, introduced itself to be Fatih's face, and proceeded almost immediately to offer us a place to stay the night.

Good old Allah, we thought, employing our new favourite Turkish phrase and gesture combo, which goes something like this:

"Alllll...ah!" one exclaims (as if He might listen a bit more intently if you elongate His name), whilst shaking head and hands as if entranced and raising eyes heavenwards just in case He should appear.

DAY SIXTY-FIVE:
TURISTIK ET LOKANTASI, MARDIN, MARDIN PROVINCE, TÜRKIYE, KURDISTAN, SATURDAY 13TH SEPTEMBER 2008, 18.17

Our time with the somewhat lecherous Fatih was a topsy-turvy kind of experience by all accounts.

Exploring the bustling city centre and the pools of Ibrahim (prophet Abraham, that is; not the Kurdish trucker) were highlights, but it was hard to keep Fatih happy for very long because language barriers ensured that we could not communicate with him in any great length or depth, and our most overriding impression of our time with the man will always be his absolute obsession with members of the opposite sex.

Not unlike our Iranian friend of old, Farhud, this lecherous chap would seldom go a minute without uttering one of his two favourite phrases towards a passing female. Number one was "çok sex" (which means "lots of sex"); number two was "çok güzel" (which means "very beautiful").

The rest of our time was spent in Fatih's office, relying upon the online translator that he had downloaded in order to communicate anything beyond his love for women. It was just a shame that the words that he chose to translate all revolved around his dream of finding a new "home" in England, receiving "citizenship" there, and wanting our "help" for this task. Therein lay the real reason why he had wanted to spend time with us in the first place.

Essentially, Fatih wanted our help to get to England, but quite what he expected us to do about it, I have no idea. Minor details didn't really seem to matter to him, such as, oh I don't know, the fact that he hasn't even got the faintest grasp of our language, or the fact that Will and I might not have the required authority, even if we were willing, to tell our government that our "good friend" should be allowed to migrate to England so that he can find an English woman to marry, and thereby achieve citizenship.

I don't want to sound too negative in my appraisal of our hospitable friend, who fed and sheltered us for two nights, but it was difficult not to be vexed by the man, who blatantly told us (through the online translator) that he desires only two things from our country: "çok sex" with a beautiful English girl and making lots of money from our economy!

When we weren't talking sex and citizenship, we were being chaperoned around the city by our sweetly, and oh so frustratingly, overprotective friend, who would shepherd us through the streets like baby lambs, holding on to our hands or waists by means of showing affection. [This did seem like a strangely tactile way for a man to show another man affection, but we assume that it is the norm in these parts.]

Our best moments together came during regular çay breaks at his beautiful apartment on the outskirts of the city. Fatih was obviously doing rather well for himself already. At only 22 years of age (although our slimy friend looked at least thirty), he claimed to earn some 60,000 euros per annum, but we expect his arithmetic to be a little suspect because this would be quite a sum for a man whose work as an air-conditioning technician (from what we can understand) seemed sporadic at best during our time together. We spent many a wasted hour in his office in town, but Fatih was never at work. All the while he would be slouched, cigarette in hand, making plans to come to England, whilst he repeated the bit about us needing to "help" him.

I apologise for my continued bad report of this hospitable gentleman, but I suppose that I never forgave him for what happened at the office yesterday afternoon.

If one were to offer Fatih the benefit of the doubt, one could suppose that he had the best intentions (after all, what is it that all young men spend their time thinking about the most?), but Will and I were horrified as Fatih proceeded to treat us to a taster of his (presumably) extensive porn collection, complete with sound effects, for ten whole minutes of nauseating "entertainment."

I was the lucky one. My head was already facing the opposite direction as I sat on a chair the other side of the screen, hounded by the noises of... Well you can guess the sort.

Will, on the other hand, was not to be so fortunate. His eyes were locked upon the screen as Fatih set about showing him items from his favourite collection, not wishing to turn away for fear of offending our sensitive friend.

It wasn't until a gruelling ten minutes later that we finally managed to explain that this sort of entertainment wasn't for us, as I, rather insensitively, suggested that he should "go and wash himself in the pools of Ibrahim again!" This was a cruel reference to our earlier activity – a tiresome ritual of thorough cleansing before we would be deemed worthy enough to enter the cave where Abraham was allegedly born. We hadn't been impressed, particularly because we were the only non-Muslim tourists to be performing this ritual, which seemed to involve washing every available orifice or crevice about ten times over.

OK, perhaps I am being a little disrespectful, but it has always vexed me how people sometimes feel as if they have to behave in a certain way or match up to a certain standard if they are to be allowed into a holy place. I'm more of a follower of the late (and, I believe, highly religious) Kurt Cobain, who famously sang, "*Come as you are*" – even if it wasn't particularly related at the time.

Fatih was understandably hurt by my rather aloof suggestion. I had taken something that mattered to him very much and accused him of failing to match up to his own standards. Yet, as much as I feel a certain sense of shame for the way in which I went about reprimanding our friend, I'm not sorry that I did so because what followed was a very interesting conversation, in which Fatih apologised, before professing a "frank adulation" of first Allah, then Jesus, Mohammed, Abraham, and all the rest... Oh the beauty of online translators!

DAY SIXTY-SEVEN:
ÇAY BAR, SEHIR, VAN, 50KM FROM IRAN, VAN PROVINCE, TÜRKIYE, KURDISTAN, MONDAY 15TH SEPTEMBER 2008, 11.19AM

I don't know what all the fuss is about really. We've been informed that we're now in the "heart of Kurdistan" (something that would ring all sorts of alarm bells back on the home front), but the only aggravation that we have experienced thus far has come from the noticeable increase in tiny kleptomaniacs.

Let me clarify that statement. It seems that the further east we go, the more of a head-turner we become, and thus the more people gawp at us with that "are they aliens?" look upon their faces. On the whole, this alien quality appears to be no bad thing (we reckon that it may well be contributing to the ease with which we're able to flag down cars these days), but the one slightly frustrating result is the tendency for swarms of little children to follow us around in the hope that we might actually be made out of money. I blame the parents (it's a sad world in which the first words that the kids are taught are "money" and "please"), but I suppose that a mixture of childish curiosity and greed – neither of which should be condemned too strongly at so tender an age – might also be a factor.

As for the older generation of Kurds, I really can't see why everyone holds them in such low esteem. Other than that terribly murderous Kurd back in Kaş, we have had no trouble with these gentle folk whatsoever, and in fact, we haven't received anything but generosity from the rest of them. Where else in the world, for instance, do bus drivers pull over and insist that you travel with them… for free?

It feels like cheating to us, but there seems to be little else that we can do. We stand there with thumbs outstretched; they pull over; we say "no money," and yet you might have to physically restrain them (a very dangerous business when dealing with Kurds, so I'm led to believe) to stop them from pulling us inside their bus.

Take yesterday morning, for example. We had made our way out of the beautiful city of Mardin – a sandy city perched spectacularly upon a hilltop, from where the plains of Mesopotamia stretch out as far as the eye can see – and were just about to start our hitching efforts towards Diyarbakir when a couple of young men approached us to ask, presumably, if they could be of help.

Inevitably, they took us to a bus stop, but when we tried the "thanks, but no thanks" tactics, they simply would not take "no" for an answer.

"No money, no money," we repeated – not strictly true of course, but *you* try explaining our ambitions to people in Kurdish. "Para yok" ("money nada") is about as far as we've got, and it will have to suffice, even if it does mean that we will occasionally have to endure the kindness of Kurdish minibus drivers like the one that took us to Diyarbakir yesterday.

And if our chauffeurs weren't bemused enough already by just what two aliens impersonating Swiss men were doing running around their country without any "para," we dealt their sensibilities an even heftier blow about an hour later when, just a few kilometres short of Diyarbakir, we asked to be dropped off in what, to them, must have seemed like the middle of nowhere.

Having spent the bulk of the journey scrutinising our map of the region, attempting to work out the best way towards Iran, we had decided that our primary target should be Van (or "*Wan*" to the Kurds – they can't do "v" sounds) and, thus, as soon as we spotted our first sign for the city, there were two shrieks of "Teşekkür ederim" (or "Gelek spas" as they say here in Kurdistan), and off we hopped.

We didn't make it all the way to Wan last night, but ended up in a petrol station about ten kilometres short in the town of Givaş, thanks to a couple of quick car lifts and one more substantial ride by a Kurdish trucker named Mehmed (which is apparently just a shortening of that ubiquitous name, Mohammed).

Mehmed himself was actually on his way to Hakkari (another potential entry-route for Iran) but, and I am ashamed to admit this, we had decided back in Mardin not to go that way for fear that we would be skirting right alongside the Iraqi border and, as much as Will wanted to pop in for a cheeky peek, I had vetoed the move on account of the gunfire.

This morning we hitched a ride on the back of a pick-up truck headed for the "sehir" (centre) of Van, which is where you join us as we contemplate the mere/record-breaking stone's throw that separates us from our next country. With any luck we'll be in Iran by the end of the day... "Inṣallah," and all that.

7. THE HAGHIGHI STORY (PART ONE)

DAY SIXTY-NINE:
MASHAD HOTEL, TABRIZ, EAST AZERBAIJAN PROVINCE, IRAN, WEDNESDAY 17TH SEPTEMBER 2008, 10.05AM

It's only the start of our second full day in Iran and we're already in a bit of a pickle. Before I can explain this not completely unexpected Iranian strife, however, there are some loose Turkish ends that need tying up...

What had seemed like an easy 50km hitch from Van to the Iranian border on Monday turned out to be an absolute nightmare of a journey because of our simple failure to appreciate that one or other of the Iranian border-crossings might not be open.

So confident were we in the ease with which we would make the remaining 50km that, having arrived in Van early in the morning, we had even hitched all the way out of town again to go for a swim in Van Lake – the rather sizeable water feature that we had skirted for much of the previous day's journeying.

Hitching out of town the very same way that we had entered it (on the back of a grimy pick-up truck), we sauntered over to the beach, briefly remarked that the area wasn't quite as clean as we had hoped, and, excusing this fault on grounds of this not being England, prepared ourselves for a cooling dip in the lake.

All smiles and sunshine, it was my turn first. Will was put on bag-watch, whilst I bounded merrily over to the water's edge and took three large strides into the water, before readying myself for a dive.

Just before fully committing myself, however, I noticed something a little peculiar floating not far from my right elbow and, upon further inspection, became concerned that, although its appearance was not dissimilar to mud, its substance might be something a little more sinister.

The water had looked a little scummy from a distance, but I had simply assumed that this would clear up a few metres off shore. Now in the midst of the scum, however, there was no denying that this really was not England, and the floating object was not one solitary piece of floating mud, but one of several thousand pieces of floating faeces – of who knows what kind of animal!

"Ahhhhh!!!" I screamed in truly feminine fashion, emerging from the water a little slower than I had entered it that I might avoid any more splatters of excrement over a torso that had been in need of a good wash *before* this experience.

Perhaps this particularly poo-infested region was an anomaly, we thought, and headed further along the shore to what we hoped might be a perfectly faeces-free section of lake. Alas, no, and it wasn't until I was waist-deep in excrement for the second time in ten minutes that I fully appreciated the extent of the crisis.

Abandoning all attempts to swim in "Excrement Lake" (as we have since entitled it), there was still time for us to mistake the swamp that separated us from the road as just an average marshland, when it was, in fact, the outskirts of the excrement; still time for us to plough on, unfazed, and emerge the other side, contemplating the fact that we must now hitch 50km covered in excrement; and still time for us to be told that our expected 50km, walk-in-the-park hitch, was going to be more like three times that distance because the Van border had decided to shut itself.

At least the unexpected extension quickened us into action and, for the third time in succession, we decided against the pursuit of a Hakkari/Iraqi direction and headed for the more remote border crossing in the north, besides the town of Doğubeyazıt.

Back on the road, our first hitch away from Van wasn't helped by that all-too-familiar sight of a surrounding hoard of children, who again seemed to know only how to say the word "money" and would shout this at us relentlessly, whilst prodding at us and probing our bags with their grubby paws.

Two drivers pulled over during our impromptu hour of babysitting, but both quickly decided against picking us up, for fear that they themselves might fall foul of the children's schemes.

So difficult was it to refrain from striking out at these pernicious pests (who were costing us valuable hitching time) that we soon gave up and hopped on the next passing bus, hopping off again a few hundred metres down the road where we could hitch without such childminding constraints. Three friendly Kurdish truckers (and a whole host of unexpected police barricades) later and we had reached the Iranian border in time to perform an off-the-cuff concert for the Kurdish border officials, before marching into a new country as the last of the day's light faded.

DAY SIXTY-NINE: (CONTINUED...)
MASHAD HOTEL, TABRIZ, EAST AZERBAIJAN PROVINCE, IRAN, WEDNESDAY 17TH SEPTEMBER 2008, 19.22

The Iranian border crossing was our worst so far. No sooner had we stepped into Iranian territory than we had been surrounded by a string of bus and taxi drivers shouting at us what I can only assume to be the Farsi equivalent of "pick me, pick me."

I suppose that we should have felt some sympathy towards these poor gents because they really must have thought it was their lucky day when they saw two fresh-faced Brits coming their way, but we were tired, still embittered by our episode at Excrement Lake, and in no mood whatsoever for their mercenary advances.

"No money! *No* money!" we replied, but these words invariably take longer than most to sink in.

"Surely they can't actually mean *no* money, can they?" the men seem to question among themselves.

Then, after the briefest pause, they begin again.

"You want go bus station?" the men enquire as we pull out the remaining hair from our heads.

"You know you catch bus or taxi at very cheap price," they continue. "You want know how much?"

Our first night in Iran was not the best. Following on from these painful exchanges, we struggled to get to grips with the exchange rates as we spent our remaining Turkish lira on the night's food and accommodation, and were then woken up at 6am to be told by our hotel manager that the bus to Tabriz (the nearest big city) was about to leave and we really must hurry if we were to catch it.

It's very difficult not to get frustrated by the number of times that we have to explain and re-explain our trip to a sea of blank faces, so most of the time we just don't bother. That morning, when we did eventually get up, we simply marched straight past the new crowd of drivers pleading with us to frequent their particular taxis or buses, before finally stumbling upon a driver who actually seemed to understand the whole "no money" thing.

Glad to be shot of a grimy border town that had rather clouded our first impressions of the country, we were just beginning to think about relaxing and allowing this new culture to charm us when the previously-held-to-be clued-up-driver (I think his name was Abdullah) started talking about money.

Panicked by the inference, we repeated that we had "*no* money," and were promptly thrown out of the vehicle by an angry Abdullah, as if we had been trying to cheat the man!

For a moment or two, we stood by the side of the road and contemplated this worrying start to hitchhiking in Iran. Was it always going to be like this? What if they simply didn't understand what we're doing? It seemed as if almost every other vehicle in Iran was a taxi, so how were we going to manage to get a free ride from anyone?

Nerves were calmed slightly by the two consecutive lifts we received to transport us to the start of the main road to Tabriz, although quite what the drivers knew of our aims and intentions I do not know. The language barrier has become a thing of great concern once again, now that we have moved into a new country, where we do not have even the faintest grasp of the native tongue.

As we waited for the next ride to come along, I thought back to my preconceptions of Iran. Don't ask me why, but I had always assumed that Iran would prove to be a desolate place with a scattering of nomadic shepherds and not a lot else. It had been Iran that we and our families had been most concerned about, but now that we were here, there were a lot more people than I had expected and none of them was wearing a headscarf or carrying an AK47. In fact, it was Will and I who probably seemed the most threatening; *we* were the strange foreigners donning Turkish headscarves by way of protecting ourselves from the scorching heat.

The road upon which we stood was dusty and the air surrounding us warm and wet, so we were glad to be taken into the comparative cleanliness of the next car, even if the driver seemed to be a bit of a maniac.

At first this boy racer had been driving so fast that he had barely noticed us before he had whizzed past, slammed on his brakes, waited until the car eventually screeched to a halt (about 100 metres down the road), jammed the car into reverse, and pulled up alongside us, hastily beckoning us to get in.

Ladies and gentleman, let me introduce you to Iran's best answer to Lewis Hamilton – a young chap whose name, rather fittingly, sounded very much like *Nascar* (the American racing association).

"Tabriz?" we had ventured to ask as we stepped into the car, but this was virtually the last time that Will or I would utter anything other than the occasional gasp of terror as, for the best part of an hour, we averaged well in excess of 150km/hr, reaching a terrifying 200km/hr at one stage, as our reckless friend rammed his foot to the floor.

Nascar would see a gap and take it; no matter how small the gap and how unlikely the chances of fitting through it (especially at such high speeds), Nascar would chance his arm – an action that itself resulted in the chancing of a whole lot more than that.

If it were thrill-seeking that we were looking for, Nascar was our man, but to be honest, that wasn't our priority. Survival was top of the list, and anything beyond that was a bonus, so when Nascar eventually found his brake pedal again, slammed it to the floor and slid onto the side of the road to wave us goodbye, parting with a big grin as if to say "Welcome to Iran," we praised mighty Allah that we were still in the land of the living.

Shell-shocked, we staggered drunkenly over to the other side of the road and ordered a meal of "any food" (giving our host the appropriate bread-in-mouth hand gesture) that they might be able to find for us during this Ramazan fast. We uttered scarcely a word during the entire scoffing of our first Iranian ("chelo") kebab, spending most of the meal taking deep breaths just to enjoy the fact that we still could.

Our final hitch to Tabriz was a much more sedate affair, spent safely enclosed in the cabin of our first Iranian lorry. We arrived here late yesterday afternoon and have since begun truly getting to grips with this fascinating country.

Perhaps what interests me most so far is that it is still very possible to hitchhike here. As per usual, we encountered the same old doubters at the border (most of whom were taxi drivers, and were thus a little biased) and a few more along the way – those who would cry out, "You'll never hitch here" or the like, but nothing could be further from the truth.

It really isn't very different hitchhiking here from how hitchhiking anywhere else in the world has been. The one striking difference from hitching in Europe, in fact, is probably just how ridiculously easy it is here, now that we have grown into our status as undisputed aliens in this, our newest domain. So far we have been treated more like celebrities than vicious crusaders and I am thoroughly looking forward to the excitement that awaits us throughout the rest of our time here. We loved Turkey and found that our stereotypes of the place were completely flipped upside down, and from what I've heard of Iran – from everyone other than the Media, that is – we are in store for a similar feast of hospitality here.

* * * * *

It is high time that I described to you just what it is that has gone so drastically wrong now that we have entered Iran. It's simple really: we have completely run out of money. Now, I don't mean "no money" in the same sense as I have been using the term towards Turkish and Iranian taxi drivers; I mean this in the factual: "we have NO money" sort of way, unless twenty pounds in British Sterling means anything in these parts. To top it all off, we don't have any way of getting any, either.

This is one of those times when the questionable amount of planning that preceded this trip really becomes apparent, i.e. we really should have checked whether or not we would be able to use our Visa cards in every country, rather than just relying upon the information given to us by all those adverts back home that tell us that it is a "Worldwide" resource. Rubbish! You can't use them in Iran, and we could have done with knowing that. Maybe then we would have taken a little bit more hard cash along with us, rather than a measly twenty quid and about 700 Indian rupees (about the equivalent of ten pounds) that Will had left over from his last visit to India.

The terrible realisation that we are, in fact, now impoverished, came not long after we had arrived in Tabriz. Having eventually located a cash point, we scoured the machine for sign of that familiar Visa mark and, finding none, casually made our way inside the bank to enquire.

"Visa anyone?" we asked, assuming that they would simply point us down the road a few hundred metres to the next, slightly bigger, and definitely better, bank.

"No Visa; this is Iran," the bank clerk replied with the same sort of nonchalance with which we had posed the question, and as if the fact that this was Iran should obviously dictate that Visas were out.

"Right, that could be problematic," we said to each other as we left the bank, having changed all the notes that we possessed into Iranian Rials, and started pondering the likelihood that we will have to get through a fairly substantially sized country (this is the former Persian Empire, don't you know!) with the lump sum of about 600,000 Rials. Whilst the five noughts might sound like quite a lot to you, let me assure you that the equivalent of about thirty British pounds is unlikely to get us very far in the three or four weeks that it will surely take us to cross Iran, before we can (hopefully) find a cash point in Pakistan...

Day Seventy:
Mashad Hotel, Tabriz, East Azerbaijan Province, Iran, Thursday 18th September 2008, 19.30

Standing out like a lemon, whilst fidgeting nervously with the map he is doing his best to decipher through thick-lens glasses, we meet Woo during our very first moments in Tabriz.

"Ooohhh hellooo," this little Korean chap says nervously, as he looks up to the welcome realisation that he isn't the only lemon in town.

"Yooou knooow wayyy tooo centreee?" he asks shyly with a voice that sounds ever more like the twit-twoo-ing of an owl than any human voice we've ever heard, lingering on every syllable and ending each word with a higher tone than it started.

Quite what Woo understands of our response I do not know but, when asked if he would like to join us in our own attempts to find the centre, he cogitates for a moment, smiles sweetly, and follows.

Our shy friend comes into his own a little more on the long hike into the centre (it proves to be further than we had thought) and speaks with an air almost of authority as he tells us that he has just finished his compulsory two-year term in the army, after which he has come travelling in order to find himself, or, as he puts it, "to find what I want doooo."

Woo really doesn't seem cut out for the army; his thin frame, thick glasses and diminutive 5ft 5inches seem unlikely to instil fear into too many opponents. To be honest, it doesn't really seem as if he's cut out for travelling either (especially travelling all alone around the Middle East), so it is with a certain parental instinct that Will and I take him under our wings for the next few days – "until he finds his feet," we say to each other.

Woo's big plan is to make it all the way from Istanbul (where he started) back to his home in Seoul, South Korea, overland.

"That sounds like an awesome idea, Woo," we tell him, and it honestly does, but we are more concerned whether or not this weak-limbed chap – who puffs away on his inhaler with unnerving regularity – actually has it in him.

Woo is still with us as we check into a room for three at the cheapest guesthouse that we can find; he is still there during our mildly frustrating (and ultimately unfruitful) search for money; and he is still by our side as we scour the streets that night for just one restaurant that might be open during this period of Ramazan, which is obviously taken a little more seriously here than it was back in Turkey.

We have all but given up hope by the time we meet Iman, who finds us midway through an attempt to vault a barrier in the middle of the road.

"Hey guys, what are you doing? Can I help you?" this smiley young Iranian man asks with concern, a strangely American twang to his accent.

"Yes, please!" the hungry William replies eagerly. "We're looking for a place to get some food, but everywhere's shut."

"Come with me. There's a kebab place just down the road," Iman replies, hopping over the barrier to join us on the other side.

"Kebabs! If I eat one more kebab, I might just…"

Before I can finish bemoaning the fact that I might turn into a kebab, Will jabs me in the ribs and gives me one of those "Come on mate, this guy's trying to help us" looks, and we are soon inside a restaurant, eating you know what, and getting to know the latest addition to our group.

Iman, 25, actually hails from the capital, Tehran, but currently lives in Tabriz, where he works for a friend of his father's in the hope that he will eventually prove that he's got what it takes to hold down a full time job. Apparently he's been in and out of work since the day he left school. He soon informs us that he is extremely unhappy with his life in Tabriz and longs to return home to be with his friends and family, but his father will not permit him to return until he has proven himself.

"What about you guys?" Iman asks. "Why are you in Iran. I have never seen tourists as young as you in my country before" – a fact that probably explains why we're given such celebrity-status here.

"Well, have you heard of hitchhiking?" Will asks, not holding out for much more than the standard negative response.

"Heach-hiking?" Iman stutters, perplexed for a moment, before lifting his thumb into the air. "Like this?" he says, waving it around.

"Yeah, that's the stuff!" I blurt out, glad simply to have found one Iranian who understands. What's more, Iman actually seems genuinely excited and impressed by our venture – a reaction that we have been longing for (and missing) for quite some time.

"Have you heard of couch-surfing?" Iman interjects.

"Er… yeah, I think we're members," I reply, remembering how a friend of ours back in Ljubljana had urged us to join this website, by which you can search for free "couches" (beds) upon which to "surf" (sleep) wherever you go. I suppose that the basic premise isn't too dissimilar from hitchhiking, in the sense that you are asking for help from people who don't need to go particularly out of their way to give it, except by offering you something that is already available.

It transpires that our excitable Iranian friend is absolutely crazy about the scheme and tells us that he is the moderator of the Tehran couch-surfing group.

"Tehran has a couch-surfing group?" we ask, surprised that this thing has taken off around the world, even and especially in Iran!

"Yeah, and I'm the moderator!" Iman proudly repeats, and it isn't long before we have told Iman all about our money crisis, and he has proceeded to invite us to stay with him and his family in Tehran for as long as it may take to devise a plan.

What an unbelievably generous offer from a man we'd only just met, but this was precisely the introduction we received to that famous Persian hospitality we'd heard so much about. Now we're just waiting for Iman to tell his boss that he's leaving, and we can begin an epic, four-man, 600km hitch to the capital.

DAY SEVENTY: (CONTINUED...)
MASHAD HOTEL, TABRIZ, EAST AZERBAIJAN PROVINCE, IRAN, THURSDAY 18TH SEPTEMBER 2008, 10.35PM

My heart is still pounding as I reel at the thought of what has just happened. Woo, Will and I just popped out for a spot of dinner at a local restaurant, when we were caught up in a full-blown argument about the price.

After struggling through arguably the worst kebab of the trip so far – certainly the worst we have had in Iran – then to be charged four times the price of the previous night's kebab was a bit rich. 75,000 Rials is a reasonable price for three people to eat out in Tabriz, so our first reaction to a scrap of paper that seemed to read "300,000" was that it must surely be a mistake, and they really must mean 30,000. After all, the currency here is pretty confusing. There seems to be this distinction between *Tumans* and *Rials*, whereby you just take one nought off a Rial and it suddenly becomes a Tuman.

Fair enough, we had thought, slightly miscalculating the figures, but still not really sure of how it worked. It seemed pretty cheap, but 30,000 Rials it was. Surely that must be what they had meant.

Preparing to leave our modest 30,000 Rials behind in the hope that a crisis had been averted, we weren't all that surprised when they scoffed and demanded ten times the price, but, given that we were spending 300,000 Rials for the privilege of staying in a hotel for three whole nights, there was

First stop, the Scarths' in Moussac

A picnic in the Alps with Christian Richelme

The tree house in Bled

Alex et Guillaume, Plitvička Jezera

Farhud smoking a narghilè, Istanbul

Unusual campsite dwelling, Izmir

Inside the Efes Amphitheatre

An amusing sign outside Efes

Türk kahvesi, Selçuk

Selami's garden, Selçuk

Selami and me

Woo's first taste of hitchhiking, Tabriz

Hitching party, Tabriz

Bazaar, Shiraz

no way that we were going to fork out the same amount for one, pretty shoddy, meal.

Our first tactic was simple defiance. We refused to pay, and attempted to explain (through a mixture of hand gestures and a calculator) that we would normally pay four times less. I hate being treated like a tourist, especially when this translates into being cheated because they assume either that you are walking money-trees, or merely naïve. We were really riled up by the entire episode, and offered them the 30,000 again, and, when that was rejected, finished by suggesting that we would pay them no more than 75,000 (the normal price).

Perhaps they were simply fed up, but when they slashed the price to 100,000 (a third of their original estimate), almost without hesitation, we knew deep down that *they* knew that *we* knew that they had been found out. The business was probably going through a rough patch on account of Ramazan and now they were trying to balance the books by cheating some rich tourists. Not on our watch; not now that we were virtually broke.

100,000 Rials was probably about a fair price, but this was no longer about the money; it was a matter of principle. Will went back to the hotel to try and find Iman to translate, whilst Woo and I stayed behind, giving the two men in charge our hardest stares.

Fifteen minutes later Will returned, but there was no cavalry. Iman was still bogged down with work. This time it was my turn to leave Will and Woo behind, returning with the first person that could speak a word of English, a teenage boy named Ali, whom I almost dragged up the stairs.

"We are very angry." I spoke slowly and clearly, giving Ali time to translate. "This is not fair. We do not have much money and you try to cheat us."

"They say they do not cheat," Ali translated in return. "You pay them 100,000 Rials and it ok."

"They *do* cheat," I replied. "We *would* pay the 100,000 Rials if they had asked for that amount from the start, but now, because of the *principle*, we will not pay more than 75,000 Rials." I nodded to the boy to translate, and, hesitantly, he did.

"We are your *friends*," I continued, veins popping out of my neck in frustration by now. "You don't treat *friends* like this." Again I nodded to Ali and, with a whimper, the poor boy translated.

Eventually the men grudgingly accepted our 75,000 Rials and off we went, thanking Ali profusely for his help. Dear Ali was almost in tears as he left, his Tabriz-ian street-cred now surely in tatters. We felt utterly wretched as we walked back to the hotel, in which we now sit, contemplating events.

The worst thing about it is that we feel so dirty – not the way one wants to feel after standing one's ground and winning the battle, on a small scale, between good and evil. That's how it feels, anyway, as we wait for Iman to come home. Tomorrow morning, with any luck, we'll finally be out of this place...

Tehran here we come.

DAY SEVENTY-ONE:
MASHAD HOTEL, TABRIZ, EAST AZERBAIJAN PROVINCE, IRAN, FRIDAY 19TH SEPTEMBER 2008, 12.33PM

Iman promised that he would be back from work no later than midday, but it is already thirty minutes beyond that estimate, and still we wait for our enigmatic friend to show up. The small matter of 600km stands in our way this afternoon, and Will and I would have been pessimistic about making that distance had we started way back at 9am!

The fact, then, that we are already three and a half hours late, and have an extra two bodies to consider, and that these extra bodies are utter hitchhiking novices, means that our chances grow slimmer the longer Iman's absence endures.

The clock is ticking and we are not amused. We've already been in this pretty drab city for three nights (about three nights longer than we would have liked) and we are eager to leave as soon as possible. To make matters worse, once again we find ourselves waiting without any means of contacting the man whom we await and, as confident as we have always been in the sincerity of Iman's offer, there is always something psychologically vexing about the waiting... Come on Iman, don't let us down now!

Whilst we wait, I have a startling observation to which I would like to draw your attention: this is the simple fact that the women here all wear headscarves, most of them dress completely in black, and none of them wear anything that would reveal the slightest glimpse of skin or hint of shapeliness.

It's fascinating, if a little troubling. Iman tells us that the dress code isn't so exteme in Tehran – apparently Tabriz is just a "very religious city" – but I suppose that we'll just have to wait and see what rules we encounter when we finally make it to Tehran...

Talking of which, where the heck is Iman?

DAY SEVENTY-THREE:
IMAN'S PAD, KARAJ, TEHRAN PROVINCE, IRAN, SUNDAY 21ST SEPTEMBER 2008, 9.30AM

I don't know how exactly, but we made it to Karaj (the sister city of Tehran – where Iman actually lives) in just one day's hitching on Friday, even though we didn't get started until 3pm, when two quick lifts (both of which saw all four of us, and bags, hilariously crammed onto the back seats of tiny cars) would see us safely to the hard shoulder of the motorway on the edge of town.

Standing there as streams of traffic whizzed by at breakneck speed (with our necks the most vulnerable), we honed in upon a stationary truck, which was pulled over a few hundred metres further down the road.

With Iman in place as translator, over we went to inquire as to the driver's destination, only to be informed that currently there was none because the truck had a punctured tyre, but if we could find him a jack then he would happily take all four of us to a place called Qazvin, which, Iman informed us, was only about 75km from his house!

Spurred on by the challenge (and the thought that all four of us might actually be able to hitch together), we started madly flagging down trucks until we found a driver kind enough to stop, lend us his jack, and wait for fifteen minutes whilst the changeover took place – this isn't Formula 1, you know.

Changeover complete, driver Mohammed seemed shocked that we had actually gone through with his stipulations, but was as good as his word. All four of us were promptly invited into the relatively spacious cabin of his vehicle, where we sat and considered how much more relaxed Asian legislations regarding number of passengers-per-vehicle were than they had been back in Europe. As far as I can gather, Health and Safety considerations go largely out of the window in Asia.

Taking it in turns to ride in the passenger seat whilst the rest perched upon the bed behind, it was by no means first-class travel, but there was room enough to avoid the development of chronic back strain as a result of our seven-hour ride with Mohammed.

The journey itself was unbearably slow. Only about half an hour into the ride, Mohammed had informed Iman that, although Qazvin was his target, he didn't expect to make it the whole way there that day. He would take us as far as he could, but then we would have to make the rest of the journey by another means.

Averaging no more than about 70km/hr on the flat, and struggling to reach 40km/hr on the uphill sections (which were frequent), this was one of the slowest vehicles that we have been in, but even so, after seven hours of non-stop driving, one would have hoped to have made it more than half-way!

It was 10pm by the time Mohammed left us at a toll station just outside Zanjan (there appears to be one on the edge of each city), and we simply could not believe that we had to do the same all over again if we were to reach Tehran that day.

Urgency was the key. Iman was put in charge again – his fluency in the language and an effervescent nature standing him out as the lone candidate for the job – and off he went, confidence oozing from every part of his body as he approached the first potential driver: a single man who had just pulled up in an old banger, which, crucially, had four spare seats.

The rest of us waited in the wings, not wishing to cramp his style, nor intimidate the poor stranger. At one stage Iman pointed over to us and the three of us smiled and waved exaggeratedly in response, doing our best to appear as friendly and as far removed from the stereotypical serial-killing hitchhikers as possible.

When Iman returned, he was keeping his cards close to his chest.

"Go on then, Iman," I urged our friend, who was doing his best to keep a straight face. "How'd it go?"

And then it came; that unmistakable cheeky grin, which spoke a thousand words.

"He's going to Tehran," reported Iman, excitedly. " I did it. I'm the greatest heach-hiker in the world!"

"You're an idiot," replied Will, not wishing him to get too carried away by his own ego, but the boy deserved his moment, and, as soon as we had explained to Woo just what was going on, we all shared high fives and a celebratory group hug.

Mr. Razim – the brave man who had agreed to take four complete strangers into his car – warned us initially that he was tired, and couldn't promise that he would travel all the way to Tehran tonight, but *you* try falling asleep when Iman is rabbiting on besides you!

This was the perfect job for Iman, keeping Mr. Razim awake, and the two of them happily chatted away until we were eventually deposited on the hard shoulder of the motorway on the outskirts of Karaj, just thirty kilometres shy of Tehran. We'd made it!

* * * * *

At 2am yesterday morning, four weary hitchhikers – all kitted out with "*Steve and Will's Hitch to Malaysia*" t-shirts – climbed over the barriers away from one of the busiest motorways in Asia (it was still absolutely packed at 2 in the morning with some of the most reckless drivers that I have ever seen) and headed safely over the bridge into Karaj, jubilant and full of pride at what had been an epic day's hitchhiking. It had been twelve hours since we had left the hotel in Tabriz and we had been on the road for over ten of those hours, but we had done it. Truly it seems that no matter what time of day you start hitching, if you have enough determination, any target is within reach.

"Shall we get a taxi?" Iman suggested, as soon as we were on the other side of the bridge.

We sighed in disbelief.

"Haven't you learnt anything, Iman?" I asked. "We've made it 600km today, and now you want to jump into a taxi!"

"But we can't heach-hike *here*," Iman replied defensively, "And it would take two hours to walk to my house. Karaj is a really big city, actually the fifth largest in Iran!"

Iman certainly seemed to have a point, but we were still flying high from the day's successes, and decided at least to give hitching a try.

The results were simply too good to be true. I love hitchhiking here. The people are just so friendly and it seems as if, in contrast to Europe, where people need a reason to pick you up, here they need a reason not to!

Four consecutive lifts took us to the bottom of Iman's hill, and still we were intent on hitching. Walking backwards up the hill, thumbs out to grab a ride, and only the second driver to pass by stopped to find out where we were going, told us to hop in, and then insisted that we simply must come round to his house for some chai, so that we might meet his family!

"He wants us to come round to meet his family at 3am?" I asked, perplexed.

"Yeah. People are very friendly in Iran," Iman assured us.

We didn't doubt it, although we were a little surprised that this man's family would still be up at such a late hour.

Our final chauffeur of the day, Kazim, treated us with such incredible hospitality that we just couldn't believe what was happening to us. Forget being treated like celebrities; it felt as if we were kings. Welcomed warmly into his home, we sat around on the floor, sipping chai and smoking these really cool little *"Bahman"* cigarettes, whilst his two nephews took photographs of us and asked us lots of questions about England, Korea, and what we thought of Iran.

We did find it a little strange that neither of the head-scarved women present (Kazim's wife and daughter) spoke a word throughout the entire evening, but despite the chauvinistic atmosphere, we men did have a wonderful time that evening, singing songs on request for our hosts, and taking that "never refuse an offer" thing to the next level.

Iman was playing the role of translator throughout the evening and we had fielded all the usual questions about families and culture, but never expected Iman to turn to us and say, without any sense of it seeming at all like a strange question:

"Do you guys want to try some opium?"

"What?" Will and I replied simultaneously, exchanging quizzical glances.

"Are you sure you mean opium, Iman?" Will asked. "Isn't that the same as doing heroin?"

"No, it's normal," Iman reassured us. "It's just part of Iranian tradition, that's all."

"Well in that case," I said. "It would seem rather rude not to!"

Will agreed, and Woo didn't seem to mind. Moments later and the women had brought in a portable stove, which was placed by Kazim, who beckoned us over in turn to breathe through a thin black pipe all the smoke that arose from the embers of an unknown black resin, which he held on a wire.

I must admit that I never imagined that I would smoke opium – least of all in such a bizarre setting – but perhaps it was the complete normality of the situation that made the whole experience seem of little consequence, and we just enjoyed the fact that we were taking part in "Iranian tradition."

This was no secretive binge in the local park. We were just sitting around in a family home and the father of the house had asked us if we wanted to sample a local speciality. "Yes please" had been our response and nothing about the situation had felt at all out of the ordinary. To be honest, the drug itself seemed completely ineffectual. We were already completely worn out by the day and perhaps one might say that the opium further enhanced that feeling, but it was difficult to tell.

When all the talking, singing, and spontaneous dope-smoking had run its course, we thanked our kind hosts, and Kazim took us the rest of the way to where we were going to stay that night. It was too late to go to Iman's house, he told us, and he didn't have a key anyway. Instead, we were taken up to an abandoned shed on the top of his hill, and finally crashed out, dead to the world, upon a pile of rugs therein.

DAY SEVENTY-FOUR:
IMAN'S PAD, KARAJ, TEHRAN PROVINCE, IRAN, MONDAY 22ND SEPTEMBER 2008, 14.09

Iman's father, Dr. Haghighi, is an intimidating man. His stubborn will and unyielding political and philosophical views, matched with a wisdom befitting his long, wizard-like white hair complete an altogether unapproachable figurehead. Divorced from Iman's mother for several years now, "The Doctor," as we have learnt to call him, belittles my notions of one day proposing to my girlfriend, suggesting that marriage means a complete restriction of freedom.

Iman took us to meet his father at his office yesterday afternoon and the change in Iman's character was immediate. Gone was the bouncy personality that screams of a child just wanting to have some fun; in came a sedate figure, who lowered his head upon entering the office and barely raised it until the moment we left.

Dr. Haghighi strikes fear into the worthiest of opponents; even his own sons recoil in terror. I suppose that it's just as well that he saw a use for Will and me, for he lost no time in getting down to business yesterday afternoon.

Iman's father runs an immigration service in the centre of Tehran, which helps want-away Iranians to flee from a repressive country ruled by a psychotic despot to find new lives in Australia, where The Doctor has connections. One of the stipulations, however, of moving to Australia, as with England, is that the immigrant must have a good understanding of the native tongue, and that's where we came in.

"How long are you boys planning on staying in Karaj?" The Doctor asked; a question to which we had no answer.

"I have a proposition for you both, providing you decide to stay around for a week or two," The Doctor continued.

Will and I remained silent, but The Doctor needed no permission to continue.

"How would you like to teach English to my best students? It is not everyday that we are blessed with the presence of native English speakers, you see, and it will help our students to perfect their language if you could teach, say, an intensive course for one or two weeks? That could be arranged easily enough, couldn't it, Mr. Rezaei?" he asked, turning to his chief, who had been sitting attentively by his side throughout.

Mr. Rezaei nodded, and screwed up his face in a nervous twitch that we did our best to ignore (probably a reaction to the stress of working so closely with The Doctor, we thought), then cautiously replied:

"Yes sir, but it might be difficult to make it happen at such short notice."

"Well, make it happen!" The Doctor snapped. "How does that sound to you boys? Obviously we would pay you for your services, and Iman tells me that you have run into a little problem in that area."

A response was scarcely required. Of course we would agree to the offer, if only to save our skin from the wrath of this intimidating man. We didn't want to turn out like Mr. Rezaei, after all. For the first time since entering the office, we were given time to speak, and our response was affirmative.

"Good. I'll contact you through Iman, and we can work out the details at a later date," said The Doctor, dismissing us with firm handshakes and telling us that Iman's mother would take care of us for as long as we were around.

What an unbelievable stroke of luck! You were probably wondering just what was happening with regard to our money situation. In truth, the answer would have been "not a lot"; there was a certain stagnation about the entire situation – but no longer. No longer will we need to rely upon our dear friend Woo to bail us out for the basic costs of living; no longer will we need to rely on the kindness of this trustful fellow, who even suggested that we might live off his money all the way through Iran and pay him back when we eventually found money in Pakistan, or even India, if that was how long it took!

This generosity typifies our dear Korean friend's kind-heartedness. What a gentleman Woo is. He might not be the biggest or the bravest of guys, but our friend has already done so much for the people who mean the most to him.

Getting ready for bed the previous evening, I had asked Woo about the giant scar that clearly runs across the bottom of his stomach, upon which I had previously shied away from commenting. The way in which this humble man responded said so much about his character.

Shyly, Woo whispered that his father had needed a kidney-transplant not long before Woo left for his expedition, and Woo had kindly offered one of his own – presumably the reason he was now taking so many pills and using an inhaler!

"Humbled" would be the word that best describes how I felt. There was no boasting in Woo's manner; just the gentle obedience of a good and faithful son.

"That's an amazing thing to do for somebody Woo," I said. Our timid friend simply smiled and shrugged his shoulders, before quickly hiding the scar under a t-shirt.

* * * * *

At the tender age of twenty, Iman's brother, Milad, has a maturity befitting a man twice his age. In fact, if it weren't for knowing otherwise, his quiet demeanour and a fully-fledged goatee beard (which hangs several inches below his chin) would suggest that it was Milad who was the older of the two.

With maturity, Milad commands his father's respect – a respect that seems ever to evade his elder brother. Iman told us himself that he doesn't really know what he is doing in life and it is this indecision and immaturity that has meant that he is hardly the apple of his father's eye.

Milad, on the other hand, is the better scholar and shares his father's passion for philosophy and chess, revealing a close kindred spirit between the two. Whilst Iman recoils in the presence of his dominating father, Milad shines, and it was Milad who had the temerity to come between The Doctor and myself when I dared to cross his path in a theological discussion on our very first meeting.

I had been challenging The Doctor's clearly atheistic stance with a few suggestions regarding his false preconceptions about Christianity, whilst he seemed completely at a loss when I suggested that there could exist an immanent, yet unseen, God who cared deeply about matters of the heart.

"Matters of the heart?" he scoffed. "I think it would be wise to talk about issues that affect the real world in which we live, rather than talking subjectively about fictitious deities and matters of the heart."

Milad interjected, suggesting that our completely opposite poles of atheism and theism would never find compromise, so there was little point in argument. This was especially true, I thought to myself, because the two men engaged in the dialogue were both such stubborn individuals. We moved on in our discussions to politics – something very close to the heart for the Haghighi household, given that The Doctor once served a significant jail-term for rebelling against the government, whilst Iman himself has been arrested a few times for similar "offences."

It has been fascinating to find out the opinions of our friends towards their own government, which is so feared and despised around the world; a government famous for the tyrannical dictatorship of Mahmoud Ahmadinejad, who once famously declared that he intended to "wipe Israel off the map." Well, as far as we can gather, the opinion of our friends is simple: they hate the man more than we do, and they hate the fact that he is responsible for so poisoning the views of other nations to their own beloved nation. They love Iran and they are very proud of their Persian history, but they absolutely detest Mahmoud Ahmadinejad, who is held responsible for the very fact that friends back home regard our hitch through Iran as one of the most dangerous parts of the trip.

The long truck journey from Tabriz to Zanjan had been the first time we had dared to ask Iman of his own political views and it was with a great deal of caution that he answered us. The President has struck fear into the hearts of his people and Iman knows only too well the potential fate awaiting those who rebel against him, having seen his father behind bars for six years already – a source of pride to Iman. This is the common ground between himself and his father. Indeed, this is the common ground between himself and his fellow-countrymen as a whole. Everyone longs for a change of leadership and a change to the face of their nation as seen around the world. With no regard for the common man, the government runs riot, condemning people to a prison-like existence. Freedom of speech has been completely stripped away; Big Brother stands over like a big, unfriendly giant, waiting for just one slip that might uncover any thoughts or feelings that go against the party line. Imprisonment awaits those who wish to rebel, as did Iman's father at the time of the revolution, which itself appears to have only made matters worse. As far as I understand it, the revolutionaries wanted to change things (as their name suggests), but all that resulted was a further clamping down by the government to avoid anything that might threaten their power.

The government cannot be blamed for absolutely everything, though. Sharia Law, the Muslim rulebook, is the reason why there are such strict rules against women in Iran. It turns out that Iman was telling a bit of a mistruth when he spoke of things being a little more relaxed in Tabriz on that front. Women here, like everywhere in Iran, are forced to cover up. I'm told that Iran is the only country in the world where this law is completely enforced. Arrest awaits the disobedient. As a result of the adherence to this law, women walk around like drones in a country ruled by men, who themselves are stripped of the freedom to do harmless things like making too much noise or dancing in public. This government certainly rules with an iron fist, but it is fascinating to see no signs of such thinking amongst the people. This is no democracy.

It has been so good to share views with Iman and Milad during our time together. It is people like them who really know what is going on beneath the surface here in Iran. When one surveys the faces of the real Iranian people, there isn't even the faintest sign of the terrorism and warmongering that we see splattered across the media in the West. Warm smiles and an unwavering hospitality are the real signs of life here. The biggest problem rests with the government, who, Iman tells us, have even gone out of their way to make the public image of the country as bad as possible so that the people lose more and more of their power to do anything about it. They cannot move away, nor speak out; and rest assured that an Iranian man will now find prejudice almost everywhere he goes because of the lies instilled by men like Ahmadinejad.

DAY SEVENTY-SIX:
IMAN'S PAD, KARAJ, TEHRAN PROVINCE, IRAN, WEDNESDAY 24TH SEPTEMBER 2008, 14.45

I am officially an English teacher in Iran!

In our first class yesterday, we thoroughly enjoyed getting to grips with the grammar. Although we do not claim to be experts in the language ourselves, we can at least take comfort in the fact that we are a good deal better than the horrendous textbooks from which the students have previously been learning. There is simply no chance that they can have been written by an Englishman – such is their drastic misinformation.

Our first class was a small affair, made up of one quiet fellow and three talkative married women in their mid-twenties – each complete, of course, with headscarves and full "body armour."

The Doctor had given us permission to talk freely about anything that we liked, so long as it didn't involve "sex, religion or politics," but it isn't everyday that one gets the chance to talk openly with Iranian citizens about their honest opinions on such fascinating topics, and we proceeded to cross each of these boundaries within the first few minutes.

My particular favourite was the question that I simply could not stop myself from asking, and which probably covered all three topics in one fell swoop: the question regarding the women's dress.

"Now, I'm probably not supposed to ask you this," I began, after a few opening ice-breakers, "but, I'm really interested in the laws regarding the women's dress code in Iran."

"Don't feel under any pressure to answer this question if you don't feel comfortable in doing so," I continued, "*But*, when you emigrate to Australia, how many of you would continue to wear your headscarves?"

I'd said it. There was no going back now, and I just had to wait and see if I was about to be lynched, thrown out, or, as I hoped, engaged in discussion.

Fortunately, I wasn't the only one who longed to discuss the issue. The three women present seemed equally eager to explain their views, yet I was completely taken aback by the results.

Would you believe that out of these three young women, only one said that she would *not* wear the Islamic dress when she migrated to Australia? The other two declared proudly and openly how important it was to their tradition, whilst also giving them power over men because they were able to choose to whom they would reveal themselves – *as opposed to the Western culture in which everyone gets a look*, I thought to myself.

However, as much as I was surprised by the response of these two women (a 66% majority, albeit with only three voters), I was not overly convinced by their answers. It almost seemed as though, even within the safe confines of the classroom, they felt obliged to maintain the teachings of their religion, and a doctrine that must have been ingrained within them from a very early age.

Of course, it is not for me to judge these women for what may well have been their honest views, but I felt dissatisfied by their drone-like responses, which spoke rather disinterestedly about a "love" for Islam and how they thought that the *rosari* (headscarf) made them look "more beautiful."

Perhaps I am just being narrow-minded (I don't profess to have entered the discussion opinion-free), but I was much more satisfied by the answer of the one woman who wanted to buck the trend. Elika spoke openly and defiantly against the rules that so restrict women's freedom in Iran, suggesting that it should at least be a "*matter of choice.*"

I agreed wholeheartedly. It is no problem for me whatsoever that a woman might *choose* to wear the *chador* (full body armour) or even just the rosari, but this should be down to her own discretion. If, indeed, the whole of the Islamic law of *Hijab* (the law that governs women to cover up in public) is based upon the notion that a woman will keep herself for her husband alone, it seems to me that it should be the *woman* that gets to cast the final vote. It is *her* body, and thus it should be *her* decision.

I could see great worth in the idea of hijab if it really were to revolve around the woman's own choice to save her beauty for her husband, forsaking all others (perhaps we could do with more of that attitude in the West, where many girls seem to wear as *little* as possible to attract as much attention as possible) but the strength of the idea must surely lie in its ability to give women the *choice*.

Just the thought that the government here in Iran have bound women, by law, not to wear anything at all that might reveal their body shape (or even just their hairline, as in the case of the rosari) seems to go against the essence of all that I believe in.

Freedom is one of the things habitually taken for granted in the West, but it is this same freedom, when withdrawn, that we would go to any lengths to recover. Freedom of speech, freedom of thought, freedom of religion, freedom of sexuality, freedom of dress... the list goes on.

Elika was in total agreement. It should be a woman's *choice* to wear whatever she wants, even if she might *choose* to wear clothes that will entice males to her beauty; this is her prerogative, and a culture that fails to see this will forever fail to convince others that it is anything but chauvinistic.

It is for no man, no government, and no religion to bind a woman to a restriction of her freedom. She should be able to act in whatever way her freedom of choice dictates.

Wow! There we have it; I'm a raving feminist after all. Who'd have thought it?

* * * * *

Besides this lengthy discussion of Hijab (which took place while the supervising teacher stood silently in the corner and gawped), we also warned our students about the difficulties that an immigrant might find in a new country.

They were eager to hear about all our experiences of immigrants in England and we suggested that it is often not until the second generation that an immigrant will truly "fit in" to the society.

"Perhaps you will be disappointed," Will suggested, "If you move to Australia expecting to find a perfect existence."

"But, if you move with the future of your children in mind," he continued, "Perhaps there is more reason to be optimistic."

As far as our experiences suggested (from a purely observational level, that is; it's not as though we have been immigrants at any stage ourselves), we concluded that the best advice that we could give would be for our friends to "*put themselves out there.*"

All too often immigrants come to England and stay caught up within their own little same-race communities. Whilst it is obviously easier to stay within this comfort zone, it is the action of making friends with natives that will truly lead to integration.

When The Doctor asked us to be teachers, I have to say that I never really expected to enjoy it, but Iran is worlds-apart from England in almost every way, making just chatting to our students about their own personal views (views that aren't tempered by any media propaganda) absolutely fascinating. For this short time, Will and I are privy to the views of the *real* Iran!

One day of teaching behind us, I hope that the supervising teacher won't advise The Doctor to strike us off because we'd love to carry on teaching, even though we are probably two of the least politically-correct individuals that they could have chosen. I wouldn't be surprised if we end up causing an uprising at this rate!

The final fifteen minutes of the lesson yesterday – during which we actually tried to teach them something – was spent distinguishing between the "w" and "v" sounds that Iranians, Iman included, so often mix up, before even trying to teach them the "th" sound – something notoriously difficult for non-English speakers.

"No, not *wee-hicle. Vee-hicle,*" we would say.

"Come on, repeat after me. *Vee, vee, vee...*"

"*Wee, wee, wee...*"

It was a lot of fun, and given that we have had no training in this teaching malarkey, I thought we dealt with the lesson rather well. We even got them to notice how we bite our bottom lip when saying a "v" sound, whilst we make an "o"-like shape with our lips when trying to say the "w" sound... I'm pretty sure we're naturals!

DAY EIGHTY-TWO:
SURPRISINGLY OPEN RESTAURANT, ESFAHĀN, ESFAHĀN PROVINCE, IRAN, TUESDAY 30TH SEPTEMBER 2008, 17.09

Two hundred people die in car accidents every day in Iran. This staggering statistic leaves me with little to add to give you an idea of Iranian driving habits; just think of Formula 1, mix in a little Go-karting, bring this onto the public roads, and I think you're pretty close. Perhaps the most startling habit that we have noticed on Iranian roads is the ever-presence of a species that we lovingly refer to as "the reversing man" – a driver who can be spotted at almost every motorway junction, reversing back up the road (using hard-shoulder or just the slow lane!) because, presumably, he happened to be driving a little fast and missed his turning!

Will's got this theory that the Call to Prayer isn't actually anything to do with mighty Allah at all. Rather, the first Call of the day tells drivers to start their engines, the lunchtime Call is the pit stop, and the final Call of the day is a call to lament the fact that a few drivers, sadly, didn't make it, but thanks everyone else for a great race.

It came as little surprise to us, then, that we had our first-ever car accident a few days ago in central Tehran. Having just lectured our students about the perils of Iranian driving, we took one step outside the door, another into an inner-city taxi, and then proceeded to have a 60km/hr collision with a vehicle that thought it best to wait until just before we passed his junction to cut across us and provide us with an obstacle. Luckily for him, he had timed it just well enough so that we ploughed into the empty rear-compartment of the vehicle, and not his own cockpit. Luckily for us, we had only a few bruises to show for it the next day. I don't know, you wait a cumulative total of 44 years' driving-time in England without a crash, and then you step into Iran and get hit within a week!

We are pretty much resigned to the likelihood of being involved in another crash in this country, having had three or four unrelated bumper-to-bumper incidents in addition to that more spectacular collision. Every time we get into a car here, we always make sure that either Iman or Milad explains to the driver that we are "too young to die." Sadly, however, this seems to sound like some kind of challenge to the racing drivers out here (almost every Iranian) because, invariably, the driver will proceed to rev his engine and do his best to give you the fright of your life. If, by the end of the drive, your hair isn't standing up on end and your fingers don't have to be prized away from the seats that they have been gripping with all their might, then they haven't done their job. Every journey feels like it might be the last. Our days are surely numbered.

DAY EIGHTY-TWO: (CONTINUED...)
IMAM SQUARE, ESFAHĀN, ESFAHĀN PROVINCE, IRAN,
TUESDAY 30TH SEPTEMBER 2008, 20.15

We were sorry to leave Karaj behind yesterday evening, but glad for the company of Iman's brother, Milad, on our journey south. A gentle sort, and quite the philosopher, our new travelling companion is completely different from his emotionally unstable brother.

As much as we grew to love Iman dearly during our days together, he really needs to learn a few life-lessons before he will ever gain the respect of his father. It is the classic story of a son who is unable to fill his father's shoes and forever flounders beneath his shadow.

Iman does not boast an impressive history. Since his eighteenth birthday (now almost six years ago), he has never stuck with anything. Be this studying in Iran, migrating to Malaysia, or just trying to hold down any one of a number of jobs that his father sorted out for him in Tehran, Iman has just given up and, thereby, completely lost his father's trust.

On our penultimate day's teaching, Will and I were summoned into Dr. Haghighi's office for a private meeting regarding his eldest son. The Doctor had heard rumours circulating about Iman's hatred of Tabriz and his desire to continue hitchhiking through Iran with Will and me (rumours which were true), and just wanted to clarify our intentions.

"Iman respects you both," The Doctor began. "I want you to persuade him that he should return to Tabriz and finish the work that he has started there. If he does that and finally gets the IELTS (International English Language Testing System) award that he has been working towards, then he will have gained my trust and can return home. I need you to talk to him. Can you do this for me?"

What could we say? We were pretty shell-shocked by the whole situation, which felt more like an Italian mafia film than real life. The Doctor played the role of The Godfather quite well, and we were suitably struck with terror.

"Err, yes. Of course, sir," Will stuttered.

"We agree with you entirely," I added. "Iman should get his act together and prove that he has it within him to stick at a task; whatever that may be."

"Very good," The Doctor replied, happy that he had persuaded two of his drones to do his dirty work. We were dismissed.

Iman had been ordered to sit outside his father's office for the duration of the interview, and had done so, head bowed, full of the shame that comes as a result of knowing that one is a disappointment to one's own father.

"What did he say?" Iman asked as soon as we were far enough away from the building so that neither The Doctor, nor one of his spies, might be able to overhear.

"It's not good news, Iman," Will told our friend, putting a comforting arm around his shoulders. "He wants you to go back to Tabriz, just for a few more months, so that you can finish your work there, get your IELTS award, and come home with your head held high."

"I am not going back there!" Iman replied sharply, forcibly removing Will's arm from his shoulders. "I hate it there with my stupid boss and his stupid job and that stupid town! I am staying here in Tehran with my friends!"

"Well, I'm not sure you can, Iman," I replied. "You've got to win your father's approval first, or you'll never be trusted to find a job here. Just stick it out for a few more months and then you can come and live here for as long as you like."

"No. I can't do it!" Iman shouted. "I'm not going back!"

Iman was a mess. His father had no idea just how tortuous it was for him in Tabriz. Iman had shared with us, in great detail, about how much he hated working there, in a place where he had no friends and worked long hours, a slave to a cruel boss.

"Well, you've got to tell your father how you feel, Iman," Will said, upon reflection. "You can't just stay silent all the time."

That was the thing. Iman would never speak more than one word in his father's presence. We couldn't work out whether this was a result of sheer intimidation, or whether Iman despaired of the effort because he knew that he was fighting a losing battle. It certainly didn't help matters that The Doctor's Number Two, Mr. Rezaei, was always in the room, prodding Iman with little comments about how he'd "never stuck at anything" and would "never make his father proud," but Iman was just going to have to stand up for himself.

"I will!" our friend sobbed. "I'll tell him... But you have to help me. Tomorrow we'll go in there together and tell him that I'm never going back to that stupid place!"

* * * * *

Sadly, when the crunch finally came, the strong, quick-witted and confident Iman that we had grown to know and love was nowhere to be found. He simply shrank into his shell once again, and took a battering from his father and Mr. Rezaei, who then turned to us to offer support for their case.

Will and I were in a tricky situation. We didn't want to betray the confidence of our friend, yet we daren't go against the explicit orders of The Doctor.

"Iman," Will whispered softly. "Sometimes we all have to do things that we don't want to do, but it won't last forever."

Iman's head remained bowed; he said nothing.

"Iman," I continued. "If you do this, just for a few more months, then you can return home and do something you really want to do."

Still Iman's eyes remained fixed upon anything but anybody else. He glued them to the table in front of him, and stayed silent. Just another drubbing, he must have been thinking, but this time it wasn't just his father on his back; now he had to listen to two of his friends gang up on him.

Watching Iman sit there, lifeless, was like watching a small child whimpering in the face of his father's discipline. The only difference was that Iman's whimpers were internal; there was no outward sign that anything at all was wrong, but inside we knew that Iman was hurting.

Having sat and listened to four individuals telling him what to do and who to be for well in excess of half an hour, Iman finally came to life, even if it wasn't quite the reaction we had hoped for.

"This meeting is stupid!" was all that came out of our friend's mouth, as he stormed out in a child-like tantrum.

I stayed behind in the office, listening to another litany of despair from Numbers One and Two, whilst Will went out to try to retrieve our sensitive friend.

Ten minutes or so later, just at the point when I had run out of excuses for Iman, in strolled our friend, giggling like a naughty toddler that has just been caught in his latest bout of attention-seeking.

Will had persuaded him to return by reminding him of his promise to stand up to his father. This time, however, Iman promised that he would keep his composure, talk rationally with his father and, most importantly, look the man in the eye!

It took a while in coming but, once the laughter (on Iman's part) had subsided and his father had hung up the phone from speaking to his latest client, Iman opened up to his father about his hatred for Tabriz and the twelve-hour working days that he regularly suffers, without any friends to support him there.

"I don't want to go back to Tabriz, sir," Iman told his dad plainly.

And, finally, a compromise was made. All that it had taken was for Iman to act like a responsible adult and tell his father straight, and The Doctor conceded.

"You do have to go back, Iman, but work only for forty-eight more days, get your IELTS qualification, and then you can come home."

Of course, this wasn't exactly what Iman had wanted to hear, but this was as good as it was going to get. Iman simply had to go back to Tabriz and make his father believe in him again. Last night we said a fond farewell to our good friend and took his brother along as his replacement as we headed for the road to Esfahan just about in time to watch the last vestiges of sunlight fade out of sight. Last night we broke all the rules and went hitchhiking after dark.

8. THE HAGHIGHI STORY (PART TWO)

DAY EIGHTY-THREE:
HOSTEL, ESFAHĀN, ESFAHĀN PROVINCE, IRAN, EID UL-FITR (THE BREAKING OF THE FAST), WEDNESDAY 1ST OCTOBER 2008, 10.57AM

This is an historic day. Ramazan has officially ended for another year and, finally, we will be able to find food and water at any time and in any place for the first time since leaving Turkey. It is funny to think that it has been exactly the same Ramazan fast that we have experienced in both Turkey and Iran, and yet the connotations of the fast have been so different for the natives of each country. It has not been the case, as you might expect, that we have necessarily found more practising Muslims here in Iran – quite the contrary. Rather, we have noticed that, unlike the Turks, all Iranians have at least to pretend that they are practising Muslims when in public, only breaking the fast within the privacy of their own homes and offices – such is the strictness with which Sharia Law is implemented here.

During our time as teachers in Tehran (which spanned a total of seven, two-hour, intensive classes over a week), we were fortunate enough to be looked after by the inherently rebellious Haghighi household, which meant that food was always readily available. Safely inside the confines of The Doctor's own personal office, the door would be shut, the blinds drawn, and in would walk The Doctor's personal assistant, banquet in hand. There wasn't much variety. In fact, the menu was exactly the same every day – fried chicken, gherkins, yoghurt, and non-alcoholic beer – but this was Ramazan, and we were glad for the simple blessing of food on the table.

Oh, how we longed for the simplest array of food yesterday afternoon as we trekked through barren Iranian desert on a long hitch from Qom to Esfahan, but Ramazan would take its toll on us that day...

* * * * *

The after-dark hitch from Tehran the previous evening had been a resounding success. We weren't ever going to make it the 450km to Esfahan in one stint, so we were more than happy to settle for a 150km ride with a friendly trucker named Alireza, who, upon our arrival in Qom, even promised to take us the rest of the way to Esfahan the following day.

Relaxed by the assurance that the morrow's hitching had been achieved before it had begun, Milad took us on a tour of a city, which, he informed us, is famous for two things: sheep's head and religious strictness.

We started off with the first. Heading straight for a mutton specialist, the only parts of the animal we successfully managed to avoid were the testicles, as brain, eyes, cheeks, mouth and hooves were soon devoured, with only a generous squeeze of lemon juice to help disguise the somewhat unusual flavours.

My personal favourites were the mouth and cheeks; brain soup just tasted like lumpy lemon soup, whilst the hooves and eyes were, frankly, repulsive. Think for a moment, if you will, about how it might feel to bite into an eyeball... I reckon it's got to be a very close second to the nauseating notion of biting into a sperm-filled testicle.

With appetites thoroughly sated by the fattiest sheep's head we'd ever tasted, it was time to get a taste for Qom's second great claim to fame.

From a purely observational level, it is not especially difficult to see why Qom is understood to be very religious. Towering above the city's skyline, a spectacular Holy Shrine glistens with rich jewels, whilst down on ground level the few women who venture out in public, do so covered in black from head to toe.

So imposing is the Shrine that it can be seen from almost every vantage point within the city, so it didn't take long for the three of us to find our way to the main entrance, where we had been told by a local that we might find free accommodation for the night.

What a good idea, we had thought; a Shrine that doesn't just offer a place for people to come and pray, but also boasts a place for the weary and homeless to come and rest. That evening, we certainly felt as though we ticked all the right boxes, but there was one tiny, infinitesimal detail that we had failed to consider: we weren't Muslims.

Confidently approaching the gates, sleeping bags in hand, we had even brushed our teeth and left our bags behind at what was, I suppose, a kind of "reception desk," but as soon as the guards laid eyes upon us, we knew that something was wrong.

None of the guards could speak a word of English, so the lengthy conversation that followed went on without us, but Milad eventually turned to us to relay the unwelcome news.

"I'm sorry guys," Milad said, a look of embarrassment upon his face. "He says we can't go in tonight because you guys aren't Muslims."

Will and I were flabbergasted, and stood silently, shaking our heads in disbelief. What a ridiculous notion that we would be turned away simply because we didn't profess a belief in the same God!

Milad seemed even more upset than we were. Here he was in his country, trying to do his best to show his foreign friends that famous Persian hospitality, only to be denied the chance to do so because of a petty discrepancy regarding religious belief!

"I hate these stupid rules, this stupid religion!" he bemoaned. Our friend was more embarrassed than angry and we tried our best to disguise our own anger so as not to add further to our friend's discomfort.

Once more Milad tried to plead with the head of security, but the best that they could offer us was a "ten-minute tour" of the Shrine, during which we would be tightly chaperoned by a machine gun-wielding guard, who would even restrict us from stepping inside a number of the most sacred rooms because they were, apparently, reserved "only for Muslims!"

Needless to say, this wasn't the happiest of tour groups to have graced the spectacular Shrine of Qom. The three of us visibly moped around the mosque throughout our brief tour without even so much as the ghost of a smile between us.

I felt physically sick as I walked. I couldn't remember the last time that I had been the subject of prejudice, if I ever had, and now here we were, denied from something so small as a couple of metres of floor space because of the simple fact we weren't Muslims. I felt like such an intruder in that Holy place, which, to me, is a little oxymoronic. Even inside the mosque the looks from the crowds of worshippers were far from heart-warming. We were outsiders (our colour alone dictated that), but to be treated as sinful infidels, unworthy even to step close to the presence of their God; this was just too much.

Surely it should be the practice of all believers to welcome visitors into their holy places with open arms. Surely God isn't supposed to discriminate between creed and colour. Wouldn't Allah want his most devout of followers to invite all others openly to meet with him? Of course, this one incident shouldn't be taken as the definitive example. I am sure that there are followers in other mosques around the world who would have welcomed us in, but on this particular occasion, I felt ashamed on Islam's behalf.

I know that it isn't only mosques in which such bigotry may be encountered, and many people feel that if they stepped inside a church, they would not be welcomed. However, from my own experience, I know that this should never be the case with Christianity. One of my favourite things about the message of Christianity is its message of grace, which teaches that every person, whatever his or her creed, colour, or belief at the time, is welcomed with open arms by God, and Christians are to mirror that same love to anyone who would seek it.

Perhaps my views aren't entirely free from bias – I have been going along to church for years now, and I'm still pretty new to this Islam thing – but, as far as I can gather, Islam offers no such message. The laborious washing rituals that go on before and after each prayer session reveal an understanding of God that requires us to tick all the right boxes of the entrance form to come into his presence. It is this freedom to come before God, as I am, stripped back to the core, that most excites me about my faith. I could never believe in a God who would turn away any child that comes in search of him.

I cannot say that the blame should necessarily lie with Islam itself because this was the example of only one mosque, in one town, in one country of the world, but our experience at that mosque in Qom did a disservice to the God of grace that I believe in. That night, we were reduced to the fate of homeless men. We slept outside the mosque upon a few dirty sheets of cardboard that we found there and awoke just in time to avoid an unwanted shower from a man cleaning the streets.

A long, arduous, and ultimately unfruitful search for breakfast that morning was capped off by Alireza's failure to pick up his phone, the consequential seven-hour slog to get us to Esfahan, and the failure there to find any restaurant open for miles upon miles of Esfahani streets on that, the final day of Ramazan. Thank goodness it's over.

Day Eighty-Three: (continued...)
Imam Square, Esfahān, Esfahān Province, Iran, Eid ul-Fitr (The Breaking of the Fast), Wednesday 1st October 2008, 20.14

Esfahan is the Iranian Rome. The city abounds with feats of architectural prowess and tonight you join us in the grand vista of Imam Square – a vast space that dwarfs European attempts at the same, whilst boasting both a quintessential Persian bazaar and yet another breathtaking mosque at its borders. Just a short walk away is the Zayandeh River, over which stretch three majestic bridges; and it is at the heart of one of these bridges (each of which is lit-up spectacularly at night) that Will and I won our first game of Hokm.

This Iranian card-game has taken us by storm since first playing a few days ago with Iman's cousins, Elham and Shabnam, in Tehran. Essentially, Hokm is a pairs version of the English card game, *Whist*, in which every card in the pack is dealt out and pairs unite to try and win tricks by laying the highest card in each suit. At the beginning of each round, one suit is selected by the "hokm" (it means "king" and you achieve such status by winning the previous hand) to trump all others, and the winners of the round are the pair to win the most tricks. The winners of the game are the first team to win seven rounds.

Believing myself to be pretty good at Whist, I didn't think that making the switch to Hokm would be too difficult, but I was sadly mistaken. Iman's cousins gave us a baptism of fire, mercilessly demolishing Will and me by seven games to nil.

Given that both of us pride ourselves at being rather good at most games, defeat was difficult enough to take in itself, but it was the shameless way in which both sisters (particularly Shabnam) lorded it over us after each winning hand that really riled me. It seems that British etiquette – regarding, oh I don't know, priding oneself on winning with humility – doesn't transcend national borders, or, at least, it doesn't make it this far east. Every trick that the sisters won was another chance for the younger of the two to stick the knife in, claiming that they were going to whitewash us with a 7-0 victory, whilst I was adamant that no such thing was about to occur.

There is nothing worse for a man than to lose to a pair of gloating women, who, for some reason, cannot appreciate that luck plays a massive part in the game. I was fuming. I kept on telling Shabnam that it was all down to luck and that if it were Will and I who had started the game as "Hokm," *we* would have been the ones dominating affairs, but *we* would have done it with a touch of grace.

Infuriated by the manner of our defeat, I made the girls give us one chance to play a hand as "Hokm" to prove my point, but, much to my dismay, they still beat us. Undeterred by this further setback, I mumbled away about something to do with the crucial part that luck had to play, whilst my tormentors gloated unashamedly. There was simply no way that I was about to allow my pride to be taken away completely and own up to the rather obvious fact that they were simply better players than us.

Over the years, I have learnt that games bring out both the very best and the very worst in my character, but there was only one winner that night. I simply cannot stand performing badly at something that I either *know* or *think* that I should win at. This was the perfect example. Whist is a game I have played many times and Hokm isn't really much different, so when we were still beaten, and beaten well, my pride took a battering. Not only was it hard to stomach that my obvious skills had gone to waste, but now these girls were prodding and poking my bruised ego's defences by taunting me in my distress.

The poor girls were just enjoying their victory, blissfully unaware that they were causing me such inner turmoil, whilst every inch of my body was seething with rage. My blood pressure was sky high and my face had turned red with fury; I was gritting my teeth with all my might and my eyes were almost bulging out of my head. It must have been a terrifying sight to behold and, eventually, Elham decided that we should call it a day.

"I don't want to play anymore," she said, with that Iranian-American accent of hers. Both she and her sister, to an even greater degree than their male cousins, have almost perfect English (Elham even teaches it), but they do have an awful American twang.

"Not with Steve like this," she continued.

Silence ensued. No one dared to speak or even turn to look at me. Fury was becoming confused for embarrassment now, as the guilt for feeling this way and spoiling an otherwise pleasant evening worked away inside of me. It was 2-2 in our second game (we had swapped partners to make it more "even"), but although I had felt as if I was calming down a little, my face clearly didn't suggest anything of the sort, and Elham had had enough.

Fires rekindling within me, I felt as if my teeth were clenched so tightly together that they might shatter into pieces at any moment.

"I'm going for a walk," I huffed, slowly picking myself up from the floor on which we played, then trying as best as I could not to slam the door on my way out.

"Ahhhhhhhhhhh!!!!!!!!" I screamed at the top of my lungs as soon as I was far enough away from the house to know that I wouldn't be heard. "What am I doing?"

I paced twice around the block before crumpling in a heap on the side of the road, head in hands. It wasn't only the game that had taken hold of me. The trip has really taken it out of me emotionally, more than I had first anticipated that it would. We meet so many people, who all make such a big impression on our lives, and then we just up and leave, potentially never to see them again.

Beyond that, perhaps for the first time since Spain, I'm starting to feel really confused about why I left my beloved Jo behind in England to do this trip. I have tried as best I can to shut her out of my thoughts – determined that I may as well make the very most of these experiences now that I am here – but it just doesn't feel right to shut out what was once such a big part of my life. It is so difficult to get the balance right between not thinking about someone too much and not thinking about someone enough.

Not only did my thoughts relate to the childish way in which I was behaving towards Iman's cousins; it related all too strongly to my feelings of guilt for what was going on behind the scenes, affecting everything that I believed in so strongly. I was losing grip on my relationship with Jo and starting to really struggle with the basic physical attraction that I felt for these two beautiful Iranian women.

You might have been wondering why my feelings for Jo have been bottled up over the last few months, perhaps questioning why a relationship that I had spoken so passionately about at the beginning might not make another appearance for almost three months. Now I'm feeling the strain of the toughest test to the relationship so far, which has come as a result of spending a lot of time with Elham and Shabnam. Although nothing has happened, or is ever going to happen with the Haghighi girls, my mind is full of guilt for even entertaining thoughts that something, somewhere inside of me, might actually want it to.

Other than teaching, the entirety of our time in Tehran has been spent with the Haghighi family and we have become really good friends with the cousins as a result. Elham, 25, and her sister Shabnam, 23, are a lot of fun to be around, but I hadn't prepared myself for the awkwardness that might follow from becoming too closely attached to these girls, and it has been a real challenge to keep myself from really slipping up and spoiling a relationship that means the world to me. You hear the phrase "Absence makes the heart grow fonder" so often, and to an extent, I would agree with it, but far too little is made of the converse statement: "Out of sight, out of mind." In my attempts to put Jo out of my mind – for fear that thinking about her too much might quash the fullest enjoyment of the trip – I have taken it to such an extreme that it is difficult to remember what is was like when we were actually together, and now I just feel horribly lost and confused.

How could I have let this happen? What am I doing to my relationship and what am I risking? It is such a difficult balance to draw between healthily not thinking about someone too much, and then dangerously not thinking about them enough. Anytime Jo comes to mind, I pause, enjoy the moment, but then try to banish the thoughts as quickly as possible, so that I don't start wishing that I was back at home. But now I have become so used to batting those honest thoughts away that I feel like a fraud for even allowing myself to think them again.

"Lord, please help me," I prayed, sitting down on the kerb and weeping into my hands as I did. This wasn't just a game; this was real life, and I was living dangerously.

"I'm such a hypocrite," I said to myself. "I chastise others for the slightest indiscretion and then all but do the same myself."

I sobbed heavily for a while, allowing an old peace to wash over me, a peace that I had missed for just about as long as I had missed Jo.

DAY EIGHTY-FIVE:
PARK BENCH, OUTSIDE MARIAM'S HOUSE, SHIRAZ, FÂRS PROVINCE, FRIDAY 3RD OCTOBER 2008, 11.52AM

As a little boy peers over my shoulder I take time to still my mind and pen the thoughts of the past few days. The boy's name is Nima and he is the thirteen year-old son of Milad's aunt, Mariam, who is the latest Haghighi family member to take care of us during our time in Iran. We're not sure about the specifics of his story yet, but we do know that Nima's father is no longer with us; he passed away a few years ago, leaving poor Nima and his widowed mother alone in a house that just seems a little large for two.

We arrived here in Shiraz at about 10pm last night, having hitched the 450km from Esfahan in a personal record of sixteen hours! Our longest day yet, we were more than a little weary by the end of our twelfth and final hitch of the day. I don't really understand why it took us so long to get here because we rarely waited for more than fifteen minutes for a lift, but I suppose that the minutes do mount up.

Come to think of it, a two-hour lunch-break probably didn't help matters. Saeed and Ali, two young farmers, gave us our fifth ride of the day and insisted that we simply must visit their farm, where we would enjoy an impromtu picnic beneath a beautiful canopy of fruit trees.

Taking a little siesta upon the picnic mat (a fine Persian rug), we became so relaxed that we barely noticed the arrival of six or seven friends of our hosts, who had presumably all come along to take a good look at the strange white boys sitting on their mate's lawn. I was the last to awake from slumber and did so to the sound of laughter.

"What's all the giggling about?" I asked Milad, who would become a thoroughly worn-out translator by the end of the day.

"Um, they just asked me if you are a woman," he answered, smiling coyly.

"Definitely tell them yes," Will interrupted, joining the hysteria that had now gripped everyone but me.

I don't know, you'd have thought that my freshly-shaven head would have been a sure sign to the boys that I was one of them, but oh no; apparently, it only further enhanced the gleam of feminine beauty sparkling from my eyes. Now, I have always known that my features most resemble my mother's, but have never appreciated the likeness to be quite so pronounced. I told Milad to assure them immediately that I was, in fact, "all man," so that I might avoid the unwanted attentions of any potential male suitor.

Beyond this teddy bears' picnic – which included fresh pomegranates from the trees above us – there isn't much else to tell of yesterday's progress, other than that it was slow. The majority of our lifts were spent in small spaces, whether this meant the already-occupied back seats of a car, the sweaty confines of a lorry driver's cabin, or even a white-knuckle ride on the rickety trailer of a speeding pick-up truck.

As one might suppose, a long day on the road gave plenty of time for stressing-out on the part of Will and me, and it didn't help matters that Milad whinges a lot more than his brother ever did. If Milad wasn't complaining about constantly having to translate for us (or simply refusing to do so), he was whining about our hitchhiking tactics, essentially suggesting that his ideas were far superior to our own. Now, whilst we would not wish to come across as arrogant in our position, it is rather difficult to take notice of the advice of such a novice when one has already managed to hitchhike quite successfully (for quite some way) without his help.

To be fair to the boy, he really was having to do a lot of translating and did have to say exactly the same things about us over and over again. I suppose that Will and I have simply become accustomed to repeating ourselves, chatting about those same uninteresting personal facts or singing those same songs on the travel guitar – a tiresome ritual for all, it would seem, except the latest Iranian driver, who simply cannot believe his luck. Not only has he stumbled across a couple of aliens and managed to induce them into his vehicle, but now these strange creatures are serenading him. *And* one of them looks like David Beckham.

I'm getting rather fed up with the number of people here who take one look at my friend's blonde hair and pretty face and ask him if he actually is David Beckham. Will normally responds that, yes, in fact he is, or at the very least, he is a close relation.

In my latest efforts to quash my friend's growing ego, I try to pre-empt drivers by suggesting that he looks like a slightly less attractive English footballer.

"Oh, don't you think he looks like Wayne Rooney?" I suggest, but it rarely works.

"No," they simply respond, taking time to think about it a little longer, until... "David Beckham!" they cry, and I hang my head because it's my fault that they even started thinking about the look-alike thing anyway.

DAY EIGHTY-SIX:
MARIAM'S HOUSE, SHIRAZ, FÂRS PROVINCE, IRAN, SATURDAY 4TH OCTOBER 2008, 21.50

There is one major facet of Iranian tradition thus far unexplained, which completely overshadowed our time in the beautiful city of Esfahan. Usually renowned for those three magnificent bridges, the enormous Imam Square, and a maze of Persian bazaars, we will always remember Esfahan because of *Tarof*.

This "tarof" is an age-old Iranian custom, harmless enough in its intent, but tricky to understand fully even if you are an Iranian, let alone if you're not from around here. I suppose one could mistake it for the Iranian version of British politeness because tarof is a strict behavioural code that underpins every social interaction. Unfortunately for us, tarof is almost entirely at odds with our own rule of never refusing an offer because one of the most important rules of the code is that people are obliged to offer you something, but you are equally obliged to reject it. The result of such a predicament, to those that don't understand it, is often a total muddle.

"Come stay at my house," someone might suggest, without the least intention of following the offer through. So when we tell them that we could think of nothing we'd rather do – as was the story of our second night in Esfahan – the person offering finds himself in a little bit of a pickle.

Awkwardly, he keeps on smiling to avoid the embarrassing admission that his offer was completely hollow, whilst thinking to himself how incredibly rude it was of us to make him feel this way.

"Well then, shall we exchange numbers and give you a call later on?" we continue, allowing time for Milad to translate.

What can he do but accept, and duly he does. We shake hands, wish each other a nice day and look forward to going round to his house later on, whilst the poor chap cannot believe that something he thought was obviously just an offer of tarof has been so abused.

This was exactly the situation in which we found ourselves on our second night in Esfahan, oblivious to the fact that there had been anything at all out of the ordinary in the transaction as we patiently waited in Imam Square for a lift that would never arrive.

We waited for two whole hours in the end, playing *Futsal* (a three-a-side version of footy that the Iranians are crazy about) on the walkways that skirt around the edges of the Square, but he never came. Milad tried calling the man several times, but, strangely enough, his phone was always switched off and Milad saw little point in leaving a message.

Perhaps your initial reaction is to spring to the defence of the man. For all we know he fully intended to come, you might say, but at the very last minute, for a whole host of potential factors, he was thwarted from doing so.

Sadly, if this is your position, you clearly don't know tarof. The fact of the matter is that this man was panicked into offering something that he never intended to give and simply didn't have the balls to own up to what had been an honest misunderstanding.

We didn't stay around Imam Square for much longer because the gang with whom we were playing Futsal bluntly informed us that they were thieves and that we were lucky that they liked us because they would have taken all our belongings if they hadn't.

"Charming!" we thought, and swiftly went on our way. Midnight was almost upon us and sleeping options were limited. We had checked-out of our hostel of the previous night because of the kind offer of hospitality that we thought we had received, and now every hostel in town would be shut. As far as we could see, only two options remained.

Option number one was to sleep underneath one of the bridges (the romantic option), but Milad insisted that our chances of being mugged or arrested would soar stratospherically if we did. So to option number two, a through-the-night hitch to Shiraz (the dangerous option), which we undertook only because we appeared to have run out of all other options.

* * * * *

Sadly it would seem that regular drivers are few and far between on Esfahani roads around midnight. In an hour's waiting, the only viable interest that we received came from a nearby squadron of taxi drivers – all of whom decided, one after the other, that it really was worth their efforts to speak to us, despite the fact that we had rejected a plethora of their predecessors.

So frustrating did this monotonous trend become that, when the first non-taxi driver pulled over, there was little thought spared to who this man was, or where it was that he may or may not be going. We had clarified the "no money" thing (the man had waved away the suggestion) and that was enough. Milad and Will dumped our belongings in the back, whilst I jumped in alongside our would-be redeemer.

"Shiraz?" I asked, not especially optimistic of the chances that this stranger might be driving the distance, but not really knowing what else to say.

The response was, well, unexpectedly tactile. Turning his head towards me and leaning in close, the man said something in Farsi that I couldn't understand, but would now suppose to be something along the lines of "I'll take you anywhere you wanna go, big boy" because two seconds later his hand had found its way to my knee and he was grinning at me inanely.

Now that the man was close to me (too close by all accounts), a strong and familiar scent powerfully wafted its ways into my nostrils. Ethanol; there was no mistaking it.

"Will, get the bags out now," I whispered back to my friend, not wishing to convey too much alarm in my tone for fear at how the drunk man might react.

"He's completely wasted and just touched my leg," I continued, jumping out of the car quicker than I had got in.

The drunk man seemed surprised by our hasty exit and stumbled over to speak with us, trying his best to keep his feet still while he confronted Milad with what I can only assume to be words along the lines of:

"What's the matter? (Hiccup)... I'll take you to Shiraz... (Hiccup)... Come on, lesssss go Shhhhhiraz."

Whilst I cannot be 100% sure of Milad's exact response, I know that none of it sounded particularly pleasant and our drunken friend limped back to his car like an injured young fawn to continue on his way to wherever it was that he was actually going.

This was not to be the end of the saga, however, as first our taxi friends, and then the drunk himself, came back to give us another go. Clearly miffed by what Milad had said, the drunk was out of his car in a shot, wobbling over to say something along the lines of (and I'm filling in the blanks here): "Hold on a minute, yousss told me yousss didn't want to go Shhhirazzzz. Then why are you ssstill here?"

It was no use arguing this time. It wasn't as if our evening had been particularly productive anyway and we were just going to have to accept the fact that our plans were doomed to failure.

Taxis and drunkard duly dismissed, we did a few laps of the local area to try and find somewhere secluded to sleep, but, finding nowhere, returned to the very same spot where we had started hitching all that time ago and glumly threw down some cardboard for the second night in three.

DAY EIGHTY-SEVEN:
MONA AND AMIR'S HOUSE, SHIRAZ, FÂRS PROVINCE, IRAN, SUNDAY 5TH OCTOBER 2008, 9.45AM

From Hafez's tomb to Takht-e-Jamshid, Shiraz is another Iranian city teeming with relics from the late great Persian Empire, and we have been given a thorough tour of every last one of them thanks to our latest Haghighi hosts, cousin Mona and her husband Amir.

We are told that it was the invading Greeks (Alexander and friends) who were responsible for giving Takht-e-Jamshid the more recognised name of *Persepolis* – which translates literally to mean "City of the Persians" – making it all the more significant that Alexander burnt it down in one of his more rage-filled moments. Ruins are all that remain.

Back in Karaj, Iman sat us down to watch a French film by the name of *Persepolis* – which satirically depicts the life of a girl growing up under the stranglehold of the modern Iranian state – and, having visited the site, it doesn't take a genius to work out why it was so entitled.

Just like the ancient city, the once great Persian Empire now lies in the ruins created by the rule of totalitarian government and imposed religion. History remains very precious to the Iranian people and they are very proud of where they came from, yet they can feel no such pride for the direction in which their government is leading them. In fact, we haven't met one Iranian who feels anything but contempt for Ahmadinejad and we have been startled by the number of people who wish to leave Iran.

It is no wonder, however, when one considers just how far the government has gone to restrict its people's freedom, exemplified superbly by the frequency with which Milad is on the lookout for the repercussions of mine and Will's mischievous behaviour.

"This is E-ran!" he screams, shaking his head in disbelief as Will and I recklessly disregard the policies that Milad and countrymen so carefully obey.

"Come on Milad. Lighten up a bit mate," we respond, tugging down his cousins' headscarves for the umpteenth time in our own mini-rebellion against the farcically strict laws.

"No. Seriously guys, this isn't funny; this is E-ran!" he repeats, and our friend is right.

William and I cannot help the fact that we are so innately rebellious. Growing up in the cynical West under the influences of the likes of Ricky Gervais has led us to be somewhat wary of meaningless regulations, but we are wrong to brazenly disregard these rules whilst under the care and attention of our benevolent hosts.

It's easy for *us* to be so carefree, Milad might point out; *we* aren't the ones who have to live in the country every day. For the Iranians, however, there can be no such relief; there is only further repression and the resulting frustration that this brings. What kind of country is it, for instance, in which the simple act of removing one's headscarf in public can have you thrown into jail?

The Haghighi household, like the rest of their peers, constantly have to watch everything that they do or say in public for fear that someone might be listening in. Shabnam told us that she once had to go through the rigmarole of a court case just because a neighbour had dobbed her in for the heinous crime of pursuing an "illegal relationship." Essentially, this meant that she had a boyfriend – something that is pretty much ruled out in Iran. It's marriage or nothing here.

Apparently there is even a rule that says that you cannot be seen in public at all with a member of the opposite sex unless you are related or married! We thought Milad was joking about this particular restriction until we saw the effects first hand.

144

It was back in Tehran and a group of us (three girls, five guys) were walking down a street together on our way out for dinner.

"Wait a minute guys," Milad said. "I just saw a Secret Police car. Hold back and we'll let the girls go on ahead because we could get into serious trouble if they saw us," he explained, and we continued along our way, tailing the girls by a good fifty metres.

Still unconvinced by the whole charade, it wasn't until we arrived outside the restaurant and saw the evidence for ourselves (a black van filled with thirty or forty disobedient couples) that we truly appreciated Milad's sincerity.

Milad told us that this was no anomaly. Apparently, he and his cousins, Elham and Shabnam, are stopped quite regularly by the Secret Police, whereupon they must pull out their ID cards to prove their relationship in order to avoid further complications.

Once more we doubted, and once more we were to see the evidence first-hand. The very next day we were wandering down the street with Milad and cousins, when a Secret Police car was spotted. Will and I were sent on ahead, where we cowered around a corner, whilst the rigorous investigation took place. Upon rejoining us, Milad assured us that it was just as well we had gone on ahead because it was one thing for an Iranian boy to be caught fraternising with two unrelated girls, but it would be quite another thing if the boy was also a foreigner!

It isn't only the shocking behaviour of meeting up in mixed gender groups that can get one into a fix in Iran. During our time in Esfahan, we actually had to beg the Secret Police not to arrest Milad because he had failed to provide them with the necessary "tour-guide" certificate that would authenticate his being with us.

"No. He is our friend," we shouted, struggling to believe what we were seeing.

"Doost, khoob doost" (Friend, good friend), we continued, showing off the Farsi that we've been picking up.

Eventually they conceded, but don't think that that made it any easier for us for the remainder of our time in Esfahan. Part of the reason why we were reduced to sleeping on the streets was because they wouldn't allow Iranians and foreigners even to share a room!

Iran is a bizarre blend of the most lovely, hospitable people, and a government that treats them all as worthless slaves. I don't think we could live here. We'd do or say something offensive and get thrown into jail in no time at all. In fact, I'm surprised we've lasted this long.

DAY EIGHTY-NINE:
ANOTHER HAGHIGHI HOUSE, SHIRAZ, FÂRS PROVINCE, IRAN, TUESDAY 7TH OCTOBER 2008, 12.13PM

Milad took his "This is Iran" thing to a whole new level yesterday when he pleaded with us not to continue hitchhiking towards the unstable Pakistani border in the Zahedan province of southeastern Iran.

"Come on guys. *We* don't even go there and we're Iranian!" he said. "Why don't you just take a bus?"

The words grated against us. "Take a bus?" It was all very well coming from a stranger (most of whom are probably only in it for the money anyway), but coming from a friend (and a friend who happened to have hitchhiked some 900km with us in the previous few days) it was too much.

Of course, Milad had only our best interests at heart, but for him to have missed the mark so spectacularly felt like a kick in the teeth. Did nobody understand us?

"You know that we *are* going to hitchhike, right? Will asked. "Wherever we go people tell us that this or that place is dangerous and that we can't hitch there, but if we'd have listened to them then we'd have stopped back in Spain!"

"But this is E-ran!" Milad whined.

"Oh, for goodness sake!" I snapped. "Would you shut up about it being E-ran? We know it's Iran and it isn't nearly as bad as you would have us believe. In fact, we happen to love this country and all the people that we've met here!"

Milad looked hurt and I quickly began to feel wretched. His family had done so much for us and now we were just going to turn around and throw it back into their faces.

"We're sorry Milad," Will said, apologising on my behalf. "We don't mean to snap, but we simply *have* to hitchhike. It's in the rules you see, and I'm sure that we'll be fine. Come on, we've made it this far, haven't we?"

You could see the cogs working in Milad's head as he thought about what had been said and I just knew that all he wanted to tell us was that this was E-ran, but, for once, our friend remained silent.

* * * * *

This morning we received an unexpected phone call from an old friend. I don't think I ever properly told you what became of our dear Korean friend Woo, but just a few hours ago we were reacquainted with his familiar owl-like warblings as our friend called up to confess that he had run into a spot of bother.

Woo left us on our very first day as teachers in Tehran, heading off on his own to visit the Caspian Sea in the north. Knowing all too well Woo's timid nature and slight physique, we had worried about him from the outset, and our concerns were about to be proved right.

What with Woo being Woo, it was a little difficult to gather exactly what it was that he was saying, but the gist seemed to be something along the lines of losing/spending all of his money, which, we concluded, probably translated as being mugged.

Poor Woo, we reflected. So sweet, so defenceless, but some cruel soul had decided to take advantage of him. Now Woo was sitting safely in the arms of the Korean Embassy in Tehran, but they clearly didn't want him any longer and had asked if he had any other friends he could contact.

Instantly, Woo had thought of us, and now he was phoning to ask whether we were still in Tehran and whether he could come and travel with us again.

Oh Woo! So childlike, so innocent. How could we refuse his frightened plea? We could hardly send him off into the apparently treacherous roads of eastern Iran on his own, could we? Even during our short phone conversation Woo mumbled something or other about "Zahedan" and "danger" (which I blame entirely upon that *Lonely Planet* thing he insists upon carrying around with him) and, without us, who knows what might happen to him there?

Hitching in a bigger group doesn't seem to have affected us too adversely thus far and, although we were secretly looking forward to being alone again, we shall just have to wait a little longer for that privilege. I suppose that it won't be so bad travelling with Woo again, although travelling with others never fails to produce its difficulties. Even with our Iranian friends, Iman and Milad, difficulties ensued from travelling together, and they speak English! With Woo it is an entirely different kettle of fish. He truly is a danger to himself and everyone around him. As sweet as he is, it is his lack of awareness and Pidgin English that will no doubt put us in jeopardy at some stage.

Oh well, at least it is sure to bring about its share of amusing tales. We are scheduled to meet Woo in Yazd (about 300km northeast of here) in a few days' time, but first we have the small matter of expiring visas to attend to. Our visas run out this very day!

DAY NINETY-ONE:
AUNT HAGHIGHI'S HOUSE, SHIRAZ, FÂRS PROVINCE, IRAN, THURSDAY 9TH OCTOBER 2008, 9.25AM

Our Iranian visas have been extended for a whole extra month and we might just end up staying here for the whole of it if the Haghighi family have anything to do with it.

We first met Iman more than three weeks ago now and his family are still taking care of us! We cannot speak highly enough of the generosity and hospitality of this family, who have had us to stay in five different homes now – each one housing an offshoot of their enormously extended family.

Apparently there are thirty cousins in all (we must have met only about ten), most of their parents are divorced (in fact, we haven't met an exception yet), and still the family remains a tightly-knit unit, oozing hospitality from its core. So much for the generalisation that suggests that families will go downhill after a divorce. Divorces seem to be about as commonplace in Iran as car accidents, and nobody seems the least bit bothered about either.

"It happens" is the familiar retort that meets any question we might pose about either phenomenon. On the car accident front, as proud ambassadors for the *British Green Cross Code*, we regularly respond with a "well, it flippin' well shouldn't do," but when it comes to high divorce rates, our homeland is in no position to criticise.

What is perhaps most refreshing about the "it happens" attitude of the people here is that this reveals an incredibly laid-back nature, which is surely one of the reasons why they are so darn good at showing hospitality to complete strangers. Can you imagine casually walking around the centre of London and bumping into an English stranger, who invites you into his home and then tells you that he will sort out a place for you to stay with his family members in Birmingham, Liverpool and Edinburgh? Oh, and he'll travel with you for one section of the journey and get his brother to go with you on the next just to make sure that you make it there OK!

The latest Haghighi household to have adopted us belongs to Dr. Haghighi's sister, who lives here with her seven children (I think it's seven, but it's easy to lose count) and has warmly welcomed us to stay for as long as we like. Miss. Haghighi happens to cook the finest Persian stews available and our days seem mostly to revolve around the eating of them.

Sitting on the floor with a tablecloth spread out before us and about ten hungry bodies crowded around, Will and I agitatedly readjust our positions to find any one at all comfortable, but do not find one before it is time to rise again. All this floor-dwelling has really taken our chair-cosseted English backsides by surprise and when we're not sitting around the dining tablecloth, we move a maximum of five metres across the room to take up a similarly uncomfortable horizontal position upon another piece of floor space – the perfect setting for Hokm, chai and shisha.

Now that Milad has returned home to Tehran we find ourselves without a natural translator, but a mixture of our improved Farsi and an awful lot of exaggerated gesturing generally seems to get the message across well enough. There is no doubt in our minds about our favourite member of this particular Haghighi family. That spot belongs solely and unequivocally to eldest son, Ehsan. The joker of the pack, this twenty-seven year-old has stolen our hearts with his comical card-playing manner (every time he wins a trick he shakes his hands in the air in triumph) and the cheeky way that he behaves towards his mother and youngest sister.

During the regular family mealtimes, when hand gesturing has been exhausted and conversation has run out of steam, Ehsan will pipe up with what has become his favourite joke. Turning towards his mother and pointing a hand towards her, Ehsan will ask us:

"Mama gambou?" which literally translates as "Mum fat?"

Miss Haghighi does indeed show signs of having given birth to seven children, but we do not feel it our place to agree, so we laugh, smile nervously and shake our heads.

This simply doesn't cut it for Ehsan, who turns to us again.

"Cam gambou?" he asks, bringing his index finger close to his thumb to signal to us that "cam" means "a little bit."

He nods in our direction again, encouraging us to agree, but we say nothing and laugh nervously for the second time.

Turning his attention to his sister, Shiva, who is a fourteen year-old with a healthy serving of puppy fat, Ehsan repeats the process and the whole family (Mama and Shiva included) burst into hysterics.

There is such wonderful warmth about the people here in Iran. Even in just the way that they speak there is a loving, almost musical, tone. Listening to a Persian speak Farsi is not dissimilar to hearing a Frenchman recite poetry. The sound of each word rolls delicately into the next and there is a gentleness underlying the tone. We love it here in Iran and it is proving very difficult to move on, especially because every time we hint at doing so, Ehsan simply will not allow us to leave.

"Farda" (tomorrow), this big teddy-bear insists, removing our bags from our shoulders and setting them down beside the stairs once again.

This is the second day that we have told Ehsan that we mean to leave, and it is the second day that we have packed our bags, asked Ehsan if he'll drive us to the east-bound road, and have then succumbed to his childlike plea for us to stay.

"OK Ehsan," we say. "Farda. But we mean it this time!"

Unfortunately it is this crucial last bit about the sincerity of our plea that passes our sweet-hearted friend by and, before long, he has come back at us with "Pas farda" – "the day after tomorrow." Now, I don't know if I've missed something here, but since when is it more desirable for a host to show hospitality than it is for a guest to receive it? Only in Iran!

DAY NINETY-THREE:
MR. FARSHI'S OFFICE, YAZD, YAZD PROVINCE, IRAN, SATURDAY 11TH OCTOBER 2008, 20.10

So this is it: our first day without a Haghighi in three weeks! We finally arrived in Yazd this evening – two days late for our scheduled rendezvous with a certain small Korean man – having left Ehsan and co. yesterday morning, only to wind up staying just 50km down the road with another Iranian family, whose offer of hospitality we simply could not refuse.

Given our tardiness, and the apparent danger of the upcoming eastern territories, I suppose it is just as well that Woo has decided not to come. We received an apologetic email from our friend last night, informing us of his decision to catch a plane, rather than face roads upon which several foreigners have apparently been abducted. Just a load of hype, we reckon, but I guess that only time will tell...

There were tears in Ehsan's eyes as he drove us to the edge of Shiraz after what had been one of our longest stays in any one city, and it wasn't only Ehsan who was upset. It truly felt as if the entire Haghighi family had been holding us hostage (in a good way) for the past three weeks – such was their insistence upon us remaining with them.

Ehsan's mother was one of the worst offenders. She had taken a particular shine to us ever since she learned that we believed in God. Even if we believe in slightly different versions of said deity, our umpteenth surrogate mother seemed happy just to know that we possessed some kind of guiding morality.

The basic premises of our faiths are the same – we believe in one God, whose mercy and grace covers over our iniquities – but there is a distinction between the way in which Christians and Muslims believe that one receives this gift of grace. Muslims believe that it is earned through good deeds and obedience to the rules of Islam, whereas Christians hold it as a matter of an undeserved gift for sinners.

This difference is more than just semantics and brings up quite a disparity between the two religions because Christians cannot believe that Muslims feel pressurised to live under the wrath of a God who carefully watches their every step and judges their every deed, whilst Muslims cannot believe that Christians believe that they don't have to do anything at all in order to be saved.

"There is no point in your religion then?" Miss Haghighi asked on our first day together – the only day that translator Milad was still available.

"You don't need to do anything at all to please God?" she continued, believing this to mean that people might abuse this freedom for all kinds of wrong.

"Yes and no" was our response. "Although we don't need to do anything to earn the grace, there is a responsibility to live a certain way because of it. Real Christians won't abuse it, and if they get it wrong once in a while, they know that they can come back and find forgiveness."

It was a fascinating conversation: two religions so very similar in their devout worship of the one God of grace and mercy and yet so very different in their responses to this deity. Miss Haghighi was not satisfied at all by our depreciation of grace, and we felt exactly the same in reverse!

It turns out that Ehsan's mother actually earns her keep through her work as a spiritual guru, but we reckon that she's more of a cross between a Muslim leader and a clairvoyant because she does seem to have a certain tendency to wander down the slightly more supernatural paths of thought. No sooner had we finished talking about grace than Miss Haghighi was asking to read our palms.

"What sort of Muslim is she?" we wondered, not expecting a follower of Islam to practice the sort of occultism that might be more at home in a superstitious sect than in a monotheistic religion.

Apparently Will and I are destined for long lives and I am either going to have two or four children (a multiple of two, she said), whilst Will is going to be rich. Quite how this can be gauged from the simple reading of a palm, I do not know, but Mama certainly got one thing right.

Turning to Will, she said: "You have a problem controlling your temper."

"Finally, someone else who agrees with me!" I joked. Will and I chuckled at what was a fairly accurate perception, but just when we were starting to wonder at the potential credibility of her insights, she went and spoiled it all by telling us that she knew this only because he had "hot hands." Come on now; you don't need to have any kind of supernatural/witch-doctoring powers to work that one out!

9. THE NOT-SO-STRAIGHTFORWARD ROAD TO PAKISTAN

DAY NINETY-FIVE:
SQ. SHOHADA, RAFSANJAN, KERMAN PROVINCE, IRAN, MONDAY 13TH OCTOBER 2008, 16.00

The journey continues, and Iran is still our home. Almost a month has gone by since we first set foot in this vast country and we have been travelling between Haghighi connections ever since. The latest of these – an old school friend of Milad's by the name of Aref – is scheduled to arrive any moment, whereupon he will pick up exactly where the super-hospitable Haghighis left off.

This is only our third Haghighi-less day and we are already feeling the withdrawal symptoms, but at least their absence has given us the opportunity to find out that there is a world outside of their family and, what's more, you don't necessarily need to be a Haghighi to be an incredibly hospitable Iranian host (although it probably helps).

So why is it that the Iranian people are so overwhelmingly hospitable? Well, we were given some insight into this question by a man named Mr. Farshi – boss and friend to a Mr. Hossein, who was our final chauffeur on the road between Shiraz and Yazd.

"A guest is a friend of God," Mr. Farshi began, leaning over the desk in his office.

"You see," he continued, "Mr. Hossein is a good man and it is the custom of all Iranians to help people in need – especially foreigners."

Sounds familiar, we thought, and this wonderful Islamic idea continues to help us out wherever we go in this country. Messieurs Farshi and Hossein teamed up to pamper us thoroughly during our two nights in Yazd – simply because we were foreigners. We were well-fed at Mr. F's place, sheltered at Mr. H's, and even provided with a free tour-guide to show us around the magnificent City of Yazd – a dust-encased dwelling, which feels like a cross between walking through a sandstorm and entering into a childhood dreamland rather as I would have imagined ancient Egypt to be.

* * * * *

As if our time in Yazd wasn't enough to prove that Iranian hospitality can exist outside of the Haghighi clan, just the day before we were treated to yet another sterling example.

Having left a tearful Ehsan behind on the outskirts of Shiraz, two lifts took us 50km up the road to a town called Marvdasht, and it was here that we met Mr. Jamshid. Beckoning us into his car – paying little regard to where it was that we wanted to go, or where it was that he was actually heading – our smiley friend took us on a short tour of the town, before taking us to his friend's house for a cuppa.

The reason for this unexpected detour was simple: we were foreigners and we seemed to be in trouble. Why else would we be standing in the middle of a foreign town, waving our arms around in the air? Mr. Jamshid had wanted to help us, but would not know how best to achieve this unless he first enlisted the help of a translator.

This was how we met Sama. A pretty young thing in her early twenties, Sama was training to be an English translator and knew Mr. Jamshid through his work as her family's lawyer. Warmly invited into yet another stranger's home, one chai turned into two and, before you knew it, we were playing Hokm, smoking shisha and had soon been persuaded to stay for the night.

I think the conversation went something like this:

Sama: "Would you like to stay for the night? It is my niece's birthday party this afternoon and we would like it if you came."

Will and I (after a short pause in which we considered the quandary between gaining only 50km in the last week and having an offer before us that we couldn't refuse): "Yes, that would be nice."

Needless to say, when party time arrived it was one of the most bizarre experiences of our lives. To find oneself not only being taken into a stranger's home (where we would be treated like kings, fed, pampered, and given a bed for the night), but then taken along to a nine year-old's birthday party as the celebrity guests – this was just a bit much!

In a room full of little girls, the only fellow male representatives were the girl's father and our favourite little person of the event – a curious, sage toddler with a powerful message written proudly across his chest: *Don't waste your energy.*

Of all the relatively meaningless English phrases that one might expect upon a jumper in a foreign country, this one fitted the subject down to a tee and the funniest thing about it all was that nobody other than ourselves had a clue what it meant. The little boy simply personified the slogan, remaining still and reflective upon his chair, whilst all the other children were expending their energy dancing.

Very occasionally the boy looked as if he was about to spring into life, raising one leg as if he were actually thinking about standing up, only to slump back again upon his chair. We felt sure that he would have pointed out the message on his jumper as his reason for being so slothful, if only he could do so without, in turn, breaking his golden rule.

Other than our simple amusement at this wonderful child, the party itself was not unlike a regular little girl's party back home. Beyond the distinct lack of males, all the usual suspects were present: a comical birthday cake (this time in the shape of a kangaroo), balloons for all to play with (except, of course, Mr. Lazy), party tunes and party hats, a fifteen year-old aunt (Sama's little sister) who was doing her best to shake things up with some hormone-induced *Beyonce* moves in inappropriately scant clothing, and the afternoon's entertainment, which came in the shape of two English lads and a guitar.

Once the niece had been suitably swept off her feet, it was back to Sama's for dinner, more shisha, more chai, yet further food, and even a second dose of Iran's finest opiate.

Before you start to worry about our probable addiction to what is apparently one of the world's most addictive drugs, there is a relatively credible story behind our latest binge.

Whilst playing Hokm with Sama and cousins in the back garden, we had been flicking through a few photographs from the trip until one particular shot took their attention.

Audible gasps and worried glances exchanged, Sama informed us of the seriousness of this particularly incriminating photograph.

"Do you know what that is?" she asked, pointing towards the substance that I could be seen to be inhaling.

Such accusation was there in her tone that half of me wanted to tell her that appearances can be deceiving, but it was honesty that came through in my answer.

"Er, yes," I replied, "But don't worry. It was just a one-off because we were told that it's part of Iranian culture."

Sama seemed content with the answer, but I was still feeling guilty as I stepped back inside the lounge, only to find, right there in front of my eyes, Sama's father and a group of his pals practising the very devilry that his daughter had been so quick to denounce!

"What's all this rubbish about opium being bad for you, Sama?" I inquired, having quickly rejoined the group outside.

"You'll never guess what I just saw, Will!" I continued. "Sama's dad's only blooming well doing opium in the very next room!"

"Well, that doesn't make it right," Sama responded. "It may be part of the tradition for the older generation in Iran, but that doesn't mean it isn't still bad for you!"

Of course Sama was right, but that didn't stop us from heading inside to join the party.

"So, it's true what they say about opium then," Will remarked. "One puff and you're hooked."

The next morning we bade Sama and family a fond and thankful farewell and made our way back to the road to Yazd. One bumpy ride in a trucker's cabin later and we had made it to the junction where Mr. Hossein found us. The rest, as they say (in France), est l'histoire.

DAY NINETY-SEVEN:
CATAMARAN, KISH-BOUND, BANDAR LENGEH, SOMEWHERE IN THE PERSIAN GULF, IRAN, WEDNESDAY 15TH OCTOBER 2008, 12.57PM

The situation we now find ourselves in is bordering upon the laughable. Yesterday we managed an epic 750km hitch from Rafsanjan all the way to the Persian Gulf. This fifteen-hour, marathon hitch saw us head east to Kerman, south to Bandar Abbas, and even a little (200km or so) west to Bandar Lengeh.

Now, why on earth would we decide to come all this way when Pakistan was but a stone's throw away from us in the opposite direction? The answer is simple: once again we find ourselves at the mercy of our second major rule – never to refuse an offer.

Ever since parting company with the Haghighis on Friday morning, we have felt that something has been missing, so when we received a phone call from Shabnam on Monday night to ask us if we fancied a free holiday on an island in the Persian Gulf, we took one quick look at a map, decided that the island could be at least construed as being *relatively* on the way to Pakistan, and immediately agreed.

The one small problem that we now encounter comes as a result of our latest piece of lost property: the small matter of one fifth of our earnings from our time as English teachers in Tehran. The Doctor paid us with five 500,000 Rial notes (each worth about £25), but somehow – whether it was lost or stolen we do not know – I managed to mislay one of those pretty valuable notes during our time with Ehsan's family in Shiraz. Now, this wouldn't be too much of an issue if we hadn't already spent almost all of the other 2 million Rials, or if we were closer to Pakistan (where, we hope, they will actually have cash machines that work), but, sadly, neither of these things is true.

In fact, we now have only 60,000 Rials to our names, which might sound like quite a lot, but actually works out as about three quid – not a lot of money when one is on one's way to the most expensive tourist resort in Iran.

Shabnam and Elham, who will join us out on Kish, are well aware of our predicament and have kindly offered to pay, but they do not arrive until tomorrow and our remaining three pounds have somehow got to last us until then.

We are in a bit of a quandary really, and, once again, it is entirely of our own creation. If only we had decided to use the 750km of hitch-ability in a more Pakistani direction we would be there by now. As it is, though, we have added about 2,000km to our journey entirely on a whim. Lord, help us!

* * * * *

Not in our wildest dreams could we have expected to reach the port at Bandar Lengeh in one day (especially given that we had barely covered 150km by lunchtime), but a 400km afternoon hitch, split evenly between a charming young couple from Kerman and a trucker named Mohammed, saw us to Bandar Abbas by sundown, and we saw no reason to stop there.

Recommencing hitching at 8.30pm, conditions were far from ideal. During the night, *recommended* hitching criteria – such as good visibility, space to pull in, and cars moving slowly – become *essential* hitching criteria and, given that we were on a motorway exit with no hard shoulder and no street lighting, optimism was all but spent. It had been a long, hard day as it was, and now we were starting out on a nigh on impossible 200km of further hitching in total darkness.

Hopelessly flailing our arms at bemused passers by, desperation soon set in. We were in the middle of absolutely nowhere, with no sign of a place to find food, water or refuge. To make matters worse, the darkness and our tiredness had combined to set us both on edge. Looking out across desert-like terrain in every direction, we felt sure that we could hear the noises and make out the shadows of bandits hiding behind hillocks, just waiting for the right moment to pounce.

Hysteria was creeping in, and we were so jittery that we took hitchhiking to a new ethical low, taking it in turns to play dead on the side of the road while the other person frantically waved for help. Yet even our best efforts at deception were getting us nowhere and we soon reverted to the wild flailing of arms and legs until, eventually, a car slammed on its brakes and skidded off onto the dirt on the opposite side of the road – just about avoiding a full-on collision with the hillock and any evildoers therein.

So elated were we that somebody had stopped that we didn't bother with our usual checks regarding whether or not the man might harbour murderous tendencies and whether or not he might want money for his services. In fact, we didn't even say one word to the man until we had been driving along for a good ten minutes, about which time we figured it best to check that a) he was actually going in the right direction; b) he didn't mind us free-riding; and c) he wasn't going to slay us and take us home for supper.

Language barriers being what they are, we were in no position to charm the man with our wit, so it was just as well that we possessed one piece of equipment that was sure to dissuade the man from wishing us harm. This "equipment" was a letter that Milad had drafted for us during our time in Shiraz – right about the time when he was worried about our safety through the ensuing eastern territories – in which he had informed all persons to whom the letter was given that we were actually very nice people who were doing this thing for charity known as "hitchhiking." The trouble was that nobody in Iran would know what "hitchhiking" was; nor would they understand what it had to do with charity. Thus, Milad explained, he thought it best to embroider the truth a little by telling the Iranian masses that they should offer us help because we were, in part, travelling in order to support world peace!

It was this dubious letter that had helped us describe our intentions in the absence of an Iranian hitchhiking partner, and it was this letter that we now passed forward to our latest, rather shifty-looking, aide. Sadly, Alireza, as was his name, was not quite as impressed as those good citizens of Marvdasht and Yazd who went out of their way to feed and to house us. In fact, the notion of world peace seemed to displease Alireza so much that he proceeded to slam on his brakes and gesture that we were to leave his car unless we could cough up some dosh – or so we understood by his aggressive tone, exaggerated gesticulating, and the rubbing together of forefinger and thumb.

"Bebakhshid (sorry)," we protested, "But why don't you focus upon all the good things that Milad has written about us? Come on, don't you realise that we're ambassadors for world peace?"

Alireza seemed less than convinced, but he didn't throw us out then and there, so his perception of us can't have been all bad. No, Alireza waited until the next town to do that, whereupon we were swiftly ejected from the vehicle and off Alireza whizzed in a huff, parting with one simple word.

"Lengeh," he grunted, pointing an arm in the direction that we had been travelling, before spinning around and zooming off the opposite way.

Our new spot matched up perfectly to our essential night-time hitching criteria, and it wasn't long before a far more smiley couple of gents had pulled over to lend a hand.

One of them even spoke a little English, which made the next bit – where they dropped us off in a deserted village – that fraction less daunting.

"Lengeh seventy kilometre, you stop here one hour, brother come you take," the "English speaker" told us, which, for those not fluent in the art of Eng-arsi, means: "Bandar Lengeh is seventy kilometres in this direction and in only one hour's time my brother will come back and take you there."

"Wonderful," we thought, and slumped down upon our bags at the side of the road, whilst we took in our surroundings.

The derelict village in which we sat cannot have been made up of more than twenty houses, each of which were sporadically dotted around the dusty streets that hemmed us in. Over on the horizon a hill dusted itself down after the latest onslaught of the wind, whilst a solitary street lamp shone down behind us to reveal the shadows of two lonely white men.

It is funny how swiftly perceptions can change. In only twenty minutes of waiting (during which the grand total of three cars and one wandering villager had passed us by), we had moved from a position of absolute confidence in our friend's promise, to one of distinct uncertainty and fear.

There was no way that we were going to sit around in this ghost town and wait for some ghoul to have his way with us. Panic prompted us to leap to our feet and shoot out our thumbs, and as if we had blown upon some magical conch, who should come our way but two local policemen, who took it upon themselves to put up a police blockade and stop all passing drivers until they had found one willing to take us to Lengeh.

An old man named Mohammed was the one to heed the call and about an hour later we finally arrived in Lengeh – some fifteen hours since leaving Aref's in Rafsanjan! Mohammed seemed like a nice enough sort, so we decided to start cheekily testing the water to see if he might know somewhere that we could stay for free that night... "Maybe with you?" we joked, knowing that the man had no grasp of English.

Mohammed didn't get it and seemed insistent that we should find ourselves a hotel, but we were desperate to hold on to what little money we had and repeated our favourite slogan of the moment: "no money, no money."

And then it came to us. The answer was simple. Ehsan had given us an Iranian SIM card back in Shiraz and all that we had to do was to call any one of our Haghighi friends and they would be able to intercede for us. Without a moment's thought, Shabnam's number was dialled and we handed the phone to Mohammed. Oh, how I wish that we hadn't...

DAY NINETY-EIGHT:
MOHAMMED'S/OUR HOUSE, KISH, HORMOZGĀN PROVINCE, PERSIAN GULF COAST, IRAN, THURSDAY 16TH OCTOBER 2008, 10.49AM

What were we thinking? Why didn't we just ring Iman? Why, of all the Haghighis that we could have chosen, did we pick Shabnam?

Mohammed drove us straight to the plush Diplomat Hotel, where we sat in the lobby, whilst Mohammed chatted at length with the owner of the hotel.

"There's something really wrong about that guy," Shabnam had told us, as soon as Mohammed had handed back our phone. "He said he's going to take you to a hotel. When you get there, go to the toilet and give me a call so we can talk in private."

To be honest, Will and I thought Shabnam was making a big fuss over nothing. What was all the fuss about? So we'd called a friend and that friend happened to be a girl. So what? No doubt Shabnam was working herself into a frenzy, but what for?

When Will eventually found his way to the toilet to give Shabnam a call, he was to be subjected to a tirade of questions.

"Where did you meet him? Why did you phone me? Do you know he asked me for Ehsan's number? And Iman's! I think he's in the Secret Police!"

"All right Shab Shabs, calm down," Will replied. "We'll be fine. We haven't done anything wrong, have we?"

"No, but that's not the point," she snapped. "You know how dangerous it is for us to mix with foreigners, especially those of the opposite sex! Why didn't you just phone Iman?"

Good question. I suppose that we hadn't really given it enough thought. It was the sisters who were the best English speakers and it was they who were supposed to meet us in Kish. Surely that was enough of a reason? Not for Shabnam. Shabi was incensed and, apparently, so too was her sister.

Once Will returned from the lavatory, we concluded that the girls were probably making mountains out of molehills again and decided to use our time more efficiently by casually strolling up to the hotel owner, Abdullah, to inquire whether he had any rooms available for the evening... "Free of charge, of course."

Abdullah was stalling. He told us that they might be able to sort us out, but we must first wait for the police to come, so that they could check our passports and make sure that we were legit.

Police? Blimey! What was going on? Why was such a fuss being made over one simple phone call to a friend? Sitting down again upon the cushy sofas in the lobby, we decided to let nature take its course. Will had told Shabi not to worry, and that was all that we could do.

* * * * *

Mohammed had long since departed when the police finally arrived to check our passports, read Milad's letter, and request a song on the guitar! Satisfied enough with what they had seen and heard, they didn't stay long, and we were left to receive a free room in the Diplomat, courtesy of Abdullah and the Secret Police.

Safely inside our room, we sent the girls a few jokey texts detailing our imprisonment and their own likely capture in the imminent future, but, once we had ascertained that they really were quite worried about us, we decided to save the rest of the jokes for each other.

Half an hour later we received a telephone call from a still-agitated Shabnam, who gave us an earful about being "stupid," getting them into "trouble," and how it was lucky for us that The Doctor had got involved. Apparently Mohammed had survived talking to Iman's father for all of one minute before apologising for his mistake and fleeing, tail between his legs.

We've got friends in high places, don't you know.

DAY NINETY-EIGHT: (CONTINUED...)
THE RED ROOM, KISH, HORMOZGĀN PROVINCE, PERSIAN GULF COAST, IRAN, THURSDAY 16TH OCTOBER 2008, 16.24

We'd evidently made such a good impression upon Abdullah at the impromptu police concert the previous night that we were invited to star as the guest musicians at his friend's wedding at the weekend, and would surely have accepted the offer had we not already made plans.

Thanking Abdullah for his hospitality (albeit rather begrudging), we took our remaining three hundred thousand Rials in hand and waltzed our way to the shipping office to try and persuade a friendly agent into giving us a free ride.

It wasn't to be. We've become rather used to this free transport malarkey and we didn't let up without a substantial fight, but eventually had to concede that this island-hop wasn't really part of the Malaysian-directed hitch anyway and we were just going to have to part with 240,000 big ones to get ourselves across.

And it was in this predicament that you found us yesterday lunchtime, sitting upon a Kish-bound catamaran, virtually penniless, rather hopeless, and utterly helpless to do anything about it. We were soon to arrive upon an expensive touristy island without any means of sustenance or shelter to comfort us. The sweetcorn sandwiches that we had managed to prize from the ship's captain were already long forgotten and we knew that a second spate of begging would soon be required if we were to survive the next stint of the trip.

Scouring the decks for any friendly soul who might lend us a hand, we never expected help to make its way to us of its own accord. However, this is exactly what happened, thanks to the friendliest face of them all – that of our favourite Mohammed to date.

Banish if you can, all previous preconceptions of Mohammeds, because this Mohammed was far superior to his namesakes. A stocky, middle-aged chap, with a scattering of wispy white hair upon his otherwise balding head, this Mohammed approached us only because he wanted to see what card game it was that we were playing.

"Hokm," we answered, but dejection must have been written over our faces because Mohammed soon inquired if there was anything wrong.

Probably just another tarof, we thought, and reluctantly handed over Milad's letter to the stranger. But no, our newest Mohammed was really interested in us, and asked if there was anything that he could do to help.

"Well," I replied, glancing nervously at my companion as I considered how strange it felt to be in such a position of dependence. "We don't have any money left."

"... Nor do we have anywhere to stay," added Will, before we both turned away from Mohammed's sympathetic eye and considered how shameful it felt to beg.

Our new friend didn't leave us wallowing for long, and moved swiftly to relieve our discomfort. Feeling for his wallet, Mohammed pulled out a whopping two hundred thousand Rials (about ten quid) and firmly placed them into my hands. My instinctive reaction was to push the money back in the direction from whence it came, but Mohammed was having none of it.

"Kheli, Kheli Mamnoon (Thank you)." The words took a while in coming. Not because we weren't thankful, but simply because we were astounded by this stranger's generosity.

Mohammed shook his head, seeking to diminish the value of the gesture, before even apologising that he could not do more!

"I'm very sorry," he said. "My family and I are flying home to Tehran tonight. Otherwise you could have come to stay with us."

Words would not come. This lovely man had brought us to tears – tears borne of a mixture of joy, sadness, embarrassment and relief – and now we just could not speak. Mohammed bowed his head towards us – a humble sign of respect to two undeserving souls – and went to rejoin his family a few rows in front.

Will and I just sat there for a moment, looking down at the paper money that was still loosely placed in my outstretched palm. Eventually my hand moved of its own accord, squeezing the notes, and proceeding to wedge them securely into the front of the money-belt hidden underneath my t-shirt.

Motionless silence resumed. Will and I were simply overwhelmed by yet another new level of generosity.

"I don't know how much more of this I can take," I said. "The people here are just too good to us."

Will nodded slowly several times, seemingly unaware of the motion, as we contemplated the abundance of good deeds recently showered upon us.

Five minutes later Mohammed came back, a warm smile across his face, and handed me another piece of paper.

"Here is our address, written in Farsi. When you have got through Customs, show this to a taxi driver and come to our house for some food."

And with that, our friend smiled, and left.

* * * * *

An hour later we would arrive at Mohammed's apartment in Kish, where we would be properly introduced to his wife, nephew and sister in law – a trio we had noticed previously only because their cumulative weight seemed enough to sink a small fleet of ships.

"I suppose we'll have to look elsewhere for some food," we had joked, as we watched these three whales waddle down the aisle. "They'll want to eat it all themselves."

Who'd have thought that just a few hours later we would be sitting in their very own apartment, feasting upon their food – of which, as you might expect, there was plenty to go around?

Humbled, soon we would be standing inside the doors of their apartment, keys in hand, waving goodbye to the kindest of hosts, who had left two complete strangers in charge of their home.

Mohammed, in parting, gave us both a warm kiss on the cheek. He certainly didn't feel like a stranger any longer. He had quickly become a friend, and his kindness extended so far that he even arranged for his wife's cousin (who lives in Kish) to come over later that evening to take us out for dinner and show us around the city.

And so it was that at about 9pm, we were taken out for yet more food with cousin Benham, and treated to a tour of Kish's version of that worldwide phenomenon: yes, yet another shopping mall. This time, however, we felt little grievance. His family had shown us enough generosity to compensate for the most calamitous of errors. We could stomach a visit to another shopping mall. After all, we'll probably be connoisseurs of malls before long, and those sorts of skills are clearly transferable worldwide.

Shopping mall cravings indulged, we ended the night with a romantic stroll along the first beach that we had seen since way back at Excrement Lake. The water was warm and, thankfully, this time there were to be no nasty surprises lurking beneath its gleaming turquoise surface. No, this was the perfect end to an altogether splendid day, which finished in the comfort of yet another Iranian stranger's home.

DAY ONE HUNDRED:
THE RED ROOM, HIRED VILLA, KISH, HORMOZGĀN PROVINCE, PERSIAN GULF COAST, IRAN, SATURDAY 18TH OCTOBER 2008, 11.29AM

"Grandad!" was all Elham could say, before her lips gave way to sobs.

The news was not unexpected, but any death is bound to cause great upset. Way back in Tehran, Iman had mentioned their grandad's deteriorating condition, and we had visited the aged man a few times during our stay in Shiraz – tremendously difficult occasions for all concerned.

Ushered past the prostrate form of an ageing man – seeing only enough to consider that this may well have been the greatest number of tubes either of us had ever seen attached to a human being – and taken into another room, Will and I felt completely out of place.

Yet, if our predicament seemed hard, much worse was the situation for family members. The first time we went, Shabnam couldn't even stomach looking at her grandad in such an unhealthy state, and came quickly to join us in the other room, where she covered her mouth with her hands, letting out only silent sobs, so as not to further humiliate the dying man.

Mr. Haghighi Snr. had been suffering from the terribly debilitating condition of Alzheimer's for several years now, and his health had been in steady decline ever since. Although the news of his death will not have shocked the sisters, they are of course upset, and I feel absolutely powerless to do anything at all to help.

Words just would not come to me as I saw the two girls breaking down in front of me. No "sorry," no words of encouragement; only a sombre grimace and a few sympathetic tears, which, themselves, may well have been unhelpful. This is family business, and nothing Will or I could do or say is going to change the way our friends feel.

The sisters have been with us in Kish for only a little over two days, but already they are back at the airport, seeking to switch their return tickets to Tehran for the first available flight to Shiraz.

The customary way to treat a family member's death in Iran seems to be for the whole family to unite as quickly as possible at the home of the deceased. I suppose that in some respects this is similar to the way in which families will travel across the length and breadth of England for funerals, but the Iranian response is much more immediate. Every family member will leave whatever it is that he or she was doing and hasten to be with the family for however long it takes until the funeral has been planned, taken place, and the family feels that all that is possible has been done to ensure that the nearest and dearest are supported.

So it is that Shabnam and Elham will no doubt be flying out of the country before Will (who is still asleep in the other room) even knows what's happening. I just don't know what to do with myself. I feel so numb, sitting here all alone in the lounge of the little apartment that has been our home for only two nights.

DAY ONE HUNDRED AND ONE:
BANDAR, KISH, HORMOZGĀN PROVINCE, PERSIAN GULF COAST, IRAN, SUNDAY 19TH OCTOBER 2008, 11.19AM

We have parted ways with the Haghighi family for what (surely now) will be the last time. Shabnam and Elham have boarded the early morning flight to Shiraz, whilst Will and I are heading (much more resolutely, this time) in a Pakistani direction.

This is the morning of our fifth and, we hope, our final day upon the sticky island of Kish, whose port we now inhabit as we wait in the hope of good news regarding what we have been told are potentially hazardous conditions out at sea – rather a strange prediction if you ask me, given that the sun is blazing down as gloriously as ever.

Our short stay in Kish has been just the respite that we needed to spur us on towards our next target. We are only sorry to have to leave this place with a slightly tainted perception of our dear friend Mohammed's cousin, Benham, who is the latest to fall foul of that old tyrant, tarof.

When the girls first arrived on the island on Thursday morning, Benham seemed more than happy to act as a go-between and even extended his generosity so far as to invite us all out for dinner later that night.

It had been a fun-filled evening for all concerned, we thought, and Benham seemed so glad of our company that he invited us all to join him watch the sunrise the following morning at six, but he never came. We waited until quarter past, and tried again and again to phone him, but there was no response.

Bemused, Will and I were determined to keep on trying because we simply could not conceive of a reason why our friend would suddenly decide not to answer our calls, especially having seemed so insistent upon our morning's rendezvous. And yet, the more we tried and failed, the more it became apparent that this might have been Benham's intention after all.

The girls didn't look in the least bit surprised.

"It's just tarof," they casually informed us, as if we should just accept it as the norm, and go back to bed.

"But it can't be," I protested. "We saw him only last night and he has been so generous to us. Why would he suddenly change his mind and arrange this meeting if he never intended to turn up?"

The same short answer came back at us.

"Tarof," said the girls, in unison, before they themselves headed back to bed.

This tarof thing is really starting to get on my nerves. What did we do wrong? Why couldn't Benham have just told us that he didn't want to see us, or at least made up some sort of excuse about being busy? Why tell us that he wanted to meet us if it was never his intention to do so? The whole idea behind this strange form of social practice boggles the mind, and we are at a loss even to begin to understand it.

We were sorry to leave our friendship with Benham on such a sour note because he and his family had been so very good to us, and we were sad that we might somehow have done something to offend or to displease them. Perhaps the poor chap simply got tired of us and didn't have the heart to tell us so. Whatever his reason, we wish he had at least declared it.

DAY ONE HUNDRED AND ONE: (CONTINUED...)
CAPTAIN'S CABIN, THE ARVA, SOMEWHERE IN THE PERSIAN GULF, IRAN, SUNDAY 19TH OCTOBER 2008, 13.21

It has taken us three attempts to crack the technique, but we're finally doing it. We're hitching on a boat! Apparently there aren't any going to Lengeh today, but we've managed to find ourselves a ride on a boat heading about 100km further west to a place called Chorak. We're already friendly with the captain of the ship, who has invited us to his personal cabin for lunch, and assured us that he can persuade one of the many truckers on board to give us a lift in the right direction. Well, I say *assured* us, but, actually, he – like the rest of the people on board – does not speak a word of English. We are only guessing that this is what he was getting at when, after we had shown him Milad's letter, and said "Bandar Abbas" and "Pakistan" a few times, the captain nodded, winked, and mouthed something in Farsi... With any luck he can read minds.

My own mind now returns to the comical circumstances that greeted our arrival at the port this morning. Seeking refuge from the unrelenting heat outside, we approached an officious-looking chap and asked, simply:

"Boat? Today? What time?", pointing to our watch at the appropriate juncture and doing what we considered to be a pretty good impression of what a human-shaped boat might look like if it were leaving a port.

The man was unimpressed and said only:

"Today. No. Boat"

"I'm sorry?" enquired Will. "What do you mean?"

The man seemed rather aggravated that we hadn't left him yet and, saying nothing, pointed us in the direction of another official.

Slightly concerned by the pessimism of the first man, we hoped the second might be better versed in English and generally a little more optimistic, but found only another frank response:

"Today, bad weather. No boat."

Frustrated now by what was simply a blatant lie, we assured him that it was, in fact, lovely weather, and that if he would just step outside for a moment, he would surely agree, and we could be on our way.

The man seemed unconvinced and only repeated himself again, a little louder.

"Today, bad weather. No boat!"

Well this just will not do, we thought. With no money remaining, we could not afford to stay in Kish for another day, even if we wanted to.

"There must be *one* boat leaving," we protested. "No passenger boat. We no want passenger boat. No passenger. We crew." A mixture of bitty sentences like these – with all the crucial words in place and none of the petty constraints of syntax – and the man seemed to get the message.

"I check phone," he said, picking up the receiver to talk (we assumed) with various ship captains.

"OK. One boat," he said shortly after, in exactly the same tone of disinterest.

Soon we were following our new friend through the port, past various different ships (which all looked as though they might very well set sail in the near future), until we reached *The Arva*. Here, our friend stopped, signalled that we were to climb aboard, and went off on his merry way, seemingly happy just to have offloaded the responsibility of two potential troublemakers.

We had never really doubted that we would find a boat – despite many suggestions to the contrary – and we have now made friends with the bulk of the cabin crew on this ship, and are confident that they will sort us out with everything that we need. We are shortly to arrive in Chorak, from where we hope to be taken in a truck anywhere in the direction of Pakistan.

Who knows exactly where we will be, come sundown? Penniless as we are, we have no idea what we are going to do for food or sleep tonight, but Persian hospitality has helped us survive thus far, and I have the sneakiest suspicion we can last another night. Our hope for the rest of today is simple: by the end of the evening we want to be as far as possible on our way towards Pakistan. Tomorrow, inshallah, we will finally say goodbye to fair Iran.

DAY ONE HUNDRED AND TWO:
HOSSAIN'S HOTEL, BANDAR ABBAS, HORMOZGĀN
PROVINCE, IRAN, MONDAY 20TH OCTOBER 2008, 12.54PM

A highly frustrating morning has found us no further along in our journey east than we were at 8pm last night. Our good friends on *The Arva* did indeed find us a ride to Bandar Abbas, but we have made no progress since then, and this is partly, if not solely, the fault of Hossain.

We first met this thirty-two year-old, son of a hotel owner, last night, upon walking into his hotel lobby to try and persuade him into giving us a free bed for the night.

"How much is it for a room?" we asked, more out of curiosity than an intention to cough up the required amount.

"Twenty dollars," came the blunt reply. He'd clearly noticed that we were foreigners. It cost us eight dollars in Tabriz and Bandar Abbas isn't exactly paradise city! From what we have seen of this grotty harbour town, we aren't going to be making plans for a return visit anytime soon, so this lofty price tag didn't seem quite right.

"Do you do celebrity reductions?" I asked, pushing Milad's letter into the Hossain's hand.

"You see, the thing is..." added Will. "We're broke. I don't suppose that there is any chance we could stay for free? I don't know, maybe if you have a spare room at the end of the night, for instance?"

Hossain raised an eyebrow. He was clearly surprised by our level of cheekiness, but we could sense him warming to us by the minute. After a moment's pause, and a quick phone call to dad, he agreed that if no paying customer had arrived by midnight, the room would be ours.

Wonderful. It was just after 8pm. Now all we had to do was to find some way to kill four hours – easy when one has a guitar and a willing Iranian audience. Next door to Hossain's hotel was a restaurant, and it wasn't long before an impromptu concert had been put together, matching the best of the local talents with the best of Britain... or just Will Jackson.

Four hours later and I was pulling my hair out, having listened (over and over again) to the same half a dozen songs that I'd heard every day since leaving home. At least the event had filled the time and, as soon as midnight struck, we were ushered upstairs for what was to be a free night in the laundry room.

OK, so it wasn't the Ritz, but we had become paupers again and were in no position to be picky. There was plenty of bedding available and we soon fell asleep, contented by Hossain's suggestion that he knew people in this town, and might well be able to get us a ride to Zahedan the next day. Actually, let me rephrase that. Hossain unequivocally *assured* us that he had a friend who would be driving to Zahedan on the morrow, but that morrow has long-since arrived and, after a further four hours of waiting, there is still no sign of this "friend," whilst Hossain just sits casually at his desk.

It is the uncertainty and the aimlessness of our plight that most frustrates us. We are not in control. Even though there are about twenty trucks outside (this seems to be a hotspot for them), Hossain bluntly refuses to allow us to talk to them, reassuring us that he will provide all we need, but there is simply no sign that his promise will be fulfilled, and so we wait, harassed by uncertainty.

DAY ONE HUNDRED AND TWO: (CONTINUED...)
HOSSAIN'S HOTEL, BANDAR ABBAS, HORMOZGĀN PROVINCE, IRAN, MONDAY 20TH OCTOBER 2008, 14.33

And still we wait. Two hours have been and gone, and the only activity worth reporting is the arrival of Hossain's brother, who must have been informed of our presence by Hossain, and has brought his own guitar so that he and Will can have a jam!

Unbelievable! Hossain is just using us as minor celebrities for his friends and family, stalling from letting us go so that he can show us off to everyone he knows.

"Hossain!" I snapped recently. "Where is that friend of yours who is supposed to be taking us to Zahedan? We have been here for six hours now, on top of the four last night, and all we do is sit and play guitar!"

The story develops into its next chapter as Hossain tells me that, in fact, it isn't a trucker friend that we await, but Hossain's cousin, who works *with* truckers. Apparently (and that's the operative word) we will be taken to the trucker stop on the edge of town (where his cousin works) and there we will "easily" find an overnight ride to Zahedan. *Apparently* we would not find any trucks going such distances during the day. They all wait until nightfall, when the roads will be clearer and conditions much less likely to result in an engine overheating.

And so I sit down again, doing nothing, and wait (again) for an unspecified amount of time. The time for losing patience is well and truly past; the time has come for surrendering to apathy. Thoughts such as, *well it couldn't get any worse anyway*, come to mind, as still we wait. Will we ever reach Pakistan? The only definitive answer that can be given is that we certainly will not do so today.

DAY ONE HUNDRED AND FOUR:
PAKISTANI BORDER HOUSE, NR. MIRJAVEH, SISTAN AND BALUCHISTAN PROVINCE, IRAN, WEDNESDAY 22ND OCTOBER 2008, 0.00AM

"If you sport, your body can be better than this." These words, spoken by the enigmatic Hossain, still haunt me tonight. I am thoroughly fed up with my ridiculous body now and it doesn't help that I am regularly confronted by comments regarding the major issues: hideous feet, scrawny frame, chicken legs, gappy teeth, puny upper body and, worst of all, my concave chest, which has become affectionately referred to as "the pitfall."

Oh, how I detest this ridiculous body. Ever since I was old enough to consider vanity, I have been unable to take it very seriously because of many a natural idiosyncrasy about my person. I suppose that I should be grateful for having a healthy body that works and, rather ironically, one that is actually quite good for sport, but I do wish it wasn't quite so hideous.

* * * * *

We finally made it out of the frustrating mire that was being stuck in a grotty hotel in the middle of Bandar Abbas, but not until well into Monday evening. In the end, Hossain's promises all failed us – every one of them. His cousin never came, he did not take us to a truck bound for Zahedan, and he generally seemed much more helpless than he wanted us to believe.

He and his brother did at least eventually drive us to the start of the road towards Zahedan (a destination that was still some 750km away) and we took care to avoid being too hard on the poor chap, given that he had clearly enjoyed our brief friendship and was sorry not to have been able to help us more.

We were left at a police blockade on the edge of the city, where Hossain had a quick word with the official to let him know of our intentions, and the fact that we didn't have any money. We thanked Hossain, and waited patiently in the police depot whilst, for the second time in a few days, a policeman was stopping drivers until he found one going our way – I think we need more of that kind of friendly officiating back home.

Sure enough, before the sun had completely set on us, we were inside the cabin of the friendliest of drivers. A young Afghan by the name of Saeed, clad in an angelic white robe, beamed at us, bowed his head, and attempted to communicate to us that he was driving home to Afghanistan, but had a delivery to make in Zahedan on his way through to Kabul.

For the briefest of moments we deliberated going with Saeed the whole way to Kabul, but decided that it probably wasn't the safest or most feasible option. If it weren't for the fact that we didn't possess Afghan visas – nor was it very likely to be one of those over-the-counter transactions – we may well have gone to Kabul, but it's probably just as well that we didn't.

The twenty-hour journey to Zahedan was relatively painless. Split into two chunks, Saeed took a pit stop in Bam (the halfway marker) at 2am for a four-hour kip – during which he kindly vacated the truck and went and slept on the pavement outside, giving Will and me the luxury of his cabin bunk. An hour before the nap, we had stopped to fill the truck with countless bags of rice (which, he proudly made known, were to be sold in Afghanistan at a high premium) and for two hours after it we had to wait in a queue for petrol. Petrol pumps are few and far between in this part of the world, so drivers must plan their routes very carefully in order not to run out. We're getting a good insight into the secret life of truckers, learning that there are certain patterns that they all follow. There must have been over one hundred trucks parked by the side of the road in Bam, and all of them seemed to be doing the Bandar-Abbas-to-Zahedan run during the cooler hours of night.

We finally arrived in Zahedan at 1pm this afternoon and gave our smiley friend (who sported quite possibly the best beard of the trip thus far) the warmest of thanks, before jumping out of his vehicle and finding ourselves in what felt much like a barren wasteland. The dusty road seemed to go on for miles in each direction and we felt unusually uneasy, remembering the words of warning that we had been fed by so many of our friends about Zahedan.

"Our parents won't even let us go there, and we're Iranian!" Elham had said.

"It too dangerous. I fly over," Woo had warbled.

There was a chilling feel about the place, but we couldn't work out if this was due mainly to the fear that had been drummed into us, and we certainly weren't going to let ourselves get caught up in the hysteria for too long.

"Let's not get carried away," we decided, "but perhaps it would be sensible to adopt a more cautious approach for our final push to the border."

The problem was that, when one is hitchhiking, there really are no precautions which one can take. Caution is thrown to the wind and a hitcher commits himself completely to the good will of each and every passer-by. We were just going to have to do what we always did and rely upon the innate integrity of mankind to see us through to the border at Mirjaveh, which still stood some distance away.

Sure enough, both the allegedly dangerous path to Zahedan, and apparently treacherous road from there to the border, proved to be gross exaggerations. The only momentary unease came in the form of the police escort that was forced upon us for the last five kilometres, when our own hitching wagon was pulled over and we were told to wait by the side of the road for an officer who would take us the rest of the way.

When Alireza, our chosen officer, eventually came, we were astonished to see that an "escort" to the border simply meant that we now had to hitchhike with one extra. We had assumed that an army vehicle was soon to drive by, whereupon we would be chaperoned the rest of the way within it, but all that happened was that we had been ousted from one vehicle, told to wait for an escort, and now our "escort" was doing the very same thing that we had been doing before – flagging down cars at the side of the road.

The trouble with being obliged to accept an escort is that this service apparently comes with a price. When we eventually made the border, our chaperone stuck out his hand and asked for money. We were incensed. We had never asked for an escort, and the escort that we were forced into having had slowed us down on a journey that we could very well have made on our own.

Instead of leading us to the border gates, Alireza, who had commandeered our passports, led us into an army guesthouse, where two other officers were sitting, watching TV. Now, not only had we lost hold of our passports, but also we were outnumbered.

"Take us to the border," I demanded. "We want to go to Pakistan. Please give us our passports back."

"Border closed today," Alireza protested, quite calmly. "You go Pakistan tomorrow."

"I cannot believe this!" I shouted to Will. "Not only is this man trying to cheat us out of our money, but now he is just patently lying to us."

"Give us our passports back!" I repeated, completely forgetting myself and squaring up to the gun-wielding officer who shielded our paperback lifelines behind his back. Thankfully, the other two guards stayed relatively inactive throughout, and simply repeated their friend's suggestion that the border was closed.

As I continued to wrestle with the officer, Will seized his chance and pinched the passports from behind Alireza's back. Storming off, Will and I marched towards the border, Alireza following close behind us and calling after us to stop.

"Border closed today," he repeated. "You go Pakistan tomorrow!"

"We'll just see about that," I muttered, underneath my breath, taking the passports back from Will and fastening them safely inside the money belt once again.

"Steve, slow down mate!" Will shouted, as I raced off towards the border. "We don't want to get shot!"

"He's not going to shoot us, mate. He lied to us and just wants our money. Come on!" I protested, as we continued to march ahead of our poor escort, who now seemed resigned to the fact that we would reach the border before him and find out that he was a fraud.

Except that, when we eventually arrived at the border, there was not another soul to be seen and a great chain hung over the iron gates, hemming us in.

"Border closed," Alireza puffed, having just about caught up with us.

Will and I just stood there, hands tightly clasping the iron bars of the gate and heads bowed in disbelief. Were we ever going to get to Pakistan? Why was the border shut? It was only about four o'clock. Would the border ever open again? Were we going to have to go somewhere else? What on earth were we going to do now that we had offended the only man who could possibly help us?

Slowly we turned around to look at the young officer. I was just about able to mouth an apology, and we scuffed our heels along the dusty floor as we trudged back to the barracks. The following thirty minutes were incredibly embarrassing. His two colleagues had not moved one muscle between them, and didn't seem at all surprised to see us again. It was just as well that they didn't know the phrase, "I told you so," because the truth of that comment might well have caused us to implode – such was the combination of tiredness, frustration and embarrassment now overwhelming us.

"I can't believe you got into a fight with an Iranian officer!" Will said to me, after we had been chaperoned into our free though unwelcome dormitory for the night.

"What do you mean?" I replied. "You were the one that stole the passports!"

"Ah come on Steve!" said Will. "You were pushing him around. What were you thinking?"

I had no response. Stretching out upon my bed – the position in which you still find me – I tried as best I could to process all that had gone on in the past day and, with it, all that we have experienced in an incredible five and a half weeks in Iran. Tomorrow, inshallah, the gates will finally open to welcome us into Pakistan.

10. A WORLD WITHOUT WOMEN

DAY ONE HUNDRED AND EIGHT:
GEONET OFFICE, QUETTA, BALUCHISTAN, PAKISTAN, SUNDAY 26TH OCTOBER 2008, 13.30

It looks as though we'll be staying here in Quetta for another day. Will seems to have contracted what would appear to be a strong dose of malaria, although the validity of my doctoring judgments has been known to be a little questionable at times. Whatever the disease or sickness that Will has developed, the fact remains that it is a chronic one. He rarely leaves the safety of the toilet seat and looks about as white as a sheet whenever he does occasionally surface. I'll miss him if he should die, but *a man's gotta do what a man's gotta do*, and I'm already pledged to continue without him should our worst fears be realised.

Exchanging Persia for Pakistan on Wednesday was quite the cultural shift. Five weeks in Iran have completely changed our perspective of a country that we once assumed to be poor and relatively uncivilized. Truthfully, Iran is very advanced indeed, rich with oil, and more akin to a Western country than its leaders would have us believe. The only major difference to the West comes through its vehement adherence to the laws of Hijab and the Secret Police.

Pakistan, on the other hand, appears to be even poorer than we expected, and the most noticeable contrast from Iran comes in the simple observations that it is, frankly, dirtier here.

Clothing is another obvious point of contrast. Whilst Iranians are more akin to folk in the West in terms of their fashion sense, most Pakistanis – at least from what we have seen thus far in Baluchistan – dress in the traditional clothes of their heritage. Every man (and it really is only men whom we see) wears the combination of baggy cotton trousers and a long dress-like shirt that hangs down below the knees. Of course, we've already gone and got ourselves kitted out in the same, and it is these outfits especially that draw us to the attention of every passer-by – including our newest Pakistani friend, Zakir, in whose office we now sit.

* * * * *

Our first Pakistani hitch saw us take an epic 600km ride all the way from the remotest areas of the impoverished Western province of Baluchistan to its capital in Quetta – a journey that certainly wasn't as straightforward as the distance achieved might suggest.

Three mini-lifts in the back of pick-up trucks took us to the top of a hill on the outskirts of the tiny border town of Taftan, and upon this hill stood a tattered signpost. Upon this signpost hung a sign upon which were marked only four destinations, and the furthest of these was Quetta (at 600km), whilst the nearest was still some 150km away.

Not possessing a map of the country at this stage (it generally takes us about a week to secure one), we really had no idea where Quetta was, but hoped that it would be in the east and figured that, wherever it was, it would be preferable to a little shantytown on the border. From the large font-size of the writing on the sign alone, we hoped and assumed that Quetta was a city and would thus hopefully enable us to find a cash machine and some fresh bottled water.

As easy as it had been to get to the top of the hill, we now faced a sizeable problem. The main road leading out of the city forked at the top of the hill – one way taking us on the "main road" (read dust track) to Quetta, the other only towards Taftan's sister village – and although there was no shortage of cars making the climb to the top of the hill, almost every one of these (predominantly made up of pick-up trucks) seemed only to be doing laps of the local area in order to carry goods between the two villages.

After some two hours of waiting (in what was fast becoming unbearable heat), the need for food and water was growing, and we possessed neither the funds nor the available resources to acquire these commodities. What's more, the only vehicles passing our way (at a rate of about one every five minutes) were buses, all of which would skid to a halt, spraying dust in our faces, whilst the conductor would shout some generic loud noises at us – something along the lines of: "Quetta eeeeeh, ohhhhh Quetta, Quetta aaaaaaahhhhhh" – before driving off again when we emptied our pockets and told them, in Farsi, that we had no money.

In this time only two trucks passed our way, and just one of these stopped. The driver kindly allowed us to share a cup of water from a cleanish looking tank, but just laughed at us when we mouthed "Quetta" at him, and signalled our intention to ride with him.

At the bottom of the hill there had been at least a dozen trucks parked along the side of the road, and we had assumed that all of these would soon be leaving to travel great distances along our way. We would take a lift anywhere really and felt sure that every truck was likely to end up in a major city.

Incidentally, these trucks are like no others that I have ever seen, more akin to Chinese dragons or merry-go-rounds than credible goods vehicles. One might easily mistake them for colourful buses or fairground rides if it weren't for the stacks of hay bales or cardboard boxes strapped precariously onto their vast, top-heavy behinds.

In any case, we had seen only two of these in the past two hours and we just could not go on like this. We were going to have to be a bit more proactive in our approach. As much as it would hurt to do so, we were just going to have to hitch back to where we had started from and find a local there who could give us a bit more information and hopefully fill our hungry bellies too.

It didn't take long to get a ride back to Taftan. After all, the problem had never been the lack of friendliness in the locals, but simply that no non-profit vehicle was going anywhere like the distance or direction that we had asked. The streams of traffic returning from village number two stopped at the top of the hill, before descending back whence they had come, and we were soon in the back of our fourth pick-up truck of the day, heading back to the start.

In the excitement that followed the chaotic border crossing (which had been packed full of people even at 7am) we had refused countless offers of bus or taxi rides to Quetta, and had even refused one bus driver who had assured us that he didn't want any money for taking us there. It was this man whom we now sought and, sure enough, there he was, just as we had left him. Sitting outside his little hut, which, we decided, was probably his bus company's HQ, the man immediately recognised us and beckoned us over.

"I said I take you Quetta no money, no problem," he said, a tone of rebuke in his voice.

Exchanging one quick glance, we shrugged our shoulders and decided to accept this man's generous offer. The long two-hour wait had dampened our spirits and our determination to travel by the more orthodox route of truck or car had diminished as a result. Well, it's not as if we broke any of our rules! In fact, it was positively in tune with the second one, and fully in line with the first. We would get this ride to Quetta, where we would be sure to ground ourselves a little better, get some money together and make a more concerted effort to hitch in a less soul-destroying manner the next time.

Even though hitching on a bus is still technically travelling for free with someone going your way, it just doesn't feel right, and we have vowed to do it only in the direst of circumstances. Surely this was one of those times.

We had no money, no food, no water, and no idea of how long it was going to be until we might find some. This kind man's offer was a Godsend, we figured, and it would be rude to reject it.

Thus, at 4pm we were crammed onto a rickety old bus – which, although the hottest part of the day was over, still felt extremely like a sauna – and were on our way to Quetta. Twelve gruelling hours later, having meandered our way through mountain valleys and across deserts, we finally arrived in our first Pakistani city just in time to see the sunrise.

Looking back, I am so very glad that we took Hossani up on his kind offer because who knows just where we would be now if it weren't for his generosity? Arriving in Quetta has indeed given us the opportunity to catch up on sleep that we have lost during our non-stop 1500km journey since leaving Kish. What's more, we have even found a working international cash machine for what must be the first time since mid-September! We are beggars no longer!

Day One Hundred And Eight: (continued...)
Zakir's garden, Hanna Urak, Quetta District, Baluchistan, Pakistan, Sunday 26th October 2008, 17.03

I sit in the garden of Zakir's beautiful village home in Hanna Urak and watch the sun finally fall away behind the mountains that surround us here, just ten kilometres outside the bustling city of Quetta. Sitting beside me is Zakir's older brother, Aref, who has kindly taken care of Will and me today and taken us to his beautiful home for the second time in two days.

We have been honorary members of the Rasheed family from the end of our very first day in Quetta, and I am now more convinced than ever that the further we go east, the more hospitality we are sure to find. From the goodwill of Hossani to the arms of Zakir in one swift, 24-hour, movement, and there was even time for us to receive a wedding invitation from a complete stranger in the meantime.

The stranger in question is Mr. Mohammed Qasim, and we met the man only because he happened not to be looking where he was going, and may have accidentally broken one of Will's ribs in passing.

Will and I were just discussing how rude it had been of this man not to apologise for his offence, when the stranger chased after us to invite us to go for a compensatory cup of tea.

This was our first taste of the milky Pakistani chai – the first time that milk has been added to tea since leaving England's green and pleasant pastures – and apparently the reason is entirely our own. It's from the colonial times, don't you know!

Other than discussions regarding the tea, which has a thicker, sweeter taste than our own (Mohammed told us that it's because they use Buffalo milk), Mohammed shared his political views in great depth and was anxious to find out what an authentic British perception of Pakistan really looked like.

"Well," I replied, "I suppose that the media doesn't really portray Pakistan too kindly. There is a lot of talk of terrorism at the moment and Pakistan is fast becoming at the heart of the troubles."

"Saying that," interjected Will, "it would be unfair and untrue to think that all English people believe all Pakistanis to be terrorists. We know that terrorists make up only a small minority of the population and do not hold the bulk of the innocent Pakistani public responsible."

Our short friend – who told us that he is twenty-five, but looks at least ten years older – seemed satisfied enough with our answer and soon began directing the conversation away from Pakistan as a nation and towards the Pashtun tribe of the Baluchistan region in the West.

"I am a Pashtun," Mohammed proudly stated. "And you two caught my eye because you are wearing Pashtun clothes." Pointing at our new Pakistani dress (dress being the operative word), Mohammed told us that they were each "embroidered by the hands of Afghani women. Pashtun women!" he emphasised.

Mohammed continued to separate himself from the Pakistan nation as a whole, which, he told us, has been around for only about forty years anyway, and he associated himself with his heritage as an Afghan from the proud Pashtun caste. It was strange to listen to a man talking of caste because the concept has all but disappeared in modern-day England, but seems very much to apply here in Pakistan.

Before long, Mohammed was our firm friend. Gone were our concerns that hospitality would fade as we made it into Pakistan. Within one hour of meeting the man, he had bought us chai, uncovered much of Pakistani history, and proceeded to invite us to the wedding of a man that he himself professed to know only slightly. It is as a result of this invitation alone that we are still in Quetta.

* * * * *

The weather's getting colder here in Hanna Urak, and I think I might have to go inside soon. Before that, however, I think I've got just enough stamina to fill you in on the steps that led us to meet Zakir – steps which eventually led us up here to this beautiful hillside village...

Either Zakir is a professional stalker, or he has the perfect credentials to consider becoming one. Whilst he claims that his initial and most devout interest in us related only to our strange choice of clothing, it is nevertheless rather disconcerting to have someone admit to having noticed us from afar and then waiting for us outside our hotel until we should reappear.

So it was that no sooner had we stepped outside the Islamabad Hotel than this stranger was upon us, and plying us with cups of tea at his office, which, conveniently, was just around the corner.

"Just don't kidnap us, all right?" we joked with Zakir as we entered his GEONET domain.

"Taliban?" we asked the two other men in the room, pointing a finger at Zakir.

They laughed, and nodded in what we hoped to be jovial affirmation.

I suppose that it might seem as though we were being quite insensitive toward this trio of strangers, but we were really rather nervous about the whole affair and decided that the best method of breaking the ice would be to dispel quickly any notion that we would think them to be anything other than decent, hospitable individuals – by suggesting the very opposite in jest.

It served us right, I guess, that moments later and our hands were tied behind our backs, scarves put in place to gag our mouths, and a shotgun was switching its aim between us. Zakir held a video camera, whilst his two friends had disguised their faces with more scarves and were demanding a ransom to save our lives...

I honestly cannot remember whose idea it was, but there was one moment when I looked across at my friend to see what we had been told was a replica shotgun pointing down his throat and thought to myself that if these men really were anything other than the hospitable sorts that we had taken them for, this would have been the easiest kidnapping of all time. We had just sat there and let them bind and gag us, before even inviting them to pretend to hold us hostage.

It's just as well that we've become quite good judges of character and that the practical joke soon came to a harmless end. If it weren't for the slightly more responsible attitude of Zakir and friends, our parents would have received a distasteful hostage video over the Internet the next day, but they told us that they could get into serious trouble for it, and we scrapped the idea... Just as well really.

This might be a good point to clarify that we do not find the idea of being held hostage in a strange country at all amusing. Rather, we cannot stand the hype that surrounds the media's interpretations of countries in the Middle East. During our time here, we have experienced nothing but warmth and hospitality, and the only response that we can offer to counter the fear-factor is to laugh about it all, and to reassure our friends that we do not consider them terrorists. Insensitive and inappropriate, we may be; ignorant we are not.

* * * * *

The cold has got the better of me and I'm back inside now, feeling a little worse for wear. Neither of us has taken particularly well to this new shift in diet and the lack of hygienic facilities in which to wash hands that have become regular replacements for utensils since entering Pakistan. This, and the severe lack of readily available (clean) drinking water, has led to the gradual deterioration that our bodies are currently experiencing. We are two particularly unwell individuals, although my body is still just about fighting off the sickness and diarrhoea that now consume my companion.

DAY ONE HUNDRED AND NINE:

THE SICK ROOM, ZAKIR'S HOUSE, HANNA URAK, QUETTA DISTRICT, BALUCHISTAN, PAKISTAN, MONDAY 27TH OCTOBER 2008, 12.27PM

Our progress eastward has been halted rather sharply. Will is still under the weather, having spent the entirety of last night in the toilet, whilst I am certainly not at my effervescent best. I suspect the cause to be either something that we ate at the wedding party on Saturday night, or an intrepid bug that has since crawled from fingers to food during a mealtime here. Inshallah, we will be fit enough to leave tomorrow because we have, once again, stayed in the same place for much longer than was originally intended.

This is our fourth day at the village, in which we first arrived, fit and well, on Friday evening, just in time to hike up one of the spectacular mountains that overlook the golden brown Urak valley below.

Mountain peaked, we returned to the muddy walls of Zakir's family home, which contains four rooms, we believe, although we have really spent time in only two. Our favourite – at least as the proportionate amount of time spent there would suggest – is the squatter's toilet-hole in the garden, whilst all other time is spent sectioned away in the *guesthouse.*

Zakir tells us that all homes in Pakistan must have a guesthouse to ensure that any visitor will be kept away from the women, who will remain inside until they can be sure that there are no guests outside. Quite the reasoning behind this we do not know, but it would explain why we have seen so few XX chromosomes running around the streets of Pakistan so far. Pakistan is a country ruled by men, after all, and their wives are precious treasures to be kept for personal use only.

"I'm sorry, but you cannot meet mother," Zakir told us earlier, when we questioned whether we might ever meet the kind lady responsible for feeding and sheltering us over the past few days.

"And every time you go toilet, tell me or brother, so we can tell women go inside."

That's just the way it is in Pakistan and, whilst it feels rather strange, and a touch misogynistic to us, we must respect that our friends are simply products of their own, specific tradition.

* * * * *

Every evening here runs the same course. After gulping down a meal made by an invisible mystery woman, it is time for the main event: a concert with all Zakir's brothers (he has eight) and friends. Will and I are only the support act, churning out all the old crowd favourites (basically anything loud and fast goes down well in Pakistan), before we hand over to the night's main event: an elderly looking gentleman (we believe him to be part of the *friend*, rather than *sibling* bracket), who has one of the most startling voices that I have ever heard.

An octave above our own, this old man whines and warbles shrill verses, before we are all encouraged to join in with the noisy chorus:

"Zorl, Mama Zorldé!"

"Zorl, Mama Zorldé!"

Zakir tells us that the song is about an old man. "Zorl Mama Zorldé" means: "the man is old, so we should leave him at home."

Rather ironic, we think, given that the soloist looks to be well into his seventies, but Zakir assures us that he is only forty.

"He has had a hard life," Zakir tells us.

The years have clearly taken their toll.

"Zorl Mama Zorldé!" has become our regularly ditty, and it was this we sang in unison on Saturday morning as we walked through the Urak valley, fishing net and prodding sticks in hand. We were going fishing, and we were going to do it the authentic way.

When we reached the icy cold water, we took it in turns to be fish catchers and fish disturbers. Two men were charged with stretching the net across the narrow stream and holding it down as best they could, so that all through traffic would find its way into the net, whilst the others took their big sticks in hand and entered a little upstream, plunging sticks underneath rocks and crevices to disturb any fish that might be hiding there and, in so doing, sending them towards the trap.

For several hours we played the same game, until our hands and feet were too numb to continue. The total catch totalled more than twenty, although there were only three big ones to take home to the stove – not that we would see any of our catch for dinner that night, for we had made other arrangements.

* * * * *

Saturday night was wedding night. Kitting ourselves out in our best Pakistani frocks, we headed back to Quetta for a wedding like no other. There was no ceremony (this had already taken place behind closed doors, with only close family and an Imam present), and there were over seven hundred guests – although quite how many of these were actually invited I do not know. Apparently it is quite normal at such events for an invited guest to bring along seven or eight of his friends to join in the celebrations.

Inside a giant marquee, we sat down to enjoy a traditional Pashtun dinner of mutton, chicken, flat bread, and an outrageously spicy sauce. As the only white guys in the crowd, we rather stole the limelight from the groom – not that we had any idea which one he was, in what was a sea of men. I forgot to mention that the bride and groom's parties are held completely separately – yet another way to ensure the segregation of the sexes.

"It is not uncommon for the bride and groom to meet for the first time at the wedding," Mohammed informed us, once we had snuck away from the party for a little chai break.

Mohammed had been both jealous and concerned, when Will and I had so soon become surrounded by a crowd of raucous Pashtun men, all of whom seemed a little high on snuff, and were doing their best to force it down our throats. Mohammed had whisked us away in the nick of time, and we used our chai break as an opportunity to ask our friend about his own marriage.

"I married for love," Mohammed proudly told us. "Yes, it was an arranged marriage, but I made sure that I met my bride several times before the ceremony, and we were lucky because we fell in love."

"How common are arranged marriages here?" asked Will.

"I think it is still very common," Mohammed replied. "Probably the majority, but more and more people of the younger generations are breaking the rules by meeting their prospective partners before the wedding, just to make sure that it will work."

"So how are the marriages arranged?" I asked, continuing to press Mohammed with questions.

"Traditionally it is something only to be arranged by the two fathers of the couple, who do not need the consent of their children, but recently this has been changing," Mohammed replied. "Nowadays a man may be attracted to a woman whose family are affiliated with his own, and he might suggest to his own parents that he wants to marry her. Then they will go and ask the woman's parents for his permission to do so."

"How much say does the woman have in it all?" asked Will, presuming that it will be very little.

"The decision rests with her parents," came the reply. "Traditionally, they will decide for her, but it has become more common for the parents to consult their daughter first."

Reassured by the idea that women did at least seem to have some say in it all, we pressed Mohammed about his own marriage again.

"So at what age was your marriage arranged?"

"I think I was only ten years old, and my wife would have been seven, but we started meeting regularly once I got to fourteen. And then we fell in love."

It was fascinating to talk with Mohammed, who truly did seem to be in love with his wife. It is a strange thought for Western minds that a marriage might be arranged apart from the two parties involved, but I do not believe that it is for us to condemn. After all, it isn't as if our own marriage system works particularly well. A 50% success rate doesn't exactly give us any bragging rights over an alternative system, just because it seems so alien to our own.

One thing that I am sure few readers would care to contradict is my opinion of the general lack of gender equality that can be seen here in Pakistan. If you ladies thought that Iran was bad – enforced Hijab doesn't exactly breathe freedom to the bones – then consider the world without women that is Pakistan. We simply haven't seen any here. We assume that they probably do exist – it would be strange to think otherwise – but, other than the meals that they have provided for us, there has been no sign of them.

Of the women that do apparently exist, we know none to have any other jobs beside housewifery and, whilst this is, of course, a very worthy vocation, surely a woman's freedom should not be so restricted that they are simply unable to choose anything else.

Perhaps I am wrong to criticise. This is but an unavoidable view from a child of the West – knowing the freedom that girls enjoy this side of equality – when, in all honesty, I have no idea how happy women really are in Pakistan...

Back at the wedding, Will could not resist the peer-pressure any longer, accepting a chunk of snuff and slotting it into the side of his mouth – only for Mohammed almost forcibly to eject the thing ten minutes later, when it came to the time for all to hit the dance floor.

Mohammed led the way, jumping straight into the heart of the action, where fifty men circled around in the traditional Pashtun step, *Atthan*. Atthan is another one of those things that looks a lot easier than it actually is. The men join together in a circle and follow a strict, and apparently simple, four-step routine, but when it came to our turn, we were soon lost in dizziness, and proceeded only to bump carelessly into the poor men on either side of us.

Just at the moment when we thought we'd cracked it, the rhythm changed. The band of drummers, led by a singular vocalist, shifted away from the waltz-like, two forward, two backward step, and the dance suddenly sprang into life. All flailing arms and pirouettes, the men twisted and twirled in explosive fashion, waving handkerchiefs as they danced in perfect synchronism.

Open-mouthed, Will and I watched in amazement. Mohammed was in his element, his tubby belly bouncing around to the beat of the drum in a way that made me think of *Baloo the Bear*, but there was no knocking the elegant movement of his nimble feet.

Long after midnight, but well before the end of the action (which would continue throughout the night), Zakir came to take us back to the office for the night. The following morning, yesterday morning, we would head back to Urak, and it was then that sickness struck.

DAY ONE HUNDRED AND NINE: (CONTINUED...)
THE SICK ROOM, ZAKIR'S HOUSE, HANNA URAK, QUETTA DISTRICT, BALUCHISTAN, PAKISTAN, MONDAY 27TH OCTOBER 2008, 16.58

A bomb went off in Quetta today, killing four people. Apparently this is no rare event here, and Zakir tells us not to worry, but that is a little hard, given that we have worked out that it went off right in the spot where we were standing only a few hours before.

The blast has shaken us, and we are beginning to feel a little uneasy about the prospect of hitching towards the infamous North Western Frontier

Province (NWFP) – currently at the centre of the terrorist conflict – especially as, being English, we could very well be mistaken for the Americans currently bombing the region.

With fighting and terrorist bombings growing in scale and intensity every day, we are seriously considering the likelihood that we will meet with some sort of serious danger at some stage. The inconsequential nature of the scare-tactics that we experienced during days in Kurdistan and Zahedan give us some cause to remain optimistic ahead of our likely departure tomorrow, but one thing is certain: friends and family at home will not be relishing this particular stage of the proceedings.

* * * * *

It's almost time for evening prayers at the local mosque, which we shall attend for the first time as a result of an invitation we received when out on a walk with our carer of the past few days, Aref – a man who needs fuller introduction.

A slightly annoying chap, Aref's favourite topic of choice is the mountains of Afghanistan, which he claims to be his own.

"Mountains, mountains, Afghanistan," his regular chorus, Aref tells us that he is really a citizen of Afghanistan because Pakistan does not truly begin until the mountains end.

"Pashtun people are Afghani people!" claims Aref. "Pakistan does not begin until you reach the plains of Asia, beyond my mountains."

"They're not your mountains Aref," we protest, but it is no use.

"Oh yes they are," says Aref. "My mountains dance for me."

"Do they really? That's nice," we respond. "Could you possibly make them dance now, so that we might see them?"

Sadly, this is where the conversation ends because, of course, the man is deluded.

You might wonder why we are being so rude to a man whose family have been very good to us in this time of sickness, but I don't think you'll mind once I have told you more about our friend Aref, and explained what his version of "taking care" of us really entails.

Poor Will spends most of the day coughing and spluttering upon his bed and all night arched over the toilet-hole in the garden, but Aref's sole response is to look at me, shake his head, and say: "Weak, weak man. If he were in my army, I would leave him behind."

Will looks up, clearly miffed, but unable to say anything because of his depleted energy levels, so it is left to me to respond.

"That's nice Aref," I say. "You do realise that he's ill, don't you?"

"Weak, weak man," Aref repeats. "He has been ill for days".

Arguing with Aref is a bit of a lost cause. The evening is the worst, when all friends and brothers assemble to see the white guys, and Aref chastises Will for being too weak even to entertain them – as if it were his duty to do so!

"Weak, weak man," he says again. "He is just like an old woman. These friends come to see him and he cannot even speak to them! How rude!" Aref concludes, pushing his thick-framed glasses back to rest upon the bridge of his sizeable nose.

Another of Aref's little quirks is his obsession with University degrees. Ever since Aref realised that I had a degree, he has been pestering me to copy it and change the name to read his own.

"If I had a degree," he declares, "I would be promoted in no time. You can do this for me, can't you?"

"Sure thing, Aref," I reply, inwardly at a loss. "I'll just go home, print one out and change the names – just like that!"

During one of Will's moments of strength, he manages to sit up for long enough to reach the table, find a scrap piece of paper and a pen, and begins to write Aref a fake degree – just to make a point.

"Where would you like your degree to be from, and what subject?" Will asks.

"What University is the best in England?" Aref replies, unable to see that he is being mocked.

"Oxford. No, Cambridge... We'll put them both down, just to be safe." Will clears his throat and dictates: "Right... I, William Jackson, Doctor of... Science at Oxbridge University, do hereby proclaim that Aref Rasheed is the proud owner of a Science degree from the Universities of Oxford and Cambridge."

"There. Finished. Here you go Aref," says Will, handing over the scrap paper to our friend, who conveys a mixture of puzzlement and appreciation and places it upon the top shelf, right next to the Holy Qu'ran.

So that's a little introduction to Aref for you. The only other thing that you need to know about the brother of our sweet-hearted friend, Zakir, is that he seems to revel in creating miracle cures out of the strangest of combinations (such as an egg yoke and one of his garden plants) and then forcibly shoves them down poor Will's throat. Good at heart Aref may well be, but boy is he misguided!

DAY ONE HUNDRED AND TEN:
ZAKIR'S GARDEN, HANNA URAK, QUETTA DISTRICT, BALUCHISTAN, PAKISTAN, TUESDAY 28TH OCTOBER 2008, 15.03

I cannot remember the last time I felt so devoid of energy. Last night my body finally decided not to flirt with sickness any longer and just to get on with it and let everything out.

Not feeling so good, I had exchanged places with my recovering companion, and stayed behind in the Sick Room with Zakir, whilst the friends and brothers headed out to enjoy what Aref referred to as "fun around a fire." Today was supposed to be the day we finally left, but I never imagined that my sickness would so quickly escalate to the stage that it did.

Zakir kindly prepared two buckets of water (one boiling hot, the other freezing cold) for me to pour over myself in the villager's own, unique version of a bath. Let's just say that I now understand why non-Europeans don't wash nearly as much as we do! The experience was horrific. The temperature at night here in the valley must be teetering on the brink of the minus degrees' mark, and getting down to my birthday suit (even with the promise of warm water to come) in such conditions, and in such a weak state of health, just sent me into hypothermic shakes and shivers.

After all Zakir's efforts lovingly to prepare a bath for me, I managed to pour only about three buckets over my head before I just couldn't take it anymore. Reaching for my towel, I tightly wrapped it around myself to make up for the significant loss in body temperature, and hurried back into the Sick Room, where there were gas heaters ready to warm me up again.

"Did you have a bath?" Zakir questioned, obviously disappointed to see so much water remaining in both buckets, having spent goodness knows how long preparing it.

"Yes I did. Thank you Zakir. I'm sorry, I just don't feel well," I sniffled, putting myself in the recovery position, whilst the motherly Zakir stroked his hand through my hair.

You know that feeling that runs through you just at the moment before you are going to be sick? Well, all of a sudden it hit me and I stumbled outside, just managing to reach the garden before my stomach erupted. Worse even than a bout of vomiting and diarrhoea that I once experienced during a visit to Malawi, this time both came at once!

Not a pleasant image, I know, but believe me when I say that it was much worse for me, and for the poor man (Zakir) who had to clean me up. I had really let rip out of both ends and, understandably embarrassed, battled against my pride before finally admitting the severity of the crisis.

"I think I've gone to the toilet in my clothes," I mumbled, head bowed.

"OK dear. Don't worry," Zakir reassured me, the perfect gentleman as ever, even if he verges on the creepy side with the level of his affection.

Who'd have thought that I would have reached incontinence at the tender age of twenty-two? Here I was, in the middle of a garden in impoverished Baluchistan, struggling my way out of sodden clothes.

"It was a good job I left some of that hot water," I said to Zakir, who graciously dealt with my soiled clothes and gave me the privacy to go in and wash myself.

Sadly, my second attempt to bathe was no easier than the first. I still felt wretched and just knew that I hadn't got it all out of my system. Just about satisfied that the bulk of my disgrace had been washed away, I covered myself up again and returned to the recovery position, where the omnipresent Zakir soon stroked my forehead again.

Last night was the longest I have ever experienced, as a perpetual pattern of vomiting and diarrhoea continued and I soon became firm friends with the toilet-hole that Will had so recently vacated. The only solace came in the fact that the vomiting and diarrhoea seemed to have decided to take it in turns, or else my body had caught up enough to work out which one was coming before it did, making the dynamics of the sickness a little more controllable. Thank heavens for small mercies!

This morning I felt much the same, managing to win a war of attrition with my stomach for just long enough to think that I'd beaten it, before the inevitable returned and my stomach reasserted itself. I'm pretty sure that the worst is now over, and I have just about mustered the strength to stagger outside to sit in some shade and pen my thoughts following a gruelling evening of stomach churning.

It's nice to get a change of scenery, after feeling all too well acquainted with the respective walls of the Sick Room and toilet hole. With any luck, this improvement of feeling will mean that we can finally leave this place tomorrow, but I am careful not to get too carried away. So far, every time we have thought about leaving, sickness has recurred quickly to change our minds. Perhaps it will be Will's turn tomorrow in what has been a season of tag-team diarrhoea.

* * * * *

I think I've just got enough remaining strength to mention briefly the wonderfully humbling encounter at the mosque last night, which took place just before the sickness... I don't think the two are related.

For a long time now I have struggled with concerns relating to the notions of Heaven and Hell – how some may be uninvited to a party at the former, and will thereby become banished to the fires of the latter. What a repugnant idea, and yet this seems accurately to be the position of many a believer today – from a whole host of religions.

The very belief that my way is the only way, in turn means that all other ways are void. *My way or the highway* is the cry of the majority of Muslims and Christians alike, but here we were, sitting in a mosque, having to think this quandary through whilst looking straight into the eyes of the most hospitable and friendly Muslim brothers. And then I am supposed to conclude that all of them are going to hell if they don't side with me? What an horrific idea! The night started with our Muslim brothers telling us the basics of their faith, through the medium of Aref's translations. We already knew a lot of the basics and told them just how similar their beliefs were to our own.

"Surely God's grace transcends the boundaries of one religion," I suggested. "Otherwise you or I must look at each other and condemn the other to an eternity without God, even though we are both devout in the separate beliefs that we honestly hold to be the truth."

The leader of the mosque agreed with my sentiments, and shared my hope that we might meet again in Heaven. What a very interesting thing it is to think about the confidence with which Christians and Muslims generally hold to their own faith, without giving any leeway to the idea that they may be wrong. The fact of the matter is that they cannot both be completely right. They may well both be a little bit right and a little bit wrong, but their pivotal claims do not allow for both to be right and, thus, would seem to turn both parties back to Allah to cry out for an outpouring of His grace. Only grace can save us!

My rather wishy-washy conclusion to the problem of many faiths and only one Way is that we can be sure only of what we know, but can believe that God's knowledge is superior to our own, and hope that He rises above our own inadequate conception of the enormous scale of His grace to save many more than we might think.

We parted from our Muslim friends with the humble prayer that "God would bring all those to salvation who deserved it," but I instantly regretted it. I was wrong to pray for those who deserve it because the point of grace is that it is a salvation that is completely undeserved. There is nothing that the most devout Muslim, Christian, Jew, or other believer could do to deserve salvation. We have only to hope and pray that God's grace will extend beyond any boundaries we can impose upon it.

11. HAVING A BLAST

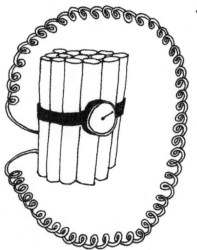

DAY ONE HUNDRED AND FOURTEEN:
PARKWAY HOTEL, LAHORE, PUNJAB, PAKISTAN, SATURDAY 1ST NOVEMBER 2008, 9PM

There is the slightest chance that this could be my last entry. Don't worry; I haven't given up on my desire to write down all the adventures that we may have until we finally reach Malaysia. However, tonight, perhaps for the first time, I am starting to doubt if we will ever really make it. Tonight, we may have met our prospective murderer.

For all this talk of the friendliness and hospitality of Muslims, for all the amazing proofs that speak of the stupidity of denouncing all of them as terrorists, we may have thoughtlessly put our trust in one too many. A casual trip to the local Lahore supermarket – in order that we might treat ourselves to a few basic home comforts after what has been a debilitating patch of sickness – turned into an encounter that we won't soon forget.

It has become quite common during our time in Pakistan for strangers to approach us and, almost without exception, the first question that they will ask us is: "Are you Muslim?" (I blame the man dresses). Thus, it wasn't particularly surprising, during our walk down the toiletries aisle, that two Muslim men approached us to ask us that same question. Normally we would humbly reply with something along the lines of: "No, but Ek Allah," which means "No, but there is one God." This answer generally does enough to satisfy the questioner, and we part with an air of mutual understanding and respect.

If only we had been in one of our more sensible moods tonight. Unfortunately, this was the first night in a long while that we hadn't both felt too ill even to think about making jokes, and so we were back to our normal, cheeky selves.

"Um... I'd say that we were half Muslim," I said, thoughtlessly. "We're all for that one God business – Ek Allah, and all that. But we can't really agree on Mohammed – thus deeming us half Muslims!"

This clever (if a little misplaced) jest was in reference to the staple declaration of Muslim faith, which we have grown quite accustomed to hearing during our time in Pakistan. It reads something along the lines of:

"*There is no God but Allah, and Mohammed's his Prophet; may he rest peacefully*" (that's a poor man's paraphrase, but you get the gist). And so, you see, we've rather taken to the idea that we are, in fact, half of the real deal. One God: sure, we can handle that. It's all this stuff about Mohammed that sees us come unstuck, and it was this point that we were trying, not so eloquently, to express.

"There is no half Muslim!" one of our Muslim brothers shouted. "You *full* Muslim! *Full* Muslim!" he raged, rolling the "l" sounds such that they seemed to follow us around the supermarket until the moment we left.

"Sorry," we replied, sheepishly, starting to appreciate that if there is one thing that you shouldn't joke about in Pakistan, it's the Muslim faith. Of course, we weren't really attacking the Muslim faith itself; we were just making a light-hearted joke that almost everyone in England would have laughed off as another one of those inappropriate, yet strangely amusing, gags.

Unfortunately, we weren't in England, and had severely misjudged our target audience. Our mumbled apologies and most sincere attempts to appear remorseful had done little to assuage the growing vexation and anger of our devout Muslim friends. When we came out of the supermarket, there they were, waiting for us.

Forcing our best apologetic smiles, we waved our hands at the two men and made for a nearby rickshaw, but our friends weren't going to let us get away that easily. Dismounting from the motorbike upon which they sat, headscarves pulled over their faces so that we could only just about make out the colour of their eyes (no prizes for guessing: they were brown like everyone else here), the leader of the duo approached us.

"Where is your hotel?" he demanded, in such a frightening tone that it sounded as though he were insulting our mothers.

"Um, it's near the railway station," I replied, hoping that I had said it either too quietly or too quickly for him to catch it. Trying to wave goodbye again, we started out for the rickshaw for the second time, but before we had made two steps, our friend was calling after us:

"I take you," he said, in that same tone. Why did everything that he said sound like a threat? It wasn't like us to be overly sensitive in the presence of strangers, but we were both absolutely terrified.

Not knowing how else we could respond to this man's insistence, we followed him back to the bike. There he ordered his companion to get off, and we were soon getting on behind this terrifying gent and speeding off in the direction of our hotel.

Why does he want to take us home? I thought to myself. Maybe he wants to know where our hotel is so that he can plant a bomb in it, just as those terrorists did a little up the road in Islamabad not so long ago. I shook at the thought and told myself that I was being melodramatic, but still could not shift the thought from my mind. Perhaps we should pretend we were staying somewhere else, and take him to another hotel, I thought, at once realising that there was no time to plan such a move, and that this would only turn our friend's rage upon some other innocent victims. Oh no! Now we're dealing with a whole new level of ethics! In saving ourselves, we would be condemning others to a sorry fate. We might be making ourselves accessories to murder!

Now it may sound as if I am making a big fuss about nothing, as I ponder the events of just moments ago, sitting now up against the headboard of my hotel bed, but the funny thing about it all is that you really wouldn't take Will and me as the melodramatic types. We have spent so many good times with so many Muslims over the past few months that our respect for these people has grown to such a level that it is almost impossible to conceive that there might be any bad ones out there... Until now.

It was the manner in which this man spoke, and the animosity that he seemed to feel towards anybody and anything, that unnerved us. We are always so eager to befriend and to put our trust in all the people that we meet, and yet neither of us liked this man, nor would we trust him further than we could throw him.

I honestly can't remember hearing our friend talking about anything other than the fundamentals of his faith and the importance of adhering strictly to its rules and regulations. His eagerness to convey a message reminded me of the sort of pride and intensity of feeling that is conveyed by raving nationalists, and the entirety of his message seemed to revolve around the dos and don'ts of Islam.

Take our friend, the lady motorbike rider (we've finally seen a few women, here in Lahore) sitting in front of us in a queue of traffic, patiently waiting for the lights to change. Hijab all in line, you would have thought that our friend would be pleased. But no.

"She should not be dressed like that!" he tutted, presumably referring to the fact that the lady's headscarf was pulled back fractionally to reveal a fringe, and, shock horror, the headscarf wasn't just black: it had some colour!

"What do you think? What do you think about these women?" he raged. Poor William was sat right up next to the madman and had to suffer the full brunt of his mutterings, whilst I was able to ignore them every now and then by leaning back and letting the much calmer tone of the wind replace their sound.

"I like women," replied Will, not knowing what else to say. "My mother is a lovely woman... Very respectfully dressed, of course," he added, so as not to aggravate the situation any further.

For the next item of his lecture, our friend started reeling off a long list of names of people we had never heard of, but whom we assumed to be Muslim fundamentalists.

"Do you know them?" he shouted, continuing to spit out names that meant nothing to us. "They are all in my family!"

He took the greatest pride in one particular name, who we supposed might be a Taliban head honcho. "*He* is my uncle," he said, and was that a smile that we detected? No, surely not; there was still something sinister about the way in which the corners of his mouth turned.

Finally, we had made it back to the hotel – our hotel – and we were released just outside of it, nervously looking at our friend as he seemed to pay particular attention to the name, location and dimensions of the building. He would know everything that he needed to know about it now. The only thing that remained was to wonder if he could see to the planting of a bomb by the end of the evening.

"I want to see you dinner tomorrow," he said, exchanging numbers with us (he went in our phone as "*Terror*") before speeding off, hopefully in order to pick up his poor friend, who had been discarded outside the supermarket.

Will and I didn't say a word until we had climbed the staircase to the fourth floor, walked along the corridor to our room, given a long look in each direction to make sure that we weren't being followed, and then stepped inside, hastily fastening the door behind us.

"Looking forward to dinner tomorrow night?" Will asked.

I nodded, solemnly. "If there is a tomorrow night..."

DAY ONE HUNDRED AND FOURTEEN: (CONTINUED...)
PARKWAY HOTEL, LAHORE, PUNJAB, PAKISTAN, SATURDAY
1ST NOVEMBER 2008, 10.40PM

Moving on from that slight detour into the realms of the (thankfully) hypothetical, I should bring you up to date on the movements that have somehow seen us transported all the way (some 1200km!) from that Sick Room in Hanna Urak to the Indian border in Lahore, bypassing Peshawar and Islamabad so that we may be out of this country as soon as is humanly possible.

Against all the odds, we were both well *enough* finally to leave the Rasheed family on Wednesday afternoon, making our way to the eastern edge of Quetta for our second attempt at hitchhiking in Pakistan.

Feeling as though we had largely failed in the manner of our hitch from Taftan to Quetta, this was our chance to make amends. Standing in what we adjudged to be a suitable spot for picking up a ride out of Quetta, we really had no idea where we were, or in which direction we should be heading. Surrounded by roads that looked more like tractor-trails than motorways, we were especially unsure whether the road upon which we stood could really be the *main* northbound road, and our first driver did little to clear up our uncertainty. A friendly chap, we learnt little more about the man than his name (Abdullah) and received no further clarification as to where exactly we were when, some twenty minutes later, he signalled to us that we should get out of his vehicle.

Well, at least we'd got ourselves a ride – our first *real* Pakistani hitch since those pick-up trucks back in Taftan. Perhaps this Pakistani hitching business wouldn't be so bad after all...

Now, I have spoken before about the friendliness of the Pakistani people, but who'd have thought that this friendliness would grow to such an extent than it would almost become an inconvenience? Funny to think of a generally positive attribute like friendliness as anything other than a good thing, I know, but try hitching with a crowd of thirty people all around you, and you'll understand what I mean.

This was exactly the situation we found ourselves in on Wednesday afternoon, in a little village just a few kilometres north (we hoped) of Quetta. Of course, none of the surrounding crowd could speak any English, and so they just stood there, open-mouthed, gawping at us. Perhaps they were expecting us to do something? Maybe we should sing them a song, or do a little dance? If only it were that easy to get rid of them.

Pushing our way through the crowd, we ended up standing halfway into the middle of the road, just to get some space, but even there we were followed. Taking a quick glance at the map, we worked out that, by our calculations, we were on what would seem to be the right path to the Punjab or NWFP provinces, and didn't really care which. Either would do. The main thing was to catch up on some distance, having been delayed by illness for such a long time.

We were hardly feeling on top of the world, as it was. Both of us had plied ourselves with that trusty friend, *Imodium*, and only hoped this might see us through to the next big city. The problem was that the clock was ticking, sundown fast approaching, and we hadn't even made it more than about twenty kilometres! Why had we left it so long to make tracks? We shouldn't have agreed to go for a final lunch in Quetta with Zakir and Aref – although it was jolly nice of them to buy us those Pakistani signet rings. If only these people would leave us alone, and give us half a chance to get a ride! Who was going to stop for a couple of white guys completely surrounded by hoards of villagers?

Probably only about fifteen vehicles passed by in the first thirty minutes and it seemed like our wait might go on forever, until, suddenly, someone screeched to a halt, almost running over a section of the crowd in the process. We almost wished he had. Poking his head out of the window, we simply could not believe it when we recognised the driver's face to be that of one of Zakir's pals from GEONET – the very same! What were the chances?

It turned out that Zakir's pal, and his brother, were on their way to visit their parents at a village 100km away, in what we judged to be the right direction. It wasn't the most comfortable of rides. Squished up against our seats because of the copious piles of luggage on board, our view consisted predominantly of baggage, although we could see the occasional passing tree flash by through a square-inch gap between our bags – but no matter. The method of travel wasn't at all important. We were just glad to be making some distance before nightfall.

The sun came crashing down on our parade midway through the drive, and we knew that it was too dark to expect to make any more distance that night. Zakir's pal treated us to a cup of chai in a village about ten kilometres away from their own, and here they pointed us in the right direction for heading north the next day. Zakir's pal apologised that he couldn't help us more, "but this is a difficult time, you see…"

Oh yes, that's right. I have made a spectacular omission from my recent log – failing to mention that, not only did a bomb go off very near to us in Quetta, but we were also extremely lucky to escape any ill effects from an earthquake that hit 6.4 on the Richter scale (I'm told that's quite a lot), the epicentre of which was said to be only about seventy kilometres from Quetta… in a north-easterly direction!

This was the first time that Zakir's friend had been to see his parents since Tuesday's tragic quake – which killed 300 people and left thousands homeless – and now we were sitting only a few kilometres away from the centre of the devastation.

Such is the friendliness of the Pakistani people that in the time it takes four men to drink a cup of chai, we had been offered a place to stay for the night with a complete stranger. Of course we were grateful, although the accommodation we received would not exactly turn out to be five-star…

DAY ONE HUNDRED AND FIFTEEN:
INTERNET INN, LAHORE, PUNJAB, PAKISTAN, SUNDAY 2ND NOVEMBER2008, 15.32

Only once did my bowels decide to wake me up for a pit stop during what was a blissfully long, and bomb-less sleep, in the Parkway Hotel last night. I'm hopeful that my diarrhoea relapse is now over, but cautious of not counting stomach-related chickens before they've hatched – these things often take a little longer than expected.

I can at least happily report that we appear to have made it through the night unscathed. Clearly our terror-fuelled friend could not get hold of enough C4 in time to accomplish our doom in one fell, hotel swoop, and we have escaped with our lives… for now at least.

We have, nevertheless, changed our hotel as a precaution, and even took the advice of one of those *Lonely Planet* thingy-me-jigs to find this little place, joining a host of other travellers at the warmly recommended *Internet Inn*.

Incidentally, it's just a stone's throw away from our terror-happy friend's favourite supermarket, so I suppose we didn't think that one through particularly well...

* * * * *

Before I can update you further upon our time in Lahore, there are about 1100km of catching up to do, and I will pick up where I left off. It's Wednesday evening and we have been invited to stay at the home of another chap called Zakir.

The deadly earthquake on Tuesday night had reverberated far and wide, shaking us from our beds in the middle of our last night in Hanna Urak. It was one of those disconcerting moments when you don't quite know if you're in dreamland or reality until everyone around you is frantically shouting at you: "Get up, quick!"

There was a second tremor, not quite as strong as the first, and then we went back to bed – own mud hut still intact, whilst we remained unaware that several hundred others had fallen in upon themselves just a little up the road.

On our way out of Quetta the next day, we hardly noticed a repeat quake whilst we were casually strolling across a bridge, just a few moments before Zakir's friend would rescue us from the madding crowd.

"What was that?" Will asked.

I shrugged my shoulders, completely oblivious to the tectonic-plate activity underfoot, until floods of villagers came rushing out onto the streets, shouting something in Urdu that was probably along the lines of: "Ahhhh! Earthquake!"

Of course, the crowds of people who fled their homes then decided to crowd around the next greatest phenomenon to have crossed their path.

"I can't believe this," one of them seemed to say to another. "First an earthquake, and now two white-faced aliens dressed in Pashtun clothing!"

A few hours later, thanks to the most fortunate of coincidental meetings, we had made it 100km up the road to the home of Zakir II, who lives in the village of Khanoudi.

Upon arrival, we were surprised to find Zakir's family huddled together inside a makeshift tent – the kind that you might expect to find in a refugee camp – that they had erected in the courtyard outside their mud-walled home.

"Earthquake. Yesterday," Zakir explained. "Not safe we go inside today. Forty eight hours after earthquake it not safe we go inside."

Zakir proceeded to give us a tour of his home – which was much like his namesake's – but we were never permitted to enter inside any room, for fear that the walls might come tumbling down upon our heads. Zakir pointed at the many ominous cracks that ran down the walls and ceilings, and shook his head in dismay.

"Earthquake?" asked Will.

He nodded, solemnly.

The quake had really shaken the people in this little village. None of its inhabitants felt safe inside their homes and we happily slept outside with the rest of them that night, sharing in the experience that had made them refugees inside their own home.

* * * * *

Early the next morning, following long goodbyes and thanks to our kind hosts – including the women of the house, whom we had been privileged to have met because, in such circumstances, there is no capacity for a guestroom – Zakir led us back to the chai store of the previous night.

During the night, between bouts of diarrhoea, we had decided to avoid the NWFP and Peshawar because of recent stories of unrest, and to make straight for the capital, Islamabad. This information we relayed to Zakir, but for all our trying to explain the art of hitchhiking, our efforts fell upon another set of deaf ears, and he sat us down outside a shop (possibly a bus station, but not quite like the ones at home) to tell us that a bus would soon come along on its way and take us towards the capital.

It was hard not to get frustrated with the continuing lack of understanding regarding our mission, but we did our best not to sound too disappointed in our thanks towards our kind host, and waited for him to be well out of sight before taking matters into our own hands.

Zakir left us in the charge of one of his friends, who seemed to have a fairly decent grasp of the English language, so it wasn't long before we began trying to explain our wishes for the second time that morning.

"No bus! We want big truck... Lorry... Camion... Islamabad." Wild gesticulations followed every word that we said, as we tried without success to explain, but our friend was understandably confused by the notion that we would not want to catch a bus.

"No Rupees?" he asked, presumably wondering if we had been robbed or lost our money – any reason that might explain why two rich Westerners could not afford the comparatively modest bus-fare.

"Cheap money," he continued. "You no pay big Rupees."

"Thank you," we sighed, reluctantly. This man was never going to be able to understand our intention. The only thing that we could do was to keep insisting that we wanted to travel in a truck. Now, where was one of those Amazing Technicolor Lorries when you needed one? I mean, it's not as if they're inconspicuous!

The map of Pakistan wasn't helping much. It was hardly the most detailed road map that we had seen, and seemed to omit helpful additions such as road names or, in fact, any lines that might join one city to the next. The next north-easterly town/village/city on the map was called *Zhob*, and it was *Zhob* we set as our next target.

After all, it was optimistic to start a conversation with a prospective driver by suggesting that we were looking to make it all the way (over 1000km, we posited) to the capital in one go. We would start small. Zhob appeared to be anywhere between 50 and 300km away, but it was certainly somewhere between Khanoudi and Islamabad, and that would be a good start.

We wondered if there existed anything remotely resembling a motorway in Pakistan. So far, all we had seen were dusty, pothole-ravaged, single roads, half of which might spontaneously decide to disappear at any one time if they should so choose.

This was not Europe; this was not Iran. We had been rather spoilt by the quality of roads thus far and concluded that it was probably good for us to be experiencing this latest dilemma, although it would be nice to know if this non-descript road really was their equivalent of a motorway to Islamabad, or if we had just become lost somewhere along the way. Perhaps there was a six-lane, concrete highway just over the other side of *them thar hills*, and we had just missed it.

For now, at least, we would have to deal with the conditions as we found them. Will stayed and chatted with the man responsible for getting us a ride – who, in some forty minutes of waiting, had done nothing except to vex us with a barrage of unwanted offers of more chai and food (the thought of anything but good old English food was enough to make our stomachs churn) – whilst I made my way out to the road and started doing that old trick of simultaneously flapping arms and legs around in a manner that might hopefully attract some attention.

It did.

A man passing on his motorbike soon stopped right next to me and piped up, in an impressive phrasing of English, the question of "whether or not" he could be of any help.

My eyes lit up at the sound of what I hoped to be a fluent English speaker, but it turned out that this phrase was just another of those that one might learn at school – as, for instance, "The cat sat on the mat" or "The mouse is underneath the table."

When I excitedly tried telling him about the hitch, the man merely looked at me with the expression that most people give us these days: one that tells me both that he has no idea what it is that I am trying to tell him, and wouldn't really care to find out anyway.

"Come chai and breakfast my shop," he says, an unsurprising return to Pak-lish, which feels more like an order than a request.

I sigh, and hang my head. One more milky chai is certain to turn the already curdling mess inside our stomachs back into an explosive volcano from both ends.

"Thank you," I say, forlorn, but unable to refuse the offer.

The man on the bike signals to one of his friends (he obviously lives nearby) and Will and I are soon hopping onto the backs of two different bikes, speeding our way up the road a couple of kilometres, until we reach our new friend's shop.

The change of scenery and the enjoyment of hitching a ride on two motorbikes is enough to raise our spirits for a little while, but neither comes close to the excitement that we soon feel upon arriving at our friend's shop, outside of which proudly stand two Pakistani Dragons, their respective drivers casually crouched down upon the dusty road, whilst their engines are refuelled. It turns out that our new friend doesn't only own a breakfast shop; he owns a few petrol pumps too!

It's no *Shell Garage*; in fact, it's nothing like any petrol station we've ever seen, but there is petrol, there are some makeshift pumps, and there are trucks outside, being filled-up for what we can only hope will be a long journey towards one of Pakistan's biggest cities.

"We want go Islamabad," Will proclaims (it doesn't take long before one's own English takes a significant turn for the worse in these countries), pointing towards the trucks.

Our new favourite Pakistani mate nods. He actually seems to understand us and moves over to the driving quartet in order to explain our request.

Nervously we wait in the wings, wondering if we should go over and give them our best "A-ssalam-O-Alekums" (they add a tuneful "A-O" to their brothers in Turkey and Iran) to show that there's more to us than being rich and Western. Look at our dresses, for goodness sake – if that isn't being culturally sensitive, then I don't know what is!

Moments later our friend returns, an apologetic look upon his face.

"Sorry. No Islamabad. They Lahore," he says, leading us away from the truckers and towards his breakfast shop.

"Hold on a minute... La-hore?" we interject, pulling out our already tattered Pakistani map to find out where on earth La-hore is. And then we spot it.

"Wait!" we shout after our friend. "Lahore good. Lahore very good!" Gone is all sense of worry; gone is all sense of pain. For a moment we even forget the decidedly uncomfortable nature of our stomachs and happily accept our friend's offer of another chai and more horribly spicy meat (of what sort, we aren't sure) with its accompanying wafer-thin bread.

Lahore is right on the other side of Pakistan. We reckon that it's got to be over 1000km away and we'd practically have arrived in India if we managed to get this ride. Once breakfast is over, our friend casually approaches the drivers again and we are soon dumping our bags into the spacious loft above the drivers' colourful cabin, and jumping inside. Forty-two hours, one thousand one hundred kilometres later, we arrive in Lahore.

DAY ONE HUNDRED AND SIXTEEN:
INTERNET INN, LAHORE, PUNJAB, PAKISTAN, MONDAY 3RD NOVEMBER 2008, 7.53AM

It would appear that we have parasites lurking deep within us, which would probably explain why our sickness has taken so long to shift. The likelihood is, the local Doctor tells us, that we picked them up through the impure water that we have been drinking since our arrival in Pakistan. Quite why we thought it a good idea to continue to eat and drink as the locals do, now that we have moved into a noticeably less developed country, I do not know. We are certainly paying for it now.

The Doctor prescribes a strong course of antibiotics for the pair of us and despairs when we tell him that we have been living on Imodium for a week. Apparently Imodium is more of a stomach-stopper than a stomach-solver. The Doctor rolls his eyes and gives us a good telling off.

* * * * *

Now, I have been a bit slack of late because a short sentence is hardly sufficient to describe the events of forty-two hours on the road, the bulk of which were spent upon the roof of a Pakistani dragon-with-wheels. We have some catching up to do...

The first stretch was the hardest. Ten hours of pretty much non-stop driving were endured inside the claustrophobic confines of new friends, Rahman and Saeed's, cabin. We spent the bulk of that first leg (during which, Will's stomach provided constant threat of eruption) arranging and rearranging our bum and shoulder positions in vain attempts to achieve any sort of comfort on the wooden bench upon which we perched.

Our first break came after about four hours of bumping along at an excruciatingly slow pace and, by this time, Will's bowels were just about ready to explode. As soon as we'd halted, he leapt out of the vehicle and stormed around the dusty village in search of a place in which he might evacuate his bowels.

This was obviously one of those places where they don't see a lot of white folk because it hadn't taken long before a crowd of fifty gawping faces surrounded him.

"Toilet! Toilet!" he screamed at them, desperately.

No response.

"WC! Double...You... See!" he whimpered, more softly.

Finally, a small boy wriggled his way through the crowd, signalled for Will to follow him, and was soon leading him towards what Will could only hope would be a lavatory. Of course, Will hardly expected the home comforts of a Western, sit-down toilet, but he could never have prepared himself for just how Spartan this "lavatory" would turn out to be.

They had gone into an apothecary's store, and out of the door at the back, at which point the boy proudly looked at Will, smiled, and pointed him out into the open field awaiting him.

Not quite sure what to make of it all, Will took one step outside, whereupon he noticed the considerable amount of excrement surrounding him, and sighed as he concluded that this was the best available toilet in the area! Well, at least it had been well used, he thought.

We are well versed in the art of squat toilets now, but random toileting in fields is still quite a new concept, and perhaps Will would have thought twice about it had he not been so desperate.

Trousers down, man-dress lifted, Will did his business, only to find that the entire crowd had come along to watch the show! One can only assume that they wanted to know if we Westerners do it in the same way that they do... OK, I'm clutching at straws, but seriously, if not why on earth would they have followed him to watch him undergo a serious bout of diarrhoea?

To make matters worse, toilet paper has become rather a rare commodity these days and we have long been bereft of supplies of that hand-sanitising gel. Thus, poor Will had to suffer one of his worst episodes to date, in front of a crowd of spectators, and now he was going to have to find some other means by which to clean himself up. It was not a happy man that rejoined me outside the apothecary's, and Will never did tell me how he got himself out of that mess. I guess that some things are better left unsaid.

Stuffing ourselves back into our friends' sweaty cabin, it was 10pm by the time we were ready for our next break and, surely now, it was time to call it a day. We scoffed some grub and made our way back to the truck, awaiting some instructions that might tell us where we were going to spend the night, but we could never have imagined what was to come.

Saeed pointed us to the iron rungs that clung to the side of their truck, and signalled that we should climb up onto the roof. Unlike the European trucks, it seems that Pakistani dragons come with a spacious loft above the cabin, which makes for a perfectly adequate bed for the night. There were several blankets laid there, and we were soon snuggling-up underneath them for what we assumed would be a few hours shut eye before we continued the journey the following day.

"This is awesome. We're sleeping on top of a truck," Will enthused, as we wrapped ourselves tightly in the blankets and gazed up at the starry skies. There was no light pollution in this remote part of the world and the stars were pulling out all the stops that night.

It had been a long day and it didn't take long before we were drifting off, but then the truck started to move!

"Oh no!" I exclaimed. "He's left the handbrake off! Actually, forget that, do we even have a handbrake?"

"It's all right," Will reassured me. "He's probably just taking us to a better spot to spend the night."

We had been driving for ten minutes before we finally worked out what was going on. Our friends hadn't sent us up on to the top of the truck so that we could get some sleep, while they themselves slept downstairs. They had sent us up here so that there was room enough for one of them to sleep on the bed downstairs, whilst the other continued, throughout the night, to drive us onwards towards Lahore.

"This just keeps getting better," Will continued. "I can't believe we're sleeping on the top of a dragon as it flies its way across Pakistan. We'll be there in no time!"

We sat up to enjoy the experience for a little while, until enough dust had been kicked up off the road to force us back to our horizontal positions beneath the blankets.

A mixture of dust and bumps ensured that our sleep wasn't the longest or the deepest, but the experience was still one that we would savour. The next morning we awoke just in time to see ourselves winding our way through the last of Aref's mountains, and we finally appreciated the significance of what we had been told – that we would know once we had reached the end of the Pashtun's Afghanistan because there we would meet with the plains of Asia.

Winding our way down one final mountain valley, we saw that, suddenly, the peaks and troughs of the previous day had given way to the flattest terrain that we had ever seen. Having told so many people about how flat England was, this was something else! Green paddy fields and grazing cattle stretched out before us as far as the eye could see, and this same scenery remained unchanged for miles on end.

Up and ready for the day by then, we proudly assumed a bird's-eye view perch on top of some boxes of apples (this was their load) that had spilled over into our private loft during the night and watched with amazement as Pakistan passed by, in what felt a little like an out-of-body experience. Here we were, thrust into the everyday lives of two Pakistani truckers, silently watching the world go by as we sat upon the top of a truck!

Our first stop of that second day came a few hours later, and Rahman and Saeed tried their best to beckon us back inside the cabin, but there was no way that we were going to prefer those claustrophobic quarters to this unprecedented chance to see the world whizz by – with free air-conditioning (caused by the actual wind) thrown in for free.

Such was our excitement that at one stage our friends practically had to physically force us to lower our heads as we began our journey through the southernmost parts of the notoriously treacherous NWFP. Just before entering into a town called D.I.Khan, Rahman pulled over, climbed up the rigging, and signalled that we should lower our heads, giving us an easily recognisable mime of the effects of machine-gun fire upon his person.

Will and I looked at each other and laughed.

"He's joking, right?" Will said, as Rahman climbed down again and re-entered through the cabin's open window.

I nodded. "Yeah, sure he is."

However, my reluctance to accept our friend's advice was not at all based upon my ignorance regarding what was a fairly good piece of acting. Rather, for some reason, I wanted simply to ignore his advice so that I could see the effects for myself. Call it a death-wish if you like, but I'd liken it more to curiosity… although I suppose that it was curiosity that saw an end to that cat, so maybe they're synonymous after all.

Not generally prone to giving in to unnecessary hysteria, we paid little regard to our friend's advice, casually whistling away as we passed through the new town, which looked much like the others, until…

There, in the middle of the road, was a military blockade. This was no uncommon thing in itself – we had become quite used to such things during our time in Eastern Turkey and Iran – but there was something different about this one. There were no uniforms. The only thing that marked out these apparent militants from the rest was that their headscarves had been pulled over their faces a little further than everyone else's, whilst they just happened to be firmly clutching hold of AK47s and sitting on the top of pick-up trucks with cigarettes dangling out of their mouths.

Before you can say "Taliban," we have hit the deck, and don't decide to surface again (other than the occasional cheeky look to see if we can see any more guerrillas) until we have safely passed through the rest of the NWFP and made the transition into the wealthier Punjab region.

The contrast is immediate. The countryside is a lush green, whilst the towns and villages that we pass generally seem more developed. Perhaps the most interesting difference relates to the road conditions. The potholed highways of Baluchistan and the NWFP are soon replaced by roads that wouldn't be out of place upon a narrow country lane in England. OK, so it's not quite the M25, but the improvement is enough to see us increase the pace significantly, and flash across the breadth of the Punjab region, arriving in Lahore in the small hours of Saturday morning.

DAY ONE HUNDRED AND EIGHTEEN:
LAWRENCE PARK, LAHORE, PUNJAB, PAKISTAN, WEDNESDAY NOVEMBER 5TH 2008, 15.46

I am sincerely hopeful that Will and I can finally manage to find a few moments of peace and quiet, as we sit upon a tree branch in what we have adjudged to be the quietest corner of Lawrence Park. Those two old friends, Peace and Quiet, have become increasingly elusive of late and, in fact, ever since we entered this country. Wherever we go, people want to talk with us and there seems to be no such thing as *alone time* in Pakistan.

The familiar sound of the call to prayer, rising up above the trees and earthen pathways that surround us, gradually fades away to reveal the squawking din of the park's airborne community. Regular passers-by – even to this most lofty hillock – disturb us with clumsy cries of "Hello," or the general shriek of accomplishment that accompanies even the most simple discoveries.

"What is this?" they whisper to each other. "Two aliens have found their way into our midst. Let us stay and watch them to see if their movements are different from our own."

Moments later, upon realising that, in fact, we are actually quite similar to them, they leave, disappointed; or, worse still, they come a little closer, just to make sure. Perhaps if they prod us, they will have a better understanding of the intricate differences between our two races.

For the moment – this blissful, fleeting moment – we are alone.

Our time in Lahore has been a time of R&R (rest and recuperation), trying as best we can to avoid the constant streams of interested passers-by and, for once, breaking our rule of never refusing an offer because, if we didn't, we would never stop drinking chai with the next stranger to approach us and ask for our hand in friendship.

"You are my best friend, yes?" they ask us, having met with us for all of one minute.

"No, you are no such thing," we long to reply. "We don't even remember your name and now you want us to be best friends with you. What does that even mean?"

Perhaps we seem ungrateful; we certainly feel that way, but depleted energy supplies have meant that we simply do not have the strength to face another hoard of locals as they harass us with an endless set of monotonous questions, which we have answered a million times already. Perhaps the most frustrating thing about it all is that we have made so many good friends on the trip and have parted company with every one of them, unlikely ever to meet again, and now, after all that, Joe Bloggs comes over to us and requests that we reassure him that, yes, in fact, he is our best mate. Of course we smile, nod, and pretend that he is right, but every time we do it drains a little bit more of that energy away from us.

* * * * *

Two men have come to join us. They sit upon my right side. Why didn't we choose a slightly smaller tree branch?

"A-ssalam-O-Alekum," one man blurts out, having patiently waited for at least twenty silent seconds, before he just cannot stand it any longer. Why haven't we even acknowledged his presence?

I force a smile, and say nothing.

"My friend, can I talk with you for a moment," he continues, clearly upset that we are being so discourteous.

Again I force a smile, and look up at the stranger. This time I speak:

"I'm really sorry, but my friend and I are just trying to take a moment to write down our thoughts. We are tired and would rather just be alone right now."

The man thinks for a moment, before responding:

"OK, I'll just sit here and watch you."

I sigh. It's better than nothing, I suppose, and it is quite ironic that this man probably has no idea that *he* is the current subject of my manuscript.

Not more than thirty seconds go by before the man interrupts again:

"Hello, my friend. Sorry, but how long do you think you will be writing?"

Again I sigh, and turn to Will, who looks up, forces a pained smile, and with it, gives me just enough strength to choke a reply:

"Look, I'm really sorry," I say, trying my best not to sound overly agitated, but really struggling now. "I said that we are writing and that we would rather be alone. If you want to watch us, then go ahead, but please don't disturb us again."

We are constantly under the tremendous pressure to act as ambassadors for our country. The first thing that people will ask us – after questioning whether or not we are Muslims – is to find out which country we are from, and everything that we proceed to say or do will help form the stranger's impression of our country as a whole. 24-7, we are called upon to act with the utmost grace and patience, and after four months of doing so, we have just about had enough.

The illness hasn't helped. We have been on antibiotics for two days now and our stomachs are finally starting to remember what it feels like when they actually hold on to some of the nutrients that we throw their way. Our waif-like appearances have caused us much distress during the course of the sickness, and regularly they have caused us to examine each other, snigger, and exclaim simply:

"You look awful," to which the other can but reply:

"Yes, I know. You too."

Thankfully, whatever parasites there were lurking deep within us have now been thoroughly prompted to head for the exit door. A good dosage of home comforts – such as regular visits to the restaurant at the *Holiday Inn*, or even (and I'm somewhat ashamed of this) *Pizza Hut* and *Subway* – has seen to that. Our bodies have been growing stronger by the day and it won't be long before we're ready to leave this city and make tracks for India. Hopefully there we will finally be able to find some peace and quiet, but I find that somewhat hard to believe.

Day One Hundred And Eighteen: (continued...)
Internet Inn, Lahore, Punjab, Pakistan, Wednesday November 5th 2008, 16.43

We must have lasted about ten minutes longer upon that tree branch before it became too much. The two men kept jabbering away and seemed painfully undeterred by our obvious lack of interest in anything that they had to say. As politely as we could, we had dealt with our harassers until they eventually left the log, but, of course, they were back inside ten minutes, bringing with them three more friends to ask us those same questions all over again. What do we think about Pakistan? Why are we here? Where have we been? Where are we going? Oh, and the most popular question of them all: What do we think about Pakistani people?

Well, in truth, we think that they are overbearing, overeager, and generally just a little bit too much, but, of course, we assume our best fixed smiles and bring out a fake line about how much we "loooooove" Pakistan and its people. They are, after all, ever so friendly!

No matter how insistent we are that we would really rather be alone, new admirers come along every few minutes, simply to gaze upon our beauty and to hassle us with questions. I think that "admirers" is actually a pretty good way of referring to the men that swarm around us wherever we go. Their admiration is only borne out of a harmless curiosity towards these new and different people in their midst (we are often told that we are the youngest foreigners that they have ever seen), but they simply have no concept of the numbers of people whom we meet and the number of times that we have had the very same conversations... again and again!

More questions follow and we've had enough. Getting up from the log, we take our journals back in hand and make for the one place that we can find peace and quiet: our hotel room. We leave our friends with another painfully censored and politically correct spiel. We feel like politicians.

"Pakistan is a beautiful country with some of the most friendly and hospitable folk on the planet. There is absolutely no sign of terrorism, nor extremism, and the bulk of the population are innocent bystanders as a few idiots wreck the image of the entire country."

Of course, this last bit is entirely true, but the first bit is just our version of diplomacy. In truth, we have found Pakistan to be quite a dirty country, which struggles with the strange paradox that comes from having inhabitants that are too friendly for foreigners to handle.

If only we had started in Pakistan, then perhaps we would have welcomed the fact that everyone wants to talk with us. It is probably only tiredness and frustration talking when we tell of the unwanted hospitality and tiresome curiosity of the locals. What strange things to complain about! What an ungrateful pair we are!

DAY ONE HUNDRED AND EIGHTEEN: (CONTINUED...)
INTERNET INN, LAHORE, PUNJAB, PAKISTAN, WEDNESDAY 5TH NOVEMBER 2008, 20.31

During our time at the Internet Inn, we have made the acquaintance of a whole host of travellers, coming to Lahore from far and wide, but it is a man from close to home that has really caught the eye. Ladies and gentlemen: it is my great pleasure to introduce you to Malcolm.

Born in Jersey, Malcolm was living a relatively normal life until one day – not unlike any other, in the sense that he was just going through the motions of his job as a soil expert – Malcolm had what, he tells us, was a spiritual experience like no other.

"I had just smoked some really strong skunk and was thinking through a mathematical pattern that had been troubling me for a little while, when, suddenly, everything seemed to make sense," Malcolm tells us.

"I was thrown into a trance and had the most intense revelation, which sent my head spinning."

Malcolm throws his arms wildly into the air and whirls them around, whilst at the same time swaying his head from side to side in order to give us a perfect representation of the kind of trance that had befallen him on that day.

"Suddenly words that were not my own came to me and, before I even knew what was going on, I wrote down the following:

"*There are Three Pillars to Paradise: Devotion, Compassion, and*

Pacifism. Whoa! I had no control over the words, but suddenly everything made sense to me."

Malcolm takes a break, brushing his long, greying hair, away from his eyes, before continuing:

"Recite Mohammed, recite!" The hands whirl around his head again and he's really trying his best to show us what it feels like to work oneself into a stupor.

"I tell you, this was God speaking to me, giving me the same revelation that he gave Mohammed centuries ago. It was the most beautiful moment. Whoa!"

Malcolm takes another puff of the reefer in his hand, and flails his arms around in the air again, his long hair reaching down to the floor, meeting legs that are crossed over into a perfectly orchestrated, Buddhist-like position of meditation. He sits there silently, swaying slowly to the music going on inside of his head, whilst Will and I look at each other, raising our eyebrows and biting our lips so that we won't burst into laughter.

Malcolm has been living in India for five years now (God told him to go there during his "experience") and is only in Lahore for the sake of extending his visa over there. During these five years, Malcolm has travelled far and wide in the country, visiting all of the most holy sites of the different religions represented there. He doesn't appear to pay a particular allegiance to one, preferring to sit on the fence in a truly post-modernistic appreciation of the benefits of each. God, he believes, has chosen him to be a prophet to the nations, professing a message not his own, so that the world may be saved.

* * * * *

"Malcolm really does think he's going to save the world, doesn't he?" I say to Will, over another dinner at the *Holiday Inn*.

We both laugh. Neither of us has said anything about the conversation since it happened, several hours before.

"The funniest thing is that every point that he makes starts in the same way." Will stops for a moment to put on his best Jersey accent:

"I had just scored some of the finest weed known to humanity and then… then The Lights came!"

Malcolm refers to the spiritual entity speaking to him as *The Lights* and we do feel it to be a little unorthodox that the Deity, in revealing itself to him, chooses to do so only when he is off his head on drugs!

At forty-something years of age, Malcolm is a strange man to get one's head around. The first thing that we ever heard him say, shortly after his arrival, was to blabber on about how much he hates Israelis because (and you'll enjoy the reasoning here):

"Every one of them is a c***."

"Don't you think you're generalising a little bit," I offer, hoping that I can change this peculiar little man's prejudice.

"No!" he replies shortly, and that is that.

If the crazed words coming out of Malcolm's lips weren't enough to convince somebody that he was a total lunatic, his appearance ought to do it. I'd reckon Malcolm is about 5ft 5inches (quite short for a fella), and the straggly hair that flows from every available follicle upon his skull combines to reach at least half the way down his tiny torso. When he speaks, he spits, and this is no doubt partly as a result of the sheer number of hairs that flow from his face, somehow managing to droop all the way from his moustache to his belly button. A lip-reader would struggle to make out a word that Malcolm mutters from behind those jagged, yellow teeth, but one assumes that it is the intensity of his spiritual journey that has led him to this grotesque position: a true pilgrim need not waste time on grooming.

Beyond Malcolm's mental musings and verbal rants, his chosen medium of communication is visual animation. It isn't long after we have met the man that he is showing us every one of his "Lights" videos in turn, until they have told us the whole story about how he sees the world.

Malcolm has two main points. Point one is that Aum (Hindu) and Allah (Muslim), when flipped upside down in mathematical formulae, are in fact one and the same, thus proving the plurality of religions, i.e. We all believe in the same God, but see Him from different sides of the same being. Point two (and this is where he really starts sounding insane) is that he has been sent to save the world from collapsing upon itself as a result of a dangerous scientific experiment going on somewhere in Geneva.

Hold on a minute! Showing us videos about the similarities between Aum and Allah was one thing, but suddenly a subliminal message flashes up on the screen:

"STOP CERN!!!"

The message repeats itself a number of times in later Lights videos and we are thoroughly bemused by our peculiar friend's reasoning.

"Malcolm, who on earth are CERN? And why do you want to stop them?" I ask, deciding it best not to go one step further and ask him quite *how* he intends to stop them.

"CERN is a European organisation of nuclear scientists that are carrying out incredibly dangerous experiments at the moment," Malcolm explains.

"They are trying to recreate the Big Bang in a controlled environment by bringing two atoms together at speeds approaching that of the speed of Light." Malcolm is becoming more and more agitated as he goes on.

"But they've got it wrong! They've got their arithmetic entirely wrong and if we let them do it then it will mean that the whole world will collapse in upon itself!"

Will and I exchange quizzical glances.

"But don't you think that they know what they're doing, Malcolm?" asks Will.

"No!" he shouts. "They *think* that they do, but that's exactly what I've been trying to show you. They don't know what they're doing because at the heart of the creation of the Universe are Aum and Allah and, if we bring them together again, the world will end."

"So you really believe yourself to be more intelligent than these highly acclaimed nuclear physicists?" I ask.

"Yes!" he squeals, "but only because the Lights revealed their message to me."

Oh, how we yearn to interrupt with an "Of course they did Malcolm," but we hold our tongues.

Malcolm continues. "It's all because these scientists are working off the back of a premonition that is entirely false. They believe that the Universe is expanding, but it isn't!"

The conversation goes on, but as much as we enjoy watching his videos and hearing the thoughts of a clearly intelligent individual, Malcolm's methods come unstuck right about the time when he starts talking about the copious amounts of weed that he has been smoking, not to mention the bit about stopping nuclear scientists in Switzerland. I'm sorry to say it, but Malcolm's just another headcase.

DAY ONE HUNDRED AND NINETEEN:
INTERNET INN, LAHORE, PUNJAB, PAKISTAN, THURSDAY 6TH NOVEMBER 2008, 10AM

If you're wondering why it is that we are *still* in Lahore, then think no further than today. Apparently Thursday is *the* day to come to Lahore and we have risked bumping into our terror-happy friend for at least two more days than we might have done, just so that we can be here to see what all the fuss is about.

The weakening effects of the parasites have now largely subsided and we feel ready to hit the road again, but have been waiting around to see today's double-headed musical spectacle. We kick off at lunchtime with traditional Pakistani music and dancing at the mosque, but the main event comes later in the evening, when we will be taken to the other side of town for a Sufi drumming session. We don't know what to expect, but if it is anything like the Pakistani cinema that we experienced last night, then it'll be worth a peek.

Our purple-haired, Geordie pal, Keith (another of the residents at the Internet Inn), is a teacher of film and cinema at the local University and he simply would not allow us to pass through Lahore without going along to watch famous Punjabi actress, Nargis, *strut her stuff* in one of the archetypal Punjabi films, *Suhagan*.

As soon as we arrived at the cinema, we were overawed by the bright lights that beckoned us in. After paying our dues we slipped inside to await the ensuing cinematic production, slightly disappointed that this wasn't the jam-packed room that we had been warned to expect, but then the music started, reaching full volume in its very first seconds, and persisting resolutely to stay at this level throughout the film.

When the pictures came, it felt as if we were watching a Bollywood film from the eighties – such was the basic quality of the picture – and the film was entirely in the local dialect, which meant that any interpretation of events would be guesswork.

Luckily for us the storyline wasn't too hard to follow. The film revolved around the story of two families and the various different marriages that took place within them. There was nothing particularly special about the storyline – in fact I guess it was a kind of Pakistani *chick flick* – but the way in which it was acted will certainly live long in the memory.

Our excitable friend, Keith, had warned us about the vulgarity that we should expect to see, and he wasn't exaggerating. The purpose of every actress on screen revolved solely around jutting and jiving in front of the camera so that she might show off her sizeable bust and behind to the whooping and cat-calling audience.

"Every actress on screen who isn't wearing a headscarf is actually a prostitute," our camp Geordie friend tells us. "But, although they may be prostitutes, they are also probably the only women in the whole of Pakistan to have any power!"

On this evidence, it isn't difficult to believe him. The camera work wasn't exactly tasteful and if it weren't for censorship laws then I'm sure this movie would have degenerated into a cheap attempt at pornography. To be honest, it is probably about as close as Pakistani men get to seeing porn anyway, which might explain the crowd's reaction.

"Whoop! Whoop! Whoop!" they yell. "Yada! Yada! Yada!"

Keith warned us about the dirty deeds that often take place underneath the dimly lit Odeon roof, and a security guard is regularly on call to flash his torch along every row that he might keep a check upon potential miscreants.

The interval comes about two hours after the film has started and we have seen quite enough. It was worth going to get a glimpse of the Pakistani cinematic experience, but I don't think we'll be going back for a second helping.

DAY ONE HUNDRED AND TWENTY:
MOTEL, WAGHA BORDER, PUNJAB, PAKISTAN, FRIDAY 7TH NOVEMBER 2008, 20.14

Our time in Pakistan has been short. Tomorrow morning we cross over the Wagha Border and experience what is sure to be a tough first day's hitching in India. As far as our sage friend Malcolm tells us, there is no hitchhiking in India.

"You won't do it in *there* boys," he splutters from somewhere beneath that furry upper lip. "You'll need more than luck to hitchhike in India! They won't do anything for free!"

I suppose that we will just have to wait and see how much wisdom there is in this pessimism, but I have a quiet and growing confidence in the worldwide goodness of humankind, which suggests to me that we will be just fine.

* * * * *

Yesterday it was our turn to enjoy the famous musical feast that takes over the streets of Lahore every Thursday. In the afternoon we were taken to the central mosque (to its underground layer), where we watched a dozen musical ensembles take to the stage in an attempt to woo the watching crowd into parting with precious rupees.

Malik, owner of the Internet Inn, had told us to take as many ten-rupee notes as we could because several times during each performance a basket would be passed around the crowd and, if we liked the act, we were supposed to cough up.

For the most popular acts it was not uncommon to see grand demonstrations of appreciation by the most impressed audience members waltzing right up to the stage to drop, one by one, handfuls of notes at the performers' feet.

Of course, we were encouraged to do the same, but, being British, chose to show our gratitude in a more understated fashion, surreptitiously sneaking a few notes into the basket as it went the rounds. On only one occasion did the performance offer enough pizzazz to see me take to my feet, but this time it was not the music that had really impressed, but the dancing of an aged man, who sported his finest robe and pirouetted in a most flirtatious fashion.

During each band's set, a few of the regulars would take to the dance floor in front of the stage and offer us the most amazing examples of traditional Pakistani dancing.

First on his feet was a chubby old man with a full head of dreadlocks, which he soon began to send spinning around his head as he twisted around in what, we were told, was a typically Sufi style of dance. The second man looked as if he had just clocked off from working at a garage. Sporting a mechanic's overalls, this strange looking chap processed towards us in what was more like a gallop than a dance step.

Then, as if these two pretenders weren't enough to bring amusement, the third arrival beggared belief. A man who must have been well into his eighties, dressed in a fine green robe that was richly embroidered with emeralds, bounded to his feet and started nodding his head to the beat of the music. We couldn't believe the amount of energy that this old-timer had, and the manner of his flirtatious dance – which seemed wholly directed towards us Westerners on the front row – was as disturbing as it was surprising. Twisting his arms around in a way akin to an Egyptian temptress, this man skipped towards us and beckoned us to dance with him. An hilariously flirtatious old gent, I was on my feet in seconds, slipping a ten-rupee note into the pouch on the front of his garment, as if this man was on a lap dancer's stage.

The afternoon's entertainment over with, the real spectacle came later on that evening as hundreds of locals (and a scattering of white folk) gathered together outside a second mosque to watch an all-night Sufi drumming session.

The courtyard was crammed full and we whities were squeezed into a corner and given a good view from some steps on the side of the shrine, where we would watch in amazement as two brothers began to bang upon their drums (which were fastened to their necks by big straps) and twist around... and around... and around.

It was the stamina of the pair that really took the breath away. They just would not stop spinning and we could not believe that they were able to stay on their feet for so long, without fainting from dizziness.

Apparently the point of the spinning is to work oneself into a trance-like state so that you might come closer to the spirit of God. Sufism is a mystic strand of Islam and it wasn't hard to notice that these weren't your regular Muslims. If the spinning around wasn't enough to show us that, then the copious amount of marijuana passed around confirmed the suspicions. At one stage a man approached us with no less than six joints in one hand and offered each Westerner a drag.

It wasn't long before a dance party had amassed around the drummers, and doped-up Sufis were vigorously spinning around to find that higher spiritual state. This was a rave like no other and we were sorry to leave well before its expected finish, but we had a new country to explore the very next morning, and figured that we were going to need all the energy that we could get.

Opium den, Karaj

Dr. Haghighi's Office, Tehran

Ehsan's house, Shiraz

Shabnam and Elham, Kish

Man dresses, Quetta

Zakir's garden, Hanna Urak

Fishing expedition, Hanna Urak

Zakir's nephew and sister

Earthquake refugees, Khanoudi

Taliban?

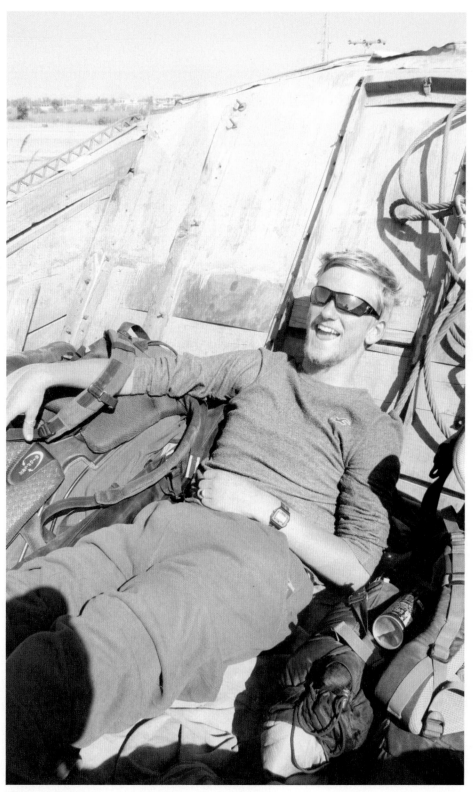

Trucktop, Pakistan

Wagha Border

12. AN INVASION OF THE SENSES

DAY ONE HUNDRED AND TWENTY-ONE:
RAJU GUEST HOUSE, JALANDHAR, PUNJAB, INDIA, SATURDAY 8TH NOVEMBER 2008, 21.12

Who says you can't hitchhike in India?

Knowing not what to expect when we finally surfaced from our beds to wander over the colourful Wagha Border, we were pleasantly surprised to be offered a lift in a matter of minutes by a Sikh trucker on his way to nearby Amritsar. There, we were deposited outside the train station and presented with the remnants of a bottle of whiskey as a leaving present.

It is becoming increasingly tricky to get this hitchhiking message across the further we go east, and we have resigned ourselves to the likelihood that most people, like dear Mr. Singh, will assume only that we long to be taken to public transport hubs.

Laughing it off this time, we shook our friend's hand, crammed his liquor bottle into Will's oversized bag, and were just attempting to navigate ourselves back out onto the right road when we stumbled across a Golden Temple.

Having spent the previous two months in Muslim countries, it is a joy to be entering the home of two other famous world religions, Hinduism and Sikhism. We are yet to come into contact with any Hindus, but we have already been moved by the kindness of the Sikhs to have crossed our path

– none more so than at Amritsar's stunning Golden Temple, and the Community Kitchen therein.

The best way of describing the truly miraculous scale of servitude that goes on there is to liken it to an hourly feeding of the five thousand. In a hall that must accommodate close to two thousand people at any one time, lines of hungry bellies are satisfied on a 24-7 basis in what can only be described as a beacon of humanitarian aid.

Joining with a queue of visiting Sikhs and a scattering of fellow-tourists (all of whom seemed equally unaware of just what was going on), we were plied with plates, bowls and spoons, and then pushed and shoved from every side for half an hour until the time came for us to eat.

Outside the Temple, a sign reads simply:

"Free community kitchen open 24 hours a day for people of every class."

What a wonderful thing to have in the midst of so holy a place! The poorest people in Amritsar can at least rest safely in the knowledge that, as long as this service continues, they will never go hungry.

* * * * *

Another spectacle to have taken our breath away in the past 24 hours was the theatrical ceremony that accompanied the closing of the Wagha Border last night. A daily performance, we marvelled at the passion that presided over the marches of the guards, and the hollering of the assigned country-criers, who, dressed proudly in the colours of their flag, did not cease from patriotic chanting until the border gate had slammed shut on their rivals.

I do not understand exactly the reasoning behind the procession – which sees huge crowds develop on both sides of the Wagha border each day – but I assume that both countries are making statements about their right to the land in the disputed Kashmir region in the North.

"Pakistan! Pakistan! Pakistan!" the toothless crier spat in his fiercest tone, obliging everyone (ourselves included) on our side of the gate to join in.

My favourite bit of the whole procession (which lasted almost an hour) was the grand finale, in which the respective senior guards marched speedily towards the gate, stared sternly at the other, shook hands, and then swivelled around to stomp their feet in defiance, offering one final glare at the other before marching off with their country's flag proudly held aloft.

"You shall not pass!" was the phrase arising from their respective ranks, as the crowd gasped in awe and appreciation, applauding loudly and echoing those well-versed cries:

"Pakistan! Pakistan! Pakistan!" This chant was still reverberating around my head as it hit the pillow last night.

* * * * *

It is funny to think that the cities of Amritsar and Lahore are only about thirty kilometres apart because the differences between the two could not be more apparent. Religion, culture, dress, food – and just about everything else – is so drastically different here in India that it feels strange to consider that Pakistan is but a stone's throw away.

Gone are the distasteful looks that were directed towards us by the most pious of Islamists; gone is the awful prejudice that cripples the women of Pakistan. Finally we can see women on the streets again! Whilst in Lahore the number of women certainly did increase – I suppose that it is only in the most rural areas of Pakistan where practice remains so archaic – it is the additional splash of colour that is the most notable difference here.

Women are everywhere again – there even seem to be more of them than there are men – and they all dress in the most wonderfully colourful and elaborate of saris and embroidered dresses. The Muslim dress code has finally relaxed and, along with it, we have found that the whole atmosphere of the country seems... generally lighter.

One thing that is slightly frustrating, this side of the border, is the mercenary attitude of the natives. To a certain extent, Malcolm was right: touts are everywhere, and we had to have our wits about us tonight in order to avoid being completely ripped-off for a bed for the night in this truly grotty town, Jalandhar.

In the end we settled for this grubby guesthouse only because they were charging us a fair price: 200 rupees (less than three quid) a night. Traipsing between hotels for over an hour, searching for anything slightly cleaner that might offer us a reasonable rate, we were quoted vastly different sums (anywhere between 100 and 2000 rupees) for essentially the same service, but found nothing worth paying the extra pennies for.

The final straw in our search came when a man offered to show us to a "cheap hotel," only to bump up the price as soon as we had arrived – by way of commissioning him for his efforts!

We had met our first tout. These people apparently roam the streets of every town in India, on the lookout for naive tourists with too much money and not enough sense, and we escaped on this occasion only because we had asked our final driver what we should be paying for a basic hotel room. He told us to pay no more than 300 rupees, so when the chap, upon racking his brains for a fabricated lofty figure, came out with "1800 rupees," we said "No thank you very much," and went on our way to settle for a soggy mattress at this, the Raju Guesthouse.

It might take us a while to get used to the money-grabbing nature of the Indian unemployed, but we have dealt with tonight fairly well, and don't mind too much that our bathroom doesn't even have a working tap, let alone a sit-down toilet. We've got a bed for the night and sleeping bags to place over the dirty sheets. The overhead light might not be very bright, but it has at least been bright enough for me to jot down a few thoughts tonight on this, our first night in India.

DAY ONE HUNDRED AND TWENTY-THREE:
RANJAN HOTEL, SHIMLA, HIMACHAL PRADESH, INDIA, MONDAY 10TH NOVEMBER 2008, 10.32AM

I sit upon a bench on the top floor of the Ranjan Hotel in the colonial hill station of Shimla – our first stop in the Indian Himalayan mountain range – and gaze upon the breathtaking peaks that stretch out before me. It is noticeably chillier in this part of the world, but there is not a snowdrop to be seen and the entire valley remains beautifully green. The sound of a thousand horns somewhat disturbs this tranquil scene, but serves as a nice reminder that this is, after all, still a part of India.

"Hitch to the Himalayas" has got a certain ring to it, don't you think? If only we had decided to stick with this original plan then the journey would now be complete, but, as it is, there is still a very long way to go, and we remain decidedly uncertain about the best route to take from here on in. Our Indian visas – acquired long ago in Sofia – mark our last prepaid border crossing, so the way ahead is wide open.

One of our drivers yesterday, a Colonel called "S.P.," recommended Burma as our "best bet." Somewhat oxymoronic to hear the words "Burma" and "best" in the same sentence without a serious disclaimer, we thought, but the Colonel assured us that it isn't nearly as bad as it's cracked up to be.

Given the ongoing instability of the Burmese government and their continuing attempts to stamp out any visits from foreigners – be they mere tourists or the most benevolent aid workers – we had not given Myanmar much thought, but it would be a real Godsend should this route prove a possibility. Not only is it much more direct, but it would save us from weeks of hazardous mountain trekking through increasingly cold climates. We have little idea regarding the feasibility of a trek through the upper regions of Nepal and Tibet into that enormous land mass that is China, and whilst we know very little about Burma – save that the country is run by a volatile militia – we can see, geographically and climatically speaking at the very least, just how advantageous this option could be.

Dreams of future plans must be put aside a little longer, however, because there is a long way to go before we need to consider future direction too seriously, and I am sure that there is much to enjoy on the Indian roads between now and then.

* * * * *

Yesterday marked only our second day's hitching in India, and I have to say that, much as we thought, it isn't proving nearly as difficult as dear Malco made out. It's a darn sight easier than it was in Pakistan, at the very least, and marks a welcome return to days gone by in Iran, when just the novelty of having a white face would seem to be enough at least to ensure that every driver stops – even if he might want money for the privilege of doing so.

Actually, it's even better here than it was in Iran because most people seem to have a rough (even if it is *very* rough) idea of what it is that we are trying to do. "Lift" (pronounced "leafed") seems to be the nearest translation and they even seem to understand our thumb-wagging actions!

Of course, this greater understanding did little to prevent our first driver – a man in charge of an empty school minibus – from taking us straight to a bus stop. Here, a squadron of touts soon swarmed around us in their most ardent attempts at guiding us into their respective money-making wagons, but we were having none of it. As soon as our unknowingly unhelpful driver was out of sight, we marched away from the bus stop until we were at a sufficient distance to feel certain that we would not be associated with other bus frequenters, and stuck out our thumbs again.

Within fifteen minutes a truck had pulled over and, after a brief conversation with the driver in which little was said, and even less clarified, we were underway on what we hoped would be a free ride roughly in the direction of Shimla.

"Rupee nahi" (which means "no money" in Urdu), Will stated, once safely under way, just to check that our driver was clear on our position, but he seemed almost offended that we'd even asked, waving away the suggestion as madness.

"Shimla?" I inquired, just to make sure we weren't heading in completely the opposite direction.

The man nodded, but it wasn't until some five hours later – when we were finally deposited beside a signpost that had *SHIMLA* written upon it in large letters – that we were truly certain of our direction. The problem was that ever since leaving those Afghani Mountains we seemed to have been surrounded only by plains upon plains of identical scenery, and it seemed a little farfetched to believe that we were even vaguely close to one of the world's largest mountain ranges.

"Where are all the flippin' mountains?" bemoaned Will, whilst we waited. "We'll never get there at this rate!"

To be fair, he had a point. We were still over 200km away and it seemed that the bulk of that journey was going to be spent averaging no more than 20km/hr as we wound our way up the side of an apparently invisible mountain. Yet, there was one thing that Will hadn't accounted for, and that was the surprise arrival of a Colonel who just so happened to be stationed in Shimla, spoke fluent English, and drove one of the fastest cars that we had been in for months.

It was a long 50km slog before we even reached the foothills, followed by an horrendously slow 130km hill-climb beyond that, but we rested safely in the knowledge that we were at least going to make it to Shimla that day and we were going to do it a hell of a lot faster than we would have been able to do in one of those Indian trucks – which are about as slow as the Pakistani dragons and don't even have quite the same strength of colour to make up for it.

In fact we cared little about the length of the journey, and tried our best to ignore the regular near misses we encountered as we crawled precariously up the cliff face. We were simply relieved to have made it to Shimla in one go. At around 9pm, some fourteen hours after leaving Scum City, we finally arrived in Shimla, at which point we could officially claim that we'd hitchhiked to the Himalayas!

DAY ONE HUNDRED AND TWENTY-FOUR:
RANJAN HOTEL, SHIMLA, HIMACHAL PRADESH, INDIA, TUESDAY 11TH NOVEMBER 2008, 11.30PM

Our time in Shimla is set to come to an end. At 9am tomorrow we plan on making our way towards the apparently "unmissible" Mcleodganj and, not for the first time, we appear to have acquired a hitching partner for the event. Evan from New York State will accompany us upon our adventure into the depths of the Himalayan Mountains, where we are very much looking forward to spending time in peaceful reflection at the home of the Dalai Lama. Who knows, maybe we'll have been converted to Buddhism after our time there? One must never rule these things out.

We felt as though we had Islam sussed by the end of our two-month stay in Turkey, Iran and Pakistan, and we are already making waves with Sikhism and Hinduism. I mean, we even visited a Hindu temple yesterday and the man tending the altar judged us worthy enough to endow us with a light sprinkling of his holy ointment and a handful of the children's sweets he was dishing out. The icing on the cake, though, was the orange goo that he proceeded to wipe across our foreheads – marking us out as newly born Hindus, I suppose.

Reflecting upon the experience now, we do not feel overly comfortable with our willy-nilly decision to join in with what we believe to be little more than worthless idolatry, but we were so relaxed at the time that our cynicism did not prevent us from sharing in what one could also conclude to be a harmless ritual with our new Hindu pals.

Today has been spent almost entirely in the company of these same pals – a group of seven engineers from Chandigard, a city at the foothills of the Himalayas. Knowing the area a little better than us (this is their regular holiday resort), our friends led us on a 10km trek, which we finished with beers around a campfire we built beside a mountain stream.

The scenery surrounding us here in Himachal Pradesh is indescribably beautiful and the friendliness of the locals has immediately made us feel much more comfortable than we had been during our brief stay in Pakistan. There generally seems to be less pressure upon us to live up to other people's expectations and we are not expected to stop and talk to every single person that passes by. India generally appears to have a much more relaxed way of life, and we are finding it much easier to fit in.

It'll be a shame to leave this place tomorrow, and to say goodbye to the lovely locals who smile widely at us as we pass by, staffs (fashioned out of tree branches) gripped tightly in our hands, but one thing we won't miss is the need to be constantly on our guard here (hence the sticks) to protect ourselves from the attacks of any one of several wild creatures that roam here.

"Monkey leave you alone if you have stick," our hotel owner kindly informed us at the end of our first night here. We were thankful for the advice because the place is awash with cheeky monkeys, who would otherwise cause havoc with their kleptomania. On our walk to the temple yesterday we saw one poor, unsuspecting soul lose his glasses to one of the little terrors. Turning his back only for a moment, the little blighter jumped up onto his back and ripped the glasses from his face, letting out a shrill shriek as it dismounted from its victim, as if to warn the chap against making any attempt to retrieve them. Presumably it was the glasses' interestingly shiny qualities that attracted the monkey's admiration, although I suppose that there is a chance that this monkey might have been high enough in the evolutionary plane to have developed an understanding of the drawbacks of his short-sightedness. I would like to think that he is currently sitting back at home with the wife and kids, proudly dictating a Shakespearean sonnet to his family just to get used to the feel of the things...

Intellectual monkeys aside, there is another set of wild creatures which have caused us great alarm during our stay in Shimla and these are the stray dogs. On our very first night here, just after the Colonel had dropped us off at the Ranjan Hotel, we ravenously wolfed down supper at the nearby vegetarian establishment and went for an impromptu stroll around the town that we might find our bearings.

It had been a long day and it didn't take long before dozens of slopes and steps had tired us out. We were going to make one final circuit of what we adjudged to be the town centre and then attempt to find our way back to the hotel. We hadn't got very far in our return journey, however, before one of the many strays (and a particularly straggly one at that) had taken a particular liking, or disliking (we couldn't tell), to us and decided to follow us, snapping at our heels and growling as we went.

Perhaps this might not seem particularly scary, or even out of the ordinary, for those of you that are used to that sort of thing, but to a man who was bitten by a dog at the age of two and has never seen eye-to-eye with the Animal Kingdom since, this was terrifying.

"Mate, what are we going to do? You know I don't like dogs!" I yelped, scampering off in front to leave Will to do his dog-whispering thing.

"Oh come on mate, don't leave me with the thing. It's clearly rabid," moaned Will, giving the mongrel in question an accusing glare. The mutt seemed hurt by the suggestion and proceeded to snap and snarl at Will's heels in growing agitation.

A man came into view a little further down the hill and I scampered over to him in search of assistance. He looked like a local; surely he'd know what to do in this situation.

Drawing closer to the man, it quickly became apparent that not only was this man a local, but he was also a beggar. The tattered clothing and considerable body odour gave me a hint, whilst the open hands and the "Please sir, please sir" confirmed it.

"Namaste," I greeted the man, who didn't seem to know which way to look in order to find me.

"Will, I think he's drunk," I called back to my friend, who was fast approaching, hound still snapping at his heels.

"Hello sir. Please help us," I continued, hoping that, even if the words that I said could not be understood, the distressed tone in which they were said might spark this man into action.

The beggar still seemed to be having trouble finding exactly where to look and, just before I wrote the man off as a hopeless drunk, I realised that he must be at least partially blind.

Reaching out to take the half-empty bottle of water in my hand (presumably as payment), the blind beggar took a second to sense the exact location of the heavily breathing stray, then threw back his left leg and caught it full in the face.

Our mouths dropped open as we heard the mutt whimper and limp back in the direction from whence it came.

"Thank you! Thank you!" we cried in unison.

"Der-ne-vad. That's how you say it, isn't it mate?" I asked Will, who shrugged. Our blind saviour seemed happy enough with his plastic bottle anyway and we hollered our continued thanks to him until he had fully shuffled out of sight.

On our way back to the hotel we picked up a few branches and fashioned them into staffs. We wouldn't go outside in Shimla again without them.

DAY ONE HUNDRED AND TWENTY-SIX:
ZILNON KAGYELING NVINGMAPA MONASTERY, MCLEOD GANJ, HIMACHAL PRADESH, INDIA, THURSDAY 13TH NOVEMBER 2008, 13.29

Mcleod Ganj seems to live up to the hippie-hype quite emphatically. On my left, an elderly Tibetan woman shuffles by to make her slow ascent up the metal staircase that hugs the wall of this picturesque monastery. We will not be staying here tonight – having already made our beds in the similarly well-respected *Om Hotel* – but I hope that we have another chance to stay in a monastery during our time in this refugee village, which is home to flocks of asylum-seeking Tibetans.

We arrived late last night, miraculously managing to hitch all the way up and down the 250km of mountainous verges in just one day's hitching from Shimla. Although the distance doesn't sound particularly impressive, let me assure you that the average speed meant that this – which might be a two and a half hour journey on the flat – was more like a twelve-hour journey, given our chosen terrain, and the vehicles in which we tackled it.

On our first day with a tagalong since Iran, Evan's inaugural hitch contained everything required to make sure that he got the fullest experience of just what it has been like for us to hitch all the way here. At 10am yesterday morning, having once again spectacularly failed to point ourselves in an easterly direction, we dragged Evan onto a westerly road and started out on what was sure to be at least 500km of additional hitchhiking.

Progress was swift. We waited a cumulative total of no more than ten minutes between our first two lifts, which combined to bring us to the midway point of Bilaspur in time for a late luncheon. Yet, that was the easy bit. We had done over 100km in a little under four hours, but that was the downhill sector. Now it was time for the challenging part.

Evan was growing in confidence and took over the reins in this second stint, making the most of his gangly arms and legs in his attempts to plead with passing truckers to stop. We were impressed with the results.

Within minutes, our lanky friend had managed to get us a lift in a truck and, his adrenaline pumping hard, didn't seem to mind too much when he found that there was enough room only for Will and me in an already-congested trucker's cabin. Jumping from the cabin door, Evan simply wheeled away to the back of the vehicle, climbed into the trailer and made himself comfortable among a hundred bags of cement.

Meanwhile, Will and I were busy introducing ourselves to the seven other inhabitants of our cramped confines, whilst we worried about the possibility that the rest of our friends might be paying customers.

"No money. No money," we repeated several times.

"Rupee nahi. Rupee nahi," we continued, hoping that these Indians could speak a little Urdu.

It seemed to do the trick. Our driver waved away the suggestion, but then we had to watch, ashamed, as, one by one, the other passengers parted with their own handfuls of petty change for the ride.

"Nothing comes for free in India." We remembered these words that Malcolm had told us and pondered our new ethical dilemma. How could it be fair for us to pay nothing when these other passengers – almost certainly poorer than ourselves – were doing so?

We had an enormous amount of time to think about just that, as we plodded our way up the mountain, averaging 20km/hr at the very most. By the time we had arrived at our trucker friends' last stop, it was already dark and we reckoned that we were still about 70km short of our destination.

A sparse scattering of street lamps provided our only illumination, but, upon becoming fast surrounded by a curious band of local children – who each tugged at various bits of our person or belongings, and mentioned that word, "Rupee," all too often – we decided we must go on.

Perhaps it was the confusion of the mêlée that led us to make what probably must go down as our most naïve hitching-mistake to date...

The driver of a small white vehicle answered Evan's frantic flailing of limbs by pulling over at the side of the road, winding down the window, and (presumably) asking if he could be of help. The problem was that the gentleman spoke only Hindi.

Well-versed in attempting to find unorthodox methods of communication, Will and I went over to give Evan a hand.

"Five kilometres," I said, loud and clear, even holding up five fingers to signify just what I meant.

The driver seemed to understand, but shook his head, holding up an additional two fingers in order (presumably) to get across the sign language equivalent of: "I go seven kilometres; not five!"

"Seven?" I repeated, copying his gesture with my own seven digits.

"He's clearly one for detail," joked Will.

"Seven kilometres it is," said I, as the three of us hopped into the vehicle. "Anywhere to get us away from these little pests!"

Seven kilometres came and went in a flash. We were in a car, after all, and must have been averaging more than double the pace that we were doing in the trucks, but then we just kept on going... and going some more.

Of course, there was no way of knowing exactly how far we had gone, but by the time we had been driving for forty minutes, and must have easily done more than three times the distance he seemed to have indicated, I knew that something was wrong. Why had he been so darn precise about the number of kilometres that he was going to take us, if he wasn't intending to stick to it?

And then the dreaded thought came to my mind that maybe, just maybe... No, he couldn't be a Taxi driver, could he?

Given the dangerous universality of the "T" word, I had to be subtle as I fronted my concerns to my two companions.

"No way man," Evan replied. "He said seven kilometres, didn't he? Come on, there's no way he's going to charge us. If he were a "T" driver then it would be his prerogative to make certain about the money, but he never mentioned it."

It was with a mixture of optimism and naivety, however, rather than wisdom and certainty, that our American friend comforted us, and Will and I exchanged worried glances as we warned Evan that the "M" word (money) was just as dangerous as the "T" word. We had been in this sort of situation before and knew the dangers when the subject of money had not yet arisen. Why hadn't we made sure of it at the start of our journey? Normally we were always repeating that "Rupee Nahi!" thing. Why not this time?

Evan's words of reassurance were enough to calm us down for a while, but with every extra kilometre that we travelled beyond our original expectation, it seemed more and more likely that we were soon going to have to prepare ourselves for an unsavoury confrontation.

Cautiously, we decided that we had to act soon, rather than waiting for him to take us all the way to our destination before we spoke up.

"Where you go?" I began, speaking as slowly as I could and pointing at him to signify "you," before opening my hands and shrugging my shoulders in an attempt to communicate "where."

No response.

"You business?" asked Will.

I know that "You business" is hardly a specific question, but this was the best that we could come up with to check if he was driving for business or for pleasure. It is these bitty phrases that we have to rely upon in desperate times. There is no point in producing an eloquent sentence to a man that can't even count to ten! Words like "business," "money" and "taxi" seem to cross cultural divides – perhaps it is because they are necessities if one is to make money off unsuspecting tourists! – but this man wasn't getting any of it.

"You go family?" I continued.

Still nothing.

As the kilometres racked up, the only things that we had managed to work out from our bemused friend – who must have been wondering why these bizarre foreigners wouldn't just leave him alone – were that he was twenty-seven years old (achieved through the raising of twenty-seven digits between us) and that his "home" (they know that one) seemed to be the place from where he picked us up.

By the time the interrogation had run out of steam and we had resigned ourselves to just sitting back and seeing what happened, we had been travelling for some ninety minutes and must have done at least sixty kilometres. There was little optimism remaining. Even the chirpy newcomer among us was getting a little scared about the inevitable confrontation that was awaiting us around the next bend.

"Come on guys. What's going on? This is ridiculous," he chirped, trying to impose a little urgency, but now it was our turn to be mute. There was nothing left to say; nothing left to do but to wait.

* * * * *

Sure enough, when we eventually arrived in Dharamshala (the place where we had told the man that we were headed because it is the big town just 3.9km down the hill from Mcleod Ganj) we were abruptly ejected from the car and promptly introduced to our friend's open palms.

"Rupee." Finally he had found his tongue. All it had taken to break that long silence had been the potential for some sweet, sweet rupees.

We stared blankly at our friend, overtaken by a mixture of fear and disappointment. It was clear what had happened now. Our fears had been realised. My, "We are going to Dharamshala. Can you take us just five kilometres in that direction?" had been mistaken for more of a, "Will you take us to Dharamshala for five rupees per kilometre?" And thus, what we had assumed to be a, "No, I cannot take you five, but will be happy to take you seven," actually turned out to be a, "Five rupees? No way. I'll do it for seven!"

Curse these language barriers! I am sincerely hopeful that this was an honest mistake upon both sides, rather than this man's cheap attempt to rip us off, but whatever kind of mistake it was, the scene that followed was decidedly unpleasant.

Surrounded by a crowd, we were aided by a kind young boy named Pavel in our attempts to explain to our driver that we were travelling all the way to Malaysia without money and that, as a result, we could not pay him for what was a relatively insignificant journey.

Pavel seemed to be the only person in the crowd to speak any English, so it was his job to play the part of translator, and this he did with great patience and goodness of heart.

"He says you pay 1,100 rupees," Pavel told us.

"1,100 rupees?" yelped Evan. "No way! You tell him that we are not going to pay that. We could have taken a bus for less than half that all the way from Shimla!"

Pavel shrugged his shoulders, giving Evan a, *don't shoot the messenger*, kind of look, and patiently proceeding to tell our increasingly animated driver what Evan had said.

Our driver talked at Pavel for a while, before Pavel turned toward us and repeated – in exactly the same gentle tone he employed the first time – that the man believed we should pay him 1,100 rupees.

"I think you pay him," he continued, his own personal advice. "This is private car, so it more expensive to bus."

It wasn't helping our levels of embarrassment that Pavel seemed to be a genuinely nice boy because we had first hurt the feelings of one seemingly honest taxi driver and now we were doing the same to those of a kind young man. This was a no-win situation. We simply could not pay the man because it seemed to negate everything that the trip was about, but we couldn't just leave the man empty-handed because he appeared to have been as genuinely innocent in the matter as ourselves.

"I think that we should make a move guys," our lanky American friend suggested. "This is not going to end well, but if we walk away then I don't think they'll follow."

We couldn't believe what Evan was suggesting. Clearly it takes desperate situations for differences in moral attitudes to show themselves. The thought of just walking off hadn't even crossed our minds.

"There's no way we can do that Evan. It's completely dishonest," said Will.

I nodded in approval. It wasn't that Evan was less morally attuned than we; it was just that he had a different concept of the best way out of an apparently un-winnable situation like this one.

In any case, we were getting nowhere, and Pavel was charged with the task of watching over us whilst the driver went and sought police assistance.

"Come on guys. We've got to get out now," Evan prompted again, as soon as the man had gone out of sight.

But we were going nowhere. Pavel had told us that if the man returned home without any money then he might be fired from his job. Once again Pavel humbly suggested that it might be easiest for us to just pay the man... at least enough to cover petrol costs.

"Ah! This is so frustrating!" I squealed. We had gotten ourselves into a right mess and there appeared to be no satisfactory answer to the situation. We couldn't pay the man, but at the same time, we couldn't refuse to pay the man either!

When the police finally arrived to take us down to the station, I think it was fair to say that each one of us (perhaps with the exception of Evan) naively assumed that the local police would be sure to stand upon those pillars of truth, integrity and justice. We never expected corruption.

Yet, the conversations that went on inside the station were utterly futile. None of our explanations (each translated by our friend Pavel, who had kindly come with us to give his support) seemed to mean anything at all to our jury. It seemed as if these policemen had better things to do with their time because they gave the matter little thought, merely ordering Pavel to tell us to pay the man.

"Well done!" I felt like saying. "We hadn't thought of that one. They must have taught you some invaluable lessons at police school because your powers of deduction are remarkable!"

Three hours had passed since the time we first arrived in Dharamshala and we were getting nowhere because there was simply no way that all parties could find a compromise, so the police decided that enough was enough; they were going to take matters into their own hands.

Forcibly ejecting Pavel from the room, the policemen turned their attentions to our bags, ordering us to empty them and offer some of our belongings to the driver as payment. We were outraged. Not only had we lost our only ally; we had also been stripped of all powers of reasoning because there was now no means of verbal communication. This was only going to end in tears.

In the mêlée surrounding Pavel's exit, I had actually got into a spot of wrestling with a bayonet-wielding policeman. Reminiscent of the incident on the Iran-Pakistan border crossing, it would appear that I have a deeper underlying problem with authority than first thought. If it weren't for the saving actions of my friend William – who literally had to drag me away from the man with the bayonet before he could skewer me upon it – I might not be here today.

Evan decided that the only way out was to pay the man. Reaching inside his money belt and carefully withdrawing 300 rupees (the amount suggested in the final compromise), he thrust the notes towards the taxi driver and we stormed out as quickly as we could, to find Pavel waiting outside, nursing his own bruises.

Reunited with our friend, we apologised for the trouble that we had caused him and gave our warmest thanks to a true gentleman, who even led us back through the centre of Dharamshala and dropped us off at the foot of the hill leading the rest of the way to Mcleod Ganj. We walked the remaining distance to our destination, deciding that it would be safer to get ourselves as far away from the Dharamashala police as possible. It was a tough old hill-climb, which took us almost an hour, but when we eventually reached the summit, we found our way to the first open bar that we could see and treated ourselves to a well-earned pint.

"You still haven't broken your rule," Evan reassured us. "I paid for the taxi.

Think of it as you guys hitching a ride with me."

Will and I used our remaining energy to force smiles, thankful for our friend's kind words, but not sure if we could fully accept them. It had never been about the money; it had been about the rule. However, if our rule was going to get us into situations like this, then was it really worth holding on so tightly to it? We were starting to wonder about the ethics of hitchhiking.

DAY ONE HUNDRED AND TWENTY-EIGHT:
ROOF TERRACE, OM HOTEL, MCLEOD GANJ, HIMACHAL PRADESH, INDIA, SATURDAY 15TH NOVEMBER 2008, 9.34AM

Our third day in this hippie-infested town gets underway, and we have still to decide upon the route we shall take beyond these mountains.

I suppose that we shall head south, first of all, but whether or not we delve into the chaotic Delhi or head straight for the Taj Mahal in Agra is yet uncertain. Either way, it seems highly likely that we will be spending much less time here than we would like if we are to accept Evan's kind offer of Christmas in Laos with the Moody family.

If that is the case, I suppose we would head towards the Nepalese mountain range in the east and then continue south through Bangladesh and into Burma – a route that would both excite and concern me. Whilst I do not possess the fear that many might attach to the unstable political situation in Burma, the possibility that we may simply face refusal at the border curbs even my bravest ambition.

For now at least, our time in Mcleod goes on, and I must admit that I have enjoyed my time here a lot more than I expected. Despite the fact that this place is overrun with dope-smoking hippies (a sub-section I have little time for), each member of the group appears to be on a deep quest for an unknown *something*, and it is their plight that endears them to me. Quite what it is that they are searching for, to many, remains a mystery, but they are certainly in a good place to allow themselves the time and space required to explore both themselves and the wider world around them. This Tibetan refugee-camp hosts gruelling, ten-day meditation courses, which give many a chance for spiritual junkies to get their *fix*.

As far as I see it, their quest comes down to the very same search that must be the fundamental issue of every life: a search for something bigger than themselves. *Why am I here? Who made me? Where can I find the meaning for my life? Is there a God?* These questions are fundamentally important for all to consider – whatever one's background or personal inclination. From a vast array of different nations, all equipped with their own fascinating story, travellers run to the hills of Mcleod Ganj to find themselves, or to search for that "force" or "other" that seems to be pulling the strings from an unknown somewhere.

* * * * *

Three such searchers have made a great impact on us during our time here in Mcleod, and each needs a proper introduction.

The first is nineteen year-old maverick, Balthazar, from the French quarter of Switzerland. A quintessential Bohemian traveller, Balthazar certainly looks the part. Free-flowing hair curls below his shoulder-blades to reveal a dress sense that simply typifies the frequenters of this region. He does not seem to own anything that was not purchased on his travels; nor does he seem to own anything that isn't at least two sizes too big for him. If he could, Balthazar would smoke weed and play the guitar all day, whilst contemplating life's greater meaning. Naturally, we have warmed instantly to this interesting fellow, who has happily taken the fourth and final space within the petite chalet in which we reside, and seems sure to become the latest tagalong on our journey east.

With little plan, other than to explore himself in a world much more spiritually alive than his own homeland, our young friend, claiming to have some experience of hitchhiking at home, is keen to see how it works in this part of the world. A rugged charmer, Balthazar has spent most of his ten-day stay in Mcleod wooing a French-speaking Canadian girl. We have yet to meet his latest love, but are continually amused by the propensity for romance that is an everyday part of the amorous Frenchman's life. OK, so Balta isn't strictly "French," but this is how he has become known by our newly acquired friendship group, here in the hippie heights. After all, French people are most famous for one thing. *C'est la langue d'amour*, don't you know? Just one word (be it in French, or in a cute English accent) and men and women alike melt before our handsome friend.

The second is a British girl by the name of Beth. A former theatre student in Paris, this drama queen has a good sense of humour, which is just as well, as she regularly has to take the flack from three invariably cheeky souls, in Will, Evan and myself. She even handled herself very well yesterday, when the three of us (Balta was off wooing somewhere) took her on a treacherously *off-piste* route over a rocky waterfall path and near-vertical hillside, as a light afternoon stroll got a little out of hand. Even this bubbly character, intrepid though she may be, professes to be lacking a certain *something*, which, to me, simply screams of an unfinished search for what I would define to be God.

The evening that followed our most adventurous hike since days gone by in Hanna Urak was filled with all the joys that are sure to be involved in an evening spent with Eleanora. Originally from Venice, hers seems to be a sad tale of a runaway sixteen year-old from a broken home. Twelve years on, the character that now greets every person she meets with a hugely affectionate embrace and a sloppy kiss on the cheek is one that is equally adorable and infuriating. You cannot help but love this eccentric Venetian beauty, but that love is tempered with a strong concern as to what lies ahead for this restlessly travelling, self-professed "perpetual spinster." It seems as if dear Eleanora has moved from place to place ever since she was sixteen, never finding one that she could call home and never caring to settle down somewhere to make long-lasting relationships – relationships that might run deeper than the loose ties that are formed with fellow travellers, who come and go unpredictably, like the wind.

Dear Eleanora is certainly searching for something and running from something else, and this seems to be the story for almost every backpacker here. I wonder what it is that Will or I might be running from, or towards…

DAY ONE HUNDRED AND TWENTY-EIGHT:(CONTINUED…)
ROOF TERRACE, OM HOTEL, MCLEOD GANJ, HIMACHAL PRADESH, INDIA, SATURDAY 15TH NOVEMBER 2008, 17.27

Still no plan has been constructed for what happens beyond these hills. We are sorely tempted by the prospect of a big family Christmas with Evan's family, but it is difficult to work out whether it is worth the inevitable rush that it would cause. If we were to go with Evan's plan, we would be dashing across India, dipping into Nepal, and bumbling across Bangladesh and Burma, in order to get ourselves to the middle of Laos for what would be a scheduled rendezvous in Luang Prabang on Christmas Eve.

I really don't know whether to settle for this first option or the second, which offers a much more relaxed amble across the aforementioned countries, including the likelihood of a Christmas date with an, as yet, unknown family in Bangladesh or Myanmar, or in fact, which option would best fulfil the aims of our venture.

Starting out, I never envisaged that we would become just another set of tourists, going from place to place in order that we might visit all the big sites, but that seems to be very much the way that we have been going recently. Perhaps the decision we take may reveal the real reason why we started this trip in the first place. What could it be that we are searching for, or running away from?

Personally, I don't really feel as if I am searching for anything. In fact, I would assert that I feel altogether *found*. Perhaps it would be easier to ascertain what I may be running *from*, which might take the shape either of my very first career (having graduated just two days before we left), or of the growing seriousness attached to my relationship with Jo. It was our first anniversary yesterday (quite an achievement for a man with my track record, whose previous twenty girlfriends lasted cumulatively less), and marriage supposedly awaits my return. Am I too young? Do I really love her enough and is my love simply so strong because it has found *some* object to attach itself to – no matter who that object might be – rather than because it has found *Jo* specifically?

* * * * *

Previous musings led to a lengthy conversation with Evan and I feel thoroughly reassured about my situation, having reflected upon the bliss that seems to follow Jo and me around during our time together – particularly the heady heights of a love-struck three months just before we left. Love surrounded us in our every move and, upon serious reflection, I am convinced that nobody comes close to matching up to Jo. Seemingly, she truly is the perfect match for me and my worries are born out of a typically masculine fear at the imminent prospect of a commitment. Nonetheless, my reasons for leaving when I did probably, somewhere beneath the surface, related to a mixture of running *away* from this commitment and running *towards* a better understanding of how secure this love really is. Four months down the line, and I honestly feel surer than ever that I have made the right choice. Jo and I are made for each other.

13. VIVE LA REVOLUTION!

DAY ONE HUNDRED AND THIRTY-ONE:
TIP TOP RESTAURANT, RISHIKESH, GANGA RIVER, UTTHAR KHAN, INDIA, TUESDAY 18TH NOVEMBER 2008, 19.00

You join me as I sip herbal tea at a table overlooking the Ganga (Ganges) as it makes its slow, south-easterly journey towards Bangladesh – a route the three of us are soon to follow. Oh yes, that's right; we've picked up yet another tagalong – this time in the form of our Swiss friend, Balthazar.

It has taken much longer to reach this point than we had originally intended when we left new friends, Evan, Beth and Eleanora, at the end of one final breakfast ensemble on Sunday morning. Our mysterious Italian friend is the only member of our group who did not leave Mcleod with us and, whilst Evan and Beth attempted their own hitch towards the disputed Kashmir region in the North West of India, Balta joined Will and me in our attempts to journey further east.

Being only five or six hundred kilometres away, Rishikesh had seemed a decent target for that Sunday's hitch. It was an optimistic target, but we could give it our best shot, and finish off the job on the Monday if we were found a little short.

All five of our travelling party joined in on the first hitch – a bumpy ride in the back of a trailer, which took us precariously close to our favourite police station in Dharmashala. Then came the split. Evan and Beth set out in what they adjudged to be a north-westerly direction, whilst Balta joined Will and me in our attempts at heading the opposite way.

Things didn't go quite as we had planned. After two hours of stop-start lifts, we had barely made twenty kilometres from Mcleod and, to be honest, still hadn't really worked out if we were going in the right direction at all. It was almost lunchtime and we had already given up any hope of reaching Rishikesh in one day, hoping only that we would make it to the other side of the mountain in front of us come sundown.

Optimism was almost spent, so when Jai pulled over in his flashy BMW and asked us – in what seemed to be a fluent English tongue – "Where do you guys wanna go?" we were more than a little relieved. This relief soon turned to elation, as Jai informed us that he was driving to his hometown of Ludhiana, at the foothills of the Himalayas, where we would be very welcome to join him for the night.

"What were you guys doing standing in the middle of nowhere anyway?" he asked, in what now seemed to have developed into an Aussie twang.

We explained, telling him the story of our adventure, before turning our attention to his own. It turned out that Jai had only just returned from a couple of years' studying in Australia (hence the twang) and had just popped up to Mcleod – one of his favourite haunts – to take part in one of their meditation courses.

Our only prior insight into these courses came from our friend Beth, who booked herself in for the ten-day experience, but didn't last a day!

"It was horrible," she told us. "I got really freaked out and just couldn't stay there any longer. They made us listen to this weird tape and we had to sit there for hours, not doing anything, and not allowed to talk to anyone. I think I was a bad influence there anyway because I just kept on laughing at the tape and couldn't handle the intense atmosphere. We had to sleep on planks of wood and were given only little scraps of food every seven hours!"

This clearly wasn't an experience for the faint of heart. One needed more than a little muscle and a dollop of will power to last the distance.

"I didn't finish the first time I tried," Jai admitted. "But I've done it three or four times now and it's really good for improving discipline and taking time out to relax."

Now that his cravings for study and meditation had been sated, it was time for Jai to look for a job. He had decided to come home in order to find one and, when we arrived at his home four hours later, it didn't take us long to see why.

In what has to be the richest area of Ludhiana, Jai lives in a huge house that wouldn't be out of place in London's *West End*. Pristinely white walls, wooden floorboards and too many rooms to count, this was not quite the slum we expected. For the briefest of moments, I pondered how awful it was that this family lived in such plenty while so many others around them were struggling to survive, but before I could get too far in my judgments, I remembered the affluence of my own background. The fact that poverty isn't necessarily on my doorstep doesn't make me any less responsible for its existence.

Our evening at Jai's wonderful family home was largely spent exploring the streets of Ludhiana, where we would be taken to… yes, you've guessed it: yet another shopping mall! To be fair to the *West End Mall*, it was probably the pick of the bunch thus far, but wasn't exactly what we were envisaging when Jai told us that he was going to show us around the city.

* * * * *

The next morning we were up at 8.30 with the hope that this relatively early start would give us ample time to reach our destination that day. Jai estimated that we had covered about half the distance to Rishikesh with him and would have only about 300km further to travel.

We fancied our chances, but by the time the family maid had treated us to a hearty breakfast, and then we had waited for Jai's mum to bring the car home so that Jai could drive us to a good starting spot, it was almost 11am. Perhaps we ought to learn, after a string of failures, that we really ought to get ourselves up a little earlier in the future. It was all very well back in Europe when the sun would stay high in the sky until long after 9pm, but the days are much shorter now.

Needless to say, we didn't make it to Rishikesh on that day, either. It was a funny old day because we always felt as though we were picking up lifts remarkably quickly and making great progress, but none was ever very fast, nor substantial, and bad light came crashing down on our parade when we were still 100km short.

If it had not been for a kind Christian man by the name of Amarjeet, I don't know what we would have done that (last) night. When Amarjeet found us, we were in a situation that reminded us of times gone by in Pakistan. Surrounded by a huge crowd of locals in a non-descript village, it was becoming harder and harder to keep our emotions in check as we desperately attempted to flag down one final, "Lord please make it a substantial lift," before total darkness ensued.

Amarjeet seemed reluctant to take us at first, muttering something about there being a problem with the police. Perhaps he thought we must have done something wrong, or be doing something wrong, to find ourselves in this situation. As it was, we piled into his car before he had even fully agreed to take us, and were soon encouraging him to start his engine that we might leave the hordes behind.

Not long into the journey, it became clear that not only did he probably have some personal reservations about picking up three strange white men, but Amarjeet had also heard stories about Indians getting into trouble with the police for picking up people like us.

"I am no taxi and I need taxi license to take you anywhere," he protested, bringing the vehicle to a standstill.

Yet there was no way that we were going to leave his vehicle because this surely marked our last hope of getting anywhere that evening. Amarjeet had already confirmed that he was heading the same way that we were (to

Dehra Dun, a city nearby to Rishikesh) and there was no chance that we were going to bail out now.

"We don't *want* a taxi," I said. "No taxi, no money. We travel for free."

The funny thing was that it seemed as though this was all Amarjeet wanted to hear. The problem with the police had come from unofficial taxi drivers picking up foreigners and charging them the earth for their services. Amarjeet just wanted to help us out.

"Free. No money. OK, good," he said, relieved and reassured, re-starting the engine.

From that moment on, our new friend cut a much calmer figure and, once we finally arrived in the large city of Dehra Dun, capital of the Utthar Khan Province, even offered us a place to stay for the night. About an hour later we arrived at *Oak Grove School Hospital* in the little village of Jharipeni, which lies just underneath the more renowned hilltop town of Mussorie. This majestic Victorian hospital (built by the Brits in 1888), whilst still very much in use for both its scholarly and medical functions, is now also the proud home of the Barnabas family.

Having been rather taken aback when our rather quiet chauffeur had invited us to stay, we weren't quite sure what to expect upon our arrival, but were soon charmed by his two young daughters and their mother, Caroline. With a smile of pure goodness, Caroline was the perfect hostess and we were set instantly at ease. Sixteen-year-old Archal was as giggly as you might expect any teenage girl to be at the sight of three young men, whilst her younger sister, eleven-year-old, Abha, seemed quite the timid sort.

An adorable pair, they had inherited their mother's smile and Amarjeet (who had grown in confidence now he was back at home) told of how lucky he and Caroline were to have found each other, and to have married for love, revealing that he thought that about 80% of marriages in India were still arranged to this day!

* * * * *

The Barnabas family really were the perfect hosts during our short stay, even shacking up in one bedroom together so that we boys might have the lounge (which doubled up as the girls' bedroom) to ourselves. The beautiful simplicity in which they lived was a great example. Amarjeet is an on-call nurse and midwife at the hospital, whilst Caroline is, in her words, a "very strict teacher" at the school. You wouldn't know it to look at this angelic creature, but there is a great deal of determination beneath that charming exterior, which seemingly allows her to hold sway over her pupils and, arguably, her husband too.

Perhaps the most fascinating experience of our night with the Barnabas's was to listen to their remarks on the state of the Church in India. We had already clocked that Amarjeet and family were Christians because of the many Christian symbols within the car and were thus not surprised to see the house similarly awash with symbols that spoke of a true Christian faith.

And yet, despite this, the Barnabas family does not attend a church because they believe the Church in India to be famous only for dishonesty and money laundering!

"The pastors all have nice houses, and fast cars, and steal the collection money for themselves," Caroline declared.

"We don't go to church," continued Amarjeet, "We live as Christians from home, reading the Bible and praying together every day."

Churchgoers though Will and I may be, it would have been really rather rich to have argued against the logic of this particularly kind family.

Yesterday was quite the day for theologising. Our very first lift came courtesy of a Sikh, who spent the entire journey telling us all we needed to know about his views upon religion and how best we might live together in a world of many religions. His was the classic post-modernist outlook: *my religion for me, your religion for you, and we'll all get along just fine* – a view very similar to that fronted by Evan just a few days before.

This position seems to be all the rage these days, and I suppose I can see why. Nobody loses out by this definition; we are all right under the giant umbrella of religious plurality. And yet, for me, this vague, relative suggestion that all beliefs are right – but only insofar as they are right for the particular person that holds them (i.e. *religion is in the eye of the beholder*) – does not leave any room for particularity. In fact, a little way along in this line of thinking and one has to exclude all sorts of definite/absolute opinions altogether. One would not be allowed to say anything at all for sure, just in case one's belief might upset somebody's differing, conflicting, or opposite belief!

"You believe what you believe only because you have been taught to believe it," the man informed us.

"You were born in England and so you are a Christian; I was born in a Sikh family in India and so I am a Sikh," he continued. "You did not choose to be a Christian; Christianity chose you."

In some respects, I suppose that I can see the logic in his argument. I agree that my chances of being a Christian were dramatically increased by my being born in England. However, I fundamentally refuse to believe that it was anyone other than myself who chose my faith. Religion is much more than a means of identification to me and I am not just a Christian because I live in a Christian country. I had to choose my faith and decided to change my life because of it. There are thousands of other young Englishmen (within or outside of Christian homes) who make a different choice.

Moving on from that slight tangent into all things theological, the following morning (this morning) we were sent off from the Barnabas's with a hearty breakfast, and then accompanied by Amarjeet on a long and mountainous walk to a spot where we might wait for a lift back to Dehra Dun, and on, ultimately, to Rishikesh.

It has taken us a while to make it here (three days in fact), but we eventually arrived at 1.30pm this afternoon, and spent two hours trekking around the city in search of the cheapest place to stay. The journey from

Mcleod was certainly demoralising at points, but we had the chance to meet with two splendid Indian families along the way and we might never have met either were it not for the tardiness of our progress.

DAY ONE HUNDRED AND THIRTY-THREE:
MOON DANCE CAFÉ, RISHIKESH, GANGA RIVER, UTTHAR KHAN, INDIA, THURSDAY 20TH NOVEMBER 2008, 9.18AM

There is something very religious about Rishikesh. Perhaps it sprouts from the Holy Ganga River, which has made its way here from the top of the Himalayas and is soon scheduled to stop off at Varanasi (a site of great religious significance for all Hindus) on its way through to Bangladesh. It is said that if a Hindu dies in Varanasi, he achieves freedom from the perpetual cycle of reincarnation – the cycle that calls all to do as many good deeds as possible, that they may receive a positive Karma score and favourable rebirth. It's no wonder that India is so highly populated, given this reincarnation business. Varanasi must be the worst: the Bexhill of India, where hundreds of old people wait for their final marching orders.

As far as I can gather, one of the major differences between Sikhism and Hinduism (from which the former developed) stems from their different interpretations of Karma. Whilst Hindus maintain that their good and bad deeds will have an effect in the life to come, Sikhs believe that the consequences relate first to this life: *if I do good, good things will happen to me. If I do not, then I should expect to reap what I have sown.*

One thing that slightly troubles me about this way of thinking is something that once famously caught out former Spurs legend and England manager, Glenn Hoddle. I doubt Glenny can have been thinking too clearly – in what was one of his more insightful phases – when he suggested that all disabled people must have done something wrong to get the way that they are because the logic behind such a thought baffles even the most open of minds.

What an horrendous and implausible suggestion! The question of suffering is one that frustrates every believer because suffering appears to be completely indiscriminate. There are no rules for who will suffer or for why they will. Suffering can strike at any time, strike any person, and in any way. Good things happen to bad people; bad things happen to good people. Surely these two truths challenge the very essence of the Hindu/Sikh reliance upon Karma – at least in terms of the repercussions in this life.

* * * * *

Yesterday, Will and I put our religious prudishness aside by becoming yogis for a day. For two of the least flexible men upon this planet, this two-and-a-half-hour experience was… stretching to say the least. And yet, both Will and I prevailed against our bodies' tendencies not to want to bend in *that* particular way for such a long period of time (he says as he somehow manages to twist his leg just one extra degree to the right), and I have to confess that we actually rather enjoyed the experience.

One aspect of the practice that we hadn't quite bargained for, however, was the lead yogi's tendency to call upon us all to chant mantras together in worship of the sun!

"Focus your attention to perceive," he would begin, over and over again, before spouting off some nonsense about the sun's holy essence.

"Devote yourselves to the sun," he continued, whilst Will and I watched on with horror as crowds of L-plated yogis slowly raised their arms to imbibe the sun's glorious radiance.

Whilst we certainly enjoyed the relaxing (and not-so-relaxing) stretches, devoting oneself to a big ball of light in the sky was one step too far. Fortunately, the huge concentration required to hold one's body in such contorted positions made it easy enough for us to pretend that we were simply misunderstanding the repeated calls for sun worship, rather than blatantly ignoring them.

"Increase your inner performance," the man yelled, before suggesting that we each had the capacity to bring inner healing to ourselves. The mind certainly is a powerful tool, and I found it fascinating to reflect upon the idea that we may be able to control our own bodies a great deal more if only we gave our minds the chance. I wasn't quite sure, however, that I wanted to give my mind quite the level of control that this man wished to apportion it. The twenty other devotees, on the other hand, seemed perfectly happy to give it a bash.

Aside from the sun-worshipping aspect, the yoga experience as a whole was harmless enough, and we certainly felt a strong sense of inner peace by the end of the last exercise. Whether or not this was a direct result of the yoga and sun themselves, however, I do not know. I have an inkling that it might have more to do with the fact that the last exercise was basically just a thirty minute siesta... Lying motionless for half an hour rarely fails to refresh!

* * * * *

Our time here in Rishikesh has given us further opportunity to consider future plans. Upon leaving Mcleod Ganj on Sunday, Will and I were hoping that we might start a month-long loop from the Himalayas down to Mumbai and Goa (via Delhi and the Taj Mahal), before heading North to Varanasi, into Nepal, across Bangladesh and Burma, and into South East Asia. Once again, our plans have changed.

Having been in touch with Evan, who is now making his way back from a short trip to Kashmir, we have decided to reconnect with him and Beth in Nepal, then to journey on through Nepal, Bangladesh and Burma – giving the dream of a Laotian Christmas a real try.

Time is of the essence if we are to complete this marathon venture in time for Christmas Day, but we're up for the challenge. I suppose that we will just have to wait for another opportunity to explore India properly. From what we have heard, it could take a lifetime truly to get to grips with this subcontinent anyway, so it's just as well that we won't be forced into rushing our impressions of the place. Tomorrow we leave Rishikesh and head for another border. Next stop, Nepal.

DAY ONE HUNDRED AND THIRTY-SIX:
ROADSIDE RESTAURANT, EN ROUTE TO POKHARA, THE HIMALAYAS, NEPAL, SUNDAY 23RD NOVEMBER 2008, 21.32

When I'm home I shall seriously consider petitioning for hitchhiking to be considered, when practised properly, as just another variation upon a full-time job. It may be no "9 to 5" in an office, but the hours can be even stiffer, and the potential for personal injury much greater. There we have it. My plan even fits in with the current climate, in which people can file a claim should anybody do so much as sneeze at them! Now all I need to do is to work out whom I can sue... As Head of the country, the Queen will be my first port of call.

We left Rishikesh early on Friday morning and have been on the road solidly ever since. Pokhara, our destination, then stood one thousand kilometres away, and included not only a border crossing, but also the small matter of a significant number of Nepalese Himalayas. I suppose that it is no wonder, then, that we have not yet arrived, nor do we seem destined to do so until the early hours of tomorrow morning. Yet, if you had told me this just six hours ago, when we stood but 150km away from the target – with a whole evening's progress ahead of us – I would have thought you mad. There is, of course, a very good reason for such sluggish progress, but before I can bring you up to speed on current affairs, I must take you back to the very beginning...

It's Friday morning and we have had one final breakfast at our favourite eatery in Rishikesh, *Moon Dance Café*. We all went for their fabulous *Muesli fruit curd* option, but had to settle for *Nescafé* on the coffee front, as there appears to be a distinct lack of filter coffee in the entire region.

Balthazar stops to flirt with one final French-speaking woman (it truly is a joy to behold) and then we begin our 5km hike across the town until we are satisfied that we have reached a suitable hitching post. The day's aim is to make it as close to the Nepalese border as we can, but our ambitions are hit with an early stumbling block: the long trek has tired us out and there don't appear to be any other vehicles besides rickshaws, taxis and buses. We've been here before.

When we eventually find our first lift of the day, it comes as no surprise that our chauffeur is actually a taxi driver, offering a one-off, pro bono service, putting his job on hold that he might take us far enough outside of the city for it to become clear to passing vehicles that we aren't just looking for a ride to the shops.

Wouldn't you know it but the very next car to come our way takes one look at us, pulls over, and we're off again. This stroke of luck is followed by a trio of mini-lifts, which take us a good chunk of the way towards our 300km border target, but things start looking a little trickier when one of our drivers dumps us off in the middle of a random town, leaving us with no instruction as to how we might get out of it, nor telling us in which direction lies Nepal.

Wherever possible we avoid getting ourselves stuck in the middle of towns because they are notoriously difficult to get oneself out of again. On this occasion it takes us more than an hour. Eventually, the young Dr. Morab intercedes by removing us from the latest swarm of locals to have crowded around us.

"Where do you wanna go?" he asks, reminiscent of our first encounter with Jai.

We are so desperate to escape from the crowd that we don't even mouth an audible response, but only mutter some nonsensical words, pile into the vehicle (driven by his personal chauffeur) and point down the road.

"We'll go anywhere," Will reveals once we are safely underway.

"Where are *you* going?" I ask, crossing my fingers in the hope that he will say: "Well, you know, as a matter of fact I'm actually driving to Nepal."

The answer isn't quite that good, but Dr. Morab is going a good distance in our direction and eventually manages to persuade his chauffeur to relax because we don't seem likely to be the hijacking types. Dr. Morab is moving house, you see, so there is a lot of stuff for potential muggers to lay their hands upon, and the chauffeur continues to eye us suspiciously for the remainder of the journey.

We travel together for about three hours in all (Dr. Morab even treats us to lunch along the way), but then it is time for us to part. The doctor kindly invites us to stay with him at his home in Naintal, but the border is still quite a way away and going to Naintal would add an extra fifty kilometres onto the following day's journeying. Thus, for once in our lives, we reject this latest offer of hospitality.

There is still just enough light for us to hold out hope of finding ourselves very near to the border come the end of the day and our hopefulness is justified moments later when two Sikhs pull over to take us a further 50km, dropping us off on the outskirts of the next big town. From here our choice is simple: we can either spend the night in this dirty-looking town and find a cheap hotel therein, or we can attempt to make it another fifty kilometres and "Sikh" refuge (sorry, couldn't resist that one) in a temple that our friends have told us will offer free food and accommodation.

It's only 6pm and, although the sun has fully set by now, we decide to carry on. One free ride in a friend of a friend's rickshaw is followed by a chilly lift in an open trailer (filled to the brim with straw) and finished off by a final car-hitch of the day. We arrive at the temple in Nanalematta at 9pm: cold, tired and desperately hungry.

It's just as well, then, that the Sikhs in this part of the world are renowned for such wonderful hospitality. There is another 24-7 community kitchen, just like the one in Amritsar, and even plenty of free rooms to house weary travellers of any creed, colour, or religion. We are truly humbled by the kindness of the two devout Sikhs who look after us. We have arrived later than anybody else and are clearly not Sikhs – nor are we even Indians – but none of this matters. Mounds of food are piled upon our plates, and then we are shown to our humble quarters for the night. It doesn't matter to us that the place is a bit of a tip; we have a free bed for the night.

* * * * *

Suitably rested and readied for a second day's hard graft, we set off at 8 o'clock the next morn, with the goal of crossing the border (still some 50km away) by midday and covering as much distance as possible within Nepal to render Pokhara an achievable target for the following day.

Target one was achieved without too much sweat. Once we had wandered away from the Sikh temple and found ourselves facing the right direction on the border road, a passing truck soon pulled over to take us to within ten kilometres of the crossing, and we completed the journey thanks to the help of some old boys in a tractor – a ride that will live long in the memory.

Piling into a trailer already occupied by ten local "hitchers," a few chickens, and a goat, we slowly bumped our way along the dusty road and were treated to a morning *pick-me-up* (something very alcoholic that tasted like a cross between Turkish Raki and the plastic bag from which we drank) and a little breakfast (one cucumber each, accompanied by generic spicy sauce).

It wasn't quite the breakfast of kings, but Will and I were able to revel in the simplicity of the moment, whilst Balthazar seemed more concerned with avoiding the bite of the billy goat, who had clearly taken a particular shine to him and could express this only through nibbling.

The tractor ride lasted only about a quarter of an hour, after which we were shown the way to wander, and wander we did for a good five kilometres, until we eventually reached the beginning of the long stretch of land that separates India and Nepal on that particular, "pedestrians only" border. I had never come across a border that allows only for foot passengers before, but it was just as well that we didn't have our own vehicle, or else we would have had a lot of backtracking to do.

The considerable walk was broken into two phases, thanks to comical immigration checks on both sides. The first was a harmless enough exercise – although it did involve a great deal of form-filling – whilst the second was a complete farce, in which two rather unofficial-looking officials set about making sure that they had every iota of our personal details, before proceeding to ask each of us for two passport-sized snaps. There would be a 2-dollar charge (which would, no doubt, go straight into the back pocket) should any of us not have any to hand.

Unfortunately, Will was the only one of our trio to have any shots to hand

and, although the money itself would hardly break the bank, it was the principle that mattered and I was going to fight for my two dollars! Whilst Will handed over his most recent snaps and Balta coughed up the dosh, I stalled in search of an alternative. Suddenly I had an idea.

"Will, have you got any older photos of yourself?" I whispered to my friend, safe in the knowledge that the officials didn't appear to be the smartest/most linguistically brilliant we'd ever encountered.

He nodded, and produced a sheet of photos in which he was a mere schoolboy, clad in a navy blue blazer and grey trousers.

A perfect match, I thought, reflecting upon the rather obvious differences in hair colour and general face shape, before handing them over to the officials as my own.

"Very nice pictures," one of them said to me, whilst stapling them barely half an inch away from the others.

Struggling not to laugh, I nodded my head and thanked him for the compliment.

"Amazing how much we change in just a few years, isn't it?" said I.

Fiasco complete, we had officially (or perhaps unofficially) crossed into Nepal and were about to embark upon our first piece of Nepalese hitchhiking. As with every new country, we hadn't the foggiest idea what to expect and the early signs weren't very promising. The lack of through-traffic at the border meant that there was not a single car or lorry in sight. The only vehicles on offer were minibuses, taxis and motorbikes – the drivers of which all made their most frantic pleas to be the ones whose pockets would benefit from escorting us to the next town, which, we had been told, was a further six kilometres away.

"Pick me, pick me," they seemed to shout (or something in Nepalese to that effect).

"No money, no money," we retorted, marching past them all as quickly as our jaded legs would allow.

We had to walk a good kilometre before the last of these schemers called it a day, but by this time we wondered if we'd made a mistake. We were hardly likely to be able to walk the length of mountainous Nepal. There must be some other way.

Motorbikes were still trickling past every so often and, before I had even given thought to just what it was that I was hoping for, I had stuck out an arm to bring one to a halt.

The driver seemed about as bemused as the three of us, as we all wondered just what the probabilities were of fitting three grown men, plus backpacks, onto a tiny scooter, which was already occupied by a relatively large (at least 5 ft 4) Nepalese man.

"Um, well, why don't we split up?" I said, thinking on my feet. "I'll go with this fella and you guys follow on when you can."

"But what are we going to do when we get there?" asked Will, aware that none of us had a working method of communication to hand. "How will we know where to meet?"

"Mmm, not sure," I replied, mounting the scooter. "Just go straight along this road until you see me. If they take a turn or stop then get off and flag down another one. Otherwise, stay on until you see me"...

How I wish that the rest of our hitchhiking in Nepal could have been so easy! I had to wait no more than five minutes (following on from what must have been a good ten-minute journey on what sounded like a souped-up hairdryer) before, first Balthazar, and then Will, turned up on their respective hairdryers, hopped off, and we all agreed that that was the most fun that we'd had hitching in ages. It was just a shame that we couldn't very well rely upon splitting up and hitching three separate lifts for the remaining 700km stretch to Pokhara. We were going to have to explore other avenues, and this did not prove at all easy.

It wasn't that there was a lack of good people willing to give us a lift; rather, there simply weren't any suitable vehicles – only the unending stream of buses, taxis and motorcycles. I can honestly say that in our first 500km of hitching in Nepal we saw five cars, which, as I'm sure you can appreciate, doesn't exactly lend itself to easy hitchhiking. As a result, we have had to make a few incy-wincy tweaks in our concept of hitching, for which I hope you can forgive us.

To be honest, our Nepalese hitch has turned into more of a Nepalese bus-blagging venture, which, at one stage would have been thoroughly demoralising, but can now be easily encompassed within our ever-expanding "hitchhiking" definition.

There is no deception involved. We are not pretending to the drivers that we will pay them and then running off; we are simply being completely honest with them (insofar as we are able) by our insistent repetition of our favourite phrase: "No money, no money," or its Pakistani/Indian/Nepalese (hopefully it's the same here) equivalent: "Rupee nahi! Rupee nahi!"

Our first day of Nepalese "hitchhiking" involved three motorbikes, one jeep (actually, I think it was a taxi-jeep) and two free bus rides, and it was during the last of these bus rides that we met our friend, Amar, who was instrumental in convincing his bus-driving pal that it was a good idea to give us a free ride and then, after travelling perhaps a further 100km, invited us to his house for the evening.

Our latest source of outrageous kindness, Amar, at thirty-one, has been working much of the past two years in Dubai so that he might earn enough money to support his family back at their home in the village of Kohalpur. His wife and eighteen-month-old daughter have had to manage without their provider for most of his daughter's young life and will continue to do so for at least eleven months out of every year for the foreseeable future.

It isn't how many English families would work, but this wasn't a choice that Amar made because it would be easy; this was a decision he made because of the need to provide for his family. Whilst it will obviously be difficult for the mother and child left at home, it is also hard on poor Amar, who has to work extremely hard for the bulk of the year, miles away from his baby daughter and loving wife.

There was little that we could say to our friend by way of sympathising that night. We could hardly tell him not to worry because it would all be "all right in the end"; nor could we spout off some rubbish about it's being for the "greater good." This was simply a very hard situation, so we put on our best sympathetic expressions and remained silent.

DAY ONE HUNDRED AND THIRTY-SIX: (CONTINUED...)
(THE VERY SAME) ROADSIDE RESTAURANT, EN ROUTE TO POKHARA, THE HIMALAYAS, NEPAL, SUNDAY 23RD NOVEMBER 2008, 11.53PM

I simply cannot believe we're still here! Remember when I told you all that stuff about being worried that we might not make it to Pokhara until tomorrow morning? Well, two hours have been and gone since then, and still we wait for our drivers to do anything! We've even been told that we've got time for a little nap!

Goodness knows how long we are likely to remain here, so I may as well use this time to fill you in on the story beyond Amar. Now, where was I...?

... The following morning (this morning), Amar supplied us with more food than we had the space to carry, and then escorted us back onto the Pokharan "highway" (read, "dusty track"). For a man in such difficult circumstances, possessing the reserves of kindness and generosity to show complete strangers such unreserved hospitality was, frankly, astounding.

Bidding our friend a fond farewell, it was back to that infamous bus-blagging and, mercifully, it was only the second passing bus that took us aboard for what would turn out to be a 250km journey, right to the foothills of the Himalayas! The driver and his conductor took a little while in warming to the three of us, but seemed sufficiently happy to offer us the first 150km free of charge and it wasn't until the final hundred that they became a little cranky.

"Come on, we'll go on the roof," we pleaded – our last resort before they would surely chuck us off the bus and leave us in some random field.

The words themselves fell on deaf/bemused ears, but the persistent pointing to the roof did the trick. Moments later and we were climbing up the ladder on the back (every Asian bus seems to have one) and doing our best to secure ourselves onto the flat platform above, taking firm hold of the roof-rack in the knowledge that it had at least been strong enough to prevent our bags from falling off thus far.

The funny thing was that the driver probably thought that he was teaching us a lesson by sending us on top, but we wouldn't have gone back downstairs unless we had been physically forced to do so. The view alone was enough to ensure our enjoyment, and if it were thrill-seeking that we were looking for, it doesn't come much better than actually putting one's body in the line of potentially life-threatening injury.

When the bus finally came to rest, up came the driver, a massive grin scrawled across his face, and giggling as if all those times when we had "accidentally" skidded around corners a little too fast and almost been thrown from our perch hadn't been so "accidental" after all.

Firmly, he took hold of our hands and shook them. Now that we had survived his best efforts to get rid of us, we could leave with his blessing.

* * * * *

Only 150km then separated us from Pokhara and we felt sure that we had plenty of time in hand to reach our destination by the end of the evening, even if the 150km that blocked our path were a set of rather large Himalayan peaks.

Starting out from Butawal at 3pm, we assumed that, at the very latest, we would arrive by midnight, but hitching really is a very difficult thing in this part of the world. That there are *no* cars doesn't get one off to a flying start, and ensuing attempts to get oneself a free ride on either a bus or a truck seem to be entirely foreign concepts here – especially when the young pretenders claiming to have "*no* money" appear to be a trio of filthy rich Westerners.

When, eventually, a truck did pull over – seemingly heeding our call for help – we were disappointed to find that the real reason for its stopping was to be filled with as much furniture as physically possible. We had served only as a most unwelcome distraction. I suppose that it should have come as little surprise, then, when they upped and left after half an hour, without apology or explanation, despite our most ardent attempts at begging for a ride.

Having spent so long waiting for them to dilly-dally around as the sunlight hours grew fewer by the minute, we were infuriated by their lack of compassion, and it didn't help matters when the driver of the second truck to come along – who pulled over as the first was leaving – seemed to be friendly with the first lot, and stopped for a brief consultation, in which we felt sure that he had been advised not to pick us up.

Again we waited for thirty minutes as this second truck took further furniture aboard and simply would not give us any sign that they were going to give us a lift, despite the oodles of room that were clearly available in a cabin that housed only three other hitchhikers and the two men in charge of the vehicle.

"Five in a cabin? Is that all? Come on, there's plenty of room for three littl'uns to squeeze in," motioned Will.

They were unmoved.

Determination was deteriorating into desperation as we approached sixty minutes sitting in the same spot, whilst we aimlessly waited for two uninterested drivers to load up. Desperation then prompted us into action as the three of us joined our would-be drivers in helping to load further furniture, whilst we persisted in asking them if they were going to Pokhara.

Truthfully, we knew very well that they were going there. The helpful thing about mountain roads – especially somewhere with so undeveloped a road-network as Nepal – is that there will only ever be one road to choose from and it can have but one possible destination. Even their best attempts at persuading us that they were, in fact, going to Kathmandu could not dissuade us because we knew very well that they would have to go through Pokhara first.

"Kathmandu, you say?" Will remarked. "That's funny. We're going that way too. Now, how's about you stop all this nonsense and give us a cheeky little lift halfway... Oh, I don't know, to Pokhara?"

Eventually, the brothers in charge of the truck yielded to our persistent pleas and signalled that we were to join the now-disgruntled throng already crammed inside the cabin.

"Pokhara here we come!" we yelled, high-fives all round (in the white-faced section at least). It had taken us the best part of three days to do it, but we finally had the finishing post in sight...

* * * * *

But that was six hours ago and I don't believe that we have made more than one third of those 150km yet...

"... So, this isn't the fastest truck we've ever been in, is it?" joked Will, as our heavy-laden vehicle began to chug its way up the first substantial Himalayan verge.

"What are we averaging?" I wondered, glancing at the speedometer, which, like many others here in Asia, suggested that we were stationary.

"We're in for a long ride," joked Will, but he was right. There was no way that we can have been averaging more than 20km/hr!

One hour later – and thus surely no further than 20km into our marathon climb – we hit traffic.

"Traffic? A traffic jam?" gasped a shocked Will. "In the middle of the Himalayas?"

In front of us stood a column of some two-dozen vehicles (consisting predominantly of our favourite combination of buses, taxis and trucks), whilst their respective drivers and passengers were busily wandering around the corner to see what could have caused such gridlock.

Leaving our truck to make our own way around the bend, we soon saw what the problem was. A truck coming down the hill seemed to have had an altercation with a bus on its way up, and the drivers were locked in a heated exchange over the minor damage that appeared to have been caused to both vehicles in the collision.

The crowd just stood there, gawping, and initially we did too. Ten minutes on, however, and we began to wonder why it was that the drivers of the two vehicles had so selfishly decided to leave themselves strewn across the entire width of the road when it would have been so easy for at least one of them to move fractionally out of the way and so enable the rest of us poor folk to continue on our own, very long, journeys.

For five minutes the spectacle was amusing, but soon it became distressing.

"What are they doing?" shouted Will. "Why can't they just move out of the way? They're not achieving anything by just sitting there. All they need to do is just move a few feet to the left and we'll be on our way."

Not in our wildest dreams could we have expected the response we received.

"They wait for police," a relatively accomplished English-speaking onlooker informed us.

"Police, photograph," he continued.

"What?" I queried. "Why can't they just move out of the way and do photographs of the damage from there?"

"No. Must stay same position so police know accident," the onlooker replied, resolutely.

"Let me get this straight," interjected Will. "We have to wait here for the police to come along so that they can take a photograph of the exact places that they finished up? Are the police supposed to come up with some kind of miraculous mathematical equation to work out whose fault it was on account of their finishing positions?"

"Unbelievable!" I screamed, shaking my head, whilst our new friend shrugged his shoulders and presumably wondered just what it was that we found so distressing about what, to him, was probably just an average day out on a Nepalese road.

An hour went by before "the police" (one man on a motorcycle) turned up, without a camera. Taking one look at the situation, the policeman seemed just as bemused as the rest of us over why on earth the drivers hadn't simply moved an inch to the left, and soon ordered them to do so.

We were on our way again.

"Only 130km to go!" I enthused, hoping to re-inject some optimism into our depleted morale.

Four hours of unbearably slow hill-climbing later – soothed somewhat by the fact that the three of us were so tired that we were drifting in and out of consciousness – we pulled over into a roadside joint for what we assumed would be a short break for some food, but has turned into something better resembling a sleepover.

* * * * *

We just cannot believe that we are still so far from Pokhara. Our predictions for our E.T.A (*Estimated Time of Arrival*) are ever increasing. What had at one stage seemed like a certain pre-midnight arrival has transformed into real concern that we might not even arrive in time for breakfast tomorrow.

Supper long since supped, we have just now asked for some clarity over this continued stagnation. Turning around to enquire of the owner of the restaurant, I asked him if we had enough time for a beer.

"Time for beer?" he repeated, with a tone that made me presume my words to be either stupid or misplaced.

"You don't leave before..." He took a moment to look at his watch, bringing its face before us and pointing a finger at an hour that looked considerably further into the future than we had hoped…

"…Four o' clock."

Our eyes almost popped out of our heads as the three of us shrieked in unison.

"Four o' clock! You're joking, right?" said I.

The man shrugged his shoulders and walked back to his chair to sip upon his own bottle of *Everest* beer.

He wasn't.

DAY ONE HUNDRED AND THIRTY-EIGHT:
HARVEST MOON HOTEL, POKHARA, KASKI DISTRICT, THE HIMALAYAS, NEPAL, TUESDAY 25TH NOVEMBER 2008, 8.37AM

There were still some four hours to kill before our E.T.D (*Estimated Time of Departure*) and we tried to make the most of them, taking our first sips of the local *Everest* brew (we were closer to that landmark than we'd ever been) and preparing ourselves for some shut-eye upon one or other of the restaurant's benches.

The truck's cabin just wasn't big enough for the three of us, you see, given that the other five members of our party had already strewn themselves across it. Yet, after a short and thoroughly uncomfortable attempt to sleep upon one of the café's benches, Balta and I decided to cram ourselves into the cabin anyway, and soon fell blissfully into blessed unconsciousness again, whilst Will – who had been happily chatting to the locals up until that point – took his turn at trying to sleep upon a bench.

Those six hours were some of the longest of the trip thus far, so when 4am came and went without a murmur from the brothers, Balta and I made it our mission to make as much noise as possible until they were forcibly aroused from their slumber.

Eventually, we succeeded, and a further seven hours later – some nineteen hours after we first left Butawal on what then seemed to be a fairly insubstantial 150km hitch – we arrived in Pokhara.

So, what's one-hundred-and-fifty kilometres divided by nineteen hours? I make it a little less than eight kilometres per hour! That has to be some kind of a record…

DAY ONE HUNDRED AND FORTY-TWO:
HOTEL DISCOVERY INN, KATHMANDU, KATHMANDU DISTRICT, THE HIMALAYAS, NEPAL, SATURDAY 29TH NOVEMBER 2008, 18.04

My first candlelit journey of the entire trip coincides with the evening of our first full day in Kathmandu – capital city of the astoundingly beautiful country of Nepal.

What images spring to mind when you think of Nepal? I know that I used to think of it as a place where one might need to wrap up warmly, whilst also equipping oneself with essential body armour to stave off attacks from any roaming woolly-mammoth and yeti communities lurking within the mountains. I certainly didn't expect Nepal to be the lush green and blissfully warm country that we have found it to be.

Truthfully, there isn't much difference in climate here from the rest of Asia (at least what we have seen of it), other than a pleasant mountain breeze, which makes for cooler days and chillier nights.

So much of our time of late has been devoted to our ongoing friendships with the awkward trio of a lanky American, a Swiss charmer and a bubbly Brit that writing time has been severely reduced, and there is much to retell.

Beth and Evan rejoined us on only our second day in Pokhara and we have since spent all our time within that quintet, separating only once to break off into two teams for a hitchhiking race from Pokhara to Kathmandu. It seems that we have started some kind of Asian hitchhiking revolution, but before I can inform you of the details of this exciting new development, I must first invite you to take your minds back to last Monday morning, and the moment we finally arrived in Pokhara...

* * * * *

Set inside a beautiful mountain range, and extending along the waterfront of Pokhara Lake, the centre of the town is aptly named "Lakeside," and it was here we ended up on Monday morning... along with just about every other tourist!

It seems such a shame to me that a town that must have once been such a peaceful haven for the locals is now overrun with crowds of Western materialists, who cheapen the once rich culture into just another street, in just another town, where yet another hoard of faceless tourists can devote themselves to precisely the same activities that they would at home. The only change to them, it would appear, is one of scenery.

It rather embarrasses me to admit that our stay in Pokhara seemed only to imitate that of every other rich white person in the vicinity. We shopped for Christmas presents, lavishly spent about four times the normal rate for every meal, and wasted the evenings away on drinking local liquor and playing pool. I did enjoy our time there, but only insomuch as I was glad to be spending it with the ever-increasingly amusing characters of Evan, Beth and Balthazar – particularly enjoying myself as I watched tensions rise between Mr. Balta and Miss Beth, between whom, it has become clear, there is not much common ground.

The first signs of this tension came during our time in Mcleod, where Beth took an immediate dislike to our Bohemian friend.

"I'm just not sure what to make of him," she remarked to Will and me over breakfast one morn.

"Go on…" Will encouraged, curious to hear more.

"Well, I just don't think we have very much in common," she continued. "He likes girls, drinking, and smoking dope. I suppose I just don't really get why you like him."

The six-year gap between the two means that maturity levels aren't quite on a par and Beth simply cannot understand which wavelength it is that Balthazar is working from.

I suppose that it is just as well, for Balta's sake, that he cares little about Beth's opinions. The two really are at opposite ends of the spectrum and he made his own feelings very apparent to Evan and me during our long trek around Pokhara Lake on Tuesday.

"I find her voice… How do you say it…? Grating," Balthazar pronounced, much to the amusement of Evan and me.

"Grating!" we repeated.

"What makes you say that?" asked Evan, eager to hear more from our amusing friend and his limited reserves of English vocabulary.

"I do not like to listen to her voice," replied Balta, recommencing his attack. "And I do not like to look at her… She has… sausage arms, like…"

Balta didn't finish his sentence. He didn't need to. Just one flick of a finger at his own arms – enough to make them wobble – and we knew what he meant.

"Sausage arms!" I repeated, shaking my head and trying desperately not to laugh.

"Top notch Balthazar!" said Evan. "I'll clap that!"

It was rare to hear someone talking so openly about his or her feelings towards another, and Evan was all for it. I, on the other hand, whilst certainly finding Balthazar's brutal honesty a source of amusement, couldn't escape from feeling uneasy about the whole situation. Beth was a friend of ours and, even if she might not be a size-zero supermodel, it wasn't nice to hear Balthazar speak so harshly about her behind her back, and rather concerned me as to what might be said behind my own back when it was turned.

Nobody is safe from (to quote the Iranians) "evil backbiting," and hearing both Balta and Beth undertake in this backbiting business so freely was, to me, symptomatic of a society in which gossiping reigns supreme. Judgment is, of course, an unavoidable fact of life. Wherever we go we are all judged upon what we say and do, and even (and perhaps especially) how we look. From the very first meeting with a stranger, we each make strong opinions based upon every word and action. Yet, it makes me wonder how difficult it would be if one's major life aim was to please everybody all the time. I know that I have certainly been guilty of this tendency in the past, and it really is rather draining to devote oneself to the impossible task of people-pleasing, daily pretending to be something that one is not in order to attract the world's affirmation… I wouldn't recommend it.

* * * * *

The waterfall that we had been seeking was proving elusive and, as the sun was soon to set, the three of us decided to head for home through a forested region that we felt sure would lead us safely back to Lakeside.

During the walk, discussions moved onto a much nobler topic, as Evan brought up the subject of the tense political situation within Nepal at the moment.

Our American friend described to us the details surrounding Nepal's current political unrest and the deposing of the King by Maoists in their attempts to bring some version of "equality" to Nepal. As far as I can gather, the major sticking-point for the natives concerns the disproportionate way in which city dwellers have gained from the growth of the economy, whilst the poverty of the rural minorities continues to deepen.

This particular thought-stream soon sent Evan off on one about his personal aim to bring an end to Third World Debt, and his vision of globalized equality. Evan believes that his utopian dream could very well be made a reality if only globalized political groups (such as NATO or the UN) would step in and cancel the debt, giving individual governments worldwide the promise of financial aid so long as the money would be put to good use.

"As long as they put the money into schools, hospitals and the tourism industry, there will be a sustainable economy and..."

This is where I butted in: "...Happiness for all! Good stuff, Evan. You'll get my vote when you run for President."

It was Balthazar who picked up where Evan left off, leading the conversation onto the overwhelming number of beggars that can be seen in this part of the world – especially in India.

"I don't know what to do when I see the many beggar," he began. "I want give to all, but not possible."

"Well you see Balta," I began, adopting, I fear, an air of superiority. "Whenever Will or I see beggars, we ask them if we can buy them coffee or something to eat. This way we are not giving them any money that might be frittered away upon drugs and drink, and they are sure to be..."

This time it was Evan's turn to interrupt.

"Sorry Steve, I think that's a load of rubbish," said he. "If you give a beggar food or money, all you achieve is to make yourself feel better. It doesn't change anything. When you leave, the beggar remains in a condition of hunger and poverty, and the cycle is merely perpetuated because the beggar has less reason to change."

I felt a little ashamed. I had never heard this point of view before and had always thought that giving a little bit of food and a smile to the homeless was my way of showing them that they were worth bothering about, when so many just turn away in disgust. Maybe I was wrong.

"Buying food or giving money to a beggar might be good in its motive," Evan continued. "But it is useless in its consequence. What use is one day's provision in a lifetime of hunger and need? If you really want to help the poor, you need to think up sustainable projects in which individual lives can be changed."

Balta, who had remained silent for a while, suddenly burst into life with his own pearl of wisdom – borrowed, he believed, from Monsieur Hugo.

"I think it was Victor Hugo who said about seeing beggar on street. When he saw him, he did not give him any money or food, but... How do you say... ? Punch him in face. Beggar complain but Victor Hugo do not apologise and punch him again. Eventually, beggar get up and punch Victor Hugo and Hugo tell him he has taught him lesson about desire to change."

"Amen brother," Evan agreed. "Exactly my point. You give a beggar a quarter, you change nothing; you give him the desire to change and to make quarters for himself, and you may have just saved his life."

"Ah, the American dream!" I said.

DAY ONE HUNDRED AND FORTY-THREE:
HOTEL DISCOVERY INN, KATHMANDU, KATHMANDU DISTRICT, THE HIMALAYAS, NEPAL, SUNDAY 30TH NOVEMBER 2008, 22.14

I don't know whether it was the depth of our philosophical musings, or merely a lack of navigational prowess, that led us to stray from the right path, but after some thirty minutes of walking, looking up to be confronted only by further forestry (which seemed to be getting thicker and thicker by the minute) wasn't quite what we had hoped for.

Potential crisis loomed, so it was just as well that we had a gangly American with an unnaturally long neck, which enabled him to spot a rooftop hovering somewhere in the distance. We made a beeline for it.

Having successfully tangled our way through clumps of stinging nettles, one beehive, and dozens of invisible leeches – until it seemed as though there were no parts of our anatomies left unscathed – we found a wall, scaled it, and landed in what could only be described as a tourist's heaven.

As it turned out, we hadn't strayed nearly as far as we had first assumed. Not more than one hundred metres from Lakeside, secluded on its own private island, lay an idyllic resort, complete with plush villas, a swimming pool, and even a hot tub. Weary as we were, Evan and I thought it only fair that we attempted to get a free swim out of our accidental discovery. The hot tub was simply too inviting to miss and we soon convinced our Swiss pal that it was a good idea to slip into the shower room, strip down to our slacks, and hop on in...

Spurred on by our successes in this particular piece of roguery, Evan and I schemed that we might yet be able to wangle even more from this plush hotel resort. It didn't take long before we had justified any moral obligations that might deter us by deciding that any wrong-doing was thoroughly acceptable because it would be a Robin Hood-esque act of defiance acted out against the world's rich oppressors.

"Evan, let's go to the bar and try and blag a free pint," I urged, speaking at least twice as fast as usual in my excitement.

"Yeah! Great idea!" he replied, similarly upbeat. "But how?"

"Well, why don't we find an empty room, remember the number, go to the bar, and charge it to that room's tab?" I suggested.

"*I'll clap that*," responded Evan, continuing in his insistence upon using a catchphrase that had once been our own, but had now grown tiresome.

"What do you think Balta?" I asked, confident that our Bohemian friend was unlikely to offer much opposition. "It's a flawless plan. We won't be doing any harm to anyone who can't afford it."

"I do not do this," replied Balthazar, bluntly. "It is stealing," he concluded, revealing a surprisingly moral backbone.

"Wow! Balta's been brought up well," Evan remarked. "Maybe he's right."

"Oh, Balta! Now look what you've done!" I said, shaking my head in disappointment. "You've gone and made Evan feel bad!"

The funny thing was that Evan and I both agreed that, conceptually speaking, stealing was absolutely wrong. However, as absolute as that agreement might appear, it wasn't difficult for a combination of two of the world's cheekiest minds to scheme our way out of the ethical dilemma and justify it all in the name of adventure. Surely nobody could lose out. We would have the excitement and thrill that we craved, whilst this rich hotel would lose an insignificant amount of money and still leave smiling at the end of the day. What could possibly go wrong?

Then, turning to Evan, I tried to reassure him.

"Come on Evan, we can't back out now! Think of it as a challenge, rather than any matter of great morality. After all, everything is permissible, right?"

This "everything is permissible" thing had become somewhat of a catchphrase for me over the past few weeks, but I was about to see just how faulty such a philosophy, when used incorrectly, could prove...

* * * * *

Looking back, I don't know how we missed it. We had managed to overlook one of the most glaringly obvious potential drawbacks of our idea. There was someone who stood to lose in this exchange, and that was our poor waiter – a young Nepali in his early twenties, who would later reveal to me that it was his first day!

To be fair to our waiter, if I were in charge and had seen the professional way in which he served us, I wouldn't hold him accountable. The fault was entirely our own.

Having confidently declared that it was "Room 43" to which we wanted the charge to be administered, the waiter seemed a little surprised.

"Are you sure you mean Room 43?" he asked.

...Oh no! What had we done? Why didn't he believe us?

"It is forty-three, isn't it Evan?" I asked, doing my level best to speak with a touch of both surprise and detachment. A frenzy of worried thoughts went racing through my mind, whilst I tried my best to keep my face as blank as a (blank) sheet of paper.

"Yeah I'm pretty sure that's the one," Evan replied, holding his own nerve well.

"Does it say on the key?" asked the waiter. "Have you got it with you?"

"Er... no. I think I left it in the room," said Evan. "Hold on, I'll just go check the room to make sure."

And with that, Evan went off to "check the room" and to "make sure," whilst I gave my best innocent smile to the waiter, whom, I felt sure, was growing in suspicion by the minute.

Saying nothing, he went to attend to our drinks as if they had been any other order, but I felt sure that I could see him whispering to his colleagues about the two suspicious characters on table such and such.

I was in the grip of intense paranoia and couldn't seem to escape. As I tried to keep my face as emotionless as possible on the outside, I was a wreck on the inside and kept going through potential repercussions in my head. I wasn't worried about the waiter just yet. Thus far he hadn't done anything wrong and any fault or potential blame lay entirely on the heads of Evan and myself. What on earth was going to happen? How were we going to pay the 900-rupee charge (almost ten quid!) for what were actually two rather revolting glasses of wine? Would the police be called in? Would we be thrown out of the country? What would become of the Hitch? Had I just ruined everything?

I had already drunk almost all of my revolting wine before Evan eventually returned, and the waiter came over to see what he had to say for himself.

"Silly me, declared Evan, coolly. "It was Room thirty-four, not forty-three. Went and got the numbers mixed up in that-there head of mine, didn't I!"

Evan chuckled as he finished.

I stared right through him, thinking him to be entirely transparent.

A pause.

"OK, no problem sir," the waiter responded. "I assumed there must be some mistake because the couple behind you are from Room 43."

And with that, he left.

As soon as the waiter was out of earshot, I asked Evan (quietly) *where the hell* he had been and *what on earth* he thought we should do now!

"I don't know man," he replied. "I thought we were leaving when I went to "check the room." I've been waiting for you by the boat for the last ten minutes!"

I can just imagine what was going through my eccentric friend's head as he sneaked out of the bar, passed the Reception, picked up his bag from the shower room, and made for the boat.

"Every man for himself," he joked. "I was just about to get on a boat when I suddenly thought I might have misread the situation."

Once I had let Evan know just what I thought of his idiocy, I brought up the more serious matter at hand.

"Oh, I found out something rather interesting while you were away," I said. "I was doing my best to sweet-talk the waiter so he didn't suspect anything, and then he went and told me that it's his first day on the job! Apparently he's from some poor village family and is desperately hoping that this job will provide him enough money to support them."

Of course! How could we have been so stupid? It was this poor young waiter who was going to cop the blame. If anyone were going to lose from our innocent little game, it would be him – and if *he* fell, he was going to fall hard.

Evan and I sat in silence for a little while, reflecting upon the seriousness of what we had done...

* * * * *

When eventually Evan spoke, it was nice for me to see that it wasn't only *my* imagination that was running wild in the heat of the moment.

"Man, we'd better get out of here," he said. "Do you think they're on to us? I bet the police will come now and, who knows, we might even get chucked out of the country!"

Seeing the waiter fast approaching, I signalled to Evan to stop talking.

"Hello, here is the bill," said the waiter, handing me a corrected slip of paper that had "Room 34" written in bold letters at the head.

"Would you like to order anything else?"

Everything inside of me was telling me to say a swift "no" and we could be on our way, but then Evan, in a new wave of confidence, blurted out that he'd like to "see the food menu please" and "could we possibly have some garlic naan to start with, thank you very much."

"What the hell are you doing?" I snapped, as soon as the waiter was out of hearing.

"Sorry, I panicked," he responded. "Do you think he's on to us...?"

Thirty minutes passed by, during which time all we felt able to do was to conjure up potential consequences for the escalating situation, grappling over the ethical dilemma we had gotten ourselves into. All the while, Evan was hassling me to "just own up, pay the bill, and get out of here, conscience clean," but I could not stand the thought of backing out having come so far. Whatever the potential downfall, somehow the urge still remained to see whether or not we could get away with it.

* * * * *

"Whatever happened to that garlic naan?" I asked Evan, realising that it was getting on for forty minutes since we had placed the order.

"Let's just get out of here," he replied and, before we had the time to think about just how we would make our escape, we were out of our seats and making for the boat.

"I just wanted some f***ing garlic naan," Evan shouted back as we made our way past reception, pointing an accusing finger in the direction of the bar.

Oh no! Why couldn't Evan just keep his trap shut? I hung my head in shame and resignation, feeling sure that we were about to be caught and taken to the police.

Rounding the corner, we reached the jetty, where we stood and waited for the ferryboat to return from the other side of the crossing. Two fellow foreigners came and stood beside us, and Evan and I joked to each other that next round the corner would be the entire bar staff, accompanied by a posse of police officers.

So when the next person around the corner really was a solitary police officer, our hearts were in our mouths and we bowed our heads, awaiting imminent arrest.

It never came.

The officer simply stood there quietly, and waited for the boat along with the rest of us. The tension was unbearable.

The five-minute boat journey was yet another chance for our imaginations to get the better of us. We felt sure we had seen a squadron of undercover cops crowding the jetty ahead of us, waiting to pounce as soon as the boat hit the shore...

We were almost disappointed that none of this wild fabrication came to fruition. There was no resolution, in either direction – good or bad – at all. We will simply never know what became of our waiter. Perhaps he will have been docked wages, or maybe sacked. Or perhaps, more likely still, nobody will have ever noticed the 900-rupee deficit that two phantom guests of Room 34 once left unpaid.

DAY ONE HUNDRED AND FORTY-FOUR:
ROOM 501, HOTEL DISCOVERY INN, KATHMANDU, KATHMANDU DISTRICT, THE HIMALAYAS, NEPAL, MONDAY 1ST DECEMBER 2008, 17.42

For the third night in a row, I write under the romantic conditions of candlelight – a result of the latest power-cut to hit the capital city of Nepal.

Oh, and wouldn't you know it, but it has taken me the best part of the day to find myself any kind of peace or seclusion in which I may write, and I have just been interrupted (once again) by my two remaining travelling companions: Messieurs Jackson and Moody.

...Ah that's better. I have vacated the room to find inspiration and solace upon the veranda outside, and now I sit at my favourite writing table on the fifth floor of this cheap-and-cheerful Kathmandu hotel. There is much left to retell, so I shall pick up where I left off and take you back to Pokhara, and the morning after our night of tomfoolery.

A midnight hike to watch the sunrise over the magnificent mountain of Sarangkot provided us with a fitting farewell to Pokhara and then it was time to hit the road again.

Having successfully hitched back to town on a school bus, we packed our things, had a quick bite to eat, and split off into two teams to begin our race to Kathmandu. For the first time since Spain – when we vowed never to do it again – Will and I were parted, going our separate ways that we might lead our novices in their own pursuit of hitchhiking brilliance.

Both Balta and Beth expressed sincere reservations about hitching with the other, so Beth and Will were paired together, whilst I would chaperone Balta and Evan.

Next stop Kathmandu. Approximate distance: 200km. Estimated time of arrival: anytime between 6pm and midnight.

"Three, two, one... Go!!!"

* * * * *

The *A Team* (obviously that's *my* team) set the early pace, securing four quick lifts in a variety of bizarre vehicles – one of which appeared to be nothing more than a large, rusty engine with wheels and a trailer – to make it to the edge of town, and place ourselves in what we felt sure to be the perfect hitching spot on the only road between Pokhara and the capital.

Progress had been remarkably swift, but we hadn't made more than about twenty kilometres towards our destination, and were aware that we were in need of a significant lift, and fast. Beth and Will would be hot on our heels, and we were scrutinizing each passing vehicle just to make sure they hadn't taken the lead.

It was only natural, then, that we were elated when there had been no sign of a passing *B Team* and, lo and behold, a truck pulled over to give us a ride. This was our chance. They would almost certainly be heading to Kathmandu and we could almost taste the sweet, sweet victory.

It was with a mixture of jubilation and disappointment (more of the latter) that we opened the cabin door to find the familiar faces of William and Bethany staring back at us. Apparently they had been picked up just ten minutes before and, after a bit of cajoling, had managed to persuade their drivers to take a further three bodies along for the ride. I don't know whether *Team A* would have been quite so charitable.

Will and I truly are inseparable, it would seem. We can't have been apart for much more than sixty minutes, and already we were reunited in the cabin of two young truckers – they were brothers, like many of the truck-pairings in Asia, although I guess that one can never be sure if the "brother" definition actually means a blood-relation or just a very good mate.

We must have travelled a good eighty or ninety kilometres with these bruvas before we were spontaneously ejected from the vehicle and pointed towards a road on the other side of the village. It seemed that we had stumbled upon one place that actually boasted more than one exit road and our chauffeurs were heading in the other direction – south, as it transpired, to India.

Our target was still some 100km away and daylight hours were fast disappearing, so the five of us hurried across the village to recommence hitching. Our quintet remained together to begin with, but at the first sign of a stopping truck, it was my *A Team* who reacted first, pinching the lift that would surely give us the best chance of victory in our contest.

Sadly, we picked the wrong truck. This particular vehicle seemed to have only one gear, and any hill-climb we confronted – there were quite a few due to the mountainous nature of our route – would be tackled at walking pace. Meanwhile, unbeknown to us, Beth and Will had jumped straight into another truck just seconds behind our own, and were gaining on us fast.

Twenty minutes of stiff hill-climbing later and our drivers felt in sufficient need of a tea-stop.

"Oh no!" we thought. "That'll certainly put paid to our remaining chances of winning this race."

Fortunately, not for the first time that day, we were wrong, for who should we see coming over the hill to become the very next patrons of that tea shop if not the participants from the *B Team*! It just so happened that our respective drivers had been travelling in convoy since the beginning of the day and, what's more, they were going to end the day in Kathmandu!

So much for our ardent attempts to race against each other. It seemed that the entire Nepalese nation was against us... or at least its truckers. No matter; at least we were going to make it to Kathmandu that evening... or so we thought.

There is a certain carelessness that creeps in during those moments when one feels sure that the winning post is in sight. We were so sure that we would soon be in Kathmandu that it simply did not matter to us *when* we would arrive, so long as we *did* actually arrive. But since when are things ever as easy as they first appear?

* * * * *

Barely ten minutes on from our chai break, *Team A*'s truck decided to break down and, in the absence of a hand brake, it was just as well that the younger brother was a man of action (or, more likely, of habit) and leapt out to place two large stones behind the back wheels, or else we would almost certainly have fallen off the adjacent precipice.

Rocks firmly in place, the elder brother attempted to give the truck some gas, pressing his foot to the floor gently and flinging the gear-stick around to try to find some kind of grip. It was no use.

Performing a hill-start in a broken-down vehicle was never likely to amount to more than a lot of noise and a few billows of smoke, and so it proved. Ten minutes later, and the brothers turned to us, shrugged their shoulders, and signalled that we were to leave.

Luckily for us, our broken-down vehicle did at least have one working headlight (an uncommon phenomenon in these lands), which proved sufficient to give us one of those most essential hitching credentials: visibility. The slowness of passing vehicles had already been ensured by the near-vertical slope upon which we stood, and our truck presented passing vehicles with a handy place in which to pull in.

Thus, any fears that might have arisen amongst our number – perhaps because of the blackness of the sky or the fact that we were in the middle of nowhere – did not have time to surface as the very first passing truck pulled over, didn't quite stop the vehicle (probably for fear that they'd never start it again), and Evan, Balta and I performed an on-the-move vehicle mount that would have better-fitted a scene from a Hollywood blockbuster.

Hopes thoroughly restored by our quick pick-up – in a truck in much better condition – and familiar enough with the frequency with which truckers in these parts like their tea breaks, we were unperturbed when our latest chauffeurs pulled over for a chai-break after barely five minutes. Even when our friends began ordering food – first for themselves, and then for us – we were undisturbed. Yet, as the minutes rolled by, our friends became more and more relaxed, and it wasn't long before I started to entertain the thought that this might be a repeat of that marathon, nineteen-hour journey, that Balta, Will and I had suffered on our last 150km to Pokhara.

"Oh no!" I whispered to Evan and Balthazar. "I don't think we're going to leave here tonight."

"What?"

"Quoi?"

"What do you mean?" they said, together.

I reminded them both of the story of that horrendously long hitch and, sure enough, after a comical hour-or-so of pretending that the three of us were the next *Coldplay* (I was the guitar player, Balta the drummer, and Evan both vocalist and... dancer!), our friends informed us that we would be leaving again... at about 2am – five hours from then!

So relaxed had we become that we weren't even particularly upset by the news and revelled in the hilarity of our pretence. Evan and I were in our element once more, reproducing our form from the other night – during our somewhat ethically-questionable wine-blagging – as we told our friends all about what it was like being in a famous English band.

"We're still pretty unknown over here in Nepal," said Evan, "but we're huge back home."

Both Evan and I were wearing our hitching t-shirts and I suggested that the phrase that reads "Steve and Will's hitch to Malaysia" referred to me (Steve), Balta (Will) and Evan ("hitch") on our latest tour from England to Malaysia.

"Ooooohhhh!" was the unified response from the crowd. Our friends were impressed.

Of course they wanted a private gig for their troubles and, growing in confidence, Evan had grabbed the guitar, handed it to me, and I began strumming random chords to try to harmonize with Evan's best attempts at ridiculous lyrics and interpretive dance.

I was in tears within only a few seconds as the lanky frame of our American friend jerked and jolted its limbs in every direction, whilst he sung about a hitchhike to Kathmandu. Quite what our Nepalese friends made of the performance I do not know, but we received generous cheers and applause throughout the five-song show, even if these were given with both amusement and disbelief strewn across their faces.

* * * * *

Showtime over, it was time for bed. We were shown into a little room at the back of the roadside diner, where we took a few precious hours of sleep, before resuming our journey to Kathmandu – arriving at 5am the following morning.

It was still dark when we arrived, so we decided not to rush our efforts to find the recommended tourist hub of *Thamel* in central Kathmandu, preferring casual strolls in the various directions in which we were pointed by a host of well-meaning (if a little geographically unaware) locals. It always amazes me how many people you can find awake in the small hours of the morning in a big city. One would have thought it was the middle of the day – such was the hustle and bustle of the city's suburbs – if it weren't for the fact that somebody had forgotten to switch on the lights.

On our walk, we passed a string of astounding ancient temples, which shone resplendently in the half-light of dawn. Having heard only bad reports of Kathmandu from our time in Pokhara, we could only assume that everything else in the city must be appalling because our opening opinions of the capital were decidedly positive.

Perhaps we were lucky because we arrived at the perfect time to view these otherworldly relics. During the day, officials charge 200-rupees-a-head for the privilege, whilst swarms of tourists mar the overall experience with their incessant noise and flash photography. In contrast, at the break of dawn, the only people present are a few locals setting up their stalls for another day of selling tiger balm or Gurkha knives to tourists. At this time of day there is a sweet serenity, almost an aura of holiness, which enshrines these ancient places of worship. Mesmerised, we stood silently for quite some time, before heading back towards Thamel – the point of our scheduled rendezvous with *Team B*.

A friend of ours back in Pokhara had drawn us a vague map of the area so that both teams might have a rough idea of where to go. In the absence of phones, the plan had been for the winning team to check into a cheap hotel, log on to the Internet, and email the other team to let them know that they had won the race and where they could be found.

Team B must have arrived hours before us, so we headed straight to an Internet café to find out where they had checked in. Having waited for an hour in order that one of the cafés might open, we were a touch surprised to find that none of us had received any word from the other team whatsoever.

Oh no! What had happened? Something must have gone horribly wrong because they should have arrived long before us. Their truck was much faster, and they were unlikely to have experienced a breakdown... Surely their drivers hadn't also decided to take a spontaneous five-hour stop for some sleep, had they?

Whatever had happened, we agreed that Team A should be crowned the official winners of the race, but something still felt very wrong. Not knowing what else to do, we followed the original plan, checking into a hotel and emailing the others to let them know where they might find us.

Entitling the email "*Team A reign victorious*," we told Will and Beth to find us at the Harvest Moon Hotel, whereupon we headed straight up to our room on the top floor to catch up on some sleep.

* * * * *

We were awoken a little after midday by an agitated banging on the door.

"Where the hell were you guys?" shouted Will, as he and Beth walked into the room. "We've spent the best part of two hours looking for you!"

"Where were *we*?" I yelled back. "Where the hell have *you* been? You should have been here hours before us, but you couldn't even be bothered to write us a little email to let us know!"

I think of the arguments that Will and I exchange as rather like a rocket launch. On the rare occasions when such a thing occurs, it starts with a great explosion, but never goes on for very long. I can remember only three arguments on the trip thus far and none of them has been about anything at all significant, nor have they lasted for more than a moment. This one was to be no different. It had been a mutual misunderstanding and we soon kissed (not literally) and made up.

As expected, Will and Beth had indeed arrived substantially before us, checking into their own hotel at about midnight the previous night. It turned out that their drivers had caught wind of our breakdown and had done their best to explain that there had been a problem with the other vehicle and we would not be expected until the following day.

Thus, when *Team B* arrived, they simply checked in, went out for a celebratory drink, and crashed out for the night, assuming that there would be plenty of time to write us an email the following morning because we surely wouldn't arrive until well into the afternoon.

What they hadn't allowed for was our decision to ditch our broken-down lorry and make off in a new vehicle. It's just as well that our second vehicle decided to indulge that infamous Nepalese trick of an overnight sleep outside a roadside eatery or we might have had much longer to worry over the safety of our friends.

As it was, all was reconciled easily enough. Will had merely been a touch frustrated because we had been a little uncertain as to where we might end up. We had given them two options and, naturally, they had tried the wrong one first. Beyond this minor hiccup, I suppose that Will was probably also a tad cheesed off by the title of our message…

Their failure to contact us had, indeed, caused us to assume the victory, and I'm sticking by it! Congratulations *Team A*: winners by the two sweetest words in the English language – to borrow a phrase from Homer (the Simpson, not the Greek): "De-fault."

14. THE RACE (PART ONE)

DAY ONE HUNDRED AND FORTY-SIX:
ROADSIDE DINER, SOMEWHERE BETWEEN MOTIHARI AND MUZAFFARPUR, BIHAR STATE, INDIA, WEDNESDAY 3RD DECEMBER 2008, 14.50

The Race has officially begun. At 4pm yesterday afternoon, Evan was enrolled as the third member of Steve and Will's hitch to Malaysia (we're going to call him "Hitch"), given his very own t-shirt, and off we set – next stop Laos!

The pressure of two major future concerns (which were to result in spectacularly contrasting conclusions) blighted our time in Kathmandu:

1. Would we receive our Bangladeshi and Burmese visas in time for us (realistically) to have enough time to reach Laos by the 25th?

2. Would we manage to worm our way out of Evan's disastrous blunder, which was spontaneously to invite Beth to join us on the rest of our journey, without giving the slightest thought to any ensuing problems this might entail?

Beth had grown more and more excited about the prospect of tagging along ever since, but we three lads had all felt immediate regret at Evan's ill-advised suggestion. It wasn't at all that we didn't like Beth (quite the contrary), but there was something that made each one of us feel uneasy, now that the prospect of a further month together had been so recklessly arranged.

"Oops!" said Evan to me, just moments after his outburst.

"Oops?" I replied, shaking my head. "Yeah, just a bit mate! You know that Will and I *have* to hitch together, don't you? So now what do you propose? It's either all four of us go together, which is, frankly, a ridiculous idea, or you and Beth will seriously have to rise to the challenge and manage to hitch your own way there."

"Mmm. Yeah. Didn't really think that one through, did I?" responded Evan. "It seemed like a good idea at the time..."

To be fair to the lad, it *had* seemed like a good idea. We had all been excited that Beth would be joining us in the venture. Quite what poor Balthazar thought at being the only one left out, I do not know, but for the rest of us, the excitement of a race across the rest of Nepal, northern India, Bangladesh and Burma loomed large on the horizon. The practicalities of such a potentially dangerous venture had not even been vaguely considered.

"Did I ever tell you what happened to me and Beth when we tried hitching to Kashmir?" asked Evan.

I shook my head.

"Well, it wasn't ideal," he continued. "After we left you, we waited around for about half an hour without anyone even stopping for us, so when we saw a bus go by, we jumped at the chance. The bus took ten hours to get us to Pathankot and Beth barely said a word throughout the journey. Then, as soon as we arrive, she starts shouting at me that she (Evan paused for a second to clear his throat, before continuing in his own unique take on a British accent) 'can't do this' and she doesn't know why she 'did this in the first place'. Before I know it, I'm off on a bus to Jammu all on my own! I don't know how she'd be able to handle Burma if she couldn't even deal with Kashmir!"

The road ahead isn't exactly everyone's cup of tea. We reckon that we've got at least 2,000km to do in three weeks and this isn't 2,000km of nice, English country lanes; this is a potentially hazardous hitch through regions that we honestly know nothing about.

When I think of Bangladesh, I think of immense poverty, so the idea that there is going to be a nice motorway running straight from the Indian to the Burmese border is pretty much a joke. And don't even get me started on my perceptions of Burma. The only thing I know about the place is that it was subject to an horrendous flood not so long ago and the ruling junta then decided that they hated the West so much that they weren't even going to allow its aid agencies to help.

This is no walk in the park; we're going to need tremendous amounts of spirit and determination to do this thing and simply cannot afford to take any risks.

And then there's the fact that she's a girl... Even if Beth were the toughest competitor we'd ever met, she would still be a liability. We have simply no idea how having a girl with us might affect our chances of getting picked up and it'd be more than just *our* safety that we'd be putting in jeopardy by taking her along for the ride. To be honest, we're just not in a position to chaperone anyone else on this hitch. We've already been lumbered with an American with a big gob. We can't afford to take any more chances.

"*And* I just don't know her all that well," Evan continued. "It's all very well spending a couple of days with someone, but having to travel for a month together is a different story."

"Right, so it's decided then?" I asked, and bear in mind that this is only about five minutes after he has unofficially invited Beth and even proceeded to rave about the idea that we will all do something to celebrate her birthday on the 10th of December when, no doubt, we will be in some remote area of Bangladesh or Burma...

He nods.

* * * * *

The matter came to a head on our second day together in Kathmandu. The four of us trudged off to explore the situation at the respective embassies of Bangladesh and Burma and it quickly became apparent that this was decision-making time. We had walked into a nearby *Visa Enquiries Office* and been informed, much to our disappointment, that, given that it was a Sunday, neither embassy would be open until the following day. Nevertheless, we had been given four sets of visa forms to fill in and were told to return early the following morning when the man would "do his best" to get all four of us visas for both countries "as soon as possible."

This was crunch time. We went to find a drink somewhere and, finally, Evan summoned up the courage to speak.

"So, about this Christmas in Laos business..." he blurted out – with the very same poise, consideration, and delivery with which he had originally invited Beth. Will and I hung our heads in disbelief at his lack of tact.

Evan was laughing as he continued.

"Well, we reckon we're going to have to go it alone, don't we boys?"

We pursed our lips and tried our best to offer apologetic smiles towards Beth.

"Right. So that's it then, is it?" mumbled Beth, sarcastically. There was a sense of real pain beneath her tough exterior.

"I need some time alone," she spat, and left, rejecting our best efforts to make her stay and talk it over.

The three of us sat in silence until the waiter came along with three mango *lassis* (these incredible fruit-shakes that they have out here in the India/Nepal region).

"I guess *I'm* going to have to finish her one, then?" Evan joked. "Can't believe it! I told you guys I didn't want anything!"

Will and I looked at each other, shook our heads, rolled our eyes, and cast them skyward in utter disbelief that our friend was *still* joking after almost bringing a girl to tears.

After we made our way back to the hotel, we found Beth sitting at a table outside our room, writing frantically in her journal. There was no response to our greeting and we were given a full dose of the silent treatment for the rest of the time we spent together.

Then, as if things could not get any worse for poor Beth, there was still time for Will and Evan to join heads and come up with one of the worst ideas this side of the turn of the Millennium: they were going throw her a surprise birthday bash that very night, to try to build bridges... I can just picture the two of them working that one through in their heads and then congratulating each other on what they considered to be a faultless plan.

Whilst Will and Evan went off to buy a present and a cake, I spent the afternoon doing my best to console Beth, who, unsurprisingly, attributed our decision to be just another one in a long line of rejections – especially by the men in her life.

"You know this isn't about you?" I said. "We are all very fond of you. We wouldn't have suggested it otherwise. We just didn't think it through that well. I'm sorry Beth – we're idiots."

"Yes you are!" she shouted. "Why are men so flippin' insensitive?"

These were about the only words that I could get out of Beth during the long hour that we spent together on the veranda outside of our room. A few tears came, but not a lot of resolution to follow. We'd screwed up, and it'd take more than my artificial apology to get her to forgive us... It might take more than a surprise birthday bash too.

* * * * *

Beth was hardly in party spirits later that evening, as we finally persuaded her that she should join us for a meal. And then it was time for Will and Evan to skulk off to prepare the surprise. It had all been worked out to perfection. They were going to pretend to go out in search of cash and then they would join us at the "Russian place" – a bar we knew that Beth liked because it was the one where she and Will celebrated their arrival in Kathmandu.

In fact, Will and Evan had run on ahead to light the candles on the cake and to prepare everyone in the room for a rendition of "Happy Birthday."

It was to this chorus that Beth, Balta and I arrived.

"Happy Birthday to..." I stopped short. The look on Beth's face was one of pure disgust. Of course, there was no stopping Will or Evan, but a deathly silence descended upon the rest.

"I need a minute outside," said Beth, storming out to compose herself after the latest turn in a long line of unfortunate and unwanted events.

"...What? That's all she's going to say?" screamed Evan, as soon as she had gone.

"Shhh. Be quiet Evan," I whispered. "Don't let Beth hear you."

"I don't f***ing care if she hears me," he continued. "This is getting God-damn ridiculous. It's all very well being a bit upset about it, but we've apologised enough times by now and she just reacts like a petulant little kid!"

"Calm down Evan." It was Will's turn to try to prevent our friend from adding any further to the poor girl's misery, but it was no use.

"No!" he snapped back. "This is one step too far. So what if she can't come to Christmas with my family? I don't just invite anyone, you know! I wanted her to come, but it's just not practical and we've told her the reasons why. Now why doesn't she just grow up and get on with it like the rest of us?"

Beth walked back in before Evan could finish his rant, but there was to be no great showing of forgiveness that night. When Evan proudly presented her with our gift (a Tom Robbins' book she'd been raving about) and offered her a slice of cake, Beth's sole response was an unimaginative statement of fact:

"It's not my birthday."

"Yeah, we all know that," said Evan, in a tone just that little bit calmer than his most extreme ranting voice. "But we were going to celebrate your birthday together, weren't we? And now we can't celebrate it on the day..."

Beth cut him short. "What? You thought it would make me feel better to throw me a party, even though it's just another reminder that I can't travel with you guys! You guys are ridiculous – just one more example of men having no idea how to deal with women."

Before Evan could react – and believe me, he *would* have reacted – Beth had taken to her feet and was on her way back to the hotel.

We would never see her again.

* * * * *

The next morning we awoke to find that a postcard had been slipped underneath our door. We recognised the design to be the very same card we had given Beth the previous evening, choosing not to write a message on the back so that Beth might use it to send home to a loved one.

Turned out she'd found another use for it... On the back of the card, scribbled in hurried fashion, was a very short message:

"Sorry not to say goodbye. Couldn't face seeing you guys any longer. Thanks for a lot of fun times and I hope you guys make it to Laos. Merry f***ing Christmas!
Beth"

DAY ONE HUNDRED AND FORTY-EIGHT:
RAJ'S HOUSE, THANAPARA, RAJSHAHI DISTRICT, BANGLADESH, FRIDAY 5TH DECEMBER 2008, 22.05

When I suggested that hitchhiking was a 9-5 job, I severely understated our current working hours. Leaving Kathmandu at 5pm on Tuesday afternoon, we travelled night and day for forty-eight hours, arriving at the Bangladeshi border at Mahadipur, just before closing time, on Thursday.

Four short pick-up truck rides saw us under way, taking us as far as the outskirts of the city, but it was our fifth ride that will stick in the memory: a lorry journey that would see us all the way to the Indian border by morning. Of course, we had to endure the usual Nepali trick of a five-hour midnight sleepover, but still arrived at the border by 7am, barely able to believe that, after only one night of hitching, we were back on Indian soil.

The second day started slowly. Laughing off the Nepali border official's attempts to charge us for leaving his country, we gulped down a welcome Indian breakfast – of roti (Indian bread), spicy sauce, and a glass of milky chai – before recommencing our hitching efforts by mid-morning.

The first truck to stop for us turned out to be a bit of a non-starter. Having travelled no more than 5km, the two drivers (probably brothers and neither of whom could speak a word of English) signalled that we were to wait whilst they went off, presumably to find something to carry on the back of their empty truck.

So tired were we from the previous night's journey – which had been spent cramped into a cabin with at least half-a-dozen other bodies – that Will and Evan were happy just to wait and catch up on some sleep. Reluctantly, I agreed to play the role of night watchman, but when, after a whole hour, there had been no sign of our drivers, the troops were roused, and we were off again.

Frustrated by the lack of passing traffic, we took a short hitch on the top of a bus (seems to be standard practice in the region) and jumped off just in time to flag down a lorry, which, we hoped, might take us a more substantial distance.

Sure enough, back-to-back truck rides saw us make good (if a little slow) progress towards our Bangladeshi target. We reckoned that we'd made some 250km by the time (about 10pm) the second truck finally dropped us off, in a dingy little town on the other side of Patna.

Worn out from our non-stop journeying since Kathmandu, we had half a mind to crash out for the night in some cheap guesthouse, but their hiked-up asking prices gave us a new lease of life. There was still about 400km separating us from the Bangladeshi border and whatever distance we could make during the night would be sure to give us a better chance of reaching our target the next day. It was Evan who was most instrumental in our decision.

"Come on guys!" he said, having scoffed at the latest guesthouse owner's attempt to charge us three times the usual rate for what was, essentially, squalor. "We've got a long way to go to get to Laos and anything we do in these night-time shifts is gonna help."

Evan's presence in our hitching party has certainly changed the dynamic. They say 'two's company, three's a crowd', and I can already see what they mean. Don't get me wrong, Evan is a likeable-enough fellow, but he is also extremely headstrong, and when three guys with similar personalities and strong opinions come together, sparks simply must fly.

Will and I know each other so well that we can gauge exactly what the other is thinking in the most stressful of times and choose not to speak when we know it will only rile the other. Evan, on the other hand, we do not know so well, and he has come into our party with his own ideas of how best to hitchhike, and seems strangely unwilling to allow us more experienced hikers to lead the way.

One good thing Evan has brought with him, however, is his incredible drive and determination, reinforced by his impression that if we're going to have any chance of making it to Laos by the 25th, we're going to have to hitch non-stop through night and day for the next three weeks!

Will and I, meanwhile, have a fairly good understanding of how long it takes to hitch between places by now, and do not foresee it taking nearly so long. The approximate 2,000km between here and Laos is a very achievable target in three weeks and does not necessitate that we must therefore hitchhike throughout every hour that the good Lord gives us.

Saying that, a few all-nighters here and there can't hurt, can they? On Wednesday night we preferred a second consecutive all-nighter to an overpriced stay in a grotty hotel room. Not even in our wildest dreams could we have imagined what would happen next, for no sooner had we recommenced hitching, than three blokes in a pick-up truck (there are a lot of them around here) pulled over to tell us that they were driving all the way to Darjeeling!

Whilst we had no particular desire to visit the famous tea-making hill-town itself, we knew that Darjeeling boasted its very own border crossing with northern Bangladesh, and that any distance these guys might take us would be a step in the right direction.

"Fifty kilometre," one of the men had said, gesturing with the five fingers on his right hand.

We could have been forgiven for thinking that this meant that, for whatever reason, they could take us no more than "fifty kilometres" that night, so it was more than a little surprising when, after three hours on the road, there was no sign of their stopping.

"Not to worry," we thought. Unless they planned to kidnap us, then we were surely heading in the right direction and it mattered little to us that we knew not where we were.

It wasn't until 7 o'clock the next morning that we were kicked out, bumped and bruised from head to toe, only fifty kilometres away from the Bangladeshi border.

"Aha!" I exclaimed. "So *that* was what they meant by "fifty kilometre!"

Those ten hours that we spent in the back of an open-topped pick-up truck weren't exactly our most comfortable of the trip. I don't know whether it was the poor quality of the roads, or the fact that the truck lacked sufficient suspension, but we were rarely asleep for more than a matter of seconds before we were catapulted into the air again by the latest bump. Huddled closely together on the hard iron floor of the trailer in our best attempts to conserve heat and protect us from the trailer's jagged edges, this was a night of unparalleled discomfort. Oh well, at least we were sure to arrive in Bangladesh by the end of the day... weren't we?

* * * * *

After an unpleasant toilet experience involving a rat – I won't bore you with the details – it was time to hit the road again. Having regained feeling in the majority of our toes, we wandered over to the other side of the roundabout at which we had been deposited, and soon found a ride on the back of one of those funny-looking trucks with no container on the back.

If you think *they* look funny, though, imagine how strange it must have looked for the locals to see three scrawny white guys taking the place of said missing container, and holding on for dear life whilst our daring driver wound his way over typically bumpy terrain without the slightest regard for the effect the experience might have upon our poor backs... or the rest of us, come to think of it!

Half an hour later and the driver pulled over, beamed back at us (it seemed as though he had found the experience rather amusing), and pointed us in the direction of another road.

"Bangladesh," he said, and off he sped.

Another few stretches, a quick gulp of water, and we were off again.

"We must be really close to Bangladesh now!" said Will.

Evan and I agreed.

The only problem was that the area was so remote that signposts to Bangladesh were scarce (or non-existent) and there appeared to be none around who could speak a word of English, nor even understand what we meant when we repeated the word, "Bangladesh," or any attempts at possible Hindi alternatives.

"Ben-ga-lee?"

"Ban-ga-la?"

"Ban-gee-la-deesh?"

"Ben-gol-o-doosh?"

It was no use.

We soon grew so desperate that, contrary to all common sense, we decided to put our faith in the hands of an American...

Evan had been surveying the area and cogitating over possible routes with his compass for much of the past thirty minutes. And then, with the most supreme confidence, he announced that he was absolutely "sure" that he knew the way.

It's a funny word that "sure"... Covers over all manner of misunderstandings!

For the next six hours (no, I'm not exaggerating), we drove in just about every direction around the Mahadipur border without ever actually finding it! It would have been hilarious to have followed our movements on a satellite navigation system and to have seen just how many times we drove right past the dusty track that led to Bangladesh without ever actually spotting it.

Finally, at 3pm – one hour before we had been told that the border would close – we were dumped at the start of said dusty track (by what must have been our sixth or seventh ride of the afternoon), and began the 10km trek to Bangladesh. That's right, this border was so remote that one literally needed to walk for ten kilometres to reach it!

We must have been walking for more than ten minutes before there was any sign of anyone else foolish enough to attempt this border crossing, so when, finally, we heard behind us the familiar sound of a rickety old truck, there was no way we were going to allow this opportunity to pass us by.

The three of us presented the drivers with an impenetrable human blockade and they had no choice but to invite us aboard.

"Finally!" cried Will. "We might just be in with a chance…"

What we hadn't allowed for was the fact that these truckers (definitely brothers) might just be celebrities in the village and would insist upon stopping to have a cup of chai with every single person we met. Yes, quite a few people actually appear to live on the dusty track that separates India from Bangladesh… I'd love to know what their postal addresses would be!

Even when the truck was moving, the terrain was such that it could move at a pace barely faster than that of walking, so when the time reached 15.40 and we seemed to have covered little more than a couple of kilometres, it was time for us to take matters into our own hands once again.

"Dhanyavaad," we cried back to our drivers, who were busily supping chai with the latest stranger, and recommenced our dash to the border.

The next vehicle to come along was a lonely motorcycle and the ever-impulsive Evan seized the opportunity by hopping onto the back.

"I'll tell the guard to wait!" he shouted behind him as he flew off into the distance.

A few minutes later another truck came along, but this time the drivers weren't quite so obliging in their response.

"Not to worry," we thought, waiting until it had driven past before chasing after it and clinging onto the ropes at the back.

For more than ten minutes we bumbled along in this fashion, feet perched precariously on the rear bumper as clouds of dust shot up from beneath the truck and covered every inch of skin and baggage we possessed.

And then we saw Evan.

His motorbike must have stopped a little short of the border and, despite his best efforts, the truckers seemed similarly unwilling to pick him up.

"Evan!" we shouted back as we whizzed past, cutting short his remonstrations. "Come on up!"

Our friend raced after us and joined us on the back of the truck, clinging on to the ropes with us until we arrived at the border.

What a sight we must have been to locals and border officials that day, caked in dust from head to toe. Although we were some fifteen minutes late, it turned out that, in true Asian style, they cared little for time restraints in these parts. It took us a little while to tick all the boxes and to complete all the checks, and we never did work out why they marked us down as "Irish," nor why they insisted upon referring only to our already-expired Nepalese visas when it came to the terms and conditions of our stay.

Not to worry; the important thing was that we had arrived. Just forty-eight hours since leaving Kathmandu, we were in Bangladesh.

DAY ONE HUNDRED AND FORTY-NINE:
TREETOP, NR. RAJ'S HOUSE, THANAPARA, RAJSHAHI DISTRICT, BANGLADESH, SATURDAY 6TH DECEMBER 2008, 16.05

Phew! What a palaver! Finally I have managed to find myself some peace and quiet, but I had to climb a tree to do it! At the top of the trunk – the point at which all the thick branches separate and wind their way skywards – I have found myself a makeshift seat, and can only hope that it will keep me safely away from the innocent pestering of the curious locals who crowd around us here in Bangladesh.

It was a grimy, sweaty business making the ascent, and three bewildered ladies had the joy of watching me, gawping in horror at the pale-faced monkey who, for some strange reason, had decided to shin its way up one of their fruit trees.

"Don't worry about me," I shouted down. "If you could just be on your way, I'd be very grateful. Oh, and whatever you do, please don't tell anybody that I'm here!"

The ladies stood silently for a moment, before bursting into hysterics and wandering off on their way, presumably taking it in turns to hazard a guess at what the monkey might have been trying to say to them and wondering since when it was that monkeys had decided to speak to humans in the first place...

* * * * *

At last, I have some time and space in which to think! After a long sigh and a moment's pause for silent reflection, I can begin to tell you the story of our time in Bangladesh thus far... Now, where was I? Oh yes, we had just completed the rigorous border checks on the Indian side of the Mahadipur border and were about to step onto Bangladeshi soil for the very first time.

Two Bangladeshi immigration officers were resting in their barracks after a long day in the office, when the three of us waltzed in through the door and demanded that they momentarily resume their services. At any other crossing we felt sure that our tardiness would be met with hostility, but not so in Bangladesh. The officers seemed positively pleased to see us! They were smiling as they went through all the rigmarole of the necessary procedures and made sure that we were all stamped up and ready to go within thirty minutes, whereupon they provided us with a free hotel room for the night!

What a beautiful country Bangladesh is, filled with the same levels of warmth and hospitality to which we have become well accustomed in this part of the world...

Oh no! Talking of warmth and hospitality, my worst fears have been realised, barely ten minutes after beginning. A young boy of about sixteen now sits to my write (see, he's even affecting my spelling!) and peers curiously into my eyes from only a few centimetres away. A broad, toothy smile accompanies his every incomprehensible word, whilst a crowd of spectators gathers at the foot of the tree, craning their necks to see the strange intruder in their midst.

"You know, there really isn't enough room for us both up here," I say to the boy, doing my best to stay calm. Why, oh why, didn't I climb a little higher? I can't believe I've been rumbled so soon.

Wouldn't you know it? Before I can protest a second child joins me, somehow finding further space upon this makeshift seat that really isn't even big enough for me.

Below us there are at least another fifteen children – ages ranging anywhere from toddlers to teenagers – and I should think that every one of them will be up here before long!

It's Pakistan all over again. Come to think of it, someone told me not so long ago that Bangladesh, rather bizarrely, used to be called "East Pakistan." Quite how two countries separated by such a great land mass as that of India can be one and the same, I do not know. Perhaps that's the reason they aren't any longer, but it seems that both Pakistan and Bangladesh still share a few unenviable characteristics.

I shall try my best to scribe my way through this invasion and focus my thoughts back upon our first full day in Bangladesh, ignoring the fact that a fourth body has now decided to join us upon our perch.

"Don't any more of you come up, will you, or we'll have the tree down!" I shout.

The usual reaction follows: stunned silence followed by hysteria. But the break at least gives me a chance to get back to the point at hand – the seeming impossibility of hitchhiking in Bangladesh...

As in Nepal, there are scarcely any cars on the road. Buses, rickshaws and a small scattering of trucks seem to make up 95% of the traffic here, so we weren't in any position to be picky as we set out on our very first attempts at hitchhiking in Bangladesh yesterday afternoon. Having not seen a single vehicle in some thirty minutes of walking, we reluctantly flagged down the first (a passing bus) and blagged a free ride to the nearest town, from where we might stand a better chance of finding a lift in a more hitch-worthy vehicle.

Unfortunately for us, it didn't get any easier. Another two free bus rides (both of which were spent sunbathing on the roof) were accepted before we managed to find ourselves that hotly sought-after "authentic hitch." Saying that, I suppose the claim that hanging off the back of a minibus might constitute authenticity is a little dubious, but perhaps you'll allow it when I tell you of the way it came about. As previously, with the buses, we had been bent on refusing the ride, but that was until we met Raj...

* * * * *

... Believe it or not, that was all I managed to write before one of my treetop companions rudely snatched the pen from my hands and ordered me to join them in a game of badminton. I do rather like badminton, so my initial frustration didn't last for too long.

Day One Hundred And Fifty-One:
Amy's Apartment, Gulshan II, Dhaka, Bangladesh, Monday 8th December 2008, 11.20am

"Don't be sorry; be sexy!" What a way to introduce oneself! This timeless phrase will forever remind us of our dear friend Raj, who saved us from our hopeless attempts at hitchhiking by taking us under his wing and welcoming us to his home in the stunningly beautiful rural village of Thanapara.

It's been a long morning and we have barely made any distance from the Bangladeshi border, even counting those three bus blags.

"Where are you going?" Raj pipes up – exhibiting what appears to be a complete grasp of the English language – whilst we wearily wave away the attempts of what we can only assume to be another money-grabbing taxi service.

"Er... Dhaka," I reply, after some thought. "But anywhere eastwards will do." I sigh.

"But it's no use; we don't have any money. I'm sorry." I bow my head and await the imminent sound of a revved engine and another potential lift leaving us behind.

It doesn't come.

"Don't be sorry; be sexy!" says Raj, with a chuckle.

"No money?" he asks, laughing off the suggestion. "Don't worry. I don't have any either. Come on, jump on while you've got the chance."

We've no idea where he's going, but there's nothing for it. For the second time in 24 hours, we're soon clinging on for dear life as a vehicle bumps and swerves its merry way along. The driver seems intent upon testing our muscle, looking back with a childish grin upon his face as he takes the next corner at top speed. We cling on desperately, trying our best to take in the surrounding beauty as we do so.

I honestly had no idea that Bangladesh was such a beautiful country. In fact, it is a lush green paradise, built upon a river delta, possessing staggering depth of colour and more trees than I've ever seen. For twenty kilometres we bump along in this vein, fears forgotten as we pass another vista of spiky-leaved banana trees and another winding path through forested undergrowth.

Finally the bus stops and we can relax. Raj jumps out of the passenger seat and rushes round to tell us we've arrived. Quite *where* we have arrived is not yet clear, but we're happy enough to go with the flow, especially now that we've found a man who has a sound grasp of our mother tongue and seems intent upon helping us.

We had assumed that Raj was the bus conductor, or at least a friend of the driver, so when he and his friend, Chandor, usher us away quickly amidst the cries of Bangladeshi voices in the background, we are a little surprised.

"Don't worry. Don't be sorry; be sexy," he repeats.

This is enough for us. Soon we're sipping chai and smoking cigarettes with two new friends. It turns out that Raj works as a freelance English translator, whilst we cannot work out what his curious little friend, Chandor, does.

It isn't long before one cup of tea has turned into five and we are seriously regretting our insistence upon accepting Raj's offer of cigarettes. When we tell Raj about our hitchhiking attempts, he claims to understand the practice and insists that we need not worry:

"You don't need money in Bangladesh," he tells us. The next minute he has kindly invited us to stay at his house for a night, telling us that we will head for Dhaka together the very next day.

"No problem at all. I will come with you and we will hitchhike together," he states confidently. "We'll get a free train down to Dhaka and a free train to the Burmese border the next day."

The three of us don't really know what to make of all of this. Surely it is too good to be true. Whilst blagging trains doesn't sound much like our original definition of hitchhiking, if Raj is so insistent that we can do it for free and knows how we can get down to Burma (so far we're map-less and simply have no idea where we're going), then so be it.

We march off into the glorious sunset together, flagging down the next rickshaw to come along, and journeying through more beautifully lush jungles until, half an hour later, we pull up outside Raj's place.

This coincidental meeting has completely changed our outlook upon our next few days in Bangladesh. By the sound of things, it won't be very long before we've made it to Burma and, as soon as we cross *that* border, it'll all be plain sailing...

...OK, maybe not, but we've made an unbelievably positive start!

DAY ONE HUNDRED AND FIFTY-TWO:
AMY'S APARTMENT, GULSHAN II, DHAKA, BANGLADESH, EID AL-ADHA (FESTIVAL OF SACRIFICE), TUESDAY 9TH DECEMBER 2008, 17.14

Today marks the annual Muslim festival of *Eid al-Adha*. Some 150,000 cows were bought over the past few days (within Dhaka alone) and all have been promptly slain during the course of this warm December day. The familiar chorus of the call to prayer echoes out over the Bangladeshi capital and reaches up to my ears as I sit, dressing-gown-clad, in a lavishly decorated flat on the 5th floor of a plush apartment block in Gulshan II – the rich quarter of this largely impoverished and overpopulated city.

Apparently there are some 14 million inhabitants here, and ninety-nine per cent of these are devout Muslims. All of those who can afford the hefty price have bought themselves a prize cow from one of twelve giant markets in the city and have kept the beast tied up in the back yard for the last few days, awaiting today's execution.

One of those cows to *meat* (my apologies) her end today was our dear friend, *Daisy*. We met her only yesterday, whilst visiting the home of the family kind enough to host us on this, the Muslim equivalent of Christmas Day, but strong bonds can be formed in short spaces of time – especially when such tragedy lies just around the corner. We gave the poor creature a name in an attempt to build some kind of attachment, even if this was to be only short-lived – much like dear Daisy's life.

Daisy had been purchased by the family of our new friend, Misha, whom we had the pleasure of meeting during our very first night here in Dhaka, thanks to his friendship with our two lovely Swedish hosts, Amy and Erika. Yet, before I can begin to unravel this web of relationships and better introduce these three new characters, I must first tell of the sad and premature end to our stay with dear Raj.

* * * * *

Raj's grandad died on our very first night in Thanapara – an event that would abruptly spell the end of our time with our friend. Our first evening had been filled with chai, cigarettes, meetings with friends, and a tour of the area – all courtesy of Raj and his rather irritating pal, Chandor.

Chandor was a bit of a cross between Zakir and brother Aref from our time in Hanna Urak, Pakistan. Overly anxious about our "state of enjoying," Chandor never stopped asking each one of us in turn whether we were enjoying ourselves. He then proceeded to ask each of us whether we thought our friends were enjoying themselves, before, to top it all off, ordering us to say things in Bangla to the different people whom we met.

Saying, "You should say him..." he would dictate either a most obvious, or else an entirely meaningless remark.

To give you a little taster, imagine you've just been introduced to a new friend of Raj's. You've shaken hands, and smiled at the man. Now you're preparing yourself to offer him a traditional greeting, but before you have the chance to gather your words together, Chandor pipes up:

"You should say him 'Salam Alecum'."

"Thank you Chandor!" you think. "My goodness! Where would I be without you?"

Your actual response is more along the lines of a heavy sigh, followed by an evil glare – which, thankfully, goes unnoticed – before, grudgingly, you tow the line.

"Salam Alecum... and all that jazz."

Chandor insisted upon grabbing us by the hand and leading us everywhere. He would ask us the most inappropriate and lewd questions regarding our relationships with our girlfriends; but perhaps worst of all was the way in which he treated his simple-but-sweet cousin, Aki.

"You should say him..." and then he would spout some nonsense to us in Bangla, which we were ordered to repeat.

The response was always the same: a roar of laughter from Chandor, a sigh and a little giggle from Raj, and a quivering of lips from poor Aki. It didn't take a genius to work out that the phrases were little more than childish swearwords. Aki was ever gracious in his response, biting his lip and remaining silent, but we couldn't bear the way that Chandor was inducing us to mock him.

Our time in Thanapara followed this same pattern of chai, cigarettes and irritation from Chandor, but the death of Raj's grandad really rocked our chirpy friend's spirits, and he was much subdued for the remainder of our time together.

* * * * *

On our first morning in Thanapara, we downed a scrumptious breakfast of Bengali delights at Chandor's family home, and made our way to the first funeral that any of us had ever been to where it is symbolically important for all to go in and pay their respects to the uncovered body of the deceased. There he was, motionless and emotionless, lying flat out on the cold, hard floor. Not a word was said for the duration of this ceremony. What does one say to a man who's just lost one of his closest allies? "Sorry" doesn't quite cut it, so we opted out of saying anything at all.

We weren't the only ones paying our respects that morning. A host of mourners had crowded outside Raj's family home to take it in turns to stand over the corpse for a few minutes. We felt like impostors. What were we doing there? Frequent outbursts of tears erupted from the many women present, but it was the unrestrained sobbing of the dead man's brother that shook me the most.

This gentle man had been trying as best he could to stay strong for the rest of his family, but as he explained to us why it was so special that there were British representatives at his brother's funeral – his brother having served in the British army for a number of years – it all became a bit too much. His tears soon flowed freely, accompanied by childlike groans from the depth of his heart.

Whilst the emotions themselves were not unexpected, it was being right in the midst of it that came as the greatest shock to the three of us. Standing over the dead body had been hard enough. An unknown personality was lying sound asleep beneath the shell of an anonymous, lifeless corpse;

mouth wide open and eyes firmly shut… never to open again.

My first observation was that this ninety-three year-old gent had aged particularly well. Yet, after my initial observations, I began to wonder about the life that this man had led – what he had done, whom he had loved and, perhaps most pressingly now that he was gone, who had loved him.

Now that he was dead, I found myself wondering what religious beliefs this man might have held – if any at all. Perhaps he was finding out, right at this minute, whether or not his beliefs counted for anything. I quickly shut these thoughts out of my head for fear that my conclusions might lead me to belittle the faith of a dead man.

The chances were that this man had been a Muslim (probably a devout, God-fearing one) and now that he was dead, I was supposed to believe, as a Christian, that this was the end for him. No pearly gates for my lifeless friend; it was down to the pits. What a despicable notion! I shut the thought out immediately and tried my best not to allow my brain to think again. For the remainder of our time with the body, I simply stared right through it and concentrated on soberly considering what a great loss his death had been to the family.

* * * * *

Leaving the mourners to make preparations for the burial later that day, Raj placed us in the not-so-safe hands of Chandor, who was given the task of taking us down the road to see *Swallows* – the workplace of the first Swedish woman to cross our path in Bangladesh… She wouldn't be the last.

Ellen was a lively character, sporting one of the most original piercings that I had ever seen. A short metal spike stuck out from the middle of her forehead, which, given that there was only one end of the spike on show, made us wonder how it ever got in there, and if it might ever come out again.

"I had to have an operation!" Ellen informed us, proudly.

"Didn't it hurt?" asked Evan, pulling all kinds of grimaces as he imagined the procedure.

"Yes, a little," she replied. "They couldn't even use anaesthetic!" Ellen seemed peculiarly excited as she relayed the details.

Well, at least the description of the operation explained why Ellen had a piercing with only one end. The quirkiness of her piercing also opened our eyes to see the bubbly character beneath the surface – a girl who had fallen in love with Bangladesh a number of years ago and, at only 24 years of age, had already decided to live here indefinitely.

The passion and determination with which Ellen spoke about her work for the Swedish N.G.O, *Swallows*, was infectious. Ellen's main task appeared to be communications-based, writing articles about Bengali women who make beautifully embroidered garments that are shipped out to many countries around the world.

After giving us a short tour of the facilities, Ellen continued to rave about her work with great enthusiasm.

"I believe we are starting to make a real change by supporting the sexual-equality movement in Bangladesh," she said. "Without our help, these women would be very unlikely to find jobs and, even if they did, they would be very likely to find themselves working in awful conditions for minimal reward."

It was easy for Will and me to draw parallels between the women in Bangladesh and those in Iran and Pakistan. On a positive note, Bangladeshi women do not appear to have to adhere so strictly to the rules of Hijab as those within Iran; nor do they appear to be as far removed from society as those within Pakistan. However, Ellen tells us that there is a great gulf between the working rights of male and of female employees here in Bangladesh, and horrendous regularity of abuse within the home.

Amongst other things, *Swallows* is striving to implement a change in women's rights, but Ellen believes that they face an uphill struggle. Apparently the situation remains as it is, predominantly, because most women in Bangladesh are unaware that what they are experiencing is anything out of the ordinary. Ellen remains hopeful that, in time, they will be able to educate the women and bring about a cultural change like that which broke out in waves across Europe and America throughout the twentieth century.

* * * * *

"The funeral must nearly be over," Evan declared, once we had been introduced to the second and third Swedish ladies present at *Swallows* that day – Amy, a "fashion spotter" from Dhaka, and her friend, Erika, from Stockholm. Soon enough Raj would be calling to let us know that he had found us a free spot on a train heading to Dhaka, and we would be in the capital by the end of the evening.

It felt a little strange to think that we were going to "hitch" on a train. Can one really hitchhike on a train? What is it that makes hitchhiking what it is? Getting a free ride's one thing, but surely there has to be an element of chance about it! Waiting for a scheduled train to arrive, and then wangling oneself onto it just doesn't seem to fit the bill.

I suppose that it was the urgency with which we wished to get through Bangladesh that had led us to agree to Raj's plan in the first place, but when Amy and Erika spontaneously presented us with an alternative, it was an offer that proved too good to refuse.

"So where are you guys going from here?" Amy asked, having been told all about our trip by the excitable Will… "Because Erika and I were talking and, so long as you don't mind a tight squeeze, we think there is probably just enough room for all five of us to travel to Dhaka together tomorrow… in the back of our car. If you'd like to, that is…?"

The offer came so unexpectedly that it took us a little while to respond, but there was no doubting our response when it came. This was too good to be true; we were going to have an authentic Bangladeshi hitch after all!

"Who knows, with any luck we might even end up with a free place to crash when we get to Dhaka," I whispered to Will, once we had accepted the offer.

Sadly, no plan is perfect. There seems always to be a loser, even in the very best of scenarios and, unfortunately, the loser in this was our dear friend Raj.

I hadn't even contemplated the notion that Raj might be disappointed when I called him up just a few seconds later to let him know the good news. But this was just another nail in the coffin for our dear friend, who had treated us with such kindness and hospitality during our short stay. When, finally, he responded, the pain in his voice was palpable.

"Oh," he said, with a heavy sigh. "But what about the arrangements I have made for us to catch the train tonight? I thought you wanted to hitchhike with me?"

Oh no! What had we done? Hadn't this man's day been hard enough already?

But there was no going back now.

"I'm sorry Raj," I said. "But we've got a lift in a car now, and it's too good to turn down."

The phone line went dead.

DAY ONE HUNDRED AND FIFTY-TWO: (CONTINUED...)
AMY'S APARTMENT, GULSHAN II, DHAKA, BANGLADESH, EID AL-ADHA, TUESDAY 9TH DECEMBER 2008, 20.20

New plans arranged, we had acquired an extra night in Thanapara, and Raj was determined to make it a night we wouldn't forget. Earlier on that day, he had asked us if we would like to try our hand at driving a Bangladeshi car, to which we had, of course, responded in the affirmative. Beyond a very short drive with Zakir in Pakistan, we hadn't driven since we had left home, and it's always fun getting used to the driving culture of a different land.

An evening of playing cards with our new Swedish friends dragged on a little later than expected, so it was almost midnight when it was time for us to head out onto the road to see what vehicle Raj had lined up for us to drive.

"Come on then Raj," I said. "Where's your car?"

We could never have expected his response.

"I don't have one," he replied.

"Come again?" said Will. "What do you mean you don't have a car?"

"Like I said," he replied. "I don't have a car."

"But I thought we were going driving tonight," I protested.

"We are," he replied. "But we just have to wait for a car to come along and then we will stop it and ask the driver to let us drive."

"Simple as that, eh?" joked Will, shaking his head at the absurdity of the situation.

Raj said nothing, but looked confident enough as he stood out in the middle of the road and waited for a car to come along.

"There is a filling station about 50km away," Raj explained a few moments later. "And cars go there every night to get gas for the next day."

Raj was right. We had waited barely five minutes before a minivan came along, and pulled over, and Raj had managed to convince the driver that it was a good idea to take the five of us (Evan had stayed at home, but Chandor and Aki were willing replacements) along for the ride.

OK, so Raj had done the hitchhiking bit well enough, but anyone could do that! There was still a long way to go before he had managed to persuade us that it was possible to convince a driver to let us take the wheel.

Raj didn't wait long before giving it a try. Scarcely had we driven one kilometre before Raj piped up, in English (for some reason he and his cronies decided to speak in English the whole time so that the driver wouldn't think they were Bengali):

"Thank you for picking us up, my friend. I actually have an international driving license and I would really like to drive your vehicle. What say you?"

The poor young driver (he can't have been much older than twenty) glanced sheepishly over to our friend, pulled over the vehicle and, unbelievably, invited Raj to trade places!

What on earth was going on?

Ten seconds later and Raj is revving the engine, twisting the strange lever by the side of the wheel that is doing its best to imitate a gear-stick, and we're off!

"I'm just going to test the brakes," Raj alerts us, as soon as we're going along at a decent pace.

Then, suddenly, he slams his foot on the brakes, sending poor Aki flying forward from the back seats, such that he almost breaks his nose on the back of the passenger seat.

"Be careful, friend," says Aki, revealing what is almost the full extent of his English vocabulary, before settling himself back into his seat.

The poor young chap in the passenger seat stares nervously at Raj and quietly asks if, just maybe, it might be a good idea if *he* drove again.

"No, no," Raj insists. "I'm doing quite well thank you. It's always important to test the brakes, don't you think?"

Will and I shake our heads in disbelief in the back, trying our best not to laugh too loudly at the poor young chap's expense.

"You know..." Raj continues, "My friends in the back also have international driving licenses and would love to drive the vehicle if that is all right."

This is getting ridiculous. The young man stares in amazement at Raj, again suggesting that it might be better for everyone if he drove. But our friend is insistent and, before you know it, first Chandor, then Will, and then I, take it in turns to get behind the wheel of the minivan, revelling in what is such a bizarre and sensationally successful hitchhike.

It wasn't until we'd made the fifty kilometres to the petrol station, stopped for some chai and driven more than half the way back, that we even considered the possibility that this seemingly-perfect hitch might have an unfortunate ending. Raj had dictated the play for the entire evening, but now it was the turn of the once-sheepish car owner to lay down the law, ordering me (I'd done the bulk of the driving on the return leg) to pull over and get out of his vehicle! We were still a good twenty kilometres from home, but this was where our driver lived and, not only would he prefer that we left the vehicle immediately, but he also suggested that we should pay up.

Will and I hadn't known what was going on at first as we left the vehicle and walked swiftly away, but Raj soon explained that it had been a monetary issue.

"Money? Why does he want money?" I asked. Five months of free rides from England to Bangladesh rather changes one's perceptions of what it takes for a journey to necessitate payment.

"I don't know," said Raj, more to avoid the question than to give an honest answer. "But that's hitchhiking, right!" he exclaimed, assuming we'd offer our support.

"No it isn't!" I replied. "Hitchhiking doesn't mean that you con a guy into thinking that you're going to pay him and then just run away. Hitchhiking means that someone is going your way and is happy to take you free of charge!"

During our time with Raj, we had noticed that he seemed to have a rather skewed perception of what it meant to hitchhike. To him, hitching certainly meant travelling without any payment, but the way in which he went about getting his free rides simply wasn't on. Raj would just get himself onto a mode of transport (be this a car, rickshaw, bus, or train) and then declare – as close to the end of the journey as possible – that he didn't have any money. That is not hitchhiking!

Will and I were infuriated by the entire affair, especially as Will was starting to suffer another of his regular episodes of stomach upset/general bodily ailments and just wanted to get back to bed as soon as he could.

Now that we had dishonestly fled from one young, unsuspecting victim, Raj boasted to us that we needn't worry because he had given the man a fake number so that, when he called the next day to demand payment, he wouldn't be able to get hold of him.

We weren't impressed.

It was fast approaching 3am and we were still a fair way from Thanapara as we recommenced our hitchhiking efforts. To make matters worse, Chandor just would not stop going on about how concerned they were for us.

"Don't worry," Chandor would say, over and over again. "We will be all right. Please don't worry."

Funnily enough – having done this sort of thing a few times before – our displeasure stemmed not from the thought that we might struggle to make it back to Raj's that night. It stemmed entirely from the way in which everything about the hitchhiking that we had done up to this point had been completely misrepresented.

There was still time for one more fracas that night, involving the two men who kindly gave us a lift the rest of the way home. Arriving back at Raj's place at 4am, it was yet another case of "Oh, hold on a minute, you know what, I thought I had some money… but somehow it's disappeared!"

Needless to say, the drivers weren't impressed, and nor were we. It had been one long day for poor Raj, so we did our best to cut the guy some slack and thanked him for the drive, but we were truly glad that it was all over.

* * * * *

The next morning it was time to say goodbye to our good friend, Raj. Despite the unfortunate events of the previous night, we had thoroughly enjoyed our time with this happy-go-lucky fellow, and wished him and his mother well as we sat for one final breakfast together – in the very same room in which we had stood to gaze at the lifeless body of his grandfather.

At two o' clock in the afternoon, it was time to depart. Chauffeur-driven by Amy's personal assistant, in one of the nicest cars we had been in since leaving home (a Mercedes 4x4), the fact that four of us had to squash ourselves into the back seats did little to curb our enthusiasm. Evan had bagged the front seat (courtesy of that lanky frame of his), but there was ample room in the back to squeeze two scrawny hitchhikers and a couple of svelte Swedes.

Used to averaging no more than about 30km/hr these days, it was nice to feel the extra *oomph* that a Mercedes can bring. Nevertheless, as a result of easily the worst traffic jam we have encountered thus far (traffic tailed back for some sixty kilometres!), it took us over eight hours to cover the 250km stretch to Dhaka.

The reason for the jam was Eid. Given that the festival was still two days away, our driver, Halal, had assumed we would be unaffected. No such luck. We had run into the kind of traffic that one might expect to see only during the Muslim equivalent of Christmas, and even then, only within a city with so sizeable a population as that of Dhaka.

Eid is a family event, you see, and Dhaka's 14 million inhabitants have hordes of relatives outside the city, who flock to the capital for a share in the spoils.

When at last we arrived in Gulshan II, and parked safely inside the private courtyard of a grand apartment block, we knew that our accommodation for the night was going to be a bit of an upgrade from the cold, hard floor of Raj's mud hut.

Even so, our eyes almost popped out of our heads as we entered into Amy's dream apartment. With *Sex and the City* written all over it, this truly is the modern independent woman's home: classy, spacious, and expensively adorned, Amy seems to have it all. I mean, forget the fact that she has a personal chauffeur for a minute. There's a paid cook and cleaner too – in the form of the intensely evangelistic, Bengali Jehovah's Witness, Bernard, who can't be more than about 5ft 5, and must weigh in at approximately seven stone.

On our first night in this freak haven of comfort and quiet, we were treated to a takeaway from the nearby *Bella Italia* franchise, followed by an evening of fine wine and coffee out on the balcony. If there are two things I will get snobbish about when it comes to beverages, these are red wine and coffee, and it probably won't surprise you to learn that Amy had outstanding examples of both. The coffee could have been a little warmer, but that was hardly likely to get us down as we were pampered in what was not only the nicest place we had stayed in Bangladesh, but also probably the nicest place in which I had ever stayed.

As we awoke the next morning to a breakfast buffet – lovingly prepared by Amy's hired hand, Bernard – we took just one minute to reflect upon our surroundings.

"Can you believe we're in Bangladesh?" Evan asked.

Will and I shook our heads.

Something about it simply didn't feel right. Sure, everyone likes to be spoilt once in a while, but, it felt, frankly, unethical to be sipping lattés and munching maple syrup pancakes, whilst, no doubt, just around the corner, a family struggled to survive.

DAY ONE HUNDRED AND FIFTY-TWO: (CONTINUED...)
AMY'S APARTMENT, GULSHAN II, DHAKA, BANGLADESH, EID AL-ADHA, TUESDAY 9TH DECEMBER 2008, 23.24

It is high time for me to introduce you to the friends we have made here in Dhaka.

We start with Misha...

One of Amy's closest allies, Misha is a man in his early thirties, who, although Bengali in origin, lived all his formative years in England. During the course of the last ten years, his work at the British Council has seen him posted in many varied and exciting places around the world, and his latest move has brought him back to Bangladesh.

Whilst he has been here for only a few months, you can tell that Misha is relishing his time back home, and he has revelled in his task of escorting us around the best bits of this bustling city – a tour that culminated in a death-defying trip to one of the twelve cattle markets to be shedding its last supplies of sacrificial fodder.

This was no walk in the park. The remaining beasts seemed to have an uncanny awareness of what was going on, tugging upon the thick ropes that bound them, and regularly butting out at passers by. These final flurries for freedom, although ultimately useless, at least provided them with the chance to wreak *some* revenge. Every year, a few humans are taken down by these still-living sacrifices, who heave their heavy heads in vengeful attacks upon all who would wish them harm. Evan and Erika came the closest of our party to fall victim to their last-gasp attacks, fortunate to escape with relatively insubstantial butts to the abdomen and skull respectively.

Misha's family had purchased *Daisy* a few days before, so our visit to the market was purely for the purposes of our touristic interest and the snap-happy exploits of budding photographers, Will and Amy – the latter of whom seemed completely oblivious to the danger she might be courting as she crept up upon each snarling beast.

* * * * *

Now, at long last, I come to the person who needs the greatest introduction: our *hostess with the mostest*, Amy.

Amy... well, where to start? There is no one quite like this free-spirited, independent heroine, who has quickly stolen our hearts with her fun-loving, mildly crazy, way of life. Perhaps a story from last night will help you to appreciate just what it is that makes Amy so special.

It all started when Misha asked us to buy his family something by means of a thank-you gesture for their proffered hospitality at the Eid celebrations on the following day.

"I know just the place," said Amy, flagging down a pair of rickshaw drivers, who would cycle us across the city for our first taste of the capital's nightlife.

Perhaps the most striking thing about Dhaka is the sheer numbers of beggars who crowd the streets here. Even more staggering in scale than the many we witnessed during our time in India and Pakistan, you simply cannot turn a corner in Dhaka without confronting another lame or malnourished street child, who will follow you around and cry after you, in the most heart-wrenching fashion:

"Uncle! Antie! Ten taka?"

Ten taka? Ten taka! This is only about the equivalent of ten English pence, but we're still not willing to part with a single Bangladeshi note.

"I'm sorry," Will and I whimper, in unison, hanging our heads amidst the growing shame of the situation.

It's not that we don't feel sorry for them. Of course we do. But, tell me, what good would it do if we were to give them that ten-taka note? The likelihood is that these poor children are just pawns for some mean old beggar pimp, skulking in the shadows to await the spoils from children whose honed acting skills (worthy of Oscar nomination) cannot fail to tug upon the heartstrings of the most resolute passers by.

Will and I force a pained smile at the children, whilst Evan probably philosophises about the deep and rich blessings that might follow if he were to give the children a right hook to the jaw.

Cynicism regarding the not-so-saintly world of begging has steadily increased following our time in India and Nepal, thanks to our falling for the infamous *milk trick* of the beggar women in Mcleod Ganj.

"Milk! Milk!" a Tibetan woman, holding a baby, screeched at Will and me as we walked up the hill on our first full day in Mcleod.

"What? She wants milk?" asked Will, looking at me in bemusement.

Following the lady to a shop, she promptly pulled down two giant bags of powdered milk and screeched at us again, just to make sure that we knew she was serious.

"Milk!"

Why on earth she wanted powdered milk we hadn't a clue, but true to our belief that there was no harm in buying a beggar some food so long as we didn't give them any money, we bought the milk, and even chose to ignore the hefty charge the shopkeeper seemed to pluck out of the air, especially for us.

"It seems a little funny that she charged us the equivalent of about a fiver for two bags of powdered milk," I reflected later on, in the presence of our other friends.

"Oh no! You didn't buy it for her, did you?" responded an alarmed Beth. "Don't you know about the milk trick?"

We shrugged our shoulders.

"Almost every beggar woman here has a baby, but they are not their own. They hire them from baby pimps and lend them out to scam tourists into buying them overcharged milk, the profit of which will be split evenly between shopkeeper and beggar."

Sure enough, the next moment, as we walk out of the shop, another random lady is screaming at us for milk. The glare she receives in return soon quietens her pleas.

"Oh, they know about the milk trick," she seems to whisper to another mother up the hill, who cowers quietly in the corner as we pass by, shaking our heads.

Let's just say that our cynicism has been deepened further now, especially after the influence of Balta/Hugo/Moody, and we have been forced to reconsider our policy of buying beggars food.

What is the world coming to when even alms for beggars is something that has to be ethically and critically weighed up each time, for fear that one might fall foul of a scam?

Amy has no such qualms. She knows exactly where she stands on the matter, and freely hands out alms to the handicapped sections of the Dhaka masses, whilst largely ignoring the children's pleas for fear that their lazy, able-bodied parents, have sent them out to do their dirty work. And yet, although she withholds monetary aid from the children, our heroine is not blind to see the child that hides inside, and last night one little girl received her Eid presents early...

* * * * *

Amy is one of the most stylish dressers I have ever encountered – probably a good thing, given her profession – and often wears the most beautiful bracelets, of all kinds and colours, which seamlessly co-ordinate with her classy saris and other Western variations upon Asian fashion.

Last night, she wore about twenty-five beautiful silver bracelets upon only one arm (we had been admiring them all day). What perfect gifts for a little beggar girl, and what graciousness Amy showed as, one by one, she gave the little girl her bracelets, until they were divided evenly between them.

"One for you, one for me," Amy said, taking the little girl through her English numeric practice, and happy to speak in Bengali if the girl was struggling.

The girl was beaming as she wheeled away, jangling those beautiful silver gifts around – much to the amazement and apparent displeasure of the remaining beggar community.

"We wanted money!" they hissed, from the shadows.

"Why give to this little girl? Why not us?" the women of the community snarled, gradually emerging from the darkness, arms outstretched, and pointing fingers aggressively towards the remaining bracelets upon Amy's arm.

One by one, Amy gave away every last bracelet to that ungrateful rabble, and she didn't even seem to mind too much when the little girl – as if intent that she must leave us with one final passing shot – called after us with that familiar cry:

"Antie! Ten taka?"

I suppose that the little girl's insistence shows something of the beggars' struggle to survive. After all, a few pretty bangles won't bring that little girl a bed to sleep in tonight, and our heroine was unaffected by her lack of manners. One smile (and what a smile it was!) was enough.

As it was, Amy's need to be generous had been satisfied, and we then made one of the fastest and most immoral transitions imaginable.

In mere minutes, we had removed ourselves from the cries of the poor and waltzed right into the material world of bars and coffee shops. The rest of that evening was spent gratifying ourselves, turning off our radars to the noise of poverty, which pleads for all the world's wealthy to give themselves and their possessions to the cause. Ironically enough, the bulk of people with whom we spent the evening worked for charities or NGOs within the city...

What is it about our upbringing that enables us to turn our compassion on and off? Isn't it just that little bit hypocritical to step off the street and into the club without so much as blinking an eye?

As we gorge ourselves in the pursuit of hedonism, there are millions of people out there (whether on the doorstep, or just a little further afield) who are struggling to survive.

* * * * *

Soul-searching aside, I can move on to tell you a little more about today's main event: *The Bloodshed of Eid*.

OK, so perhaps I'm being a little unfair in imposing such a brash and negative slogan upon this day of great import within the Muslim calendar, but, then again, we are spending a lot of time with vegetarians.

Both Evan and Erika fall into this unfortunate bracket and so disgusted were they by the ritual that Erika chose to remain at home, whilst the enigmatic Evan was moved into all kinds of facial contortions during the slaughter, first, of a small, defenceless Billy goat, and then of poor old Daisy.

Still, there is a beauty that shines out from underneath the spilt blood – that of the heart of sharing, which rises up from the crimson streets. One third of today's spoils are to be given to the poor, whilst the other two thirds are to be split evenly between poorer relatives and the slaughterer's family themselves. If only every family were like Misha's and would live up to their calling to share, then this Muslim Christmas would be a day *most* enjoyed by those who deserve enjoyment the most.

Our respect for Misha has steadily increased during our time together and we found our own generosity challenged when he prompted us to give his family 500 Taka (about £5 each) so that, when the beggars came knocking later that day, they might leave with more than just their staple food for the week.

As for the slaughters themselves, in case you were wondering, it wasn't only Evan whose face screwed up and who couldn't refrain from shrieking. The rest of us Westerners – for whom this was the first time we had ever seen an animal killed in front of our very eyes – were stunned into an uncomfortable silence.

The vocal chords are the first to go – thereby avoiding an endless stream of unbearable moans from the animal – but this only adds a strange surrealism to the experience of watching an animal's head being slowly sawn from its neck, whilst the torso lays quivering for several minutes beyond the time when the onlooker sincerely hopes that the animal's pain might have ceased.

I found it too difficult to watch the initial slaughter of the goat, whose legs were tied together, whose body was pushed over, and whose head was sawn off, as his eyes were directed in the vague direction of Mecca. And yet, by the time it came to Daisy's turn, some strange, slightly sickening, detachment had possessed me, such that I could stare at the demise of a dear friend without even so much as a flinch.

This might have had something to do with the fact that I had been made to video the event (by Evan of all people) and only saw it happen through a tiny screen on his camera – the type of screen on which I have become accustomed to seeing all kinds of atrocities.

Gallons (and I think I'm being literal here) of blood oozed from Daisy's neck, painting the street a thickly-coated, vibrant red. There is a moment at Eid, short and sharp, at which the murder of an animal changes to become merely the chopping up of a large piece of meat. An animate creature, once full of life, becomes food for the plate within a matter of seconds, as the mind does its best to close off those feelings of sympathy and guilt, and to focus upon the gastronomic gain.

One step away from the scene of the crime and we're back in Misha's house; one step outside again and we're witnessing the chopping up of a lifeless, faceless piece of meat.

Billy and Daisy have gone.

Without going in to too much more detail – realising that some of you may be more squeamish than others – I can happily report that Daisy was delicious, and Billy quite edible.

And despite my many inferences to the contrary, I can honestly say that we felt truly blessed to have been able to witness such an event with a family for whom it has no connotations with our Western perception of animal cruelty. Misha and his extended family showed us tremendous warmth and hospitality throughout the event and, after eating more food than our stomachs could comfortably bear, we said our goodbyes, parted with our 500 Taka, and returned to Amy's for a few hours of much-needed rest, in preparation for part two of *The Race*, which recommences tomorrow.

Teknaf is the destination, now that one of Misha's pals from the British Council has assured us that we might just be able to cross the border into Burma from there, Bangladesh's most southerly tip. According to many reliable sources in important positions here, it is legally impossible to do what we are about to attempt to do, but Misha and friends believe that lots of people still do it, and so must we.

I now recall stories of charity workers smuggling themselves into Burma on boats, sneaking in despite the Junta's best efforts to keep them out. OK, so we're not quite aid workers, but I'm still pretty sure that Burma could do with a bit of Steve and Will (I'm not so sure about Evan), and we mean to give it our best shot.

15. THE RACE (PART TWO)

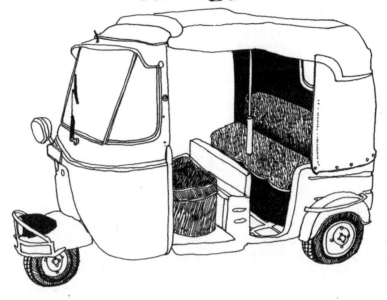

DAY ONE HUNDRED AND FIFTY-FIVE:
OFFICER'S MESS, END OF JETTY, MAUNGDAW, MYANMAR, FRIDAY 12TH DECEMBER 2008, 17.55

Somehow or other we find ourselves just a few steps away from official Burmese territory, engaged in a heated debate with members of the Junta about whether or not we should be allowed into their country.

So how did we end up here? Well, I suppose that it all started as a result of our decision to go for a sunset stroll along a Bangladeshi beach...

The journey to this southernmost point of Bangladesh's eastern peninsular took longer than expected. Setting off after one final spread of Bernard's bounties, it was hard to leave Amy's luxurious quarters behind, but the clock had been ticking fast while we were sleeping in Dhaka, and we had a long, long way to go before the 25th.

Up and raring to go by 6.30, we somehow managed to fritter away three hours before we finally made it out of the apartment and onto the maze of roads that would eventually lead us away from Dhaka. Bags packed and reunited with their old friends (our tired shoulders), we were in that all-too-familiar position of leaving friends and security behind, and heading off into the unknown. Whilst we may have done it a hundred times by now, it never gets any easier.

Getting out of Dhaka, on the other hand, did prove surprisingly easy.

Having been misdirected by another member of the trusty British Council (the Director, no less), we were redirected by a Bengali couple, who informed us that the man had been mistaken and that we should hitch in completely the opposite direction. They were right.

Two quick lifts and we had made a few further kilometres south, and stood on what was starting to look like the outskirts of the city. Waiting patiently for the next big ride to come along, it was no more than ten minutes before we saw that hope-inducing sight of a rickety old truck bumbling its way towards us.

As if by flinch reaction, our arms were soon flapping madly around in the air (directed, of course, by the effervescent Evan), as they seemed determined not to let this potentially significant lift pass us by. I don't think that the three Bengali men inside the truck's cabin can have had the foggiest idea what we wanted when they pulled over and greeted us with the broadest of smiles, but we didn't mind. We were happy enough just to have got their attention and, before they could even think about protesting, we were climbing the rigging on the side of the vehicle and finding ourselves suitably precarious positions atop the truck's old and rusting frame.

Clinging on to whatever handle we could find – on what was an unhelpfully cylindrical good's carrier – we took a deep breath of the not-so-fresh air around us, and began to befriend many a Bangladeshi doing the very same thing as ourselves (hitching on top of a vehicle), if only by a different name.

We have found ourselves on many a truck or bus roof during the past few months, but none topped this relatively short stint, during which we crawled our way through the holiday traffic and entered into surreal conversations with fellow hitchers, making particular friends with the rooftop travellers atop a bus in the lane beside us, with whom we exchanged some of Evan's unwanted clothing for apples and cigarettes!

It was just as well that we had taken such joy from this first semi-substantial lift because the rest of the day was a slog. We struggled hard enough just to get ourselves to the first target – eighty kilometres away – of a town called Camilla and, after we arrived, had to deal with one of those unfortunate fellows who expects money for his services.

"No money!" Taka Nahi!" we protested, shrugging our shoulders as we sought to walk away from a potentially volatile situation.

The man was unimpressed, clearly feeling that he had been on the wrong end of some underhand tactics by a trio of stingy Western rich-kids, but there was little we could do. We had barely enough money for lunch as it was, and didn't feel like getting into another heated debate for the sake of what was only an honest misunderstanding.

"Taka Nahi," we repeated, and slipped away to buy ourselves some roti with the remnants of our Bangladeshi Taka.

* * * * *

How had it got to lunchtime already? Surely we hadn't travelled only eighty kilometres in an entire morning of hitching! Heading back out onto the road, we were in dire need of a break.

Another thirty minutes of standstill, before, finally, help arrived – in the form of one of a number of trucks heading south after the festivities of Eid. Into the trailer we climbed, doing our best to ignore the terrible stench of what smelt like a cross between rotten vegetables and... dead cow!

There were bloodstains on the wooden floorboards! We knew all too well what this meant. Either we had jumped into the back of a truck filled with bloodthirsty bandits, or our smiley new friends were just another family to have bought and slain one of Daisy's distant relatives.

Sure enough, several hours later, upon our arrival in Chittagong (another 150km south) we were warmly welcomed into the home of one of our drivers to see the evidence of Eid first-hand. It is common knowledge here in Bangladesh that it is nothing short of the *duty* of a host to provide their guests with some food, and there are no prizes for guessing what kind of food would be on the menu in this and every household across Bangladesh for the next few weeks.

After downing a few cups of chai and the latest in a long line of bizarre alcoholic spirits – which, like the rest, tasted foul and strong – it was the main course that brought the major entertainment...

Will and I had been happily devouring another of Daisy's relatives (cooked very nicely if you ask me) for some minutes before we noticed that our dear friend, Evan, hadn't even lifted his fork.

"Evan! What are you doing?" I whispered, between mouthfuls. "Why aren't you...?"

Before I could finish speaking, Evan butted in: "Why do you think, you moron!"

It had been a long, hard day and I was too busy replenishing my belly's waning reserves to remember Evan's ethical dilemma. Our poor vegetarian friend had been sitting there nervously ever since we had arrived, contemplating how best he might politely refuse this family's hospitality. It had been the same during our time at Misha's, but this time we didn't have a Misha to explain the situation to our offended hosts.

Of course, our Bengali friends had noticed Evan's abstinence much earlier than Will and me, and an explanation was going to have to be given quickly.

"Can't you just eat it?" asked Will.

"Yeah, come on man," I agreed. "It's not going to kill you. Never refuse an offer an' all that..."

Evan said nothing for a while and just sat there glaring at us.

"Look," he replied. "I'm a vegetarian, so I can't eat meat."

Another awkward silence...

"Well then, there's nothing for it," I replied. "We're just going to have to tell them about your chronic dysentery..."

Hands placed upon stomachs, and pained expressions assumed, we pointed at Evan's belly, and said, simply: "problem."

I don't know why, but in every country – no matter how poor the level of

English comprehension – someone always seems to understand the word, *problem*, and so it proved again.

Raucous laughter ensued, and, more importantly, we had reassured our hosts that it wasn't any fault within their cooking that had caused Evan to be so picky.

* * * * *

Those of us who weren't suffering from chronic stomach-related illnesses joined in an outdoor game of badminton with our new friends (they bloody love badminton here; you see more people playing badminton than cricket!) and then it was time for us to leave.

We'd made it to Chittagong, but Evan had worked himself into another paddy about how much further we had to go if we were going to get to Laos in time for Christmas (I reckon he was just bitter about his illness), and he wouldn't budge from his view that we simply *had* to make more distance that night.

Will and I would have been much happier to accept an offer to stay with our new friends in Chittagong, but Evan was surprisingly insistent, and then there was the fact that we hadn't actually *received* an offer yet. If we bided our time, it was unlikely to be very long before they would either have to kick us out (stupendously unlikely) or invite us to stay, but Evan was being grouchy.

Thus, we wished our hosts a final "Salam Alecum," and attempted to navigate our passage through the surprisingly sizeable city of Chittagong towards the next major road leading south. Any inroads into the 200km that still separated us from Cox's Bazar (the next big city on our journey to Teknaf) were sure to make the following day's journeying that little bit more manageable.

Of course, it was Evan who spearheaded our hitching efforts – standing well out into the middle of the road and flapping those elongated arms towards anyone who might come our way – but, for all his efforts, we weren't going any further that night…

Having become so preoccupied by the task, it came as quite a shock when a young Bengali man tapped me on the shoulder and began speaking to me in fluent English tongue.

"Hey. What are you doing?" said the voice of Souheil, son of the owner of the nearby *Lord's Inn* – an establishment we had previously noted only because the bright light from its neon sign had been illuminating us.

Comforted by the presence of an English-speaker, I soon opened up about our attempts to "hitch" down towards Myanmar, telling Souheil about the basic gist of the journey that had been, and the urgency of the journey that lay ahead.

"I see," he replied. "But you can't get a lift now. It's very dangerous to do this at night."

"You hear that, Evan?" I said, taunting our friend with a tone of remonstration.

"There are lots of bandits around," continued Souheil. "It isn't safe. You must follow me."

The young man clearly had our best interests at heart. How could we refuse?

Moments later and we had been taken into his father's hotel and shown to our room for the night (free of charge, of course), but I'm afraid that any notion you might have about a penthouse suite are, sadly, misguided. Even their normal rooms were fully booked, so we were escorted into an empty storeroom, given one mattress to share, and encouraged to take some rest in what turned out to be a den for bloodthirsty mosquitoes! (They say that it's the thought that counts...)

Grateful though we were to Souheil for the "thought," it was hard to show any great level of thankfulness when we awoke at 6am to find that we had suffered literally hundreds of mosquito-bites. During the night we had faced an agonizing dilemma – locking ourselves inside mosquito-free sleeping bags (and potentially suffocating to death in the unbearable heat of the night), or, exposing ourselves to the elements, and so placing ourselves at the mercy of these buzzing bugs whose incessant hissing alone was sufficiently terrifying to keep us up all night.

Our official line, of course, was toned down.

We told dear Souheil that we had had a "very pleasant night" and would be "sure to tell folks at home about the generosity of *The Lord's Inn*" (here you are), but, in truth, we felt no better off than we might have had we hitched unsuccessfully throughout the night and been attacked by bandits in the process!

Grievances aside, we considered that Cox's Bazar must at least be an achievable target for the morning's hitching (given how early we were starting) and that if we were to make it there by lunchtime, then maybe, just maybe, we might make it to Teknaf, and even Myanmar, by the end of the day...

* * * * *

Did you know that Cox's Bazar is the longest beach in the entire world...?

...No? Nor did we. You'd have thought that Australia would have got that one wrapped up, but apparently Bangladesh has it. I don't know how they work it out. Apparently it has something to do with having an unbroken stretch of sand, and Cox's Bazar claims to have one hundred and twenty kilometres' worth of such a stretch – or so our penultimate driver of the day informed us. He also told us that the Bengalis believe it to be something so spectacular that they are even nominating it to run as one of the candidates for the modern *Seven Wonders of the World*!

After a difficult morning's hitchhiking (involving one truck, three cars and the roof of one of those minivan thingamajigs), it was 2pm when at last we arrived at one particular segment of this colossal stretch of sand, and there was nothing else for it but to wash off the grime and sweat of our previous two days by having a quick bath in the sea.

Will and I couldn't believe how long it had been since we last went for a swim in the sea (we're talking Kish!), and even Evan decided that we had worked long and hard enough to deserve a little bit of R&R on this apparently world-famous beach.

Families travel from all around (all around Bangladesh at least) to visit this popular resort, typically taking two or three weeks off to make the most of their stay, strolling along the sandy beach, sunning themselves in the scorching summer heat, and bathing in the Bay of Bengal.

After two hours, we'd seen enough.

A dip in the ocean is a dip in the ocean wherever you are in the world and we cared little for the idea of spending the evening in an overpriced tourist zone – however wonder-worthy Cox's Bazar claimed to be. And so it was that at 4pm (allowing ourselves just about one remaining hour of daylight) we decided to embark upon the 112km hitch that would eventually take us to Teknaf, and with it, the prospect of Myanmar…

DAY ONE HUNDRED AND FIFTY-FIVE: (CONTINUED…)
OFFICER'S MESS, END OF JETTY, MAUNGDAW, MYANMAR,
FRIDAY 12TH DECEMBER 2008, 19.36

The story of the events that followed could take up the whole of this book, but I'll try to be brief.

We started on what we were almost ninety-nine-per-cent sure could probably be defined as "the right foot." We were wrong. The excitement of acquiring a hitch in only a couple of minutes – with a family that spoke a fair bit of English – must have caused us momentarily to lose our senses because, without realising it, we veered off the main road to Teknaf and continued down a winding, single-lane track that better resembled the path you might see at a farmyard than anything that might lead us towards Burma.

So engrossed had we been in discussions with an elderly spinster – who had clearly taken a particular liking to Evan – that we were completely oblivious to the misdirection, and felt slightly stunned when we were dropped off at what seemed like just another tourist resort about twenty-five kilometres south from where we'd started.

It didn't help matters that the sun had long since set, and that one of the children in our last lift had had kittens because he claimed to have seen a snake.

No matter. We were just going to have to give this new route a shot. At least we'd made some distance in what would appear to be roughly the right direction. We couldn't have gone very far wrong because we'd been travelling parallel to the sea – a route that must eventually lead us to Myanmar.

After one quick look at our new map, we decided that we were right to be relaxed. Even if this road didn't quite look the same as all the other main roads we'd encountered, perhaps this was it – *the* road to Burma. After all, there couldn't be many people using it now, could there?

* * * * *

Determined to cover as much ground as possible while we still had the energy to do so, off we trotted along this dusty track to Burma, waiting for that first vehicle to pass us by...

...That we were still waiting some forty minutes later confirmed our suspicions that we might just have taken a wrong turn somewhere along the line, but it was too late to go back now. We couldn't face backtracking another forty minutes – and then an unspecified amount extra – to find out where we went wrong. It was *this* tiny track that we had chosen (albeit unconsciously) and it was *this* tiny track that was going to lead us to Burma. And so we just kept on walking... and walking some more.

It must have been almost 7pm before we saw the first sign of life. Having not seen a single soul in the past three hours – no car drivers, truck drivers, bus drivers, minivan drivers, or even any curious little villagers – it was more than a little surprising when we turned a corner to be greeted by a cacophony of noises arising from a group of about one hundred children!

A garish blue and yellow banner hovered proudly above the entrance to what we assumed must be some kind of summer camp or school. Floods of children ran haphazardly around, and a scattering of adult men (presumably the teachers) casually sat supervising.

I suppose that it was the geographical positioning of the school (i.e. in the middle of nowhere) more than anything that set our minds off on an imaginative journey that would eventually condemn these adult males to be the cruel captors of these children, who had been taken against their will to suffer all kinds of torture and abuse.

It didn't help our excitable imaginations when ten young women came out of one of the huts (potentially a classroom or a kitchen) with a look of sheer terror upon their faces. The women, who must have been between fifteen and eighteen years of age, were all strikingly attractive, but none seemed capable of any emotion other than fear. Solemnly they bowed their heads and traipsed past us, without so much as casting even one look towards the men, besides whom we were now sitting.

It all made sense now. Surely these six men had taken these ten women captive to breed a new Aryan race of warriors, who could be used for whatever sick purposes they saw fit...

Of course, our strange imaginings should be taken with a pinch of salt. We were very tired from a long journey and never expected suddenly to come across so many people in such a remote area, having not seen even a single soul for the past three hours. I suppose we've probably just watched too many films.

But no, there was something wrong about it; something strange about the remote location; something troubling about the fear in the eyes of the women and children who would flee if you so much as motioned your hand to greet them. This was no ordinary school. We didn't know quite how we'd found it, but the whole experience made us feel uneasy. Any thoughts we had of staying around for the evening were soon dispelled by the notion that we might be… slain in our sleep. Isn't that always the way these things go?

I can just see the headlines now:

"Three intrepid explorers uncover drug-fuelled den of immorality, but pay ultimate price when heads are lopped off."

OK, maybe not, but we weren't going to hang around. Smiling sweetly so as not to arouse suspicions that we might be on to them, we gave the men our best "Salam Alecums," before speeding off on our metaphorical bikes.

Come to think of it, a bike would have been pretty handy at that stage, but alas, we were bereft of anything that might resemble transport. It wasn't surprising really. The road didn't exactly match the standards of what one might deem "roadworthy." Every now and then the track would just disappear, and we would have to cross over the next river or ditch by use of a rickety bridge or a thatch of thick forest undergrowth. With every new quirk in our surroundings, we considered the growing probability that we had taken a wrong turn somewhere along the way, but we had come much too far even to think about turning back.

* * * * *

Another hour had gone by before we spotted another sign of life – this time in the form of a nondescript hut not far from the ocean's shore. Knowing not what to expect – but hardly presented with a wealth of alternatives – we approached the hut cautiously to ask its inhabitants if they knew the way to Myanmar.

"Which way Myanmar?" asked Evan, as an officious-looking gentleman approached us, wearing officious-looking clothing, and carrying an officious-looking rifle. I think he was in the army.

The man said nothing, content just to survey us with great suspicion, before beckoning two of his mates – who matched the description of the first entirely, and proceeded to survey us in the same silent manner.

"Myanmar?" one of them asked, after an uncomfortably long silence.

Oh no, what had we done? Why had we mentioned Myanmar to three men who were clearly in the Bangladeshi army? I paused for a moment, before replying.

"Yes, Myanmar." I said, attempting to speak as if this were the most ordinary question in the world.

"This way? That way?" asked Will, continuing in the pretence of nonchalance, whilst pointing his arms in different directions along the beach.

Again, silence.

Either these men spoke no English, or they were intent on making us believe that this was so. Whatever the case, they clearly knew *what* Myanmar was; now all we needed was for them to tell us *where* it was.

"Myanmar, please?" said Will, in a tone that was almost apologetic.

It seemed to do the trick. The marginally-more-talkative soldier pointed us in the same direction we had been travelling, but seemed strangely insistent that we take the beach rather than the dusty track – so insistent, in fact, that he mimicked the action of shooting at us if we did not comply, before handing us a packet of biscuits as a parting gift.

"Seven kilometre" he said, with the hint of a smile, gesturing us away.

Quite what it was that he was referring to at a distance of seven kilometres, we will never know. Surely it wasn't Myanmar. Unless we'd taken a spectacularly effective shortcut, there was simply no way that one relatively short lift and four or five hours of walking could have seen us cover more than one hundred kilometres.

"It must be the next big town along the way," said Evan, confidently, yet without really having a clue.

"If you say so Evs," I replied, doubtfully, as off we marched under the watchful gaze of the bright full moon.

* * * * *

It would appear that appreciation of direction and distance are not major strengths of the inhabitants of that strange stretch of land between Cox's Bazar and Teknaf. We walked for a further two hours along the beach and saw no sign of another town – let alone those faint, unrealistic hopes that we might actually be closing in on Myanmar.

The rising of the tide had forced us back into what, at narrower sections of the beach, was little more than a couple of metres' width of dry land.

"I can't do it any more," moaned Will. "What's the point, anyway? There's no way this is the right way, so we're just going to have to backtrack the entire way tomorrow."

"What else are we supposed to do?" I snapped. "We can't turn back now."

"Well, I'm not walking any further," Will replied. "Let's at least get some sleep and go on in the morning – when we can actually see where we're going!"

It was agreed. We had no idea of just where we were and couldn't remember exactly how long we had been walking, but certainly long enough to render the prospect of backtracking extraordinarily painful.

It proved harder than expected to find a suitable spot to sleep. We weren't worried so much about being hidden away or anything like that. The challenge was to find a spot of sand high enough so that the incoming tide would not drown us while we slept.

Eventually we settled on a little mound in front of a copse. It wasn't the most comfortable of spots, but it doesn't take me very long to fall asleep at the best of times, and we were all so tired out from our efforts that we were all asleep before we even had a chance to worry about the effects of the rising tide as it crept towards our heels...

* * * * *

I don't know how long we had been asleep when he came, but it can't have been much more than a matter of minutes before an unseen Bengali man greeted us with the most aggravating of interruptions.

"My friend."

The words hit us like a bullet from the black.

"What is it?" I groaned, expecting that this was just another one of those relentless cases of Bangladeshi curiosity.

"Can't you see that we're asleep?" grumbled Evan, turning over onto his side.

"…My friend?"

There he was again. Why wouldn't he just go away? I think I must have fallen asleep between his harmless-but-oh-so-annoying greetings. The number of times we are referred to as friends by complete strangers… well, there's been a lot anyway, and we were simply not in the mood to make another "friend" in the middle of what had already been a very long night.

"What is it?" asked Will.

"My friend, you follow me. It not safe you here now."

It took a few moments before I had summoned up sufficient strength to respond. Sighing long and hard, whilst scraping away the dust that had formed around my eyes, I muttered my response.

"How far we go?"

"Half kilo. Half kilo," the man replied, eagerly. "You come, my friend house, half kilo."

"Ahhh! I can't be bothered," shrieked Will. "I don't even think I've got enough energy for another bloody half kilo – whatever the hell that is!"

But the man wasn't budging, and we were soon on our feet again, lugging tired limbs, and loads that felt increasingly heavy, across an endless stretch of sand. We must have followed our new "friend" and his two companions for… well, a lot longer than the time it would normally take to walk half a kilometre.

After we had been walking for what must have been well over an hour, we had had enough.

"How much further?" I screamed.

"Half kilo," our friend replied, as indifferently as if he had just instructed me about the time of day.

"Half kilo!" I repeated. "You've got to be joking! We've already been walking for an hour to your mystery half kilo destination, and now you're telling me that we are no closer?"

Our new friend seemed a little surprised by the outburst, giving me the hurt look belonging to a man who doesn't know quite what he has done to cause such aggravation.

"Half kilo," he repeated, and carried on walking along as if we were casually enjoying an afternoon's stroll along the beach.

When another thirty minutes had gone by and there was still no sign of anything that might resemble "friend house," it was all becoming too much.

"That's it. We're not going any further," said Will.

"Where you friend house?" asked Evan, sarcastically. "We very tired. We go sleep now."

This time our friend finally comprehended how exhausted we had become and ordered one of his friends (who happened to have a motorbike) that he was going to have to take us the rest of the way, one by one.

When at last we arrived at "friend house" – after about another half a kilo – it was hard to hide our disappointment when we were shown to three wooden benches outside a small hut, and told that we had arrived.

"This friend house," friend number one informed us.

"Oh, is it now?" Evan retorted.

"Friend sleep this," he said, pointing inside the hut. "You sleep this"; another point – this time towards the benches. And that was that. Friend number one seemed happy enough to have taken us to the house of friend number two, and waved a hand at us, bidding us farewell until the following morning.

"No way!" I protested, as soon as friend number one was out of sight. "I can't believe we've just walked for ninety minutes to sleep like this!"

Will and Evan were too fed up to respond.

"This is a joke," I said, continuing in my rant. "It was more comfortable on the beach. Come on, let's find somewhere back there."

My friends took little convincing. We were all frustrated, and couldn't avoid feeling that we had been cheated. A few moments later we were back on the beach, and had found another generic mound of sand for our pillow. The tide seemed to have ebbed a little – not that we cared much about the possibility of drowning in it by then anyway. And, as if someone had flicked a switch inside our heads, in an instant we were asleep.

DAY ONE HUNDRED AND FIFTY-SIX:
PLEASURE HOTEL, TEKNAF, COX'S BAZAR DISTRICT, CHITTAGONG DIVISION, BANGLADESH, SATURDAY 13TH DECEMBER 2008, 8.45AM

Oh the romance of sleeping underneath the stars upon a beach in the middle of nowhere. And, as if that wasn't good enough, we were about to attempt to smuggle ourselves into Burma the very next day – if only we could find where exactly Bangladesh ended and Burma began. Perhaps we were there already. That would have been a fine piece of misdirection, but alas, we had to face the facts: we were still very much on Bangladeshi soil and had no idea of how we might leave it. Well, at least we'd found ourselves a place to sleep... I did feel tired, and...

Out like a light – I think that's the expression. And it was very true of the three of us after that unexpected, almost interminable, night of beach trekking.

If only I could start this next paragraph with a simple phrase such as: "The next morning we awoke, freshly invigorated and ready for the next chapter of our adventure." But no, that would be a lie. What I actually have to write is quite different...

* * * * *

...Was I dreaming? Something appeared to be prodding me in the midriff. No, I must be dreaming. If I turn over I'm sure that the pain will go.

What is that? I'm sure of it now; something is actually prodding me, and this time it's moved up to my chest.

Oh no, not again! I open my eyes to see five curious Bengali faces peering down at me.

"Oh, leave me alone!" I sigh, rolling over again and pulling my sleeping bag over my head.

Ah, that's better. I think they must have gone. Well, I don't really care too much anyway. I'm just going to fall back asleee...eeeep.

"...They've got my bag!" an American voice shrieks.

"What?" I respond, opening my eyes for a second time. "What's going on?"

"Hey! Drop that!" the voice calls again. "Guys, help! They've got my bag!"

I'm pretty sure the voice is Evan's, and he doesn't sound very happy. Oh well, I'm probably just dreaming again. I roll over and have just about nodded off again when the screaming dream voice returns.

No, wait. This isn't a dream. It's Evan, and he's in trouble!

By the time I've sat up and pulled my sleeping bag away from my face enough to see what's going on, Evan is clutching onto his bag tightly with one hand, whilst, with the other, he gathers belongings that have been strewn a few metres away.

"What's going on?" asks Will, rolling over and inadvertently burying his face into the sand.

"Yeah, what's happening Evan?" I ask.

"I don't know," he replies. "I was fast asleep, when suddenly I felt my bag coming out from underneath my head and these five guys were running off with it. I screamed to you guys for help and I guess that must have scared them off because they just dropped it and ran away."

* * * * *

If this had been the middle of an ordinary day, one might have expected the three of us to be more alert in our response. As it was, however, our legs were shot through from the previous day's efforts, we had no idea just what time it was, or for just how long (or how little) we had been asleep, and we weren't in the mood for moving anywhere just yet.

"So, what shall we do?" I mumbled, noticing that Will had already nodded off again, whilst Evan appeared to be joining him.

"I don't know, man," sighed Evan, turning over in his sleeping bag.

"Well, shouldn't we go somewhere?" I asked. "I mean; they just tried to steal your bag, didn't they?"

Before Evan could respond, or any one of us could make a decision (it was probably going to result in going back to sleep anyway), one had been made for us.

The shadowy figures of five men marched up our mound and encircled the three of us. One of the men mumbled something in Bengali, and gestured that we should get onto our feet.

"Mobiley!" he said, reaching out his hand and beckoning that we give him a "mobiley" (I think he wanted a mobile phone).

"Rupea!" he shouted. "Rupea?" We're in Bangladesh, aren't we? Why did he want Rupees?

"No rupea, no mobiley," we each responded, in turn, but the situation wasn't looking favourable.

The man's gestures and groans grew more insistent by the minute, but we had only one phone between the three of us (my very old Nokia, which was hidden safely inside the zip beneath the cover of my bag), and had no more than about one hundred Bangladeshi Taka (safely zipped away inside the money belt stuffed down my trousers), which was hardly going to buy him a house... or whatever it was that he was after.

Scouring the faces of the five men for a moment, they looked just like regular guys. The ringleader had pulled a scarf up over his mouth and hair to look a little bit like our terror-happy friend from Lahore, and one of his cronies had done the same, but the other three seemed like ordinary men, who didn't even really want to be there. Nevertheless, they were there now, so they'd better start acting mean...

To be completely honest, whatever approach it was that they were going for was having the desired effect. The three of us were scared witless, even if we didn't have the means with which to change this fear into any kind of monetary gain for our new friends.

"Sorry. No Taka. No mobiley," I said, showing the ringleader the 100 Taka I had in change, whilst Will and Evan outstretched their own empty hands.

And just like that, the man had had enough. Yelling something in Bengali, as he knocked the little collection of Taka out of my hand, he signalled that we should leave.

We didn't need telling twice. The three of us scurried away as quickly as our weary legs would carry us, but we weren't about to break into a trot, for fear that this would be the ultimate sign that we were, in fact, terrified.

"They've got my glasses!" Evan protested, as he blindly felt his way along.

It was a good job that we were on a beach, I suppose, because it's hardly the most taxing terrain to navigate. But for the moment, Evan was more concerned with his loss.

"Bastards!" he cried. "I want to go back."

"No Evan!" I said. "Don't be an idiot!"

It seemed that our not-so-friendly friends had caught wind of Evan's pleas for a reunion. We turned around to see five men running towards us, screaming what were presumably rather nasty things at us in Bengali.

It had the desired effect. We couldn't very well run off. There were five of them, and we had our heavy bags weighing us down, and were almost entirely exhausted.

"Yes?" enquired Will, calmly. He may as well have asked them how we could be of assistance!

"Mobiley! Rupea!" the ringleader shouted, even more aggressively than the last time.

And this time, the second man with a headscarf had brought along a little helper. There it was; we could hardly miss it – a two-foot long machete that he was busily thrusting towards my two friends, whilst I was given the marginally more attractive option of dealing with the unarmed, but equally aggressive, ringleader.

The ringleader gestured that we should drop to our knees, whilst he and his mates busily patted the outsides of our bags for any evidence that they might find something of value on the inside.

Oh no! He'd spotted something in my bag. Mr. Knife was soon at hand, turning his thrusting towards me as the ringleader accusingly held aloft my Nokia phone charger.

"Rumbled," I thought. I'd have to give it to him now!

"OK, OK," I conceded, opening the top of my bag.

The two aggressors crowded around to watch my every move as I unzipped the hidden compartment and pulled out my old Nokia phone, handing it to the ringleader.

"Rupea!" he repeated.

"No rupea! I insisted. "I'm sorry!"

"Oh, come to think of it," I continued. "Give me that phone back for a minute." And with that I reached out, grabbed my phone, held it up to the eyes of the man, removed the SIM card, stuffed it into my pocket, reassembled the phone, and handed it back to my surprisingly unconcerned assailant.

"Phew! That could have turned out differently," I thought, but we weren't out of the rough just yet. Mr. Knife was still very much at large and had stealthily made his way back over to Evan and Will, whilst the ringleader carried on in his attempts to extract any "mobiley(s)" or "rupea(s)" that *they* might be hiding away.

"We don't have any!" shouted Evan, who was still peeved about his loss.

"What about my glasses?" he continued, seemingly unperturbed by the knife that was hovering precariously close to his face. "Do you have them? Do... you... have... my... glasses?" he said, in the most patronising of tones, whilst giving them his best impression of how a pair of glasses might look upon his face.

You could never guess what was to follow...

Every one of us – muggers included – started searching for the glasses! It felt to me a little bit like the modern version of that Christmas-Day football match between the Allies and the Germans during the Great War. Here we were, still very much engaged in battle, and yet strangely united in our quest to help a man find his spectacles.

Search over with and, unfortunately for our optically-challenged friend, unsuccessful, it was back to business. Will was the next to receive the fullest attention of Messieurs Ringleader and Knife, who probed the most inward depths of his bag to try and find some reward. Luckily for Will, he was able to conceal his rather expensive camera below a pile of dirty clothing, and the muggers moved on again, to Evan, who would not stop going on about those glasses.

Hold on, what was that? Had Mr. Knife stumbled upon something? Eureka! His eyes lit up, as there before him was a small, shining, silver object. What could it be?

At first, I wasn't quite sure whether or not Evan could even see what had been discovered, but Evan was soon reaching out his hand to Mr. Knife, pleading for him to give him back his camera.

Dutifully, Mr. Knife obliged, and Evan proceeded to flick through the pictures on the screen, taking our muggers through a few precious moments we had shared in their country.

I simply could not believe what I was witnessing. First the glasses, and now this! Evan certainly knew how to play to a man's sensitive side! The ridiculous thing was that it worked! Not only did Mr. Knife give Evan full permission to keep his camera; he then had the audacity to offer his hand to us to be shaken! Of course, we accepted (never argue with a man holding a knife), and then, after one more animal howl from the top of the lungs of Mr. Ringleader, we were sent packing.

A second cry, and we did, this time, break into a trot and did not stop until we were safely around the second corner (just in case they changed their minds again and came back for a third onslaught).

For the third time that night, we found ourselves a lofty mound of sand and succumbed once more to sleep. This time, however, I can happily inform you that we were not interrupted again.

DAY ONE HUNDRED AND FIFTY-SIX: (CONTINUED...)
TEKNAF POLICE STATION, TEKNAF, COX'S BAZAR DISTRICT, CHITTAGONG DIVISION, BANGLADESH, SATURDAY 13TH DECEMBER 2008, 11.21AM

Sleeping on a beach is never likely to produce the most restful of slumbers and such efforts are not helped when your first and second attempts have both been scuppered by the rudest of awakenings. So it was that we awoke as the very first rays of light shone overhead, stirring ourselves as quickly as our weary frames would permit us – aware that the beach bandits of just a few hours ago lay right around the corner – and starting out on the sandy road to Burma once again.

We reckoned that we must have walked in excess of thirty kilometres the previous evening, but whether or not we had been walking in any kind of helpful direction was yet uncertain. It helped matters considerably that we could now see further than five metres in front of us and we were determined to focus upon the positives of what was the start of another day.

"Well, it could have been a lot worse," said Will.

"That's easy for you to say," Evan snapped. "I can't see anything now those bastards took my glasses."

"All right Evs, calm down," I replied. "I reckon you just lost them. What on earth would they have wanted with a pair of prescription lenses?"

"Well, what else did they take?" asked Evan, eager to change the topic.

"They got my watch," said Will.

"And my phone," I continued. "But they didn't take anything else, so I'd say we got off lightly."

"I couldn't believe it when one of them offered to shake my hand," said Will.

"I know!" said Evan. "And did you see the part where they were going to take my camera, so I flicked through a few pictures – tugging on the strings of their sentimentality a little bit – and then they just gave it back to me!"

We all agreed. They had been rubbish muggers.

Now that we had escaped with the bulk of our possessions and, most importantly I suppose, our lives, there was the small matter of locating Burma. A little weary of the never-ending stretch of sand, and eager for a change of scenery, we left the shore and, only a few kilometres further along a dusty path, we chanced upon a little village.

Perhaps this was the village that the army officer had spoken of some twenty kilometres before. After all, the Bengali people hardly seem to have the most accurate sense of distance and time.

We hadn't eaten anything more than a packet of biscuits between us since lunchtime the previous day, so we were glad to see a little food hut opening so early in the morn. The 100 Taka that the muggers had spurned was just enough to buy us another packet of biscuits, but it was the store owner's answer to our question that had spurred us on the most.

"Teknaf?" Will had asked, pointing this way, and that. "Twenty kilometre? Ten kilometre?"

The little man thought for a moment (and by the time he responded, a great crowd had found their way to us and taken up their regular spots in the traditional Bengali/Asian tactic of surrounding foreigners), before confidently pointing us in the direction that we had been travelling and giving us a kilometric target of just seven fingers.

"Seven?" I queried. Why was it always seven?

Surely we hadn't walked the best part of 100km the night before. No; that would have been impossible. But whatever this man had meant by holding up his shrivelled fingers, the thought that we might be getting somewhere towards our target gave us enough motivation to continue.

Of course, we were now no longer alone. The crowd (made up predominantly of small children) that had amassed to stand and gawp at our strange faces decided that they clearly hadn't seen enough and must surely follow us until we reached our destination... wherever that may be. We decided upon a new name for what is becoming a regular band of merry followers. They shall now be referred to as "*The Fellowship.*"

"Greetings Fellowship!" I stated authoritatively as soon as we had agreed upon the name, before briskly turning around and, in so doing, sending the children sprawling in every direction.

It's strange to consider what these children must think of us. Of course, they will rarely have the chance to see real-life aliens on their own turf and one doubts whether many of them have the opportunity to see them on the television either, so we were the closest that these children may ever come to celebrities. Perhaps that was why they were so wary of our movements and why just the smallest of noises or gestures from one of us could send them running frantically for cover.

When the children had recovered their composure and returned to hear the rest of my speech, I continued.

"Thank you for gathering here today Fellowship. A great journey lies ahead for all of us, with unknown perils awaiting us around every bend in the road. I do not expect all of us to survive, but, for those who do, you will have the chance to join me and my brothers here in the realms of true greatness."

The children listened attentively to my Shakespearian rallying cry and happily followed after us until they could see that we weren't planning upon stopping anytime soon, before gradually breaking off, one by one, until the three of us were left to walk in peace.

* * * * *

A couple of hours later we had arrived at the village to which the store owner had probably been referring. OK, so it wasn't Teknaf, but we were encouraged just to find a village big enough to boast some kind of recognisable infrastructure, including actual, real-life roads. We hadn't seen a car since 4 o'clock the previous afternoon and had walked for miles and miles since then. Thus, when we were greeted by the familiar squadron of rickshaw and taxi drivers (all clearly eager to rip us off for a short journey) we were surprisingly cheerful.

"No thank you, kind sir," we responded to the great din of noise, which was like music to our ears. "We intend, rather surprisingly to you I suppose, to make the rest of this journey on Old Shanks's Pony."

Hunger pangs were kicking in good and proper by the time we arrived in what could be considered the centre of this strange, bustling little town. All the money that we had left had been frittered away upon those biscuits, but we simply *had* to eat something.

Slumping down inside a typical eatery at the side of the road, we rested our heads upon our folded arms on the table in front of us and considered what had been, and what was still to come.

"Come on guys; we've still got to get ourselves to Burma," said Evan, in encouraging tones.

Will and I let our eyes do the talking, flickering disdainful looks towards our eager American friend, before allowing our weary heads to bow again.

A Bengali waiter soon approached us, asking us if we would like some chai.

"Well, that's a difficult question," I responded. "In terms of pure wanting alone, I can certifiably respond in the affirmative. Whether or not we would actually like to place an order for chai is another matter entirely..."

Will cut me short in my rant, helpfully informing the waiter of our distinct monetary want: "Taka nahi."

You know, for all the frustration that comes as a result of attributing different Fellowships wherever we go, we were truly glad when one quickly formed around us in this strange new village, especially when one member of the party introduced himself with a warm handshake, sat down beside us, told us that he was an English teacher in a local school, asked us why we had no money, and quickly ordered us some chai and some breakfast.

Will and I lifted our heads for a moment to offer this kind man a thankful smile and an automatic "Dhanyavaad," before quickly allowing our skulls to slump upon the table once again.

Evan was a more respectful recipient of this generosity, engaging with the English teacher in a long discussion of the scattered details of the previous night, and speaking with the kind of urgency and energy that belied our exhausted state.

Oh, how I wish that Evan had simply kept his mouth shut! Whilst we were very happy for the free food and drink that his admission produced, we would rather have gone hungry for the rest of the day than have suffered the rigmarole that followed.

* * * * *

The Bengali people are a proud race (like most others I suppose), so when our new friend heard that one of his countrymen had abused our trust and treated us with such outrageous inhospitality that we had even been mugged (and at knifepoint too – Evan was very clear on this point), he was understandably upset.

"What stolen?" our friend asked solemnly, with a slightly surprising lack of eloquence for one with such a profession, but then again, this was a very remote area.

"I so sorry this happen," he continued. "I so sorry."

Evan was in his element now, reeling off every last minor detail about the mugging and even adding his own artistic touch to events.

"They stole all our money, my camera, Steve's phone, Will's watch and even took my bloody glasses!" he said.

Our new friend shook his head. "I so very sorry. How much money take?"

Will and I raised our heads nervously, awaiting Evan's response. If he told the man the truth and revealed that we had not actually lost any money, perhaps our new friend might consider us to be making a lot of fuss about nothing. Evan had already lied about the loss of his camera, which the thieves had rather sweetly given back to him. What was the harm in one more lie...?

"I don't know," Evan began, reaching around in his brain for a figure of complete fabrication. "What was it?" He turned to us, but we were staying well out of this. "About five hundred Taka, I think. You know, not too much, but it was all that we had."

Great! Now Evan had done it! Why were we lying about an event that *had* truly happened and *had* truly been awful, even if they hadn't taken very much? We had suddenly gone from a position of complete honesty and morality to one of complete fraudulence and cowardice.

It served us right that for the next three hours we would sit in the police station, going over the exact events of the night before. And, of course, now we were in the unfortunate position that we *all* had to lie about it. If we admitted Evan's falsehood then the police would doubt everything about our story and that might even get us into trouble for wasting police time... well, OK, maybe not – this was Asia after all! But still, we couldn't very well change our story now, so 500 Taka it was, and a camera... Oh dear! Why had he done it? Why had he lied?

Perhaps it was my nervousness playing tricks on me, but I felt sure that the police were suspicious of us. Why did they keep asking us the same questions over and over again? Where had we been? Why were we there? How much was taken, and how did it happen?

Why had Evan lied about what had been a relatively minor incident? Nothing had really happened to us in the end, other than a little bit of a scare. And now we were wasting valuable time in this police station. I was more than a little agitated when midday came around and we still hadn't moved.

"What are we waiting for?" I yelled at the policeman in charge.

"We... want... go... Myanmar! We... go... Burma... today!" I said, slowly and clearly, so that the man – whose English was even worse than the teacher's – might understand.

Clearly displeased with the patronising tone with which I had spoken, the policeman sat still for a moment and then told me "we wait police chief telephone."

* * * * *

Finally, the call came and we were taken outside and escorted out of the town in the back of an army jeep, but any hopes we might have entertained that we were about to be taken to Myanmar were quickly dispelled as we approached a junction and proceeded to turn in precisely the opposite direction!

At first we had simply assumed that we were being taken towards Myanmar.

"This is the way to Myanmar, right?" I shouted, towards the very same policeman who had already taken a lot of flak from me in the office. "We need to go to Myanmar before the border shuts! OK?"

But we could tell, just by looking at the man's face, that something else was going on.

"Which way Myanmar?" I screamed, determined that the man would respond.

When he reluctantly pointed in the opposite direction to that which we were travelling, my rage reached boiling point. Will and Evan were staying rather docile throughout the proceedings, but my determination that we must reach Myanmar that day had turned me into a monster.

"Why?" I yelped. "Aren't you supposed to be helping us? Isn't that what the police are for? Why are you making this so difficult for us? We only want to get to Myanmar! Look, we got robbed last night, for goodness sake! *We* were the ones robbed; *we* were the ones wronged. Why do we have to do what *you* want to do? Just let us go to Myanmar!"

"All right Steve," Will whispered to me. "Calm down mate. This is the Police. We're just going to have to deal with it."

Of course I knew my friend was right, but that hardly helped matters. With every extra kilometre that we drove away from Myanmar, my resentment and impatience was rising closer to boiling point and I felt as if I was about to burst. My face must have been quite the picture that day – at least enough to turn the poor policeman's face as white as a sheet.

After some thirty kilometres of backtracking – just long enough for us to see every last kilometre of last night's effort going completely to waste – we stopped. We soon found out that the reason for this infuriating back-tracking was that every incident that happens in Bangladesh must be dealt with by the police station within the specific area in which it occurred. Apparently our description of a generic strip of beach had led them confidently to conclude that we needed to drive almost all the way back to Cox's Bazar to resolve the matter. Needless to say, I was more than a little ticked off.

Once we had finally found a policeman who spoke a decent level of English (the aforementioned "police chief" himself), we dealt quickly with the proceedings and told the man of our disappointment at seeing all our hard work put to waste.

The man was very courteous towards us – perhaps more so than my attitude deserved – and had soon ticked all the right boxes, apologised for his colleague's misunderstanding, and arranged for us to be chauffeur-driven all the way back past the village and to the border-crossing at Teknaf.

All it had taken for us to achieve this turnaround in fortunes was to explain how little we had been adversely affected by the whole mugging event (in fact, on the whole, we had found it rather amusing) and to plead with the authorities not to go out of their way to search for what were probably no more than opportunist fishermen looking for a quick and easy source of cash. Finding none upon us, they hadn't treated us very harshly really. The whole knife thing was, of course, unfortunate, and we hadn't enjoyed being made to bend down on our knees, but all in all, we reckoned that our molesters were good at heart.

"Please, whatever you do," pleaded Will: "Do not let these muggers suffer the fate of that man outside in the courtyard."

My friend was referring to the black and blue carcass of a man, whose body was lying openly in another of those army jeeps, having been found guilty of a petty crime and beaten to death by fellow villagers. We couldn't bear the thought that our opportunist friends might be subjected to the same punishment – especially since Evan had told a few mistruths.

"Please sir," Evan said, continuing from where Will had left off. "Do not punish these men. Do not look for these men. We are fine and do not want anything to happen to them."

The police chief seemed happy enough to meet our request and apologised once again for everything that had happened to us, wishing us a safe and speedy passage to Myanmar.

If only it had been that simple…

* * * * *

Making the border was easy enough, and the police escort made sure that we passed through Bangladeshi customs without too much trouble. They even paid for a ride on a fishing boat to take us to the Burmese border, which, it turned out, was a good hour's sail away.

As the only passengers on this, the last boat to Myanmar that day, we were able to sit and contemplate the crazy events of the previous twenty-four hours. Who would have thought that we would have been through so much during the hours that came between the last sunset and the one that we were then enjoying as we merrily floated across to the next, unknown land.

"Who'd have thought it was going to be this easy to get into Burma?" I enthused.

"What was all the fuss about?" agreed Will.

It was only Evan who was staying understandably pessimistic. "I don't know guys. I won't be sure of it until we arrive."

"Oh come on Evs. Lighten up a bit," replied Will. "We've done the hard bit. We've made it through the Bangladeshi customs too, so they can't send us back now."

"He's right Ev." I said. "I'd give us a ninety-per-cent chance of success now. Oh, I'm so excited! I can't believe we're actually going to do this. I can't wait to write home and tell people about how easy it is to get into Burma!"

But when are things ever as easy as you imagine them? Evan was right to be pessimistic. Somehow, in the confusion caused by a hectic twenty-four hours of strange happenings, we had completely forgotten that our intention had always been to *smuggle* ourselves into this country because we weren't actually *legally* permitted to cross it. How could we have omitted this crucial fact from our calculations? How could we have been so naïve?

When we arrived on the jetty with beaming smiles upon our faces and proudly waved our Burmese visas in front of the guards, their response was stern and simple.

"No. You no cross this border," the chief border official informed us, with such nonchalance that you'd have thought he did it for a living.

We were stunned into silence.

"What do you mean?" I asked, after some minutes. "We have valid passports and visas for your country."

To be honest, I knew what the problem was, but we couldn't admit defeat now that we had made it all this way.

"You have British and American passport. You no cross this border. I sorry." The man spoke with such a friendly tone, but the words that he was saying were like daggers in our sides.

"No. There must be a mistake," said Evan. "We have visas. Look, here. This is a visa for your country and we have just been permitted to leave Bangladesh to come to Myanmar."

The reply was the same: "I sorry. You no enter." The man wasn't going to budge on this point. There were about five border officials and a barbed wire fence separating us from the next country, whose land we so desperately wanted to explore. A small Buddha taunted us from the top of a hill, showing us a glimpse of a new and exciting religion to discover – so close and yet so unattainable.

For four hours we sat by the jetty and tried our best to charm the officials into giving us passage into their country, but to no avail. We had made friends with the staff by the time we were forced to leave, but they simply could not help us.

"I sorry," our friend repeated. "We want help you, but we trouble with Junta if help."

We were in a quandary. We so desperately wanted to persuade our friends that all would be well; they'd just let us in and we would never mention a single word of it to the Junta. It would be as if we'd never been there.

But if we did this, what could be the ramifications for these sweet-natured border guards? We had heard so many good things about the Burmese people – what lovely, hospitable hosts they are – and the glimpse of the friendliness that we could see in these officials was making it even harder for us to admit defeat.

The kindness of our new friends extended so far that they even gave us our first taste of Burmese cuisine as we were invited into the soldiers' quarters for dinner. But this was to be our last taste of Burmese cuisine... for the time being at least.

Finally, we accepted defeat and stumbled our way back down the steps of the jetty and onto the boat of the poor Bengali fisherman who had been constrained to sit and wait there throughout the proceedings.

An hour later – some six hours since leaving Bangladesh for what we thought would be the last time – we were back. We hardly exchanged a word to one another throughout the return trip. What did all this mean for the hitch? Was the dream over? At least our dream of a Laotian Christmas had now surely died. The race was over. We had failed.

16. CHRISTMAS IN DHAKA

DAY ONE HUNDRED AND FIFTY-EIGHT:
AMY'S APARTMENT, GULSHAN II, DHAKA, BANGLADESH, MONDAY 15TH DECEMBER 2008, 11.10AM

We have hit a brick wall; it goes by the name of *Myanmar*. For the first time in the entire trip we have been forced seriously to contemplate the growing possibility that we may not actually be able to finish this mission, which started now more than five months ago. Back in Dhaka, we have found refuge in Amy's apartment whilst we work out just what it is that we are going to do...

Our trip down south ended with a night at the *Pleasure Hotel* (sounds worse than it is), courtesy of the Bengali police force. Upon spectacularly failing to get into Myanmar the legal way, we briefly reconsidered the option of smuggling, even having one of those hush-hush conversations with a not-so-legally-minded Bangladeshi policeman, who contacted one of his not-so-legally-minded friends, who, in turn, would tell us about some not-so-legally-minded activities.

When said felon arrived – a local fisherman by trade – his words didn't fill us with the greatest confidence.

"He says you no find fisherman who take you," our policeman friend translated. "He says they shoot when see you and do no care if you Bangla or *Badeshi* (the term given to white people here in Bangladesh). It not easy you cross Naf River. They lot Bangla and Myanmar police. They torture you."

As tempting as run-ins with trigger-happy policemen and the Burmese Junta sounded, it took us little time to accept our friend's alternative suggestion.

"We pay you go back bus Dhaka."

And that was that. Seconds later we were driven to the bus terminal on the outskirts of Teknaf, squeezed ourselves onto a jam-packed Bengali bus, waved our friend goodbye, and watched with sombre regret as we first drove past the fishing port, and then proceeded to travel alongside the Naf River, staring longingly across at the land on the other side, whose borders seemed so near, and yet remained so frustratingly unattainable.

* * * * *

Twelve hours later we were back at Amy's house, where Bernard greeted us with one of his famous breakfasts. Strength somewhat recovered, we headed straight for the Burmese Embassy... What a pointless exercise that turned out to be.

For more than an hour we refused to go anywhere as we conversed with two security guards, who peered disinterestedly at us through a window no larger than one square metre. Their answer was simple: we cannot cross into Myanmar overland unless we obtain special permission, which, in the unlikely event that it might be granted, could take us between one and three months to receive.

Even though we attempted to use our charm and powers of persuasion to warm these obstinate guards into some kind of compromise, they simply refused even to bother trying. They wouldn't even let us inside the gates, for goodness sake, complaining that the procedure would involve too much trouble. Apparently they'd need to start off by contacting the Foreign Affairs Minister in Dhaka, who would then have to plead with a high official in Myanmar, who would himself have to convince the Ministry of Defence in Yangon; and then, they said, would come the Junta. All in all, it wasn't worth the great streams of effort and paperwork required to receive what, in all likelihood, would only be a refusal anyway.

Thus, without really wishing to wait for anywhere up to three months in Dhaka, still to be rejected entry into Burma, it would appear that we have to consider fresh options.

One idea that came to Will was the romantic notion of flying into Yangon, and then hitching back to visit our friends on the Bengali border, before heading back across Myanmar and into Thailand – thus completing the line, albeit in unorthodox fashion.

This dream was promptly quashed, however, by the dual realisation that a plane ticket to Yangon would cost us each about £250, and that we would have to fly via Bangkok. Given that we had dreamed of not paying a single penny to reach Malaysia, this much money – to thrifty travellers such as ourselves – seems like an absolute fortune, whilst it is farcical to consider flying from Thailand into Burma just so we can then hitch back again.

A second option, fronted by Evan – who still desperately clings on to the dying dream of our Laotian Christmas – is that we catch a plane to Luang Prabang, spend Christmas with the Moodys, and then hitch back into Myanmar from the other side, thus joining up the dots in another way.

Whilst this is certainly an attractive offer, I just don't know whether Will and I can see ourselves stepping onto an aeroplane before we reach Malaysia. Having travelled for one hundred and sixty days without the use of any paid form of transport, boarding a plane now would negate all we have achieved. Our most ardent rule – the fundamental decision not to pay for transport until we reach Malaysia – still holds true, and binds us, somehow, to find another way of making it overland.

The third option, then, would be to attempt to hitchhike around Myanmar. When we first left home, we never expected to travel through Burma anyway. What we had originally earmarked was a more northerly route through Nepal, Tibet and China, ending by dipping down through Laos, Thailand, and into Malaysia.

Now that we have failed to go *through* Myanmar, is it worth reconsidering this third option? It certainly wouldn't be easy. We would have to hitch all the way back up to Nepal, somehow find our way through the Tibetan mountains (which, apparently, may well be snowed under until March anyway), tackle the small obstacle of acquiring permission from the respective Tibetan and Chinese governments to do so (they're hardly handing visas out on plates), and then, of course, there is the matter of navigating our way, by hitchhiking alone, through what is one enormous country. If we take on this challenge, we will by no means be certain to succeed.

Essentially, no attractive options remain. Surely there isn't any chance that we will throw away over five months of gruelling hitchhiking by chucking in the towel and settling for a plane ride. However, there doesn't appear to be any other feasible alternative. Our options are as follows:
1. Selling out.
2. A frosty trek through impassable Tibetan mountains.
3. Waiting aimlessly for months on end for the Burmese Embassy to pull their finger out, only to be told that we cannot pass.

I really do not know how we are going to solve this dilemma because we do not appear to have a leg left to stand on. All attractive options have vanished in the face of this Bangladeshi mire, in which we *still* stand. The Burmese brick wall is all-encompassing; we've hit a dead end.

DAY ONE HUNDRED AND SIXTY:
AMY'S/OUR APARTMENT, GULSHAN II, DHAKA, BANGLADESH, WEDNESDAY 17TH DECEMBER 2008, 14.15

The mood has quietened somewhat. The combination of Evan's departure – our friend left early this morning to catch a train to Calcutta, from where he will fly to Bangkok and scurry up to Laos, his own Christmas dream still intact – and the final blow in our pursuit of Myanmar, has been to see our remaining options drastically diminished. There will be no Christmas with the Moodys (for us at least) and there will be no hitchhike across Myanmar.

The Burmese door was slammed firmly shut in our faces only an hour ago, as we (for the third day in a row) made our way to the Burmese Embassy, stood outside those tightly guarded gates, and attempted to communicate through a window opening that really cannot be bigger than one square foot in size (I was overly generous in my previous estimation). Taking it in turns to press our faces tightly up against the window, so as to attain a better view into the bizarrely secretive depths of the Burmese Embassy, we pleaded with the gate attendant to allow us at least to speak to the man in charge.

"Please just phone the Visa man and get him to come and talk to us," Will protested, but to no avail.

"He no here today."

The response was frustratingly familiar. When was he ever *here*? We had heard the same response yesterday and the day before, so even our most determined efforts were only ever doomed to failure. For some reason we had it in our heads that this sort of thing was easy to overcome; all you needed to do was show a little persistence and, eventually, they'd come around to the idea. But this kind of thinking simply doesn't translate into Burmese. They might as well have displayed a big "No Entry" sign over that tiny window frame, for all the use it was trying to talk with the men behind it.

Thoroughly cheesed off, we held up our hands in defeat and gave them a goodbye gift, which resulted in our being swiftly escorted off the premises by a man wielding a bayonet.

To the tune of "*We wish you a Merry Christmas*," we stepped back from the gate, and cried out, in full voice:

"We... wish you would come and talk to us!
We wish you would come and talk to us!
We wish you would come and talk to us!
Just let us come in!"

There goes that option then; I think it's fair to say that we've safely seen to it that we won't be receiving any letter of permission into Burma anytime this side of the next millennia.

No Laos; no Burma. What do we have left? Our remaining options would appear to be the frosty Tibetan trail, or... well, there's always the possibility that we try our never-say-die attitude at the airport in Dhaka, just sitting it out until someone gives us a free flight to the other side of Myanmar. But, to be honest, I can't really see that one working.

For now at least, we will stay here in Dhaka. Amy left us the day before Evan – to head back to Sweden for Christmas with the family – and has kindly given us free rein over her apartment in her absence. Tired out from what has already been an extremely lengthy journey, we cannot face any further failure just yet. We're going to take some time to ourselves whilst we rethink our options, and wait around in Dhaka for a lonely Christmas time to come around.

* * * * *

There is one more thing that I must tell you about our hostess, Amy, which thus far has remained unsaid.

Perhaps the best method of revealing this surprising characteristic is to share with you the way in which this thirty-five-year-old Swede reacted when we told her that we could "never refuse an offer."

"That's quite a dangerous statement," said Amy, during the final moments before we parted for the first time.

"Only in the wrong hands," I replied.

"Well, perhaps if you ever come back," said Amy, "I might make you an offer you couldn't refuse... You know, it isn't every day that you meet two attractive young men... at... the... same... time." Amy slowed down as she whispered these last four words, and then giggled with girlish glee.

I can honestly say that I have never met a woman quite like Amy before – I doubt one even exists. Tell me, what kind of woman, at the age of thirty-five, could even conceive of tempting two innocent young men to partake in a threesome?

"I think our girlfriends might have something to say about that!" replied Will.

"Oh, I don't mind," said Amy, with a coquettish smile. "I won't tell them."

What a terrible thing to say to two vulnerable young men, who had been parted from their respective girlfriends for the past five months. But worse, perhaps, was the lack of caution with which we acknowledged the remark. I suppose that we felt relatively secure in the belief that we would never see Amy again, but that was until the Burmese blockade ensued. Back in Dhaka, we returned to the home of our temptress and simply did not see her advances coming... until it was too late.

Two nights ago, Will and I both succumbed to Amy's ongoing seduction, and are now wrestling with the ethical crisis in which we have landed ourselves. Will and I both have girlfriends at home and, to make matters worse, I had only just decided that I wanted to propose to mine as soon as we are reunited – a fact of which I made Amy well aware.

"Oh, don't worry," said Amy, comforting me as I sat upon my bed, head in hands. "I won't tell her."

There it was again! How could she be so cold?

"It's OK," Amy continued. "Your heart is with your girlfriend, but you have been away so long. I know that you love her."

"Oh, that's all right then!" I thought to myself. So long as she knew that I loved Jo, I had nothing to worry about!

"I'm great at showing it, aren't I?" I said, feeling horribly numb. "You'd better go to bed."

"OK, if you're sure," replied Amy. "But don't worry. It was only a kiss."

Only a kiss! No! This scapegoat for my guilt just would not do. What shame I felt! No tears flowed, but I felt the same dirtiness I had known after previous indiscretions – only this time I had done it to my beloved Jo!

Tell me, what kind of man cheats on his girlfriend just because he is restless after five months apart? What a weak man I am, and how undeserving of Jo! It hurts me to know how much it will hurt her when, inevitably, I have to share my shame; it hurts even more to know that she would be completely justified in leaving me because of it.

Was it really worth it Steve? A bit of kissing and caressing with a Swedish temptress – is that worth risking a potentially everlasting relationship for?

Obviously it is not, but somehow this train of thought is difficult to grab hold of during those first few moments when a beautiful girl shows an interest and then begins massaging your leg.

Oh how weak I am! My only solace comes from knowing that many men have been in my situation and have done the very same; but this hardly justifies an unforgivable sin. I now face the real fear that Jo may, quite justifiably, decide to break up with me. At the very least, she will struggle ever to trust me again. What an imbecile I can be sometimes; women are my weakness.

DAY ONE HUNDRED AND SIXTY-THREE:
OUR APARTMENT, GULSHAN II, DHAKA, BANGLADESH,
SATURDAY 20TH DECEMBER 2008, 8.45AM

It's not long to go 'til Christmas now and Will and I still sit here in our new apartment in Dhaka. Nothing much has changed on the options front, which is at least partly due to the slothfulness that has overtaken us in the past few days. A forlorn state has come over us as we consider how sad it is for us to be spending this family-centred festive season alone in Dhaka.

We have made very occasional trips out of the house – to buy ourselves some basic food (Bernard's on holiday) or to frequent a local Internet Café to find out the latest news on the Nepalese border with Tibet and China. Unfortunately for us, instead of concentrating upon the *one* option we must take, our options actually appear to be growing – making the task of choosing between them progressively harder.

Not only was the Burmese door shifted ajar once again yesterday – Amy got in touch with us to give us the details of a friend of hers, who happens to be a tour guide in Myanmar and might just be able to help us get in – but we were also told about the possibility of catching a boat from the port in Chittagong, which would take us either into Myanmar or to any one of a number of countries on the other side.

* * * * *

Whilst options have been steadily on the increase, so too have our friendships with members of the local community here in Dhaka, making sure that our stagnant state doesn't completely depress us. A chance encounter with a rickshaw driver named Shonju has, surprisingly, opened up a web of new Badeshi contacts in the area, even introducing us to a local church that has offered us lunch on Christmas Day!

Shonju is a friendly young man with a keen eye for Badeshis. Most of his clients are ex-pats, and although he claims that this is merely a chance coincidence, Shonju possesses something of a business-head upon those thin shoulders and I am sure he knows that he can make that little bit extra if he drives only rich Westerners around all day. We have grown quite close to the young rogue over the past few days – he was our chauffeur on regular trips to the Burmese Embassy – and last night we even had the privilege of paying a visit to his home.

Down a tiny back alley in a dingy area of Dhaka – strangely enough, it's just around the corner from the hub of Western materialism that is *Gulshan II* – Shonju rents a small "house" (no bigger than the smallest bedroom you could find in England), whose walls are made of mud and whose roof is a sheet of corrugated iron, in which he somehow finds space for himself, his wife, and their two children to live.

"Me, my family, something cold in winter," our young friend tells us, in his broken English.

Shonju didn't learn his English at school; every word has been learnt from encountering the Badeshi community here in Dhaka. Although his English is far from perfect, Shonju can speak enough of it to communicate what he wants to say, making particular use of four key words: *something*, *problem*, *Allah*, and *me*.

Every evening Shonju will drop us off at our plush apartment and arrange to meet us the following morning, and every time we ask him how he is, he will always manage to answer with the use of these four key components.

"Me something problem. My Allah, he help me, but me, my family, something cold, something problem, something no money."

That is about as far as our communication goes with Shonju, who kindly offers us a free service on his rickshaw, saying that we should pay him only if and when we want to do so.

"You, me friend. Me something no want you pay. You pay me something, my Allah and me happy. My family something no money. You help me, my thank you Allah."

I don't know if his allegedly free service is just a ploy to get us to give him that little bit extra when, inevitably, we do finally pay him, but we like Shonju enough not to mind giving him what rarely amounts to more than twenty taka (about twenty pence) per journey.

As I've said before, it is customary for hosts to offer their guests something to eat when they arrive, and this was no different when we visited Shonju's humble home. His elderly mother took charge of his tiny, grubby children, whilst his wife cooked an egg-based, omelette-type dish, on a portable gas stove – the sort of thing that you or I might take camping once in a while.

"Me sorry. Me, my family eat something problem. You no like, it no problem me my friend. My Allah, he help me."

Of course we didn't mind that this was no gourmet restaurant and thanked Shonju and his kind family for their generous hospitality.

"Thank you. Me you friend. Me help you, you me help, something better, my Allah, me thank you. Jesse he help me."

My apologies if you can't exactly grasp Shonju's every word, but we're in the same position. The basic gist of his sentences always refer to some problem that he and his family have – normally monetary – but how friends like us, his Allah, and a good friend of his named Jesse are making his life that little bit better.

* * * * *

Jesse is an American man, whose family moved here six months ago to work as missionaries in Dhaka in whatever way they feel called. His wife Rhonda and their four young children (Rhonda is pregnant again, so there is a fifth on the way) are settling in slowly to what is an existence inconceivably different from that to which they were accustomed back at home in the US. At the moment, Rhonda is playing Mum at home with the four kids, whilst Jesse has taken up work in a local school, which just so happens to be about one minute's walk from Amy's apartment block.

Yesterday, Shonju made sure that we would meet his good friend by cycling us over to pick Jesse up from work. Soon Shonju had coerced Jesse into inviting all three of us back to his apartment, where, of course, Jesse would be obliged to feed us.

As the evening progressed, we got to know this intelligent American man and his warm-hearted family, who have taken Shonju under their wing ever since they arrived here, already agreeing a system that will one day see Shonju's dream of having his own rickshaw realised. Currently Shonju is having to pay 80 taka per day just to rent one, which, when he barely earns as much during the average day, will never be enough to offer more than the most basic support for his family.

Jesse has given Shonju a fresh incentive by promising that – so long as Shonju works hard and saves twenty per cent of the money required to buy himself a rickshaw – Jesse will step in and cough up the money for the remaining eighty per cent. My mind returns to our dear friend Evan and his idea of sustainable loans ("micro-credit") that would allow people in the poorest of countries to make a living for themselves. Evan and Jesse would have got on very well indeed. If only Evan were still here with us now; if only Evan and I had parted on better terms...

Evan was becoming irritable during his last few days in Dhaka and seemed intent upon malicious argumentation about anything and everything. To be fair to the poor chap, he had received one of those unfortunate phone calls from his beloved back at home, informing him of her new man in the most blasé of fashions – as if he should be happy for her.

Needless to say, Evan didn't react well. He had been planning to surprise Miss Autumn by returning home earlier than expected, declaring his undying love for her, and even moving to central New York to be with her.

As soon as Evan was off the phone, he went straight for the bottle, drinking silly amounts of the leftover booze in Amy's apartment, whilst Will and I did our best to console him.

"I'm going to get violent tonight," Evan told us. "It isn't a good idea for me to drink when I'm in this state."

We didn't quite understand what our friend was trying to tell us, but did our best to keep him away from any more alcohol. It was no use. Evan was determined to drink himself silly that night, taking his mind far, far away from any thoughts about *her*.

* * * * *

"…His eyes seem vacant enough. Perhaps the drink is actually doing him some good," we think, as our poor friend slumps into a sorry state on the floor. But in a flash, he's back on his feet, bouncing around like some character from a comic book.

"I think I need a hair cut," he says. "What do you think?"

Unsure what the best answer might be in response to our excitable friend, we nod our approval. Little did we know that a "hair cut" in his view means going into the bathroom, slashing at his face with a razor, chopping off random clumps of hair from behind his head, and then taking the razor to his forearms.

"Evan! What are you doing?" screams Will, as he enters the bathroom to see our friend's bloodied state.

"What do you think?" he responds, holding out his arms.

"Oh no!" I cry, entering the fray only in time to see Will wrapping some tissue around Evan's wounds. He looks a real mess.

"Come on mate. Let's go watch a film," says Will, leading our friend through to the lounge, before surreptitiously removing his glass from underneath his nose.

Just what brings a man to do this to himself, I do not know. My only guess is that Evan sees all his problems as of his own making and believes that only he can pay the price for his failings. Self-harm is his release.

I am sorry to say that my last words to Evan were unkind. The following morning – the morning of Evan's departure – I awoke at 6am to make sure he didn't miss his train to Calcutta.

Standing over Evan, I had to shout his name and to shake him a number of times to elicit any kind of response and, when it came, it was hardly polite.

"God! What's wrong with you?" cried Evan. "Why are you just standing there, staring at me?"

My final words to our American friend (with whom we had shared so much) are not fit to be repeated.

DAY ONE HUNDRED AND SIXTY-EIGHT:
OUR APARTMENT, GULSHAN II, DHAKA, BANGLADESH,
CHRISTMAS DAY, THURSDAY 25TH DECEMBER 2008, 16.25

Merry Christmas everybody! I cannot believe that Will and I find ourselves all alone this afternoon – present-less and thoroughly lonesome on this annual day of fun, festivities, carols, presents and good food.

With no family in sight, and no presents underneath the absent Christmas tree, Will and I can at least find solace in the fact that we had a church to attend this morning, carols to sing therein, and a luncheon lovingly prepared by church members to be shared by all and sundry – even by a few straggly hitchhikers.

Lunch wasn't quite your traditional Western spread of turkey, chicken, sausages and bacon, but whilst it was a little disappointing to be eating curry for Christmas, we were happy just to avoid an otherwise inevitable Christmas Dinner of scrambled eggs back at our apartment. We've been offered a second helping of Christmas Dinner at another American family's home tonight. Shonju is coming to pick us up in a little over an hour to take us for what we have been promised will be a meal much more like the ones we are used to.

Somewhere over the sea, I think of a few more Christmasses taking place without us. At home, the family gatherings are all in full swing by now – albeit without the integral ingredients that Will and I might bring – whilst over in Laos, we trust that Evan has been safely reunited with his family. The Moodys will, no doubt, be singing those carols that we were promised when we first started out on our Laos-bound voyage, way back in Kathmandu. I can just imagine Evan's not-so-tuneful voice spoiling an otherwise melodic sound, and yet still filling each member of that happy household with a warm dose of Christmas joy.

Still, all is not lost. We may not be at home with the family; we may not be in Laos with friends; but somewhere, in the midst of all this peculiarity, we have found the most important ingredient: Immanuel – *God with us*. Perhaps it is easier to find the real meaning of Christmas when all normality has been stripped away.

We're bringing Christmas back to Dhaka!

DAY ONE HUNDRED AND SIXTY-NINE:
OUR APARTMENT, GULSHAN II, DHAKA, BANGLADESH,
BOXING DAY, FRIDAY 26TH DECEMBER 2008, 11AM

We stamped our passports yesterday (yes, the same *yesterday* that marked our very first Christmas away from family) with what can only be described as pretty dodgy attempts at faking official entry stamps into Myanmar.

If only the stamping had gone as well as it had done in rehearsal, we might still hold out some hope that, when, finally, a Burmese official does ask to see our passports, he might actually believe that they were stamped by somebody with more authority than ourselves.

You may well be wondering how it was that we landed ourselves with a fake Burmese Immigration stamp-machine anyway; you might also be wondering what on earth we are planning to do with it, now that we have so brazenly gone ahead with the stamping procedure.

The answer to these questions is simple. We had already been told of the possibility of entering Myanmar by unofficial means (i.e. smuggling and the like), and it just so happened that one of our new church-going friends in Dhaka gave our smuggling ambitions that new lease of life on a day when we felt particularly fed up being stuck here in Dhaka still.

"Now, my wife's probably not going to like me telling you this," our mate Dave began, glancing nervously at his wife, Pritty, to see her shaking her head in expectation of what was to come.

"Go on Dave," we replied, earnestly seeking some excitement to drag us out of our stagnation.

"Well," he continued, "You guys want to go through Myanmar, right?"

We nodded excitedly. Surely this man wasn't about to open up a seemingly tightly fastened door for us again.

"Well, all I'll say is that, here in Bangladesh, it is possible to get any – and I mean *any* – kind of stamp you want," said Dave.

"Go on," we encouraged, still unsure of just what it was that Dave was suggesting.

"So, for example," he continued. "Say you are an aid worker, unable to get into Burma, even though you are going to do them a great service.

"And say you just happen to know some guy, who just happens to know some other guy, who just might happen to know a guy who makes stamps.

"And say this guy might be able to make a stamp for you that looks remarkably similar to those they give out on the borders in Myanmar.

"Then say you happen to be found in the deepest jungle of Myanmar, and the man who finds you wants to see your authorisation, so you show him the stamp some guy got for you, who happened to know some guy, who knew some other guy who knew about stamps.

"Well, don't you think it'd be rather tremendous if the official took one look at your stamp, and then let you get on with your aid work, without any further interference?"

Will and I needed no further encouragement. Since our dinner-date at Dave and Pritty's on Monday, we have been to find some guy who knows another guy who knows about stamps; we have taken this guy a photocopy from Amy's old passport – which just so happens to have a perfectly legitimate example of a Burmese entry and exit stamp – and we have paid the man some money, received our very own rubber stamps (one for entry, another for the date), and we have now stamped our own passports.

* * * * *

The entry date on the stamp is today, so we'd better get cracking. We've got some ground to make up if we are to convince border officials that we entered Burma in Yangon on the 26th December. Then again, I suppose it'd take a little while to get from the capital to the furthest stretches of forest in the West (where we shall attempt *Operation Smuggle Part II*), so maybe we don't have to rush so much after all. We've just got to give ourselves enough time so that, one month from now, we have got ourselves into Myanmar, hitched across the country, and surreptitiously made our way out of the Thailand border in the North.

If you're wondering what happened to the other options and why it has taken us so long to decide upon the very same thing we decided the *first* time we headed down to the Burmese border, well I suppose that the answer is threefold:

1. We are tired of being stuck here in Dhaka.
2. The China route seems just a couple of thousand kilometres too far.
3. We just cannot bring ourselves to explore the plane route until we have completely run out of all other options.

Watch out Myanmar, we're coming. And this time, we might just be ready.

17. IF AT FIRST YOU DON'T SUCCEED...

DAY ONE HUNDRED AND SEVENTY-ONE:
THE LAUNDRY ROOM, THE ESTRELLA ETERNA, CHITTAGONG PORT, CHITTAGONG, BANGLADESH, SUNDAY 28TH DECEMBER 2008, 23.04

Arriving outside Chittagong Port late yesterday afternoon, we spent the bulk of the next 24 hours working on a plan to get us over to the other side of the ten-metre high, barbed-wire-topped walls, which hide the secrets of the ocean safely behind their impenetrable shield.

Now that we sit aboard the *Estrella Eterna* (bound for Japan), you might well wonder how we managed it. You might also wonder – quite legitimately – how, having raved on so much about smuggling into Burma, we are now inside a port, attempting to find ourselves a ride on a cargo-ship heading... well, *anywhere* away from Bangladesh.

Allow me to explain...

Kissing Dhaka goodbye for the second time yesterday morning, we had two plans in mind. Our passports had been stamped for *Plan B* – the smuggle into Myanmar – with the thought that it probably wouldn't matter whether or not we used them, but *Plan A* was always going to come first... one has to be chronological about these things.

Plan A was one that had been growing in our minds ever since our first trip to Jesse's church, where a teenage boy (I think he was the son of an ex-pat missionary) had informed us of the possibility of catching a ship from Chittagong to any one of a number of destinations on the other side of Myanmar. Since then, we had done all the necessary Internet research, emailed a bunch of shipping agents, received no replies, but still felt sure that it was worth a shot.

I must admit that it came as quite a shock when, upon arrival at Chittagong Port, the border guards wanted to be given a good reason as to why they should allow us the special privilege of entering one of five closely-guarded gates.

"Well, I'll tell you why..." I had begun, at each gate in turn (we were shipped from one to the next). "Because we have hitchhiked here from England!"

There would be no response, but I would carry on regardless:

"That's right! I know you don't have the foggiest idea what hitchhiking is, or even, perhaps, what England is. Nevertheless, I'm going to keep on telling you that we have done it, and would very much like you to allow us to enter into your port so that we might have a cheeky little word with a few ship captains... No? We can't? You surprise me."

We tried everything – from pretending that we were good friends of the various captains to suggesting that we were errant members of the crew – but it wasn't going to work, and we ended the evening at the home of one of the officials at Gate 1, who pitied our obvious desperation.

* * * * *

The next morning (this morning), we were up early to try our luck at visiting the various headquarters of shipping agents in the region. From Danish shippers *Maersk Line* to humbler Bangladeshi businesses like *PIL*, we must have tried about half a dozen places in all, but it was the same story with every company:

"We are very sorry, but there are very strict rules about these kind of things. Ever since the rise of terrorism, we need to log every single item or person on board the ship and it would take months to obtain permission for you to travel with us."

Disgruntled after an entire working day wasted, we made our way back to those friends at Gate 1, and pleaded with them to give us some reward for our persistence, but it was the same story at every gate. Our friend wrote something in Bengali on a little piece of paper and sent us away to Gate 2 – the only gate we hadn't yet tried.

What was the point? We'd received the same response at every gate – we would need a special pass to get into that port, signed by the "Port Chief" himself. We had already spoken to said chief, but relations had been strained somewhat by a little white lie that I had told.

When he had informed us that he needed the authorisation from a shipping agent to allow us entry into the port, I had told him that *Maersk Line* had given us that very permission. This wasn't strictly true. In fact, all that Maersk Line had said was that they could do nothing without the permission of Mr. Port Chief, which, frankly, we had thought ridiculous... hence the lying. Needless to say, Mr. Big Wig was less than impressed and we were kicked out of the office.

Arriving at Gate 2, it was with the most reluctant wave of our friend's piece of paper that we approached the border guard, and awaited the latest in a long line of rejections. But wait... What was he doing? Was he waving us on? We couldn't believe it. With the simple wave of a scrap piece of paper, we had been ushered into this apparently impenetrable port!

Trying hard not to appear overly surprised by our success, Will and I exchanged looks of bemused excitement, and walked at a slightly-quicker-than-average pace until we had turned a corner and felt sure that we were safely out of sight.

"Yes!" yelped Will, overjoyed.

"I can't believe it!" I responded, giving my friend a huge high-five, and a big hug. This was it! We were going to get on a ship... We just knew it.

* * * * *

I suppose that in some respects we were right. We are on a ship, are we not? And yet, the story so far hasn't dealt up the fairytale ending that we were envisaging...

Buoyed by the relative ease with which we had strolled past the final port officials, we were sure our efforts would not be in vain. Once we had navigated our way through a maze of narrow pathways to find the water's edge, we did not know where to begin, as a line of about a dozen cargo ships stretched out along the harbour front.

If our heads were telling us that someone was on our side in these proceedings, imagine what reassurance we felt when the very first ship that we approach was destined for Malaysia!

As we crept up the stepladder of the *Cape Scott* and introduced ourselves to the Filipino crew, we did not consider for even one moment that there could be the slightest chance that they might refuse us.

"You're going to Malaysia!" I shrieked, with growing excitement.

The friendly Filipino crew all smiled and nodded, but that was because they had misunderstood our intentions. As soon as Will had informed them that this was quite the happy coincidence because so were we, their smiles soon uncurled.

"I'll go check with the Captain," replied one of the crewmen, with a dubious shake of the head, whilst another explained the strict regulations that rendered it highly unlikely that we would be able to travel with them.

"I'm sorry man," he said, "but not even our families are allowed to travel with us..."

Sure enough, when the first crewman descended the ladder, it was not good news:

"The Captain says there's nothing he can do... I'm sorry guys."

Stunned into silence, Will and I didn't know what to do. Wait a minute, we thought; there must have been some kind of mistake. This wasn't part of the plan. We'd made it into the port – Lord knows how hard *that* was; we'd found our way straight to a Malaysian-bound vessel with the friendliest of crew, and felt instantly at ease. The next thing on the agenda was for them to accept us aboard and we could be on our way to Malaysia, no questions asked...

"You're going to have to get down now guys," said the apologetic First Mate, who appeared surprised that we hadn't already made the move ourselves.

"No!" I replied. "We've come so far (I was welling-up)... Could we at least speak with the Captain ourselves?"

The First Mate agreed, but it was of no use. The Captain presented us with the very same response – they would like to take us, but they couldn't.

"Try another ship," the First Mate called after us as we stepped back down the ship's ladder.

Somehow it didn't feel right. How could this be happening? We had made it so far, found ourselves on a ship going precisely where we wanted to go, and now we were getting off it again! We took a quick look around for a suitable place to hide, but it wasn't going to happen. A dozen Filipinos were watching our every move. They wished us well as we left, but we could tell that they were glad to be rid of us.

* * * * *

The next few ships we try are dead-ends. One is bound for India, whilst the other is apparently bound for Sri Lanka. We approach both vessels by first asking if they are going to Malaysia and, on reflection, decide this isn't the best way to go about it. Whether they are going that way or not, they can probably guess what two Westerners carrying backpacks might want from them, so it is in their best interests to lie.

We change our approach by asking where it is that *they* are going, but it is the same story with vessels four and five: one is bound for Japan, the other for another port in Bangladesh. We have been inside the port for over two hours by the time we have tried every ship in sight, but feel no closer to succeeding than when we began. It's getting dark and we haven't made any progress since leaving that first ship, which had the friendliest crew by far. We've just got to go back and give it another shot.

Now, you might assume that the walking between the ships was easy. Let me assure you that this is not the case. We are not talking about five-metre gaps between the ships – this is no car park. We are talking about sizeable, hundred-metre gaps – sometimes longer – between these enormous vessels, which themselves take us about five minutes to cross.

By the time we eventually return to the *Cape Scott*, we're exhausted.

"Sorry to bother you again guys," says Will, as we clamber aboard, feeling, for just one moment, that strange sense of arriving home.

We can't believe that this is only temporary. As soon as we are aboard with our Filipino buddies, there is a mental shift telling us that we are no longer in Bangladesh; in fact, we have arrived in Malaysia. But no, it isn't to be. The best our friends can do for us, when we tell them our lack of success, is to alert us to the possibility that the ship bound for Japan is likely to be stopping for fuel somewhere along the line, and may just be doing so in Malaysia!

They are wrong. The *Estrella Eterna* – crewed by another group of friendly Filipinos – is refuelling off the coast of Singapore. But this is good enough for us. We don't care if they take us to Japan, for goodness sake! We'll go anywhere... anywhere to get us out of Bangladesh!

And yet, once again, our attempts are unsuccessful. There is nothing that any of these Captains can do. You can see in the eyes of our Filipino friends that they genuinely want to help us, but their hands are tied. They will risk losing their jobs if they bend the rules to accommodate us.

"Well, what do we do then?" I ask one of our new friends on the *Estrella Eterna*. "I can see only two options remaining. One: we smuggle into Burma. Two: we stow away on a ship! Which one would *you* choose? Which one of them is least likely to result in death?"

Our friend ponders the question for a moment, before answering. "It is better to stow away," he says. "There are rules at Sea; if you find stowaways, you must treat them kindly... Either that or you throw them overboard."

There's nothing for it then. Thanking our friend, we quickly leave the *Estrella Eterna* and head back to the *Cape Scott* for the third time. It departs at 2200, leaving us a little under an hour to learn and to implement the ancient art of stowing away...

It doesn't go well.

* * * * *

Skulking around in the shadows cast by a warehouse directly opposite the vessel, we wait patiently for the right moment... but *you* tell me what the "right" moment is for sneaking onto a ship. We've never done this kind of thing before and have no idea what we are doing.

One thing I'd definitely do differently next time is not to wait until so shortly before departure. Dozens of workers are loading huge containers onto the cargo ship, whilst the crewmen are all busily undertaking their final "stowaway search."

I'm not making this stuff up; there really is a stowaway search as almost the final action before the ship leaves. In front of us, all we can see is a flurry of activity – hardly the most quiet, inconspicuous setting for our very first stowaway attempt.

"When shall we go?" I whisper to my friend.

"What?" he whispers back.

"I said, when shall we go?" I repeat.

"Oh. I don't know," replies Will. "I was waiting for you... It's not looking too good though, is it?"

For a moment, we allow ourselves to chuckle at the ridiculous situation that we find ourselves in. What the hell are we doing here? At what stage in our lives did we ever conceive that we might find ourselves in some random port in southern Bangladesh, attempting to stow away on a ship bound for Malaysia?

There's not long until the ship departs. We take our final deep breaths, and then strive assertively towards the boat.

It doesn't look good.

Directly in front of us, not far from the very point where we have aimed to board the ship, we see two crewmen.

What do we do now?

We can't exactly turn around. All eyes are on us now and if we turn around, someone will approach us, take us out of the port, and the dream will be over.

There's no turning back. Perhaps the men haven't noticed us. Maybe, just maybe, we haven't been spotted.

We've reached the side of the ship now and it's just low enough for us to make the jump.

One, two, three... we're on.

Oh no, here they come. The two crewmen spot us instantly and come directly for us. Without a word, we look at each other and split up.

Will turns a corner and cowers in a dark doorway not far from where we got on, whilst I make a break for it, darting round the opposite corner, up some stairs and... straight into the two crewmen.

Oh no! What can I do now? I give them an apologetic grimace and turn to run in the opposite direction, eventually finding myself a secluded doorway in which to cower.

Seconds later and the men have found me. To be honest, I don't think they ever really lost me.

"Shhh!" I whisper, putting my index finger to my lips. "Don't tell anyone."

The joke's lost on them. They might have liked us when we first met, but that was before we tried to stow away on their ship! Shaking their heads in disappointment, they beckon me out of my doorway and lead me out from whence we came.

But where did Will go? Maybe *he* had better luck. Wouldn't it be amusing if he managed to stow away on a ship bound for Malaysia, whilst I was stuck here, all alone in this Bangladeshi port?

Oh no, there he is, cowering in that same doorway. As we walk past him, I give my friend a defeated smile and a shrug of the shoulders, and he follows me as we are escorted off the vessel for the third time.

* * * * *

Not long after our unceremonious failure, we decided to give up all remaining stowaway ambitions and to make our way back out of the port.

However, when we got to the gate – the very same gate whose guards had so casually allowed us in – and waved the very same piece of paper towards a different guard, he merely looked at us with disapproval and ordered us back inside.

"Well that's just great, isn't it!" Will exclaimed, as we turned to head back towards the fleet of ships that had rejected us. "What do we do now?"

It had been hard enough to get into the port when we were strangers outside it, but now that we were inside, it was proving impossible to get out! Thus, we did the only thing that we could think of doing, and headed for the ship aboard which were our only remaining friends this side of the gates. Back we went to the *Estrella Eterna*.

Back on deck, our friends couldn't believe that we had actually tried to stow away on that other ship; nor could they believe the predicament in which we now found ourselves – of being utterly stranded inside the port. Graciously, the Captain gave orders for us to be brought a hearty meal and given a room for the night – on the one condition that we left as soon as morning came.

To think that we currently hide behind a cabin door, which is fastened shut by a huge bolt... To think that this boat is heading for Singapore... Would it be so bad if we steadfastly refused to come out in the morning in the hope that they would leave us be until we were safely out at sea? If only the Captain hadn't been so kind to us! There is simply no way that we could repay his kindness with such ingratitude. Tomorrow morning we will leave, and go... well, I just do not know where.

Day One Hundred and Seventy-Two:
Landmark Hotel Restaurant, Chittagong, Bangladesh, Election Day, Monday 29th December 2008, 18.14

I haven't felt this demoralised since the first morning of Benicassim festival, way back at the start of this venture. At that time I was feeling the sort of teething pangs that accompany the beginning of any new adventure – or the beginning of anything at all really – but now I find myself subjected to real concerns about the here and now. The understandable fear of the unknown that I felt at the beginning of the trip has been replaced by the overwhelming fear of the present that I feel now. We have struck a serious string of dead ends during our unexpectedly lengthy stay in Bangladesh, and it doesn't do much for the peace of mind. I am experiencing what I like to refer to as a "mental crisis."

Ever since we were refused entry into Myanmar – way back on December 12th – there have been many questions asked, and many options suggested, but no satisfactory answer discovered. We cannot go into Burma, fearing, quite justifiably, that we might be killed; the China-Tibet route (after everything that we've been through) just seems like one journey too far; and the

Chittagong shipping expedition has hit a morbidly dead end.

Having spoken to some five captains face-to-face and inquired as to the destination of a further ten ships in the past twenty-four hours, we have failed miserably even to come close to any offer of assistance in our quest to get to Malaysia.

It was with great reluctance that we skulked away from the last in a long line of ships to turn us down this morning, shuffling our way across the breadth of the port until we found our way back to our old friends at Gate 1. Duly surprised to see us approaching from the seaward side of the gate, at least our friends knew that we were legitimately supposed to be on the landside of this harbour, and hastily ushered us back into the country, no questions asked. They must have been able to see from our faces how thoroughly miserable we were.

* * * * *

Back on Bangladeshi soil, we were greeted by the eerie silence and empty streets that personify Bangladesh on Election Day. Hopelessly flagging down a rickshaw to take us back to the centre of town, we were stunned to see that almost every shop, hotel, business or restaurant had its shutters down, the owners taking a thoroughly deserved rest on this momentous day – the first election since the caretaker-government took charge two years ago.

This put paid to any hope that we had of trying to get back in touch with all those shipping agencies, or even any hope of contacting the British High Commission in Dhaka to come to our aid. Both avenues were closed.

Thoroughly fed up by what had been an exhausting previous twenty-four hours – on top of what had already been an excruciatingly dull couple of weeks in Dhaka – we decided to find ourselves a restaurant in which to relax, take some time to think through our options, and give my head the chance to begin the meltdown process.

The thing is that we have been in Bangladesh for too long (to think that we tried to leave the place seventeen days ago and we are still here!) and, as if that wasn't bad enough, there doesn't appear to be any way out. Where can we go from here? What are we even going to do tonight? I'm finding it a struggle to shift my thoughts away from endless negativity, even for a moment.

"Will? Mate? Help me. I'm having a crisis." These words, spoken just seconds ago, reveal the extent to which I feel helpless right now.

My friend isn't doing so well either, but at least his brain hasn't completely switched itself off.

"It's all right mate," he tells me. "We'll find a way out somehow."

To be honest though, that's not enough. Will might be able to summon the right sentiments to make me feel fractionally better, but his words just seem hollow. We're in this together and neither of us can truly see a way out. Perhaps you might assume that seasoned travellers such as we might be immune from such panics, but that's just not the case. Sometimes adrenaline runs out, and a bleak, no, a hopeless future rears its ugly head and bleeds even the most eternal optimists dry.

We have no friends to contact here – other than our pals back at Gate 1 – but the last thing we want to do now is go back to that port. *Cape Scott* and the *Estrella Eterna* will be well on their way by now. It pains us to think that they are very soon to be arriving in the very place that we so desperately crave to make our own. It is frustrating also to know how much space there was on both of those ships, and to think that they wouldn't have minded (were it not for these ridiculous regulations) to have us come along for the ride. Worst of all, it hurts to know that we have come so close to achieving our ultimate goal and yet remain so painfully far away.

For the moment, we have found a refuge here inside this restaurant (the one place that's actually open) and hide away from the streams of political supporters that have now taken to the streets. What's that they're chanting?

Our waiter informs us that there's a new President in town and they are proudly chanting his name. Apparently Mr. Zillur Rahman is the new President of Bangladesh – he certainly seems popular here in Chittagong, judging by the raucous celebrations and choruses going on outside our window at the moment. Either that or they are angry... It's difficult to tell.

Perhaps this country's new dawn will lift the gloom surrounding our own current state of affairs. Restlessness and fatigue have plunged us into a pit of despair. What's more, I feel utterly pathetic and ashamed to be wallowing in such self-pity. My sudden state of misery has taken me quite by surprise. I can't remember the last time I felt so helpless.

"Come on Steve. Lighten up a bit. We've hitched all the way to Bangladesh, haven't we?" my friend encourages me. "And it's been bloody good for the most part, hasn't it?"

Of course, Will is right. These last five months have been an incredible and unforgettable adventure, full of the most extreme highs, but there has also been time for the most desperate lows, and it is hard to find one's way out of the mental mire in times like this. My crisis remains.

Day One Hundred and Seventy-Four:
Hotel Al-Abbas, Teknaf, Cox's Bazar District, Chittagong Division, Bangladesh, Wednesday 31st December 2008, New Year's Eve, 8am

It's make or break time.

Getting nowhere fast in Chittagong last night, we impulsively jumped onto the next bus to Teknaf and awake the next morning ready to undertake Episode Two of our attempt to smuggle ourselves into Myanmar.

What have we learnt since the last time we tried this? How far have we come in what has been just less than three weeks since our first shambolic failure? Well, we've got ourselves fake stamps, about ten pounds-worth of

Burmese currency (borrowed from the leftovers of Amy's last trip), and about 200 US Dollars. Apparently it's just as well we didn't get in last time because, as in Iran, Visa cards don't mean much in Myanmar. Yet, other than these rather minor details, I suppose that it would be fair to say that we haven't come very far at all.

Perhaps we've grown in confidence, but the driving force could better be described as recklessness. We certainly feel determined actually to *attempt* this smuggling thing second time around, but this is probably mostly as a result of the escalating levels of frustration and fatigue that we have been suffering from lately, which peaked at my crisis of two nights ago.

The impenetrability of Myanmar has proven a real spanner in the works and we certainly feel that it is high time we moved on. When we first arrived here and hitched the length of the country in ten days, we never anticipated that we would still be in Bangladesh three weeks later! But now, the other side of Christmas, and on New Year's Eve no less, we find ourselves still stuck inside these Bangladeshi borders, desperately eager to escape them by any means possible!

The way ahead is unknown, and potentially very dangerous, but we did try our best to do this the right way and can hardly be blamed for the failings of the Burmese government. It's not our fault that the only way to get into Myanmar is through slightly less-than-legal pathways.

Let the smuggling recommence...

DAY ONE HUNDRED & SEVENTY-FOUR: (CONTINUED...)
HOTEL BAYWATCH, COX'S BAZAR, BANGLADESH, WEDNESDAY 31ST DECEMBER 2008, NEW YEAR'S EVE, 11.55 PM

What better way to usher in the New Year than to tell of yet another spectacular failure at getting into Burma...

It had all started so promisingly. After an hour's discussion with our old friend in the Teknaf Police, we discovered that the sea route seemed unlikely to succeed (he re-emphasised the tight security on the Naf River and the unlikelihood of finding a fisherman willing to risk his life), but were told of an unguarded forest region, a little north of the river, in the narrow neck of land that adjoins the two countries.

"There, no guard," he assured us. "There, twenty kilometre forest and then you in Myanmar."

That was all we needed to hear. Two hours on a bus took us back to Cox's Bazar (we've had enough of hitching in Bangladesh, having hitched round the country twice already), from where we took a couple of micro taxis towards the forested Naikhanchari region. By 3pm we had come to within five kilometres of this apparently secret and totally unused border crossing.

Everything had gone so well up to this point that we simply did not conceive of the possibility that there might be any glitches to our perfect plan. Our friend in the police had been so confident that the forest was unguarded and we didn't care to worry about the minor details of making our way through twenty kilometres of forest without the use of any compass, or a map with any greater details than a nondescript area of trees; nor did we care to contemplate the likelihood that the bulk of this journey would need be made in pitch darkness, without even basic food or water supplies.

And then there was all this talk of "landmines," which the Burmese had apparently scattered all the way along the border.

"And what better place to scatter landmines than in a forest?" I joked, as Will and I neared our probable doom.

"No matter," Will replied. "We'll find ourselves a stray goat and have him walk in front of us. That way, we'll be only as culpable as the rest of them butchers back at Eid."

Ah! Gallows humour! An ever-present when one fears that the end is nigh, but the fact was that we didn't have a goat, nor a compass, nor a map... nor anything helpful at all really.

All in all, one could say we weren't particularly well prepared, so it was probably a good thing when, midway along our five-kilometre stroll to the border, we happened to meet a man in surprisingly official-looking gear for an "unguarded border region."

Were we seeing things?

No. There he was, unmistakable in his camouflage, leopard-spotted outfit – all browns and yellows, just like a Bengali Tiger. He had spotted us coming a mile away; for we were hardly inconspicuous ourselves – what with our bright white faces and a trailing *Fellowship* of some fifty children.

"Where you go?" the leopard-spotted man asked us.

"Oh, um... nowhere special," replied Will.

"Yeah, we're, um... just off to see a friend actually," I said. "He lives just down the road."

"You know it Burma there?" the fake feline enquired.

"Really? We had no idea!" replied Will. "Well, it was jolly nice to meet you and thanks for your advice. Now, if you don't mind, we'll be on our way."

He did mind. Before we could take one more step, the man had stopped us in our tracks with a firm forearm and a shake of the head.

"You no go Burma," he said bluntly.

"You see, that's all very well," I replied, "but the thing is, we really do have to go to Burma now. Thanks for your time and we'll just be on our way."

Again, there it was – that same shake of the head. What was it with these Bangladeshi authorities – or authorities of all kinds really – and their insistent shaking of heads?

"Come with me," the leopard said, leading us off a little way along the path to Burma.

Happy enough at least to be heading along in the right direction, we reckoned that we couldn't be more than a couple of kilometres away from Myanmar, and had already spotted some handily-placed undergrowth dwellings, which might make for good hiding spots later on.

Sadly, all future plans soon went out of the window when the promise of an unguarded forest region was uncovered for the fallacy that it was. Just around the corner, there sat no less than fifty camouflaged guards, doing very little, but certainly not about to let us waltz into Burma. No manner of pleading or protesting was going to help us now.

Ten minutes later we were back at the local police station, where we were held for questioning for several hours, after which the police chief arranged for us to be escorted safely back to the beach at Cox's Bazar.

"But please sir," I pleaded. "We don't want to go to the beach. We want to go to Burma!"

"I'm sorry," he replied. "You no go. If see you they shoot you. You go Cox's Bazar. It safe there."

And thus, here we are – still safely inside the arms of a country we have been so desperately trying to flee for the best part of a month. We have been ordered to return to Dhaka tomorrow, whereupon we should research "other ways" of getting to Malaysia. To be honest, I've almost given up all remaining hope of ever reaching that Promised Land...

Happy New Year everybody! I truly hope that wherever you are, you're having a better time of things than we are. For Will and me, the only remaining positive is that we have managed to live to see the beginning of another year.

DAY ONE HUNDRED & SEVENTY-FIVE:
BEACHSIDE, COX'S BAZAR, BANGLADESH, THURSDAY 1ST JANUARY 2009, NEW YEAR'S DAY, 17.03

Did we listen to our friends in the Bangladeshi Police and decide not to pursue the smuggling route any further? Of course not! Did we succeed in finding a way of entering that forbidden land? No prizes for getting that one correct.

We spent the entirety of our 9-5 day in Fishery Gat (an apparently-famous fishing dock, most notable for its shifty fishermen seeking to make a quick buck by helping foreigners get into Burma), but said shifty fishermen are surprisingly difficult to locate. The closest we came to succeeding was to spend a hugely frustrating couple of hours deliberating with two men who eventually declared themselves to be "tour guides." Throughout the proceedings they ignored our constant pleas for doing things *illegally*, until the very last moment when they turned to us, apologised, and told us that they couldn't help us.

That was the final straw.

This is it! Finally we are completely giving up all hope of ever reaching the secret paths of Myanmar. Tonight we return to Dhaka (again) and set about seriously and hurriedly planning our way out of this country once and for all.

The airport is to be our final destination in Bangladesh. We will leave all other options behind and try our level best to hitch on a plane. We only hope that we may have a little more success in this method of leaving Bangladesh than we have had in all others. There will be no famous smuggling or stowaway success for us. We will leave by air, whether or not it will feel like cheating to do so.

As long as we manage to hitch the ride – an ambition that seems highly unlikely – then our greatest aim will remain intact. To be honest though, it would appear that the likelihood is that *Steve and Will's Hitch to Malaysia* will be forever remembered as a hitch to Bangladesh, a flight over Myanmar, and then a final hitch from Bangkok to Malaysia.

Morale has slipped to an all time low on account of recent failures and we are intent upon making this next leg of the journey a much more fun-filled and generally more enjoyable affair. There have been far too many setbacks of late and we feel that an upturn in fortunes is long overdue. Our memories of Bangladesh, beautiful though the country may well be, will always be blighted by that Burmese brick wall.

DAY ONE HUNDRED & SEVENTY-SEVEN:
JESSE & RHONDA'S FLAT, NEW DOHS, DHAKA, BANGLADESH, SATURDAY 3RD JANUARY 2009, 17.03

Words cannot express how relieved we are feeling tonight. An upturn in fortunes was what we had been praying for, and a much more than average upturn is what we have received.

Returning to Dhaka in the small hours of yesterday morning, Will and I made straight for Dhaka International Airport, hell-bent on the idea that we were not going to leave that place unless it was on a plane.

With no idea of quite what to expect – nor any previous idea regarding how one might go about getting a free plane ride – we took one quick look at the Departures board, noticed that the first plane to the other side of Myanmar (Thailand specifically) was scheduled to leave at 1.45pm (about five hours on from that moment) and decided that we were going to be on it.

Confidently approaching the Thai Airways check-in desk, we assumed that all we'd need to do was to explain the tale of our adventure, ask if they had any free seats, and willingly agree to take them off their hands.

"Hello there," began Will, charm radiating from his very being. "Do you have any spare seats on the next flight to Thailand?"

"You do?" he continued. "Wonderful. Now, how shall I put this...?"

"Allow me," I interrupted. "Well, I suppose that in some senses you could consider this to be your lucky day because we are actually looking for two free seats to Thailand!"

"Now if you'd be so kind as to present us with two free boarding passes," added Will, "Then we'll be on our way."

The lady sighed. I think she'd heard these kinds of requests before.

"I am sorry. We cannot give out any free tickets today," she said, without the slightest inkling of remorse. "There is nobody here with enough jurisdiction to authorise such a thing because it is a Friday and our managers are on holiday."

Holiday? What sort of an excuse was that? Fair enough; we knew all too well that Friday was the Muslim holy day, sacred to Muslims in the same way that Sundays used to be for us, but surely there must be somebody in authority who could at least be available to take an important call, despite the minor problem of this being his or her holiday.

No. It was the same story wherever we went. All important parties of every airline we approached (we spoke to four) proclaimed complete ignorance as to how they might be of help, telling us to come back on Sunday when their manager would be more than happy to speak with us.

At one stage we had even convinced an obliging Japanese businessman to use an abundance of air miles to pay for our flight to Bangkok, but even then the lady behind the desk at *Thai Airways* denied having the authority to process such an odd request.

We simply could not believe it. Our already-rock-bottom morale sank even further. Five hours after we had arrived at Dhaka International Airport, we were leaving again. Shoulders slumped, we flagged down the next rickshaw to take us back to the centre of Dhaka.

* * * * *

Oh how we loathed seeing those familiar streets. How on earth had we ended up in Dhaka yet again? Tears were in our eyes as we pondered the growing inevitability of having to wait a further two days of aimlessness in Dhaka before we could even speak to anyone who might be able to help.

"We've got to get out mate!" I pleaded to Will. "Come on, I've had enough! Please! Let's just hitch back up to Nepal and go through China and Tibet."

By the time I'd finished speaking, several tears had trickled out from those brimming ducts of mine, so desperate was I not to have to stay in Dhaka for yet another depressing day... Anywhere else would do – just not Dhaka!

"No mate!" Will snapped. "Come on, we haven't even scratched the surface of this plane-hitching plan yet. We can't just give up already. I don't think I've even got it in me to face hitching all the way back up to Nepal just to be turned away like we were in Burma."

"Please Will," I protested. "I can't do this anymore – all this waiting around for nothing. How are we *still* in Bangladesh? We have been in this stupid country for almost a month now. We're never going to get out!"

"Mate, I can't do it," replied my friend. "There's no way I've got the energy to hitch back up to Nepal and then face another couple of months getting through China. We've got to at least try a little bit harder before we resort to that! Please! If we haven't got anywhere by the end of Sunday, we'll reconsider."

Grudgingly, I agreed. Will was right. We hadn't exhausted the plane-hitching thing yet. I was just feeling overwrought because of the efforts of the last month and assumed that if we kept on moving then we wouldn't

Evan, Beth and Will, Mcleod Ganj

How Tibetan monks spend their time in Mcleod Ganj

Cattle Market, Dhaka

The Fellowship

Our Cattle Market tour guide

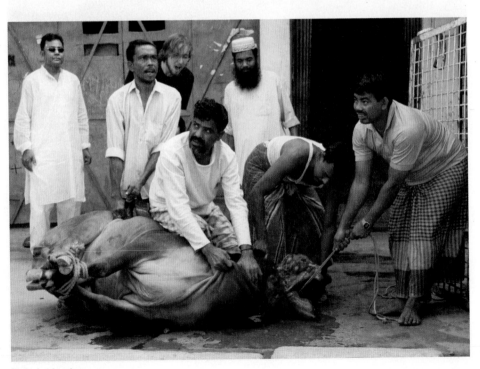

Daisy's demise

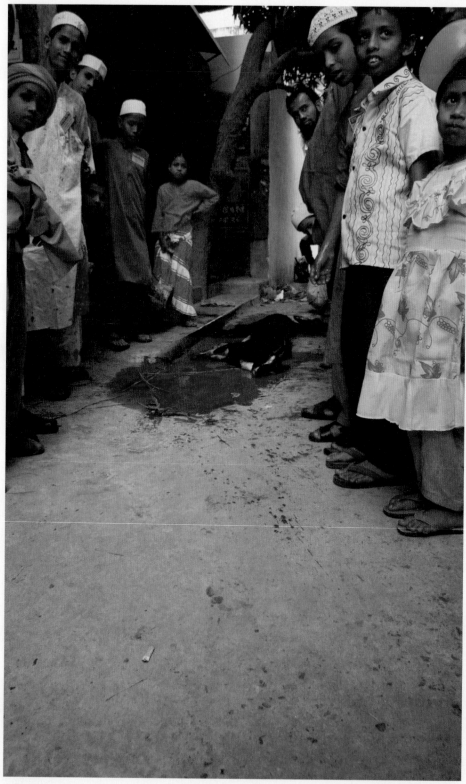

A family event

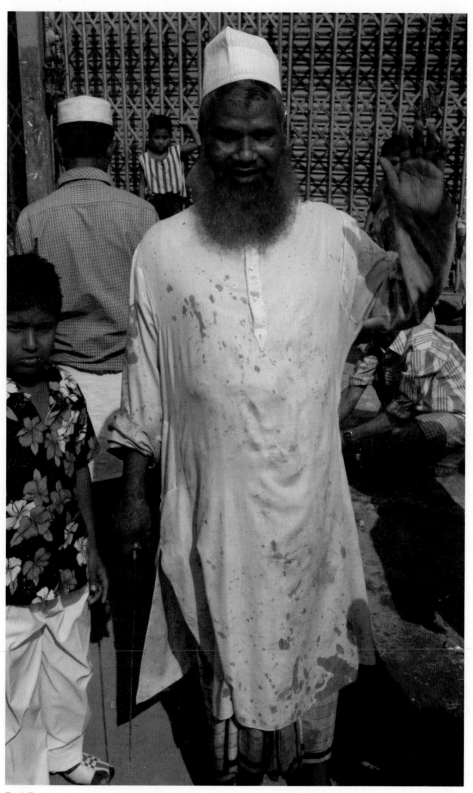

Red Beard

Boat to Myanmar

The dream that never was

Kuala Lumpur, Malaysia

Malaysian chai, Penang

Letting the hair down

have to think about how thoroughly miserable we felt. But no, here we were, in Dhaka again, and I was going to have to wait around until Sunday at the very least before I could plan on heading back to Nepal again... after the plane-hitching thing had, inevitably, failed.

* * * * *

We spent the bulk of the rest of the day grumbling to each other about how ridiculous it was for everything to come to a standstill at the weekend. Could you imagine this same sort of thing back at home? But there was light at the end of the tunnel.

It had gotten to 3pm by the time we had headed back to Gulshan II, checked if Amy was back from Sweden (she wasn't), scoffed some food in a cheap Chinese restaurant, and then suddenly remembered that there was one good thing about Fridays in Bangladesh – Fridays weren't holy days only for Muslims; Christians, too, had services on this Sabbath and oh how we needed a church service now!

Back on a rickshaw, we headed straight over to Jesse and Rhonda's, who kindly told us that we could stay for as long as we wanted, so we dumped our bags, and grabbed the next rickshaw over to the church.

Arriving, we felt slightly ashamed. The last time our friends had seen us, we had spoken adamantly of our intention to get into Myanmar, but here we were again. And yet, all disappointment and embarrassment was washed away as soon as the service began as, for the first time in a very long time, we stood before God, and wept.

There were no words, but suddenly an incredible peace had washed over us. Now that we were completely stripped back and thoroughly broken before our God, He could come in and give us peace.

I have been so incredibly adamant that I wouldn't let this book become overtly Christian, for fear that it might scare away the less religious, and yet there is simply no way that I can ignore the hand of God over us in these last few moments in Dhaka.

* * * * *

The next morning – this morning – we trudged over to visit the sole airline whose management would apparently work on a Saturday. With not a care in the world, bags and burdens totally lifted from our weary shoulders, we made our way to the HQ at GMG airlines.

Perhaps for the first time on the entire trip, neither Will nor I cared what the future might hold. If God wanted us to hitch through Nepal, China and Tibet, then so be it; if He wanted us on a plane, who were we to stand in His way? Careless and free, I can honestly say that neither of us even really minded what the people at GMG might say when we were ushered into the head office for a little chat, but I won't pretend that we weren't thoroughly swept off our feet as soon as Mr. Erfan Haque (the man behind the desk) revealed his astonishment at what we had achieved (he actually knew what hitchhiking was!), and proceeded to offer us two free tickets to Malaysia!

To be honest, Will and I reacted in the only way we knew how: we sobbed. Tears streamed down our faces as we looked at each other and let the blissful joy of the moment set in. We'd made it! We couldn't believe it. From Dhaka to Malaysia with a click of the fingers, and after all the efforts and frustrations of the past month!

For six long months we had been travelling free of charge from England towards Malaysia. All that now stands in our way is a three-hour flight to Kuala Lumpur. We leave on Tuesday. Malaysia, here we come.

We've done it!

⋆EPILOGUE⋆

DAY ONE HUNDRED & EIGHTY-TWO:
THE MANHATTAN FISH MARKET, SURIA KLCC SHOPPING CENTRE, PETRONAS TOWERS, KUALA LUMPUR, SELANGOR, MALAYSIA, THURSDAY 8TH JANUARY 2009, 17.14

It's not quite *Around the World in Eighty Days*, but hitchhiking from England to Malaysia in *one hundred and eighty* isn't bad going. We have been in Kuala Lumpur for two days now, soaking up the success of the past six months in what has been a rather surreal end to the adventure.

There wasn't one atom between the pair of us that had hoped to end our trip with a plane ride, but we had tried all other options and found only dead ends. The relief of knowing that we tried our best doesn't quite do enough to diminish the disappointment of our failure to get in or around Myanmar, but ending the trip by flying over it doesn't feel all that bad, especially having heard from our dear old friend Woo that the Nepal-Tibet border is closed. Thank goodness we didn't give in to my spontaneous desire to hitch back that way! Despite our disappointment at the means with which we finally arrived in Malaysia, we can still hold our heads high and proudly say that we did make it all the way here by hitchhiking, without paying a single penny for transport!

On the 6th January, at about 8am Bangladeshi time (the flight had been delayed by a couple of hours in what was a fitting end to life in Bangladesh)

343

we took off from Dhaka International Airport, treated to two "Business Class", front-row seats (which had all of about two feet of leg room between them, but were fractionally better than those given to the hordes of Bengalis behind us), and arrived in Kuala Lumpur in time for lunch.

I think the flight was three hours in total, which still seems a fair old length of time to be airborne, given how long it had taken us to decrease the distance between Malaysia and ourselves over the past six months. Now that we have arrived, as soon as we feel suitably settled into this strange new land, we are intending to hitch back up towards Burma from this side and thereby completing as much of the line as possible, leaving us with the deficit of only about 1000km within Burmese soil that were, simply, impassable.

* * * * *

When we first arrived in the impressive Kuala Lumpur airport lounge, we wore the inane grins that accompany two tired yet triumphant travellers after an incredible six-month expedition across a significant portion of the world, although our pride was tainted somewhat by the embarrassment we felt for wearing our hitchhiking t-shirts as we arrived at our final destination through an airport.

As we made our way into Malaysia proper for the very first time, the 25°C heat that greeted us gave us an all too obvious example of the thing that we would miss the most in this particular transition. Transferring seamlessly from winter to tropical temperatures because of one measly plane ride simply felt wrong. Where was our chance to appreciate the gradual contrasts that take place between two lands? Climatically and aesthetically speaking, we feel robbed. It has reminded us how special it is to notice those differences – sometimes so stark (as with the transition between Iran and Pakistan); other times so fluid (as with your average border crossing within Europe). But there is to be no gradual transition from Bangladesh to Malaysia; we simply have to deal with the dramatic, wholesale changes of culture, time, climate and atmosphere that unsurprisingly reveal Dhaka and Kuala Lumpur to be quite different. We honestly do feel robbed of the chance to see skin tones gradually shift, temperatures surreptitiously rise or fall; there is no chance for us to notice the distinct similarities between the languages of bordering countries, nor the subtle changes in scenery. Perhaps it is this that hurts the most, even more than the general guilt that accompanies our every remembrance of stepping onto that plane – albeit free of charge.

On the hitching front, it would appear as though we are in for a good ride now that we are this side of Burma. Our solitary hitch thus far took us less than five minutes to acquire, and then saw us swiftly progress (and by "swiftly," we're talking Iranian speeds) all the way from the airport (some fifty kilometres outside the city) into the heart of KL in less than thirty minutes.

Of course there was an element of luck in attracting such a fast driver on our first attempt (they don't come much faster than twenty-year old, boy-racer, Hyder), but it was nice simply to enjoy the fact that he actually knew what hitchhiking meant. As soon as we'd waved a thumb in his direction, he had stuck his thumb up in kind, slammed on the brakes, and beckoned us in.

"Where d'ya wanna go?" the young man inquired, with a faultless American accent.

And then there was the drive itself. Reaching speeds of up to 200km/hr on blissfully pothole-free, three-lane carriageways of beautifully palm-tree studded Malaysian highways, this was a contrast like no other we'd seen. When I think of Bangladeshi, Indian, Nepalese or Pakistani roads, the first word that comes to mind is "uncomfortable," or maybe "slow." But even the rich nation of Iran didn't boast such classy streets as these – streets that scream of a country on the up; we liked Malaysia instantly and felt glad to have randomly assigned it as the finishing point for our adventure.

The climate here is taking some getting used to. We feel chuffed to be free to wear shorts and sleeveless t-shirts once again, having spent months in devoutly Muslim cultures when the slightest showing of indecent attire could have you locked up. Although we have been in hotter places along the way, we have never been in a country this humid before. The moisture in the air is thick, clinging to you like a warm coat and even making breathing that little bit more challenging. Walking pace has slowed considerably for fear that any quick movement might cause us to experience an arrest somewhere in the region of the cardiac muscle, whilst the random distribution of heavy rain brings an air of surprise to an otherwise dry and uncomfortably sticky environment. Given that I can remember being rained on only three times over the last six months, it feels strange to have experienced more than that in just a couple of days here in Malaysia.

It's just as well we're here in January, I suppose; apparently the heat is much worse at other times of the year. We're not talking your average four-season climate here. Our friend Hyder explained that there are only two seasons in Malaysia, which alternate six times throughout a year – one is hot and dry; the other hot and wet! Thank goodness we're here in the latter or it might become too much.

DAY SIX HUNDRED & FORTY THREE:
NEW HOME, HAMMERSMITH, LONDON, ENGLAND,
WEDNESDAY 14TH APRIL 2010, 11.45AM

Every good story needs a fairytale ending, so here's mine...

Tired out from what had been an exhausting six months on the road, Will and I headed straight for a remote island off the west coast of Thailand for a week of rest and recuperation, before hitching our way a little further up the coastline to the Ranong border with Myanmar for what would be our second short-lived Burmese vacation. At least our brief visit allowed us to ensure that we had hitched as much of the journey as physically possible and this was enough to make sure that we had cleared our consciences in time for one final hitch down to Singapore to see the *Prodigy* – who kindly gave us free tickets for our troubles.

Will left Malaysia on February 12th, to be replaced by a much more attractive travelling companion, in the shape of my long lost girlfriend, Joanna. It didn't take me long to propose. By the 19th we were engaged (on another paradise island, since you're asking) and were married at the turn of the year. Now, what better way to end the story of one adventure than to tell of the beginning of another? On Tuesday, Jo and I will set off with two others on the very first *Afghan Road Challenge*, driving from England to Afghanistan to raise funds for Kabul-based charity, *Afghanaid*. Once you've caught the travelling bug, it really is rather difficult to stop.

MANY THANKS TO EVERYONE INVOLVED IN MAKING THIS BOOK A REALITY.
FIRST AND FOREMOST, A SPECIAL THANKYOU TO MR. WILLIAM JACKSON - WITHOUT WHOM THE EXPEDITION WOULD HAVE BEEN A LOT MORE LONESOME, AND GENERALLY LESS WORTH RETELLING.
THEN, OF COURSE, THERE IS MY WONDERFUL, NOW WIFE, JOANNA, WHO HUNG IN THERE THROUGH THICK AND THIN, AND EVEN STUCK BY ME WHEN I TOLD HER THAT I WAS GOING TO TRY AND SMUGGLE INTO MYANMAR... AGAIN. A TRULY FAITHFUL WIFE!
HEARTFELT THANKS TO THE GRAMMATICAL STOOGES THAT ARE MY MOTHER AND GRANDFATHER, WHO HELPED MAKE SURE THE BOOK WAS SLIGHTLY LEGIBLE.
AND FINALLY, A BIG THANKYOU TO MY FATHER FOR ACTUALLY GOING AHEAD AND PRINTING THE THING.